THE COMPLETE GUIDE TO PLAYING BLUES GUITAR
COMPILATION

Book One: Rhythm Guitar
Book Two: Melodic Phrasing
Book Three: Beyond Pentatonics

JOSEPH ALEXANDER

FUNDAMENTAL CHANGES

The Complete Guide to Playing Blues Guitar
Compilation

Published by www.fundamental-changes.com

ISBN: 978-1-78933-038-0

Copyright © 2018 Joseph Alexander

The moral right of this author has been asserted.

All rights reserved. No part of this publication may be reproduced, stored in a retrieval system, or transmitted in any form or by any means, without the prior permission in writing of the publisher.

The publisher is not responsible for websites (or their content) that are not owned by the publisher.

www.fundamental-changes.com

Twitter: **@guitar_joseph**

Over 10,000 fans on Facebook: FundamentalChangesInGuitar

Instagram: **FundamentalChanges**

For over 250 Free Guitar Lessons with Videos Check Out

www.fundamental-changes.com

Contents

Introduction	5
Chapter One – The Basic 12-bar Blues Structure	8
Chapter Two – Open-String Blues Riffs and Variations	15
Chapter Three – Using Dominant 7 Chords	23
Chapter Four – Extensions to the Dominant 7 Chord	29
Chapter Five – Common Variations to the 12-Bar Blues	33
Chapter Six – Blues Turnarounds	38
Chapter Seven – Rhythmic Placement with Triplet Blues	42
Chapter Eight – Rhythmic Placement with Straight Blues	49
Chapter Nine – Melodic Fills between Chords	56
Chapter Ten – Intros and Outros	63
Chapter Eleven – Shell Voicings	67
Chapter Twelve – Drop 2 Voicings	71
Chapter Thirteen - The Minor Blues	76
Chapter Fourteen – Other Blues Forms	78
Chapter Fifteen – Conclusions	83
Introduction to Book Two	87
Chapter 1: Blues Guitar Soloing Basics	89
Chapter 2: Rhythmic Divisions	101
Chapter 3: Rhythmic Displacement	118
Chapter 4: Developing Lines and Creativity	130
Chapter 5: Range and Other Positions on the Neck	146
Conclusions	159
Appendix A – Bending in Tune	160
Appendix B – Vibrato	163

Introduction to Book Three	166
Part One - Chord Articulation: Playing the Changes	168
Chapter One: Outlining the Chord I to Chord IV Movement	168
Chapter Two: Outlining the Chord IV to Chord I Movement	178
Chapter Three: Outlining the Chord I to Chord V Movement	182
Chapter Four: Outlining the Chord V to Chord IV Movement	189
Chapter Five: Chord Changes and Arpeggios in Every Position	197
Part Two - Scales and Soloing Schemes	201
Chapter Six: Scale Choices for the I Chord	201
Chapter Seven: Scale Choices for the IV Chord	214
Chapter Eight: Scale Choices for the V Chord	222
Chapter 9: How to Practise	235
Other Books from Fundamental Changes	239

Introduction

What does it mean when someone says they play blues guitar?

The sheer variation in musical style within the genre of The Blues is almost immeasurable and it would be impossible to cover everything in just one hundred pages.

The roots of The Blues as a well-documented musical style in popular culture are in the 'spirituals', 'work songs' and 'field hollers' sung by African-Americans in the era of slavery, and in the years that followed emancipation. As a result, The Blues is rich in African-American rhythm, harmony, melody and phrasing. One of the most important melodic structures that retains a strong link to this time is the performance of *call and response*, or 'antiphony', where a musical question is sung, and then answered by different voices.

Since the first recorded reference to The Blues (Antonio Maggio's *I Got The Blues* in 1908), the musical form has grown, spread and evolved into many different sub–genres. From early *Delta* blues, through to *Texas* blues and later contemporary rock, virtually all the music we hear today owes its origin to The Blues.

Chronologies of The Blues are widely available and this is not the place for a history lesson (although Alan Lomax's *Land Where The Blues Began* (1993) is a good place to start). However, it is essential that anyone wishing to study modern blues guitar understands the roots of the language.

While the following list of names may not be to your personal taste, please spend time listening to early performances of The Blues. Some of the recordings are poor, and maybe don't include a guitar, but you should be able to identify elements in these early musical roots that influenced the work of more contemporary guitarists, such as B.B. King, Stevie Ray Vaughan and Robben Ford.

I consider the music of the following early blues musicians to be essential listening:

- *Bessie Smith*
- *Ma Rainey*
- *Big Bill Broonzy*
- *Blind Lemon Jefferson*
- *Charley Patton*
- *Leadbelly*
- *Lonnie Johnson*
- *Robert Johnson*
- *Son House*

As guitar construction improved towards the 1950s, and as guitarists became more proficient at solo lead guitar, many of the household names associated with guitar-based blues found fame. Assisted by the public's easier access to recorded music, performers such as T-Bone Walker, John Lee Hooker, Muddy Waters, Howlin' Wolf and B.B. King helped shape the stylistic sound of guitar blues. Once again, any recordings by these performers and others in the late 1940s – 1960s are essential listening.

While these eras helped to define the sound of blues guitar music, the late 1960s to 1980s were the period during which the modern guitar blues style became the foundation of hard rock. Bands like The Yardbirds and Led Zeppelin, featuring guitarists such as Jeff Beck, Eric Clapton and Jimmy Page, drew influences from the Afro–American performers listed above, and forged blues into the rock music we know today.

Jimi Hendrix's ground-breaking albums *Are You Experienced* and *Axis, Bold as Love* in 1967, along with other albums by Beck, Clapton and Page, created the illusion of the Guitar God in the minds of the public. It is significant that the musical language of all four guitarists, and that of many others, was based heavily around the language of the blues.

In 1983, Stevie Ray Vaughan released *Texas Flood*, which has become a defining example of the Texas Blues Guitar style.

While this is far from a complete history of blues guitar, and there are some notable omissions, I highly recommend Martin Scorsese's masterpiece, *Martin Scorsese Presents: The Blues*, a seven DVD box set of the most important blues figures of the last hundred or so years, to help you learn more about the roots and political struggle of The Blues.

With so much musical diversity in just this one genre, it's hard to know where and *when* to begin. There are, however, many topics that are required knowledge and applicable to most styles of guitar blues.

I'm writing this series of books to help break down the language used in modern guitar blues from about 1950 onwards. This is by no means a chronological study, and to make things manageable the series of books is divided into three parts.

Book One: Rhythm Guitar

While there are relatively few blues chord *structures*, there are a multitude of approaches we can take to embellish this standard harmony. We will also examine common riff patterns and *straight* versus *triplet* feel rhythm guitar playing. You will learn the differences between Major and Minor type blues progressions and many different chord *voicings* to use to add great depth and interest to your playing.

There are chapters dedicated to *turnarounds,* open-string riffs and melodic fills (solo phrases) that help us move smoothly from one chord to another.

We go into considerable depth about how to play rhythm guitar with a singer or other solo instrument, using sparse *shell* voicings or higher register *drop 2* chords.

We even study some common non-12-bar blues forms such at the *8-,* and *16-bar* forms.

The largest section of Book One studies the rhythmic *placement* of chords. The aim is to open your ears to the subtlety of *when,* not *what* you play in the bar. In both triplet (12/8) and even (4/4) time we look at how to play on *any* subdivision of the beat so we can play with subtlety and finesse. You will learn to drop chords into the groove wherever you wish and will learn that one small rhythmic drop can be much more powerful than a whole bar of unfocused chordal filler.

Chord extensions are also tackled. Instead of playing just simple Major chords we will cover Dominant 7, 9 and 13 chords comprehensively, plus look at some great opportunities to use *altered* chords. All in all, *The Complete Guide to Playing Blues Guitar - Part One* aims to answer every common question about blues rhythm guitar.

Book 2: Melodic Phrasing

This book deals with soloing in much, much more detail.

"Melodic Phrasing" is a new concept in blues guitar soloing: Instead of teaching you hundreds of hard-to-remember blues licks, it teaches you to form your own unique vocabulary from basic building blocks of time and rhythm. The focus is on moving away from lick-based playing and developing your own spontaneous improvisation skills. In this way, you will develop a unique voice on your instrument while mastering the elusive skills of blues guitar phrasing.

Covering, but quickly moving on from the essential 'nuts and bolts' of blues playing (accurate bends, expressive vibrato and glissando), Melodic Phrasing looks in depth at the rhythmic fragments that are at the source of every blues guitar line. By mastering and combining these rhythms you instantly form your own unique blues guitar language and develop your own personal style.

There are extensive chapters on note placement – how to play what you want, exactly when you want. The possibilities become endless when we consider music in this way. You will develop a whole new level of awareness of the subdivisions of the beat and learn to twist the same licks into thousands of different, powerful phrases.

Lick displacement is also covered in minute detail – how to move the same line by 1/4, 1/8th or even 1/16th notes to disguise its origins and make it sound fresh, new and personal. This is one of the big secrets of blues guitar phrasing, especially when used across chord changes.

Much time is spent teaching you to organically develop any lick in a strong, musically creative way. This kind of musical development is at the roots of all blues improvisation and is imperative to developing your own musical voice.

You will also master *question and answer phrasing* and begin to use it as a vehicle to develop your own solos.

Book Three: Beyond Pentatonics

"Beyond Pentatonics" shows you how to break away from the Minor pentatonic soloing rut that many blues guitarists quickly fall into.

The first half of Beyond Pentatonics shows you how to target the most powerful notes from each chord in a blues progression to deliver the greatest emotional effect.

Every chord change is covered in minute detail, with clear diagrams and dozens of great licks to learn. You'll quickly find yourself playing emotive, original solos that you never thought possible.

The second half of Beyond Pentatonics, gives you many possible scale choices for each chord in the blues progression. Essential scale choices are given for the I, IV and V chords, with theory and important concepts clearly explained.

There are over 125 pieces of authentic blues vocabulary, plus many tricks of the trade to help you incorporate these compelling sounds into your solos.

There is no better, more detailed book to teach you the secrets of blues guitar soloing.

These three books are now available in a compilation edition from Amazon.com

Listen carefully, take your time and above all, have fun!

Joseph

Get the Audio

The audio files for this book are available to download for free from **www.fundamental-changes.com** and the link is in the top right corner. Simply select this book title from the drop-down menu and follow the instructions to get the audio.

We recommend that you download the files directly to your computer, not to your tablet, and extract them there before adding them to your media library. You can then put them on your tablet, iPod or burn them to CD. On the download page there is a help PDF and we also provide technical support via the contact form.

Kindle / eReaders

To get the most out of this book, remember that you can double tap any image to enlarge it. Turn off 'column viewing' and hold your kindle in landscape mode.

Chapter One – The Basic 12-bar Blues Structure

As much as it is a cliché and the starting point for a million guitarists, the standard *12-bar blues progression* is essential knowledge for any guitar player. It is the basis of countless songs, and has been in the musician's repertoire for longer than living memory.

We will begin by looking at the most common 12-bar blues form before looking at common alterations, additions, and riffs.

While it is hopefully obvious, the form we are studying is named the 12-bar blues because as a musical structure it is 12-bars long. In its most basic form, it contains just three chords and all of them are taken from the Major scale that you may already know. These chords are formed on the first, fourth and fifth *degrees* (notes) of the Major scale.

For example, in the key of A Major:

A B C# D E F# G#

We use the chords A Major, D Major and E Major.

The degrees of a scale are always described by Roman numerals:

1 = I

4 = IV

5 = V

So, in the key of A Major:

A = I

D = IV and

E = V

When we use Roman numerals to describe scale tones it doesn't matter which key we are in, we can always use them to explain the relationships between chords. In a sense, it is musical algebra because we describe the relationships between chords rather than the chords themselves.

In modern Western music (especially pop, rock and blues), chords I, IV and V are the most commonly used chords in all songs.

The simplest 12-bar blues progression uses just chords I, IV and V. While it might not be the most exciting rendition of The Blues you will ever hear, it is important to know the foundations of the progression before launching into the many possible variations.

Study the following chord chart. I have shown both the letter names and the Roman numeral description of each chord, along with an open position chord voicing so you can play along with the audio example.

Example 1a:

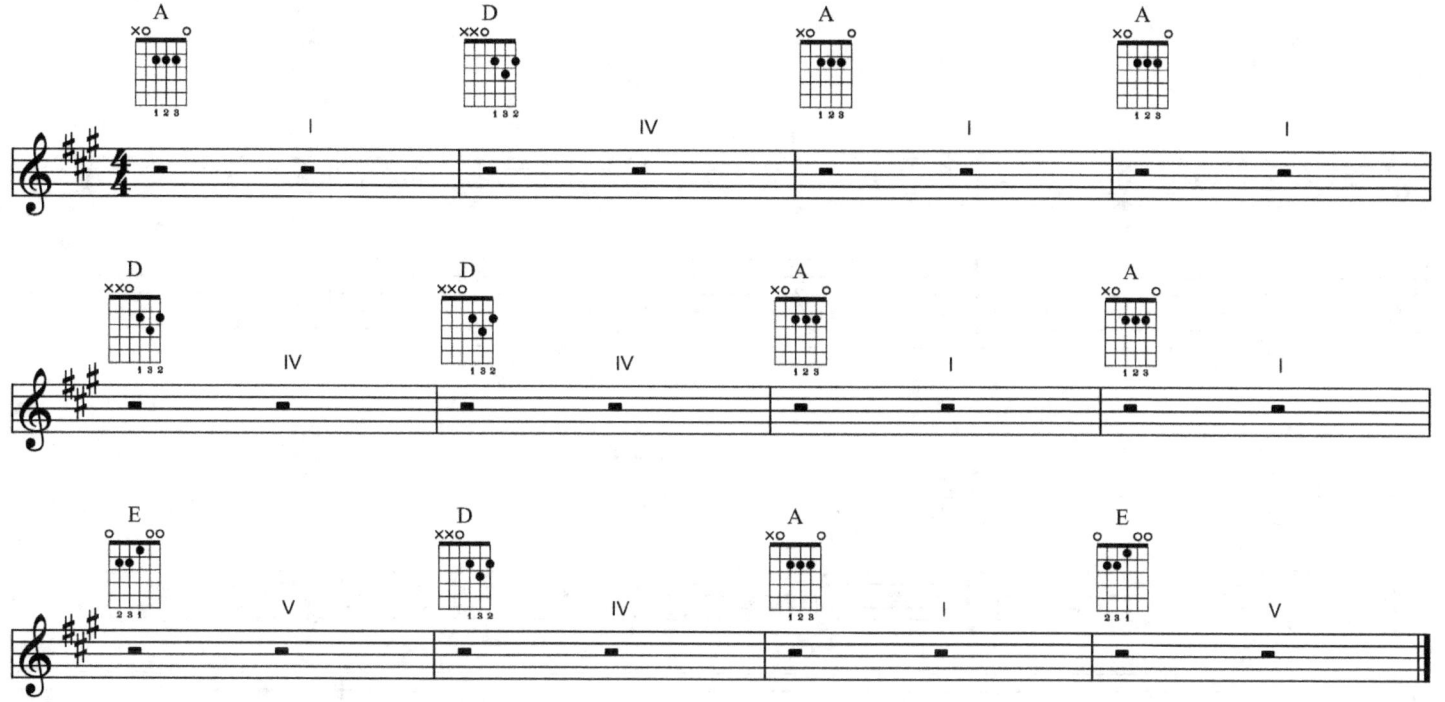

Broadly speaking, there are two main musical feels used in blues rhythm: *straight* (or even) feel and the *swing* (or triplet) feel. The triplet feel is more common and can be heard in famous blues tunes such as Stormy Monday (T-Bone Walker), Blues Power (Albert King), or Five Long Years (Buddy Guy).

The straight blues feel is important and used in many songs, such as Scuttle Buttin' (Stevie Ray Vaughan), Messin' with the Kid (Buddy Guy) and Crying at Daybreak (Howlin' Wolf). It is more common in rock and pop songs than in, what a traditionalist might consider to be, *true* blues. However, the straight blues is an easier place to start.

The first exercise is to play the correct chords just on beat 1 and beat 3.

If you don't understand the notation, listen to the audio examples and try to play along with the recorded versions.

The audio files for this book are available to download for free from **www.fundamental-changes.com** and the link is in the top right corner. Simply select this title from the drop-down menu and follow the instructions to get the audio.

Example 1b:

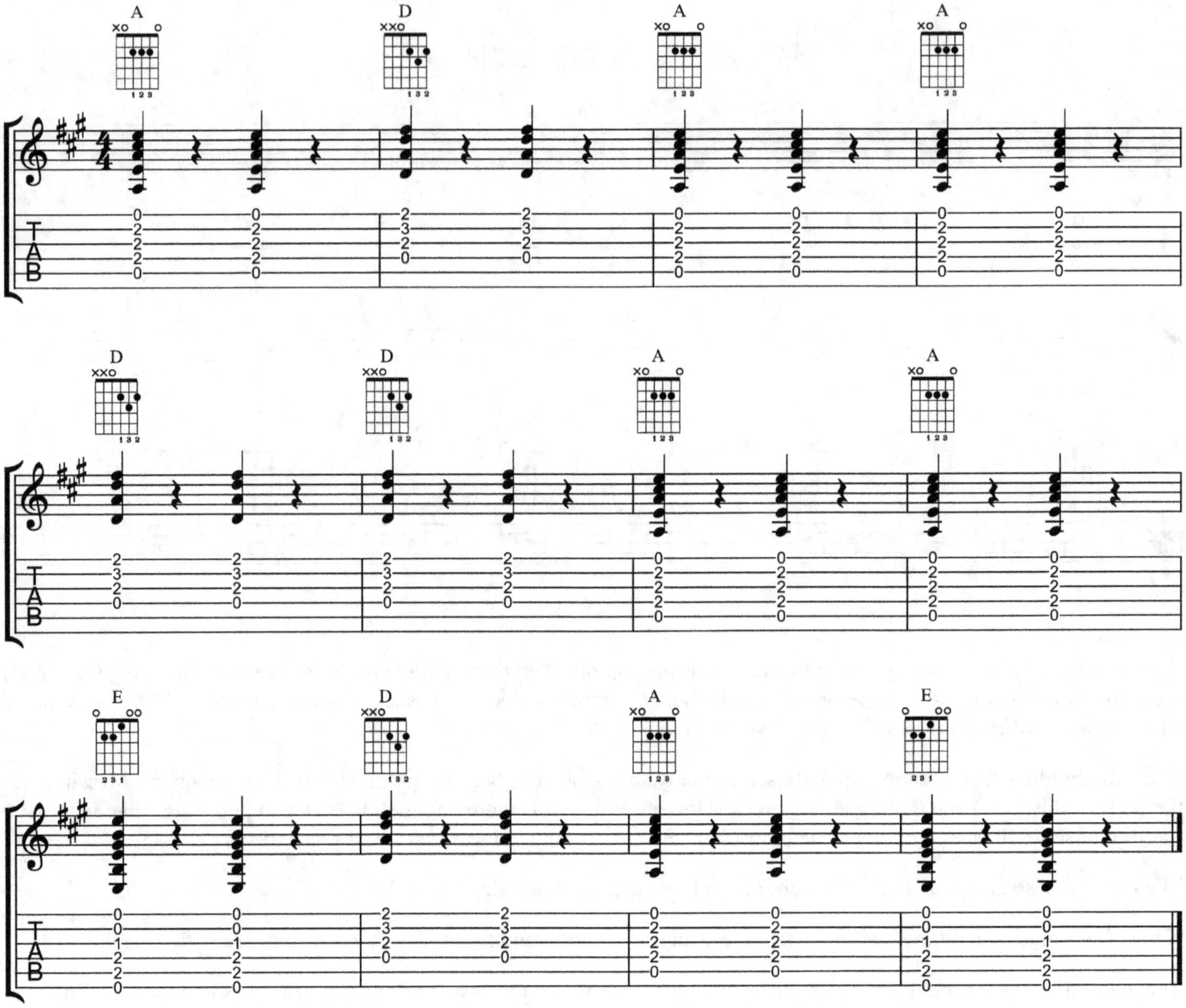

The next exercise is to strum on just beats *2 and 4* as shown in **example 1c:**

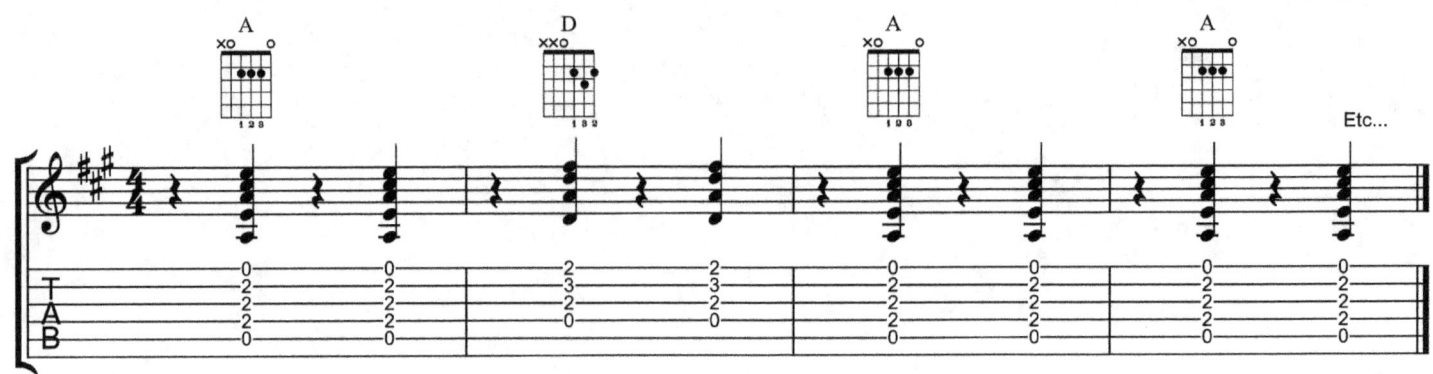

Finally, try adding a bit of a groove to the rhythm guitar by playing on one of the *off-beats* (half way between the main pulses). Listen to the audio track if you're not sure of how this rhythm sounds. In the following example play on beat 1, beat 2 and the off-beat of beat 4. (4&).

Example 1d:

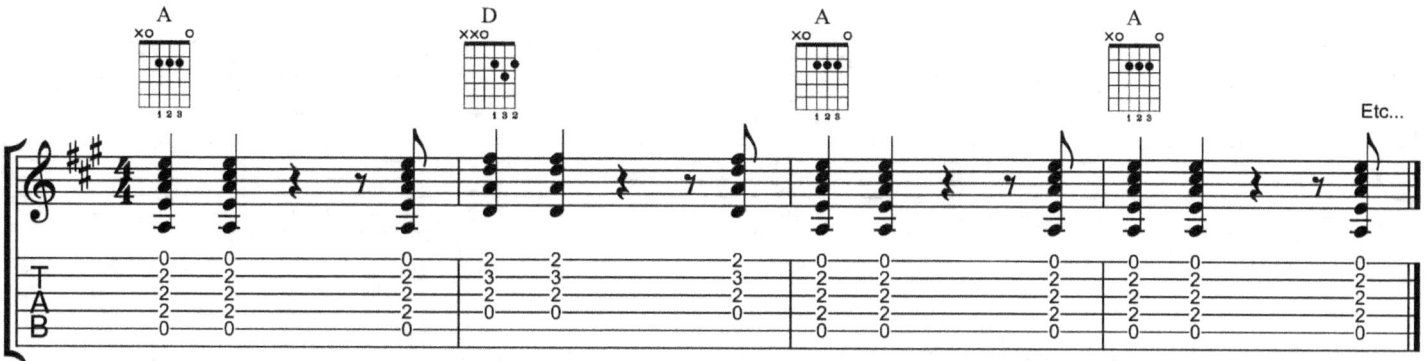

Examples 1a-1d are all examples of a *straight* blues feel. Each beat is divided evenly into two equal halves and this musical feel is found often in rock and pop music. You can count *"1 and 2 and 3 and 4 and"* throughout the progression.

We will look at more ways to subdivide the bar and free up your playing in Chapter Seven, but for now keep amming along with Backing Track 1 and see if you can find more places to hit the chords. Be led by the groove of the backing track and use the bass and drums to guide you.

The Triplet Blues

The triplet blues has a more laidback, lazy feel at slow tempos, although it can get quite bouncy when we speed things up. Each of the four main beats in the bar is divided into *three* even subdivisions giving a total of twelve quavers (1/8th notes) in a bar. This is what the *time signature* at the start of the following bar of music means: Twelve 1/8th notes in the bar. It is musical convention to group them into threes.

A bar of 12/8 looks like this:

There are plenty of ways to divide a bar of 12/8 and we will explore these in Chapter Eight, but for now let's stick with some of the more popular grooves.

We can still play on beats 1 and 3.

11

Example 1e:

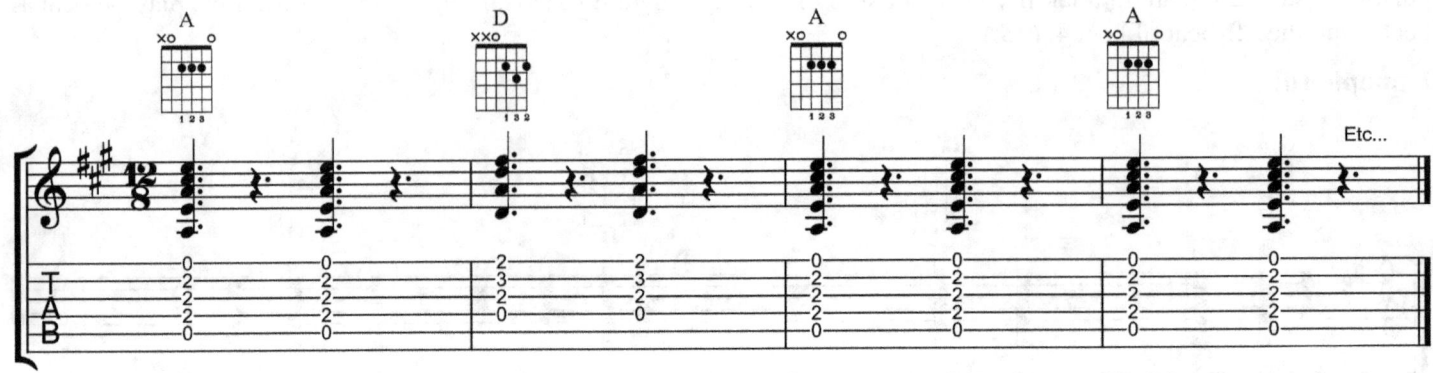

Listen to example 1e before you play it. The rhythmic feel is a bit bouncier so you might find it a little harder to place the chord accurately. Even though you're still playing on beats 1 and 3, the musical feel is very different. This triplet feel is common in blues and R&B.

Now play on just beats 2 and 4.

Example 2f:

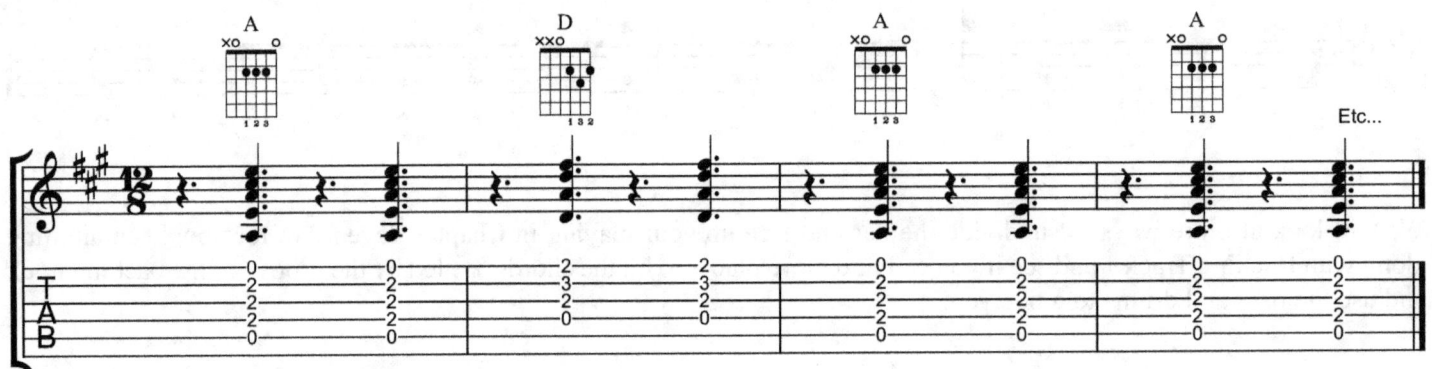

The final 12/8 example (for now) teaches you to play on the *first and third* 1/8th note of each beat. This is one of the most important basic blues rhythm patterns. As always, listen carefully to the audio examples to help you lock in with the musical feel.

Example 1g:

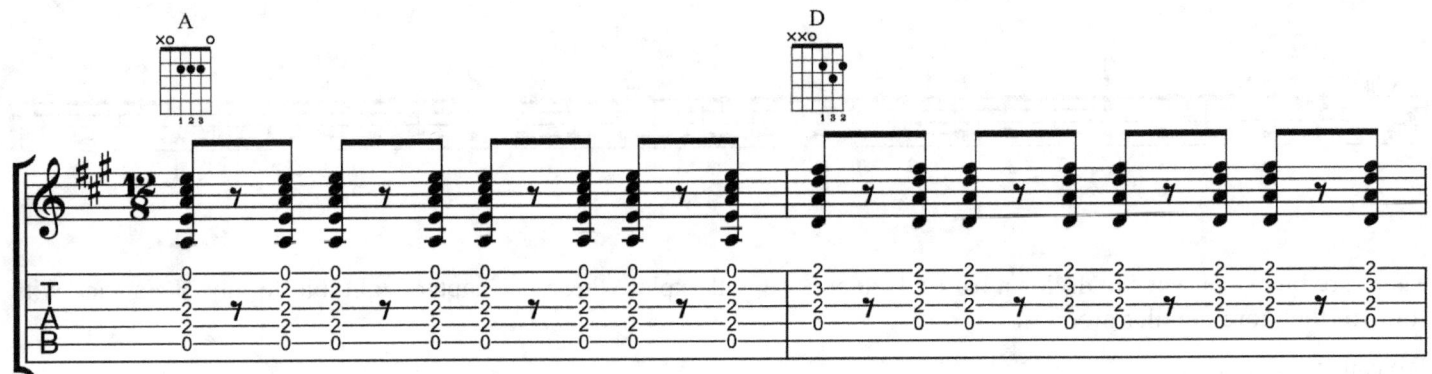

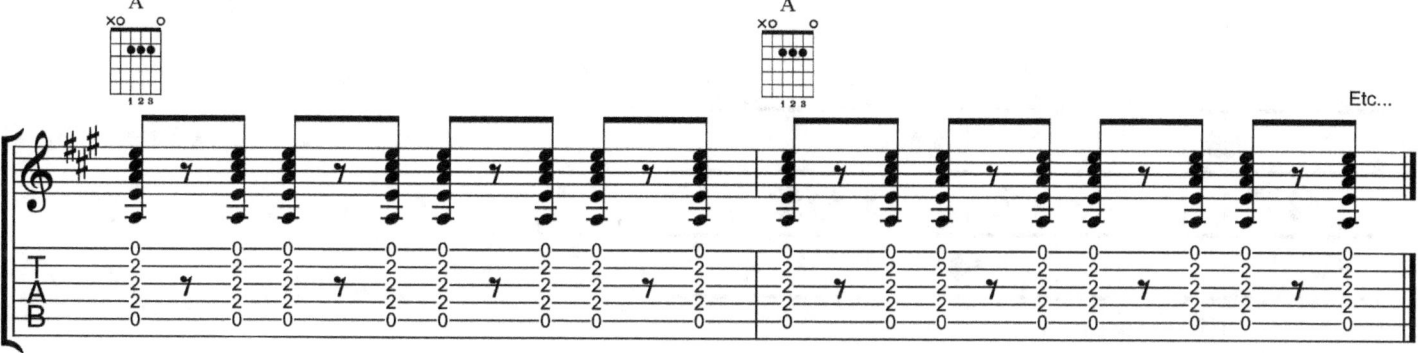

In terms of playing technique, it can be a great help to rest your strumming hand lightly on the strings to produce a muted, choppy sound. This will help to articulate the chords more clearly. You may also wish to let the first note of every beat ring slightly longer to create a less aggressive sound.

Example 1h:

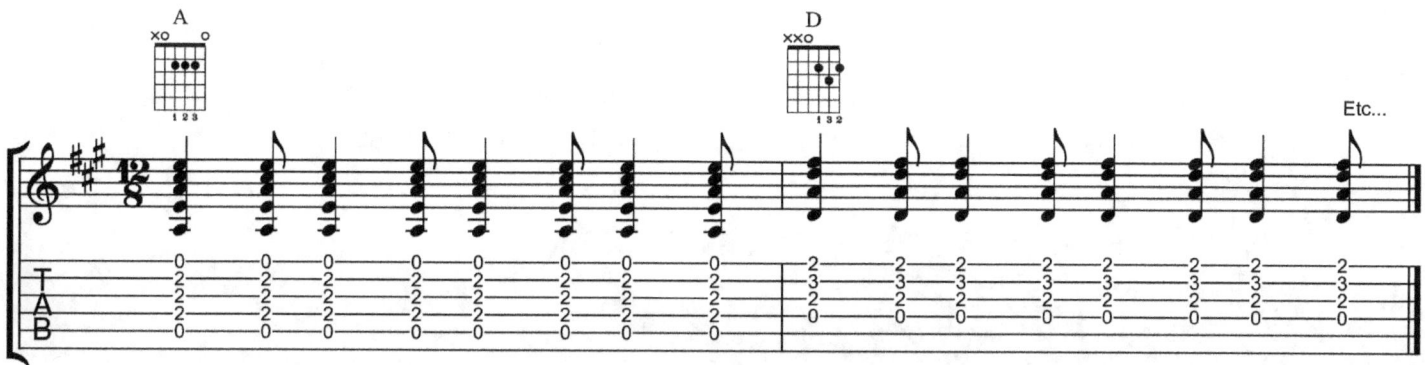

Spend time experimenting with these rhythms and see what you can come up with. Listen again to your favourite blues songs and work out whether they are played in a straight or triplet feel.

The examples in this chapter have all used Major chords. Work through the chapter again but this time substitute each chord for its equivalent '7' chord:

For example, instead of playing A Major, play A7. Here are the chord shapes you will need:

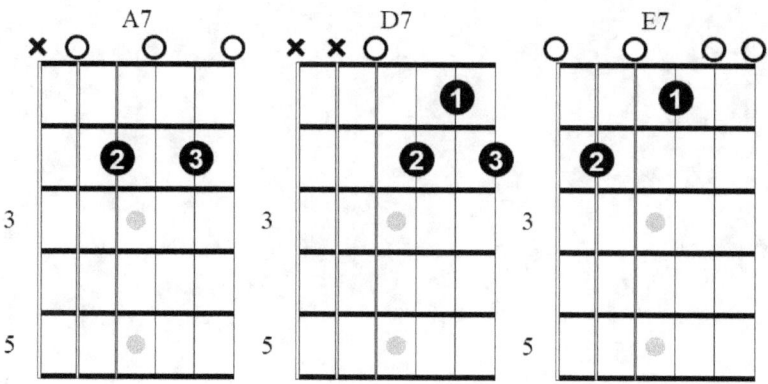

Finally, play the 12-bar blues progression using *Minor* chords:

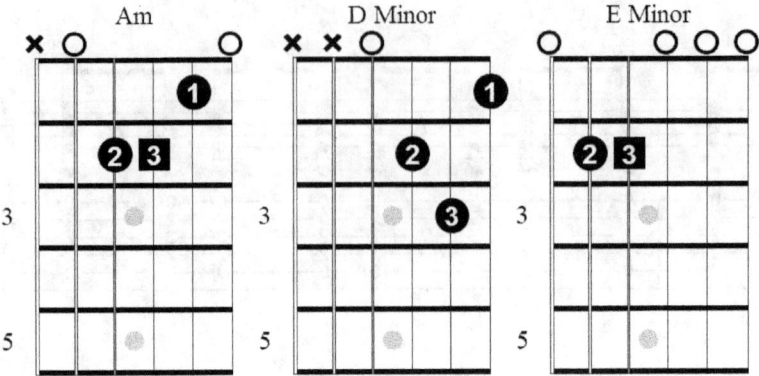

Notice how the *quality* of the chord dramatically effects the mood of the song.

Chapter Two – Open-String Blues Riffs and Variations

While it is essential to know the structure of a 12-bar blues, our rhythm guitar playing will quickly get stagnant if we stick to just playing chords.

It is a common technique to create riffs and open-string bass lines while simultaneously outlining the chord changes, as shown in the previous chapter. In this chapter, we will explore some classic examples of open string guitar riffs.

The following examples are played as *triplet* feel rhythms in the audio examples, however you should experiment by playing them as both straight and triplet feels.

Example 2a is a typical blues riff that can be used anytime there is an A Major chord (Chord I) in the progression. This idea has been used by *every* blues guitarist at some point so you need to learn it. Your picking hand continually strums the bass note (A) on the 5th string *with* a moving note on the 4th string.

Use the 1st and 3rd fingers of your fretting hand to rock backwards and forwards between the alternating notes.

Example 2a:

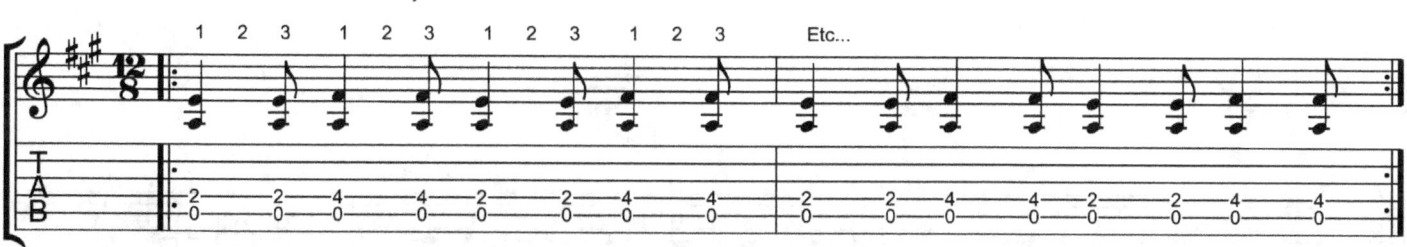

Listen to the audio example and play along with it to internalise the triplet feel. The first strum of each two-note group is longer and the second is shorter.

If we count '1 2 3 1 2 3 1 2 3 1 2 3' through each bar, the first strum lasts for the counts of 1 and 2, and the second strum lasts for just the 3rd count. Count aloud as you play along with each audio example.

To play this blues riff on the D Major chord (chord IV), simply shift the pattern onto the 4th and 3rd strings. We're playing *the same* riff, just moved over one string. Make sure you keep the unplayed bass strings quiet with a bit of palm muting.

Example 2b:

Finally, to play this riff for the E Major chord (chord V) shift this pattern onto the bottom two strings.

Example 2c:

Practise switching between each of the previous three examples. When you're ready, you can use these riffs to play through a whole blues progression.

Example 2d:

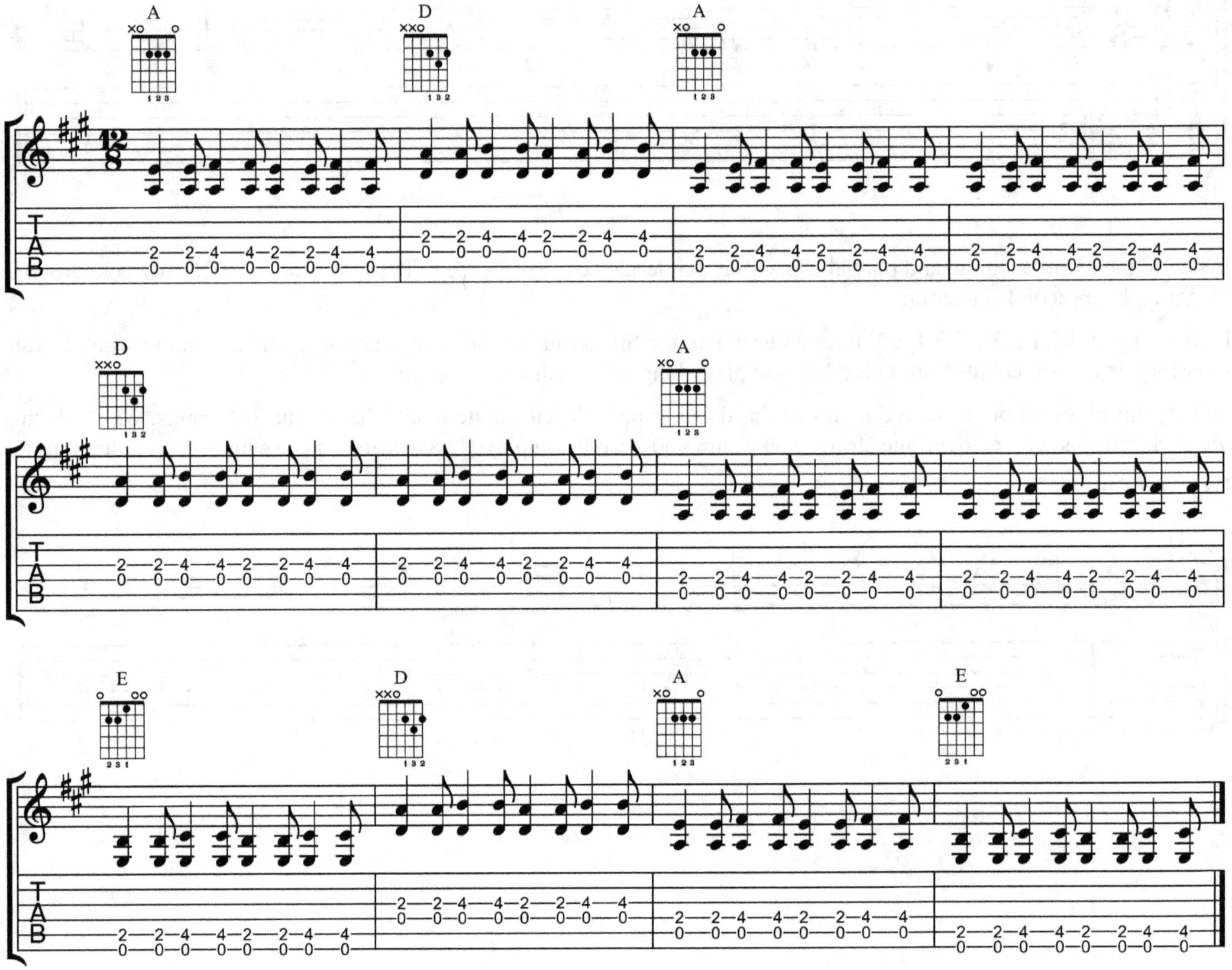

This simple pattern adds great depth to the guitar part when we play blues rhythm and is much more interesting than simply playing chords.

There are variations to the basic pattern that can be inserted anywhere to add even more interest and variation. Subtle variations in the rhythm guitar part can help give the soloist creative ideas and build the groove of the music for both the band and the audience.

In this example use your *little finger* to stretch out and play the 5th fret of the fourth string on beat 3. Move this idea through the chord changes as we did in example 2d.

Example 2e:

The next variation adds a hammer-on idea on the fifth string.

Example 2f:

Again, this riff can be used on the A, D and E chords by simply moving it across string groups as you learned earlier in the chapter.

Another classic riff in the style of John Lee Hooker uses 'pull-offs' to create a descending bass line at the end of each bar.

Example 2g:

This next example combines previous ideas and uses a bass note on a lower string to give even more movement in the guitar part.

Example 2h:

As always, practise moving this idea through all three chords.

Until now, all the bass fills have taken place on the final few beats of each bar. We can easily shake things up a bit by adding a fill on beat 2.

Example 2i:

A great approach is to split each chord into two parts to *displace* the bass line.

Example 2j:

Once you have a few of these riffs under your fingers, mix and match them in a 12-bar blues progression. All the ideas are freely interchangeable so slot them in wherever you feel they work.

One possible example out of the thousands of permutations is shown below. I've added a couple of new fills to keep you on your toes!

Example 2k:

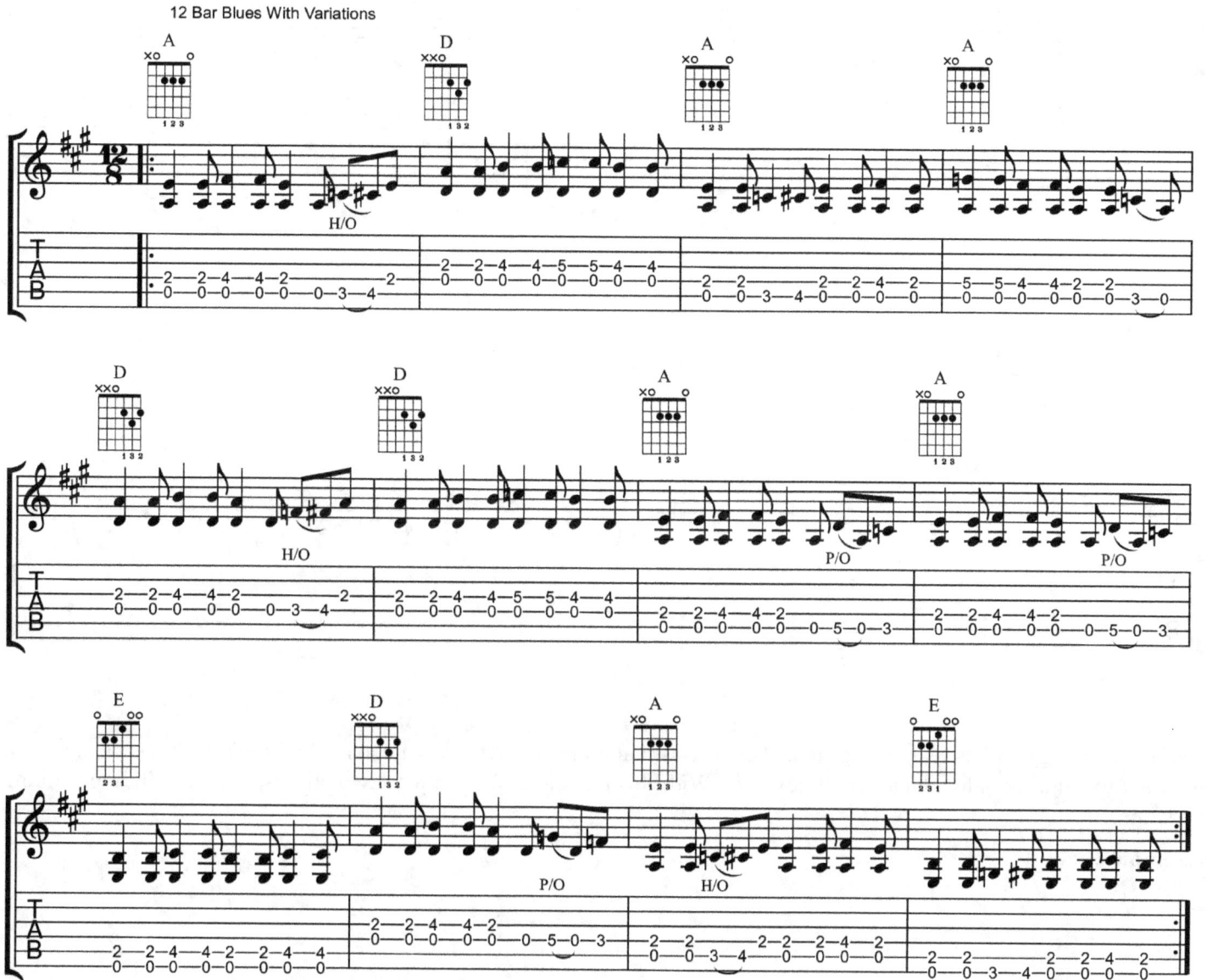

To get inspiration of what can be achieved with this simple rhythm guitar technique, listen to Pride and Joy by Stevie Ray Vaughan. There's only one guitar playing on that intro!

In Pride and Joy, Stevie Ray Vaughan combines the kinds of bass lines we have studied in this chapter with simultaneous chord playing. This hybrid of chords+bassline is typical of the Texas Blues style. Let's look at a few short examples understand this kind of playing.

E Major is normally the most common key for a guitar-based 12-bar blues for many reasons, but one of the main ones is that we can use the open E string to form bass lines as we play chords. Here's one way to add a bass line to an E Major chord in 12/8. Use strict alternate picking on this idea to help you get into the feel of the riff.

Example 2l:

We can also apply this idea to an A Major chord:

Example 2m:

Another reason guitarists like to play in the key of E is that all the open strings are available to play. This is handy when we want to hammer onto a chord from nowhere. With this technique we can play two chords in a bar with the walking bass line.

Example 2n:

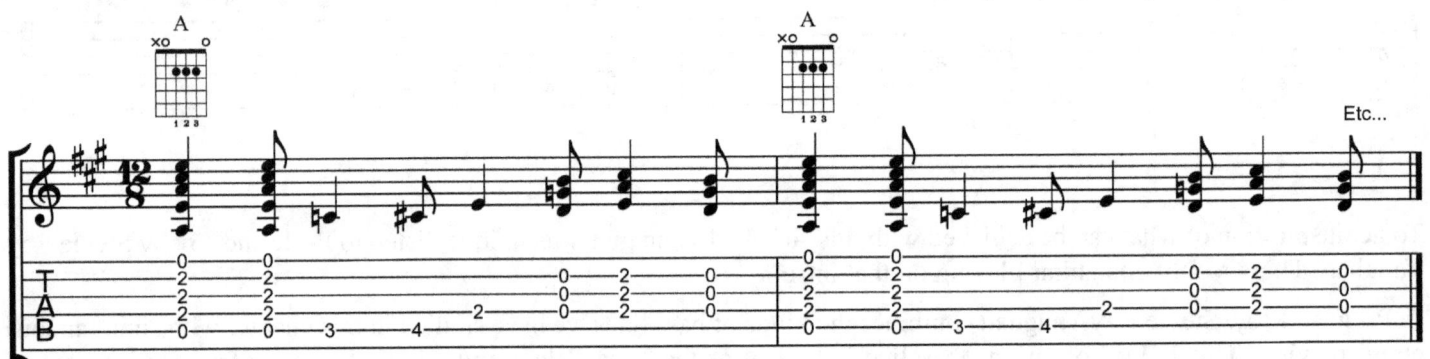

Another approach in this style is to use two different chords in one bar. The next example is heard as a riff in E Major despite the strong A Major chord late in the bar.

Example 2o:

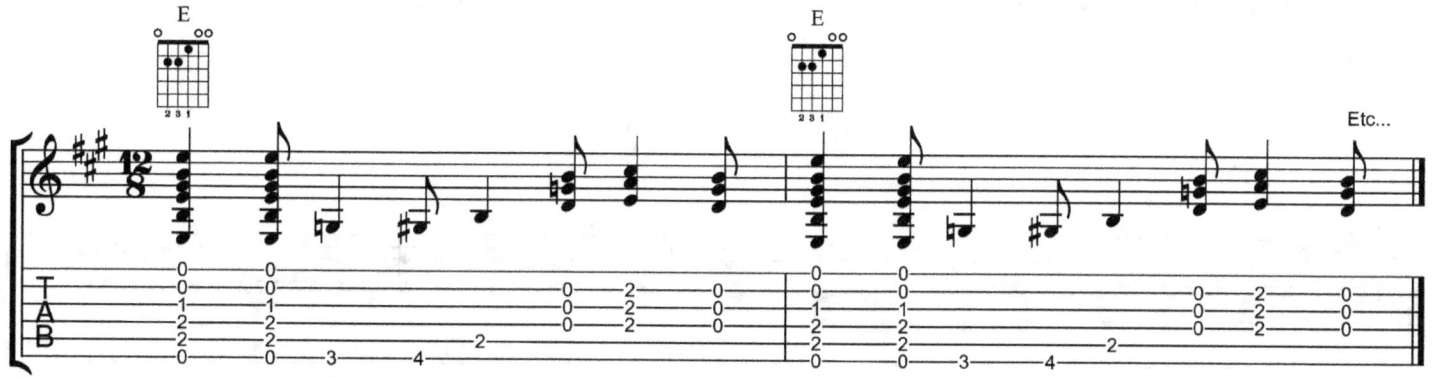

Another great Stevie Ray Vaughan bass line to check out is the one from the track, Rude Mood.

Listening to bass lines can be a great source of ideas to emulate in your playing. Try stealing a few!

It's important to point out that on the turnaround section (the final four bars), the final V chord is often *delayed* by up to two beats. Play through example 2p to learn this important technique in the key of A.

Example 2p:

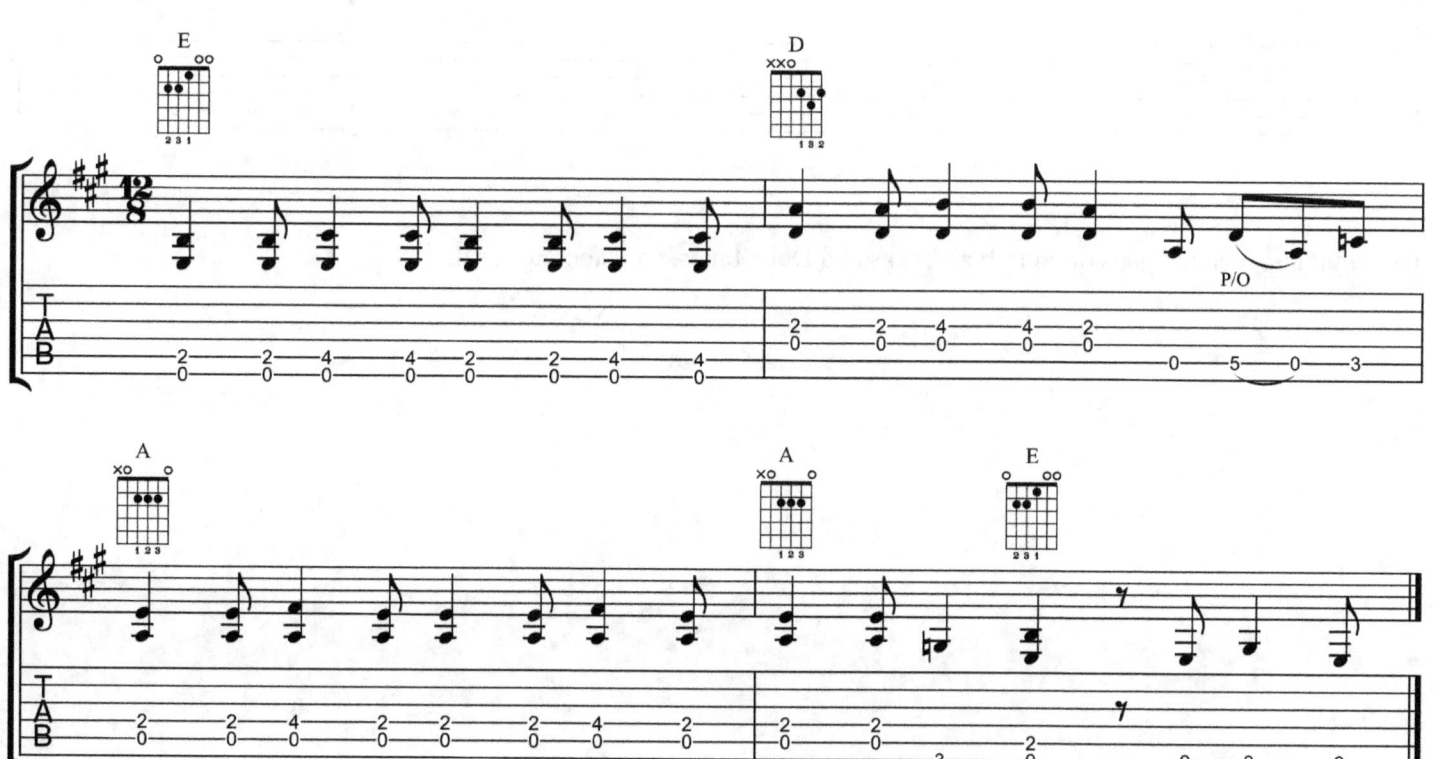

The displacement of the final V chord can occur due to a turnaround lick that starts in on chord I in bar eleven (bar three in the following example). Notice how the lick in the A Major delays the V chord (E).

Example 2q:

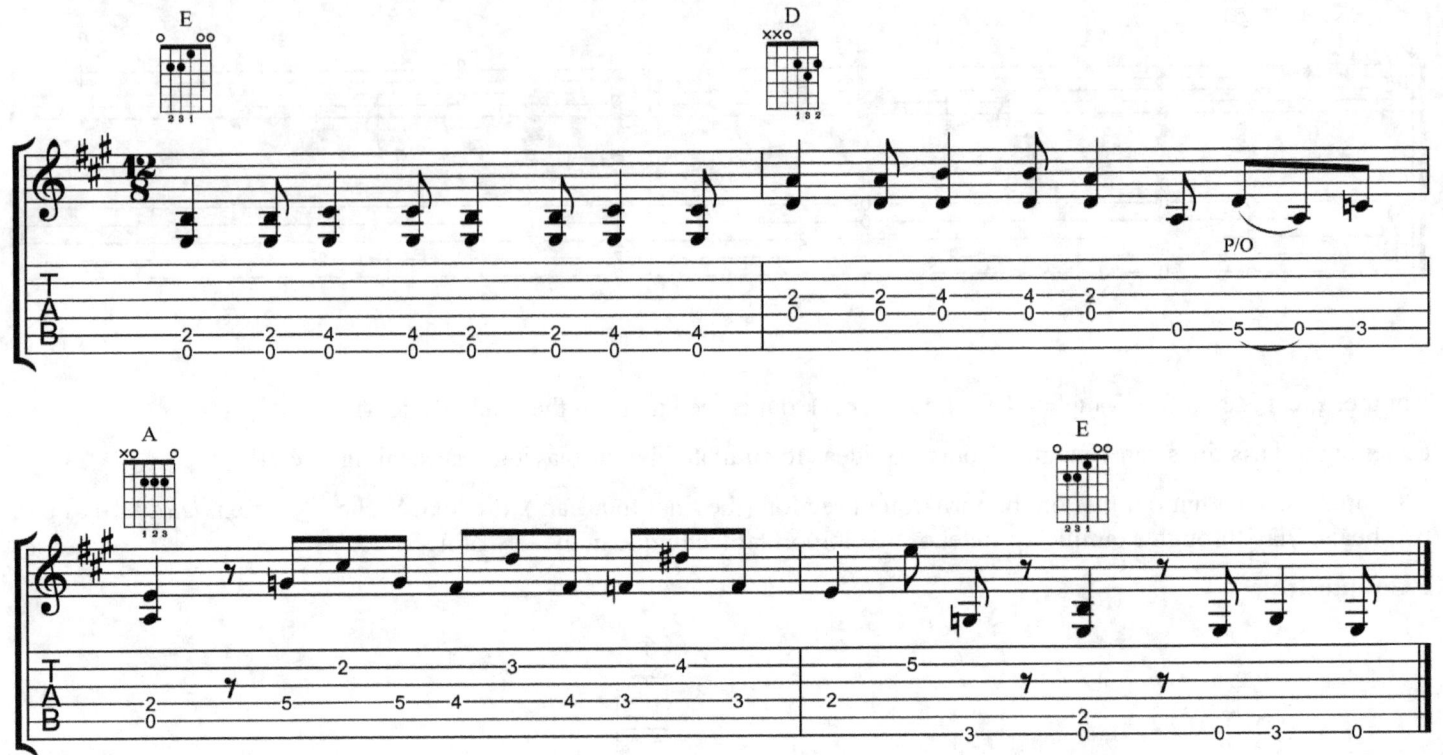

This rhythmic idea happens often in both Texas and Delta blues, so listen out for it.

Chapter Three – Using Dominant 7 Chords

While the 12-bar blues derives from chords I, IV and V in the Major scale, it is common to substitute these Major chords for any other chord quality you wish. The most common substitutions are to use Dominant 7 (7) and Minor 7 (m7) chords.

We briefly covered open position Dominant 7 chords in Chapter One:

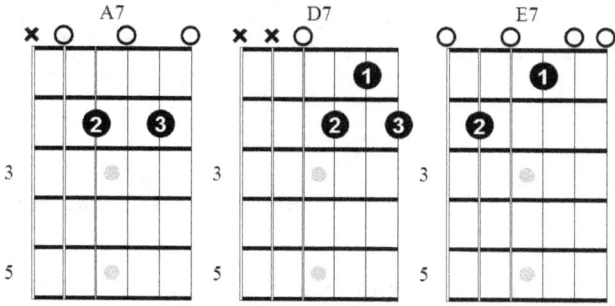

The next example shows how to play the 12-bar blues using Dominant 7 chords instead of Major ones.

Example 3a:

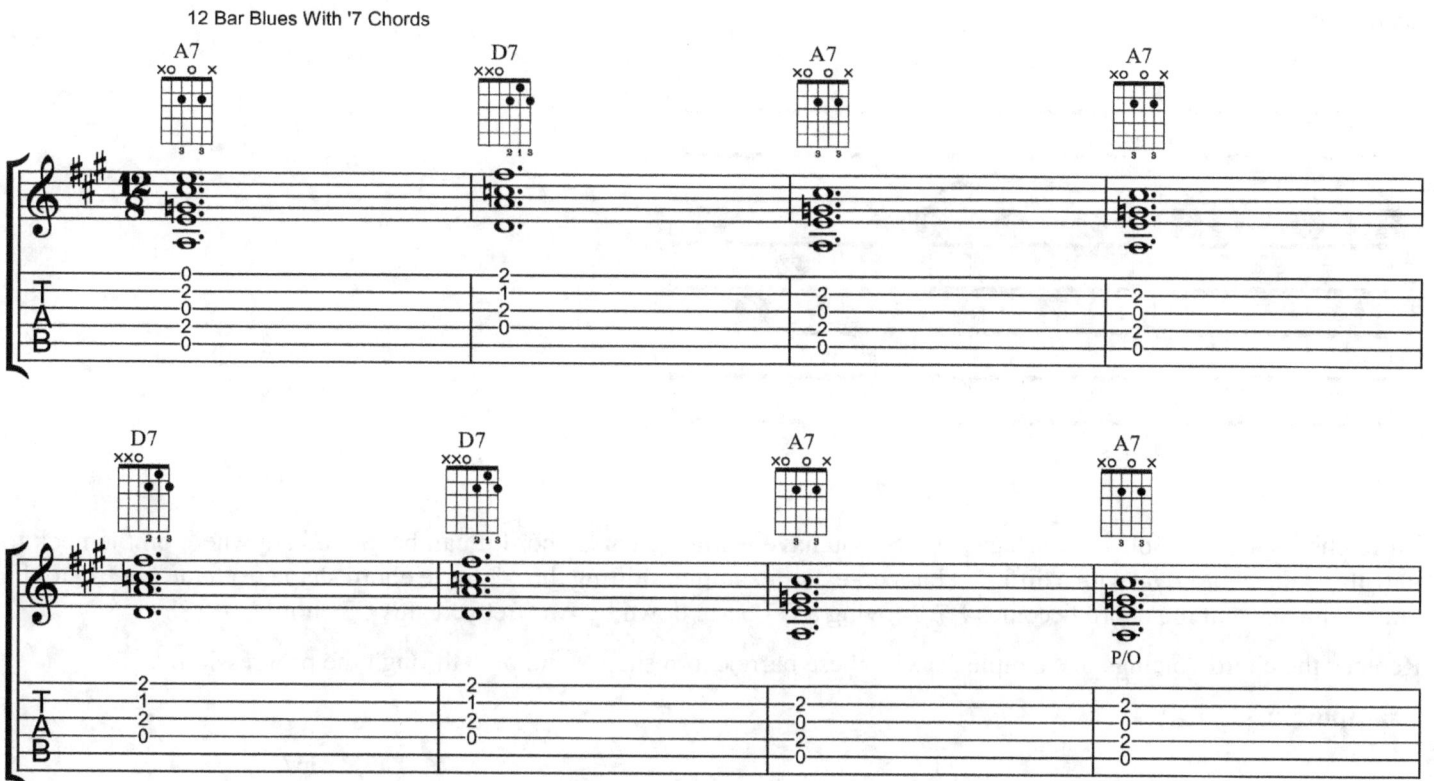

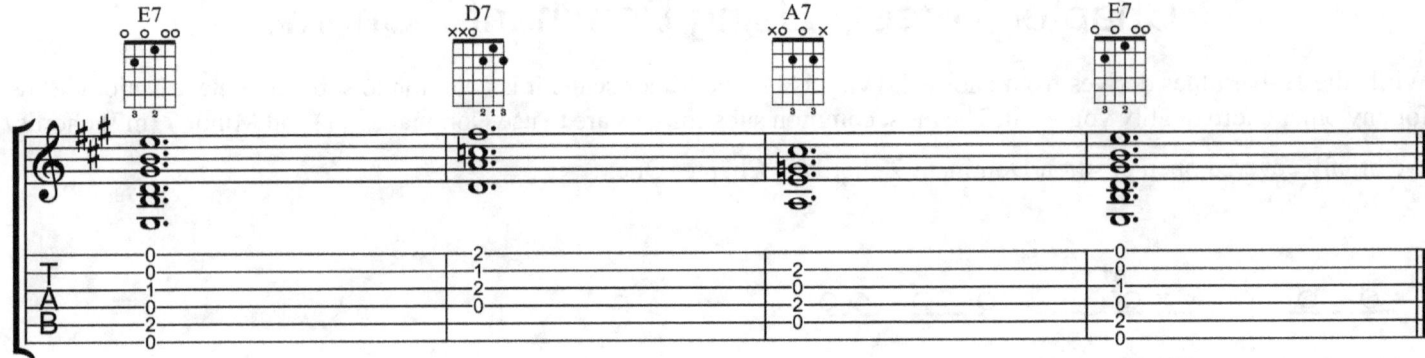

Notice how the whole mood of the music has altered from being happy with Major chords to being a bit more laid back and smooth with the Dominant 7 chords.

All the riffs you learned in the previous chapter work over this progression so try combining the chord and bass line approach we learned in Chapter Two with the Dominant 7 chord approach.

These open position chords are important to know, but to expand our ability to play The Blues in *any* key we need to learn to play *barre* chords.

The first shapes to learn when moving to barre chords are given here,

Example 3b:

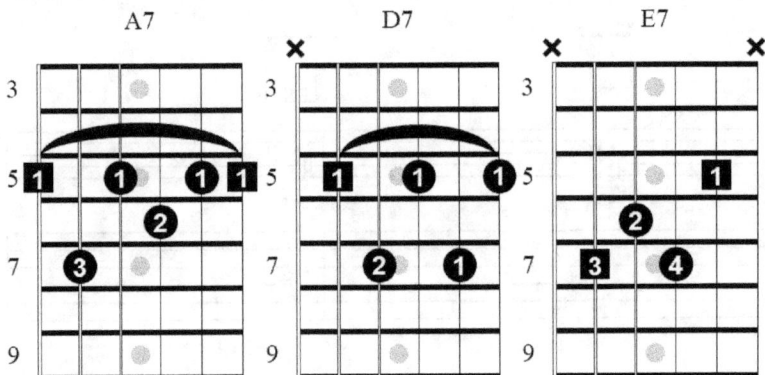

Barre chords are movable chord shapes. Once you have learned a barre chord it can be moved anywhere on the neck to play the same chord *type* with a different bass note. For example, shifting the A7 barre chord shape from the 5th fret to the 7th fret means that the chord becomes B7. Moving a D7 barre down by two frets creates C7 chord.

Replace the chord voicings in example 3a with these barre chord shapes and play through the progression.

Example 3c:

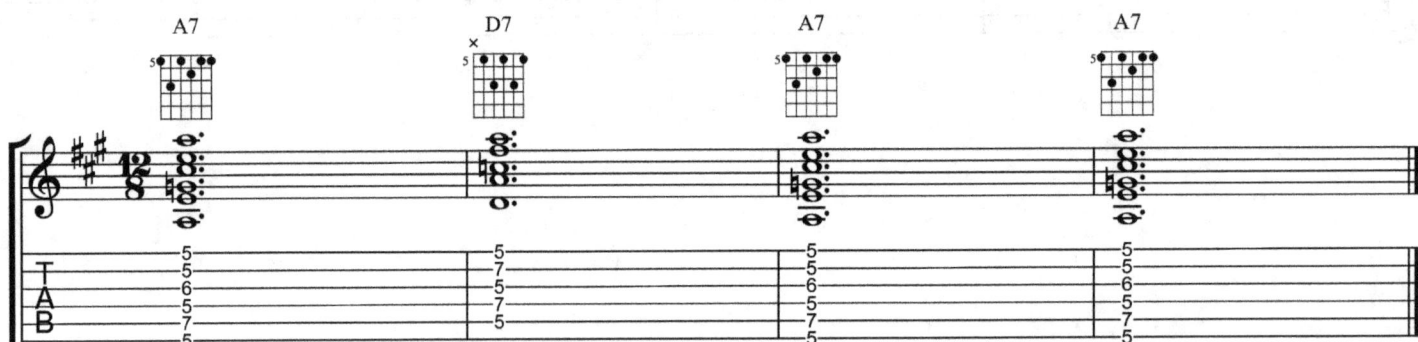

Let's add some rhythmic movement to the 12-bar blues by splitting each barre chord into a bass note and a chord stab to add interest and texture to the rhythm guitar part. Continue the following pattern throughout the 12-bar blues.

Example 3d:

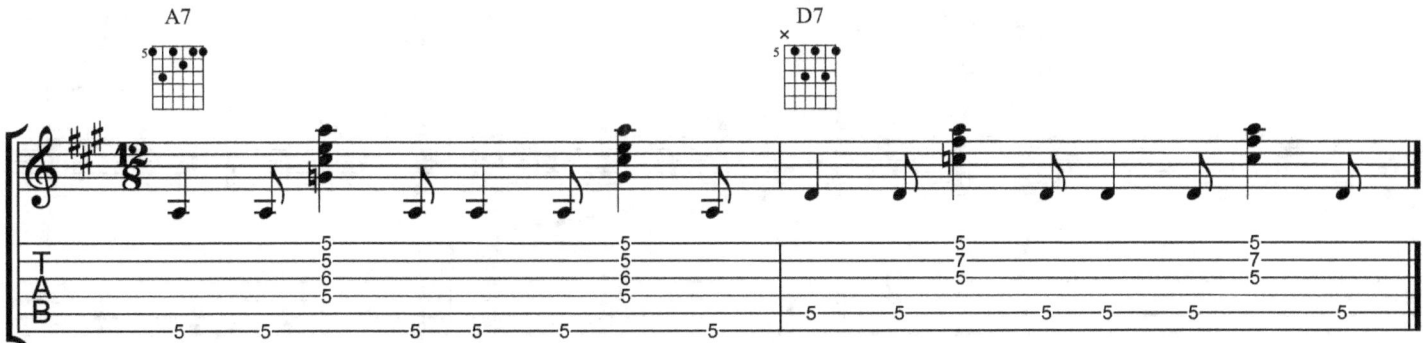

I normally use *palm muting* on the bass notes to give a more percussive effect and then let the chord ring for slightly longer to create a multi-layered texture in the rhythm guitar part. You can hear this idea in the audio example.

A common idea in blues rhythm guitar is to slide into the barre chord from a semitone below. If the slide is done from a weak beat to a strong beat you can always use this technique.

The technical challenge is to make sure that the chord you are sliding from, for example Ab7, rings through into the following A7 chord. The trick is to find just the right amount of pressure that allows you to hold the chord down while sliding it a semitone. The full six-string chord shape is held in every slide, however I normally just strum the top three or four strings.

Use your first finger to play the final note in each bar to help you get into position for the next barre chord. The whole 12-bar progression is played in example 3e, but only the first two bars are notated. Listen carefully and apply these slides to each chord in the progression.

Example 3e:

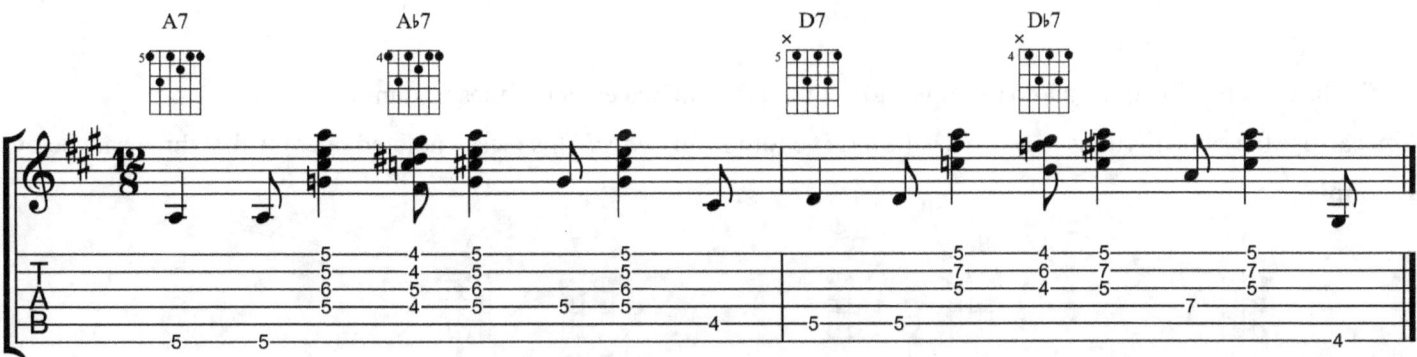

Here is another idea that begins just before beat one.

Example 3f:

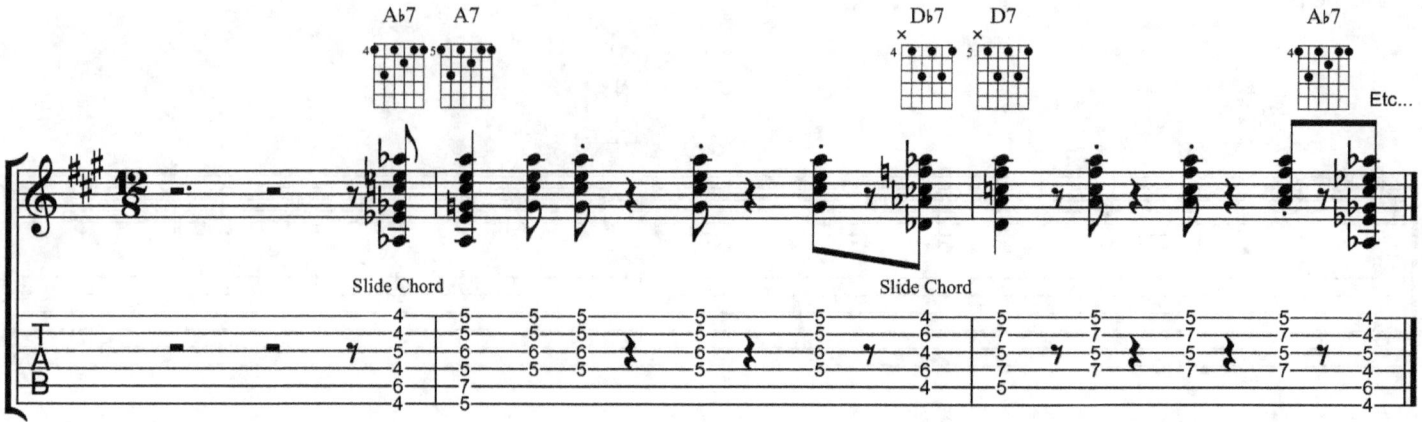

You can also slide two semitones.

Example 3g:

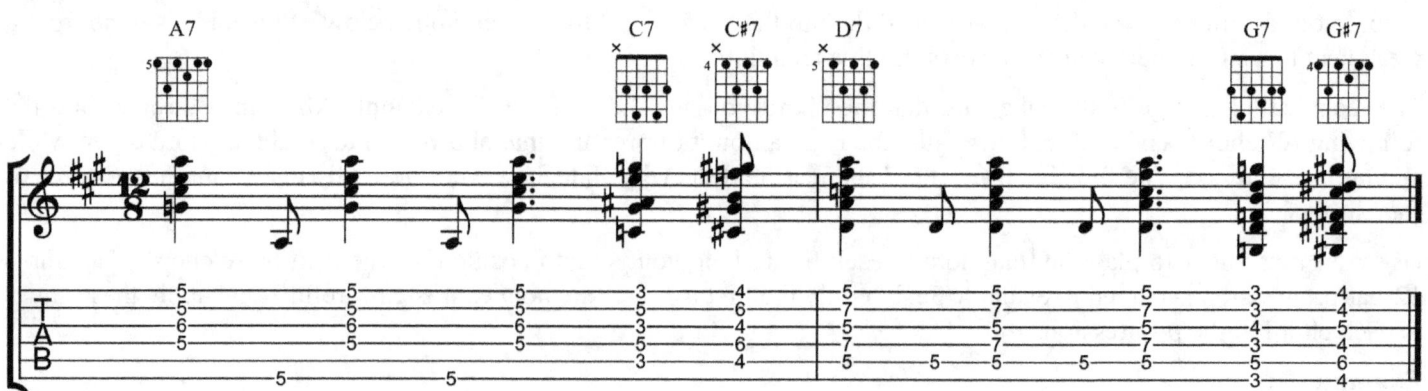

Again, listen carefully to the audio examples to get the feel and placement of these examples.

You can use the same rhythms to approach the target chord from *above*. This idea is notated over the first three bars below.

Example 3h:

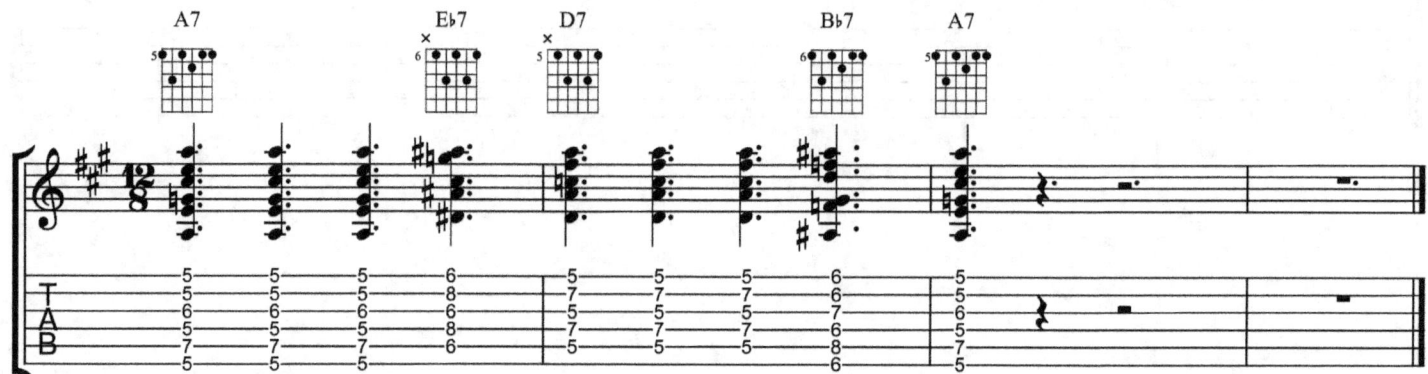

We can apply the earlier open-string riffs to barre chords. Some of the following examples require quite a stretch in the fretting hand, so if you find that you can't reach, try dropping your thumb lower on the back of the neck and remember you don't have to hold *all* the notes in the chord. It is quite acceptable to just play the bottom two strings if the stretch requires it. Here is the basic blues riff with the A7, D7 and E7 chords.

Example 3i:

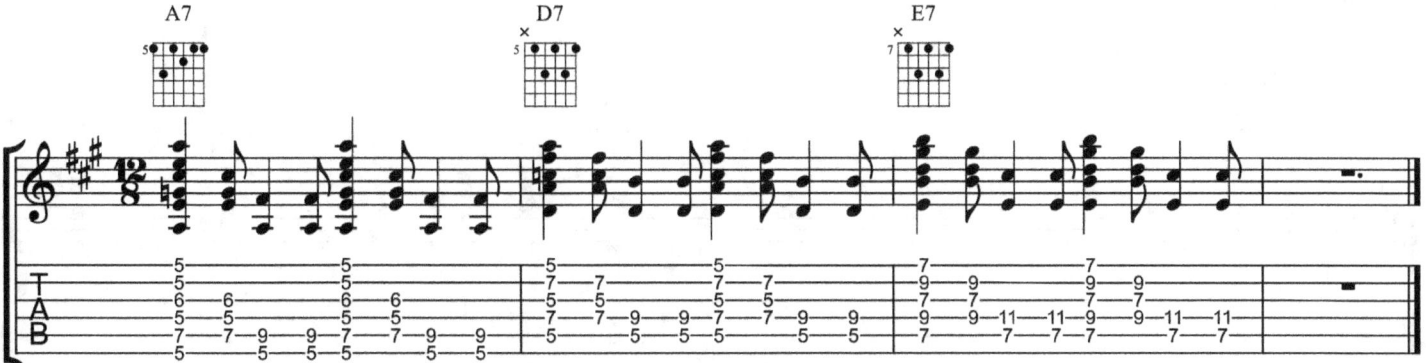

We can use an even bigger stretch with our little finger.

Example 3j:

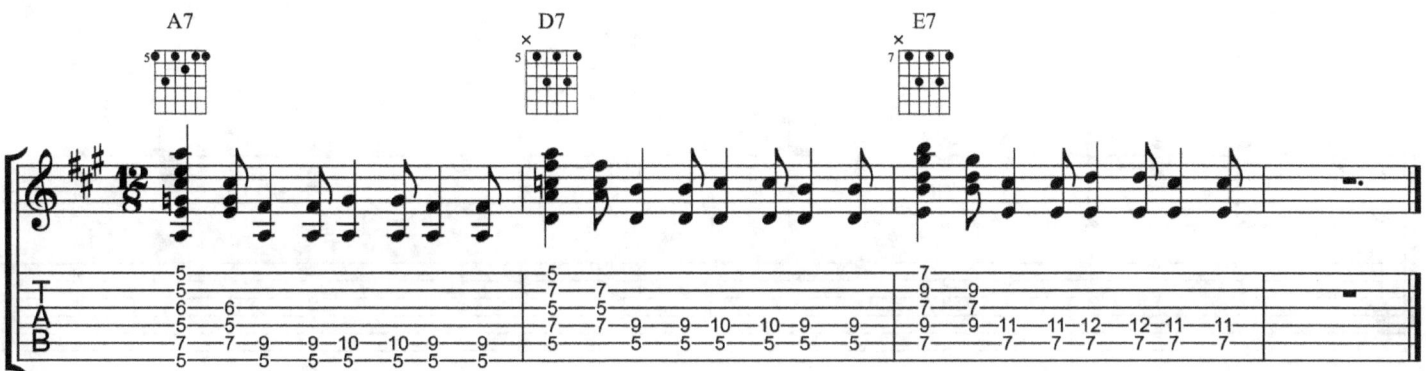

We can even add a sliding chord for extra movement in the rhythm part.

Example 3k:

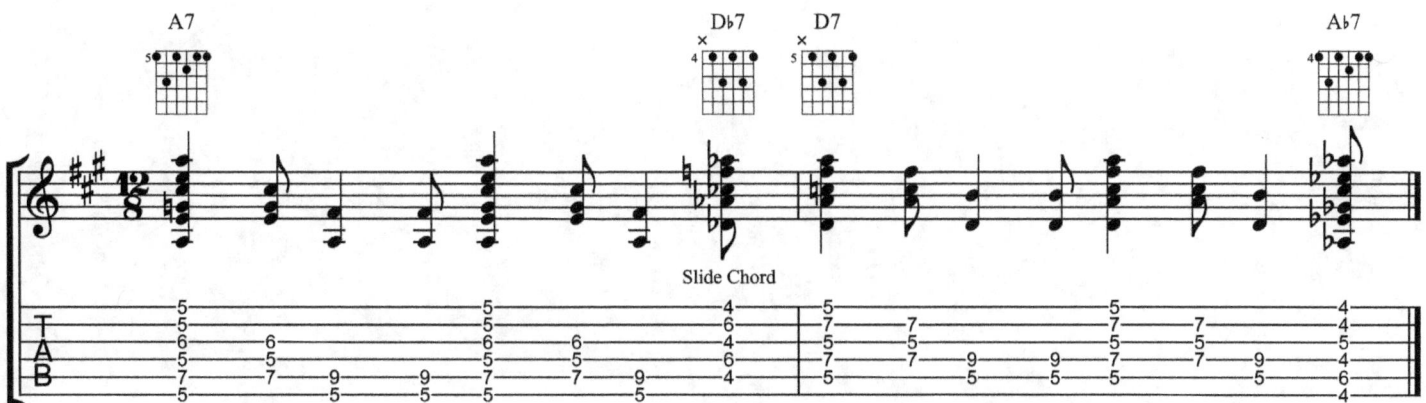

The movement in the rhythm guitar part can be at the top of the chord, not just in the bass. The following examples work well when we play rhythm underneath a guitar solo but can be a little too busy when there is a vocal melody.

In the following examples, use your little finger (pinky) to add a moving melody note at the top of the chord. With my picking hand, I use my thumb to play the bass notes and my index, middle and ring fingers to play the three note block chords.

Example 3l:

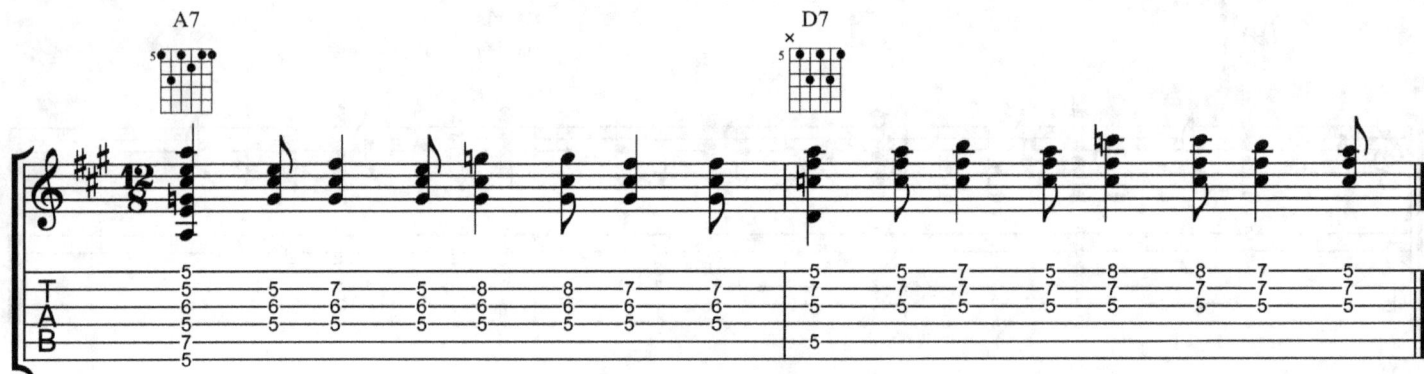

Example 3m:

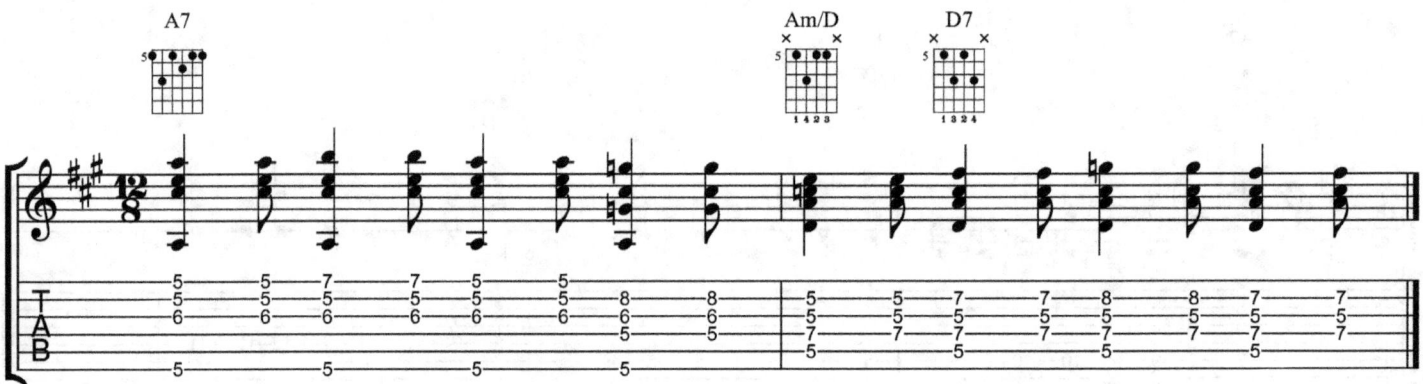

We can find many melodies to give subtle movement to the rhythm guitar part, just by moving our little finger. Ideas like this can give a lot of interest to the song, just be careful not to get in the way of the singer or soloist.

Chapter Four – Extensions to the Dominant 7 Chord

Dominant 7 chords are often used in The Blues, but we can use *any* chord from the Dominant 7 *family*.

This isn't a theory book, so to keep things simple the Dominant chord family includes 7s, 9s, 11s and 13s and these are all normally interchangeable. For example, if you see an A7 written there is often no reason why you can't substitute it for an A9 or A13 chord. You need to be more careful with Dominant 11 chords so we will avoid these for now.

Think of Dominant 9s, 11s and 13s as *extended* Dominant 7 chords. While the basic Dominant chord quality and function are the same, these extensions add depth, colour and interest to our music.

Here are some useful voicings for Dominant 9s and 13s for chords I, IV, and V.

Note that the voicing of A9 here is *rootless*. This works best in the context of a band situation where the bass player plays the root.

Example 4a:

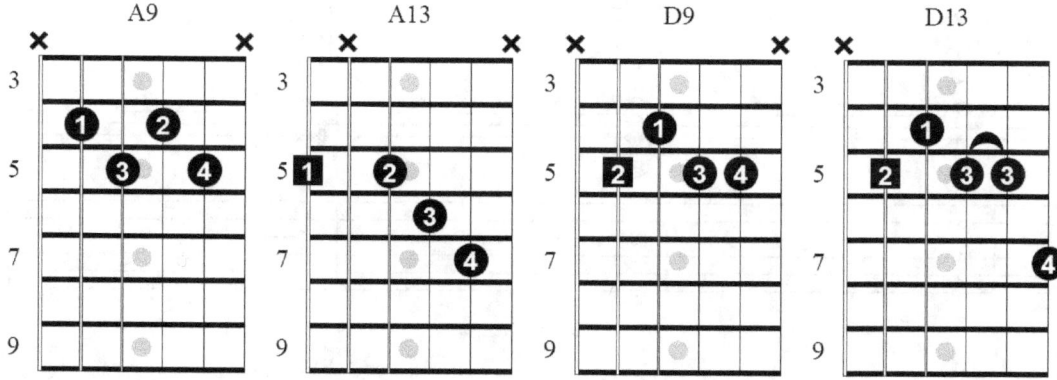

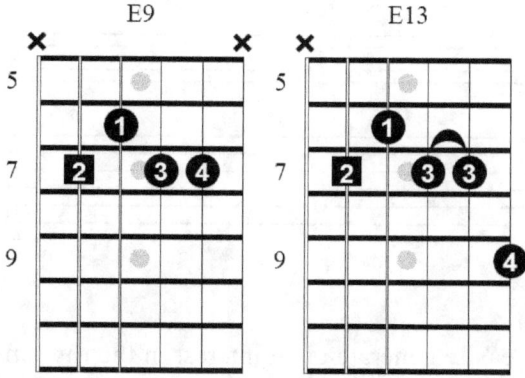

We will begin by substituting some of the original '7' chord voicings in the 12-bar blues with *extended* chord voicings.

Example 4b:

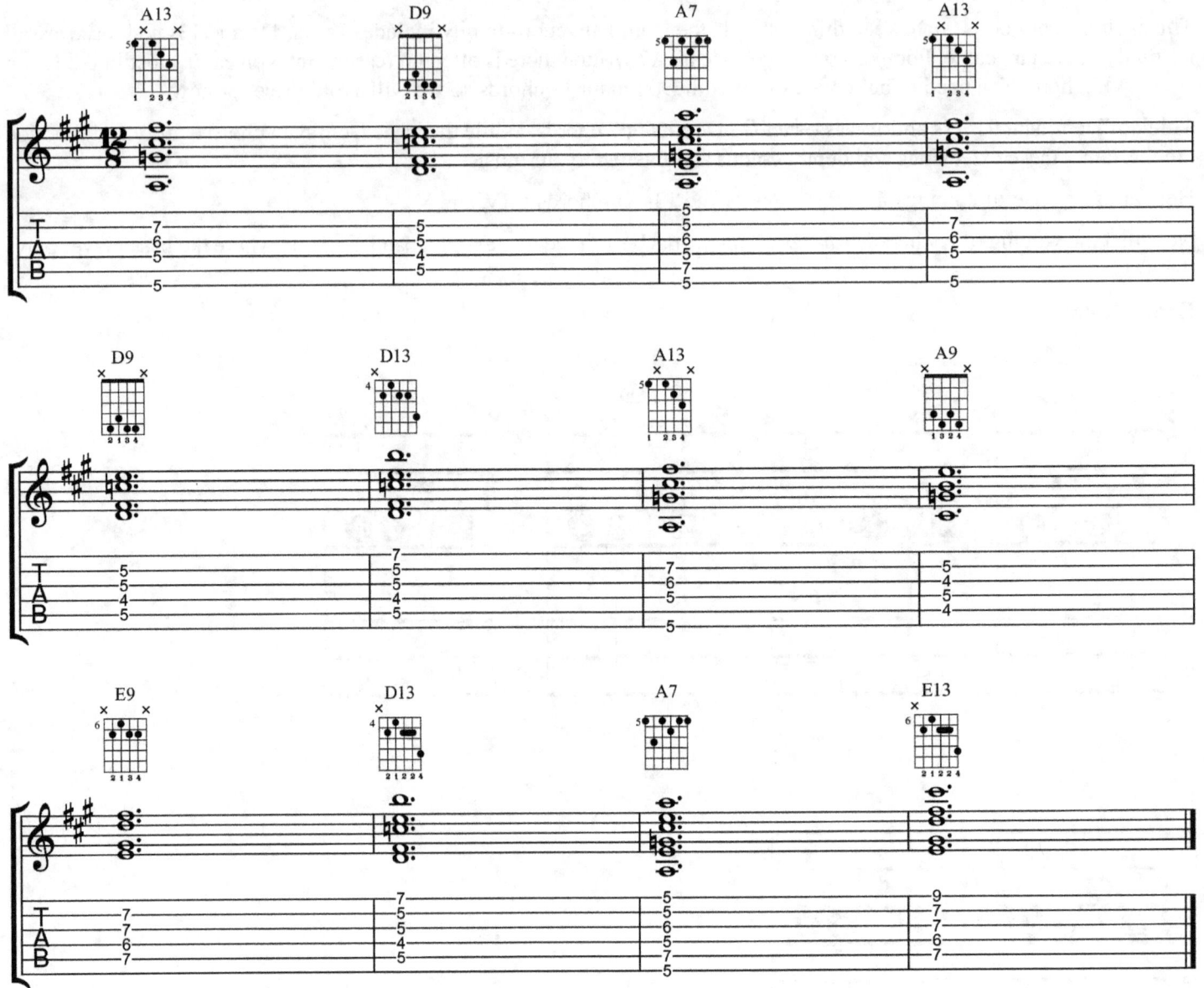

By using the idea of approaching each chord by stepwise movement we can easily generate great interest in the rhythm guitar part.

Study example 4c to hear how this kind of movement decorates the chords in the previous example.

Notice that I freely change between approaching each chord from above *and* below.

Example 4c:

It is acceptable to change between chords from the same family in the same bar. For example, you could play this:

Example 4d:

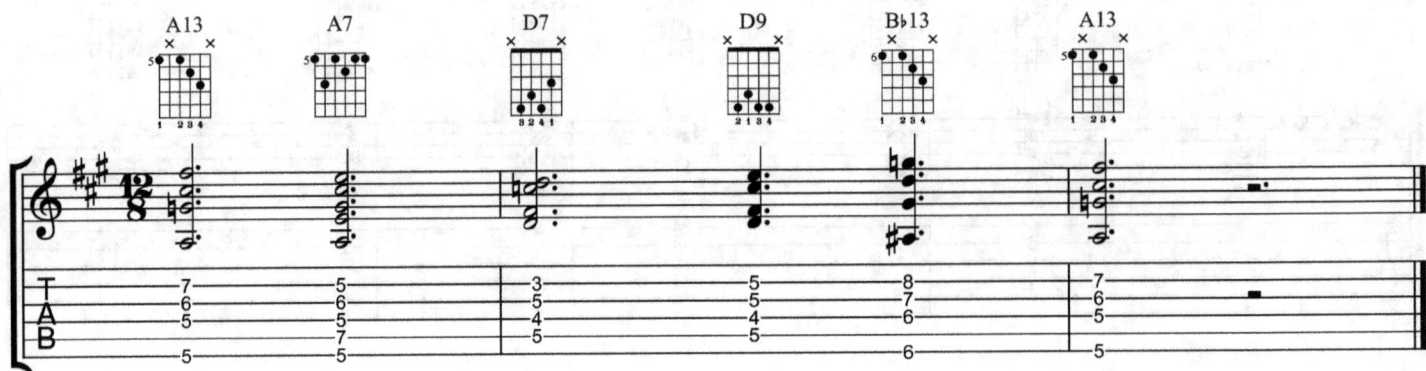

Listen to the melodic movement this creates on the second string and look out for the semitone movement from above in bar two as I approach the A13 with a Bb13.

The key to internalising these chord ideas is to practise rhythm guitar with a backing track. Backing Track 4: Triplet Blues in A, isolates the drum and bass parts so you can provide your own rhythmic accompaniment on the guitar.

Focus on changing smoothly between chords in time, and experimenting with different extensions for each chord. For example, I like to play A13 for chord I and D9 for chord IV, but you may come up with many different combinations.

Practise changing between chord voicings and moving between different extensions of each Dominant chord in each bar. Finally, practise the bass line examples from Chapter Two, and be sure to listen to the bass and drums in the backing track to *lock in* with their feel.

Chapter Five – Common Variations to the 12-Bar Blues

There are many common chord variations that can be used while staying within the 12-bar blues structure. You will find the alterations in this chapter used in hundreds of blues tunes and you will hear them all the time on classic recordings.

Let's add some variations to the first four bars of the tune. A common idea is to go to the (V) chord in the second half of bar three. In example 5a I approach some chords by step, but the thing to notice is the new E9 in bar three. Adding chord V here helps to break up the static two bars of A7 in the original 12-bar blues progression.

Example 5a:

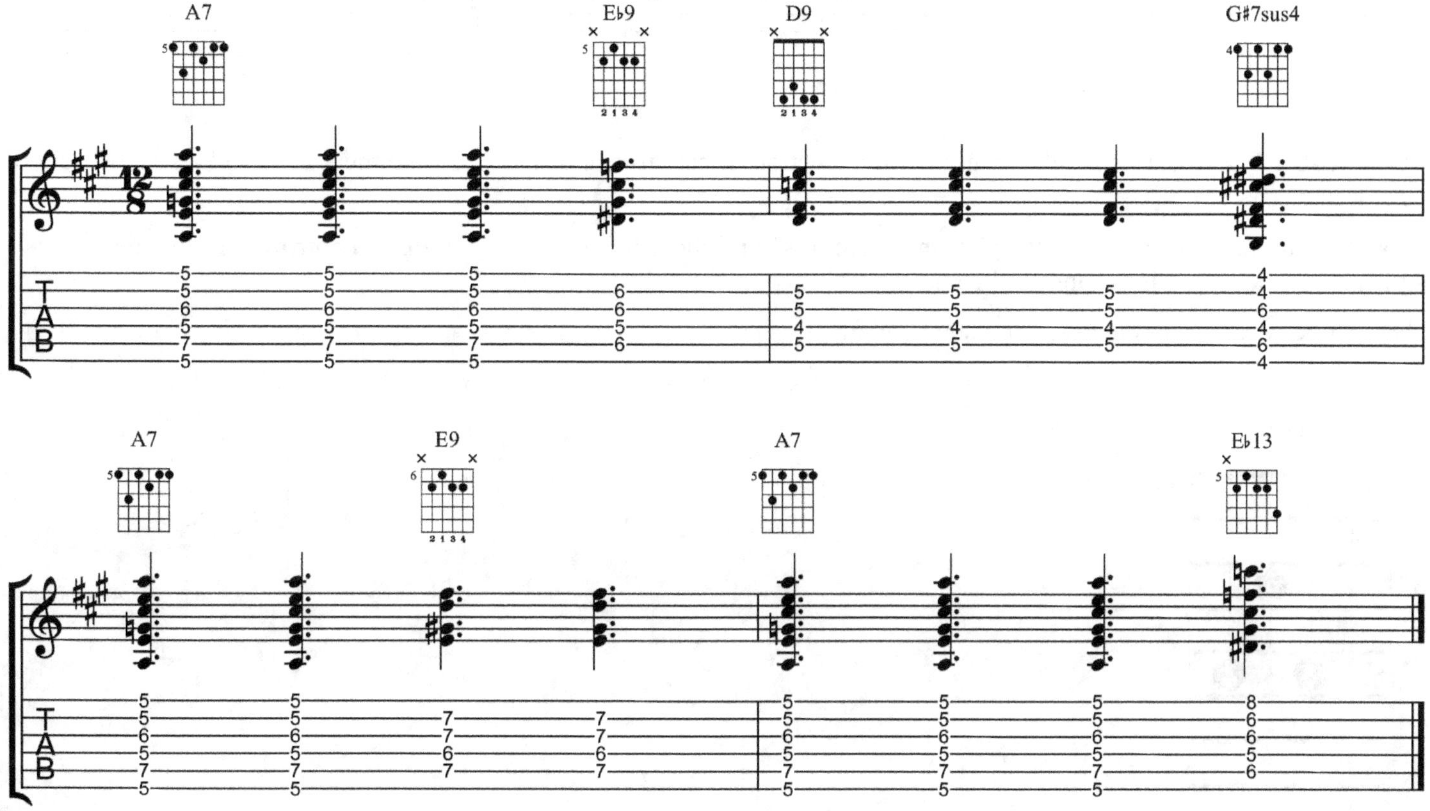

Instead of playing the E9 chord in bar three it is common to hear a Bb7 (A Dominant 7 chord built on the bII of the scale). This is idea is used in T-Bone Walker's Stormy Monday Blues.

Example 5b:

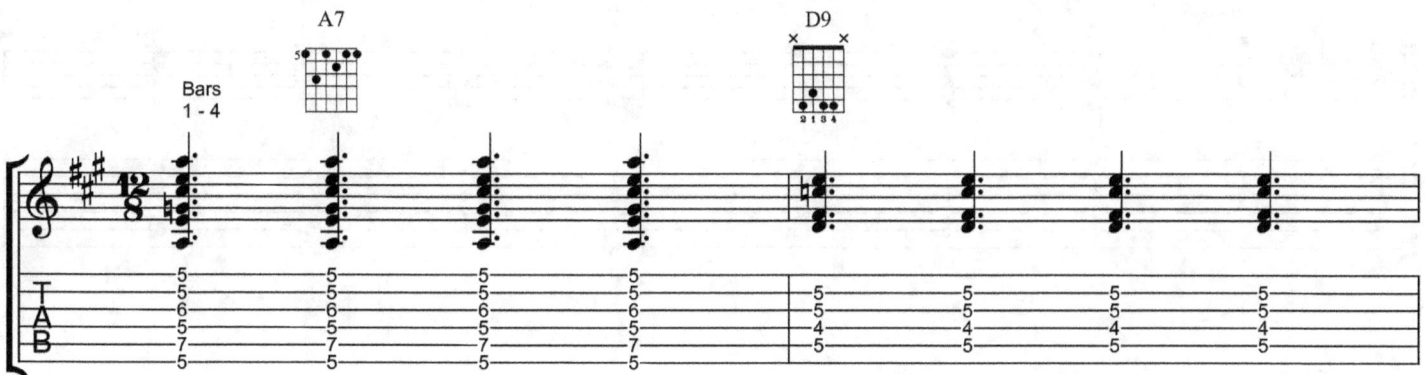

33

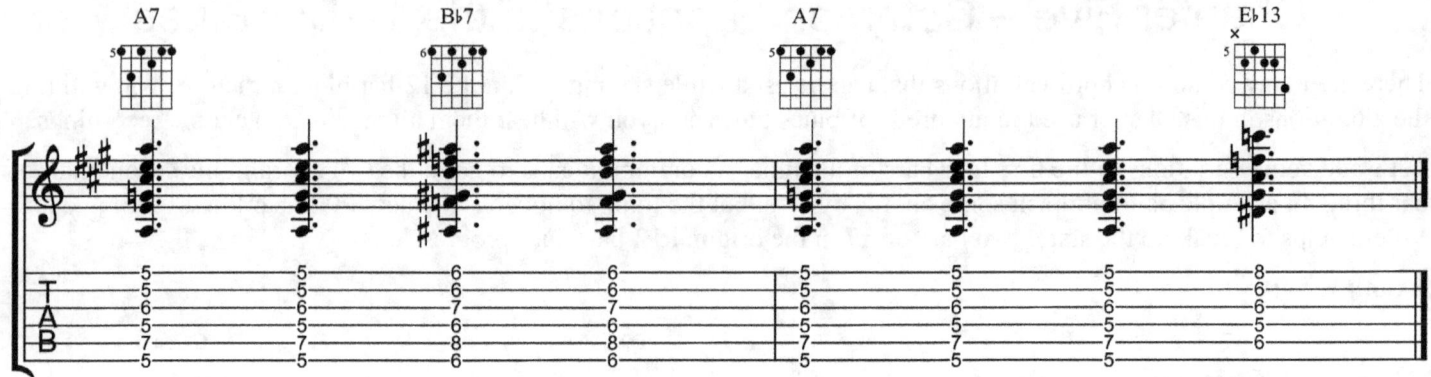

In the 12-bar blues there is another static two-bar section in bars five and six. This time there are two bars of D7 (chord IV).

To add harmonic movement, we can play an Eb diminished 7 chord in bar six. This is an idea borrowed from the jazz blues style and sounds great in a standard 12-bar.

Here is one way to play the Eb Diminished 7 chord:

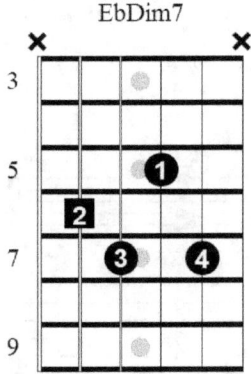

Can you see that this chord is just like a D7 chord that has had the root raised by a semitone?

Example 5c:

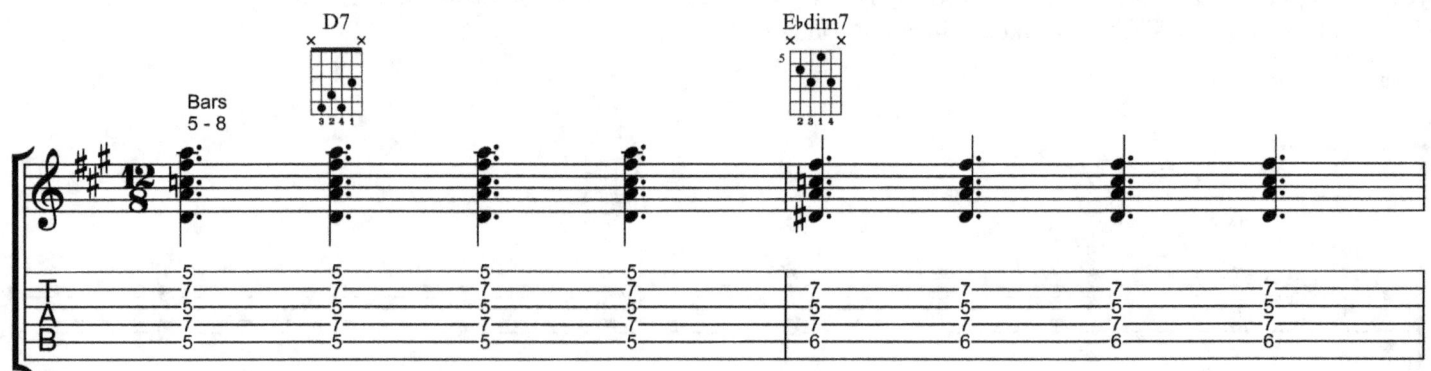

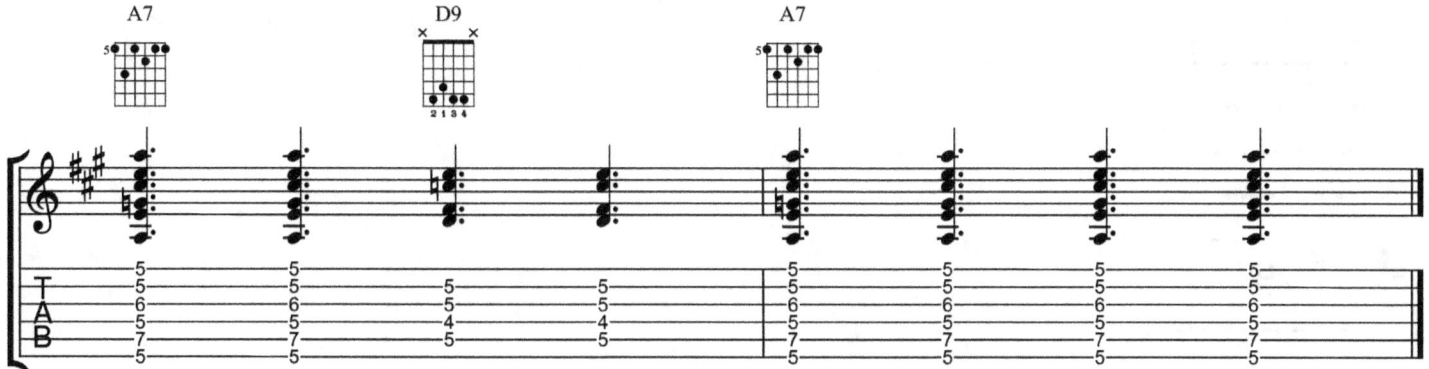

One way to break up the two bars of A7 in bars seven and eight is to add an F#7 (chord VI7) in bar eight. Once again, this idea is borrowed from the jazz repertoire but is often used in a Texas style blues.

Example 5d combines the Eb Diminished 7 chord and the added chord VI into one example. The second four bars of The Blues progression could look like this:

Example 5d:

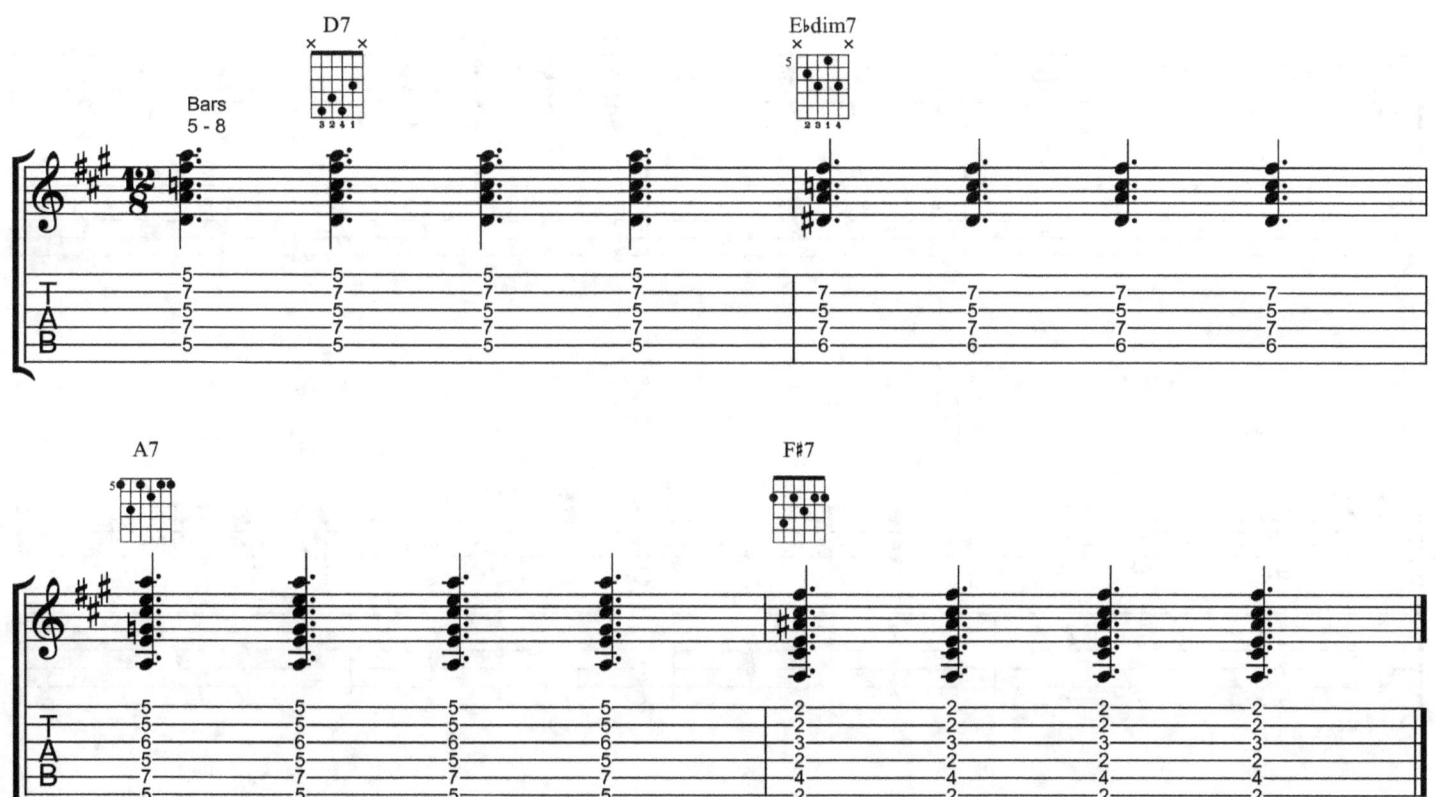

The F#7 can approached by a stepwise movement if you wish.

When we use chord VI (F#7) in bar eight, you can probably hear that the harmony wants to go somewhere different from the usual V chord (E7) that is normally played. The traditional way to follow chord VI in this context is to play chord B Minor 7 (iim7) in bar nine.

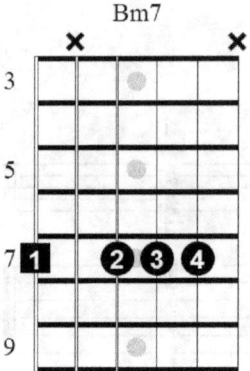

When it occurs in bar 9, the Bm7 delays the appearance of the important Dominant chord by one bar.

Example 5e:

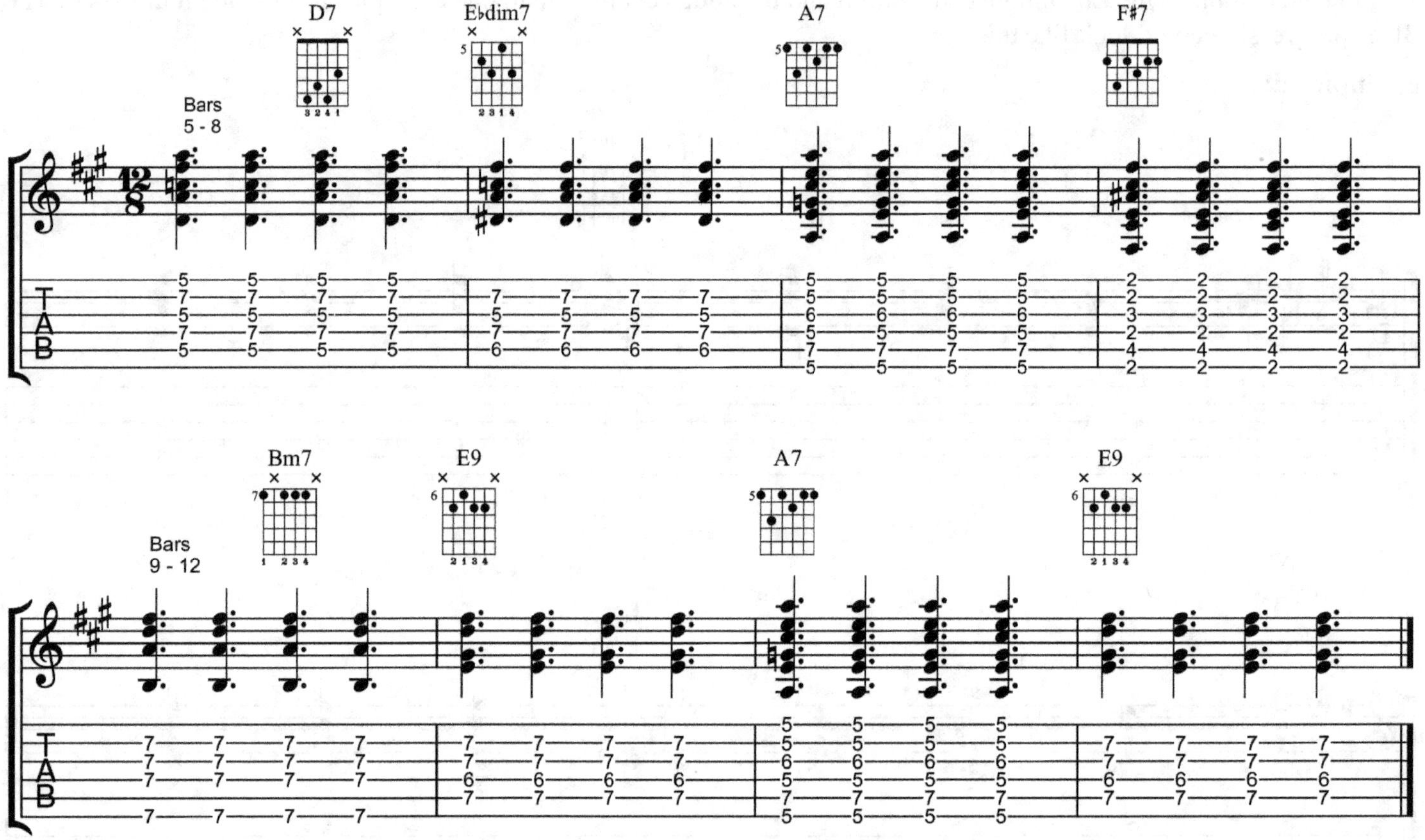

Another great way to delay the E7 (V) that occurs in bar nine is to substitute it for an F7 or F9 (bVI) chord. These are some of the most important variations that occur in the first eight or nine bars of a traditional 12-bar blues progression.

Example 5f:

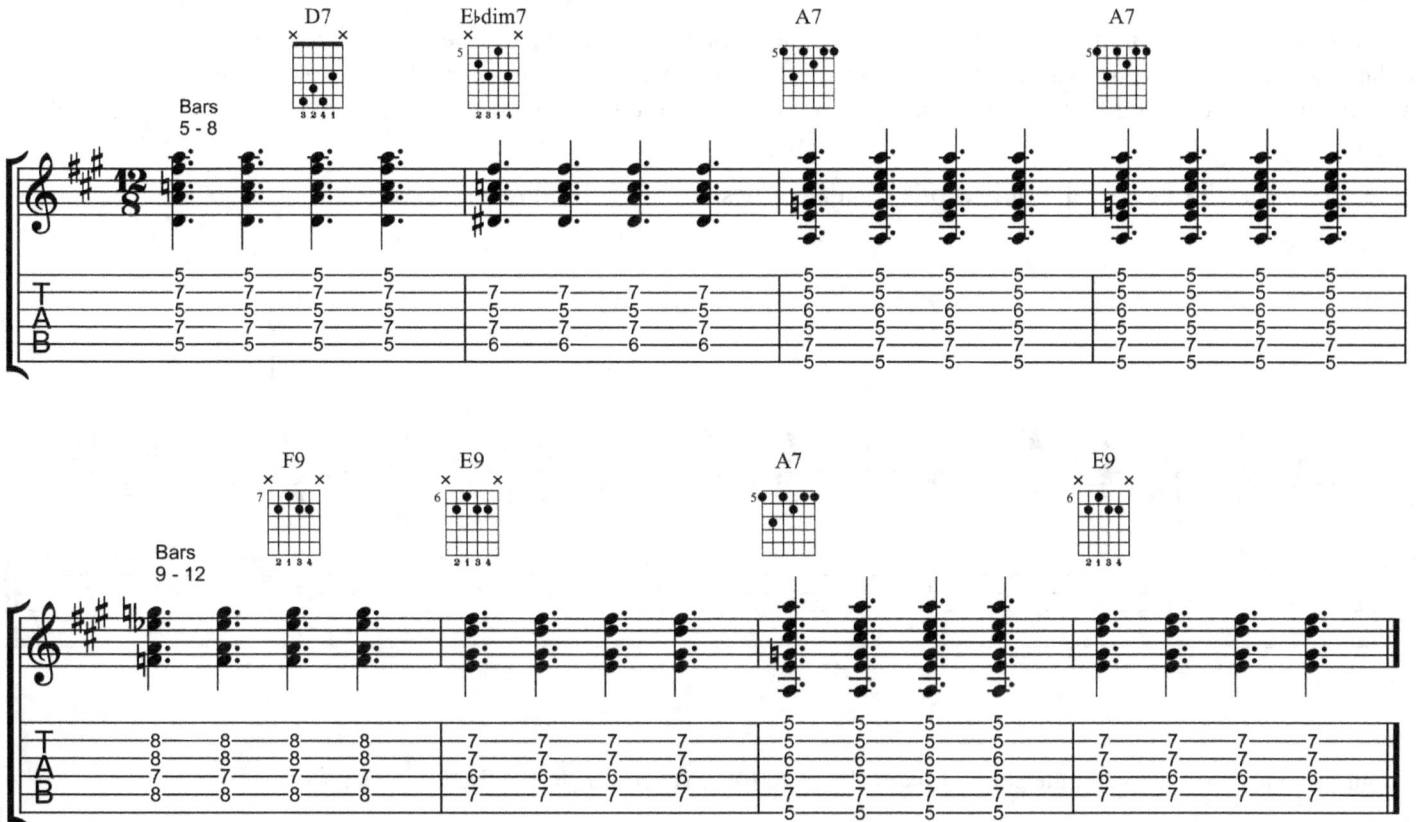

Another way to add movement to bars seven and eight is to apply a chord sequence made famous by T-Bone Walker in Stormy Monday Blues. It's easier to see on paper than it is to explain in words so study the following example.

Example 5g:

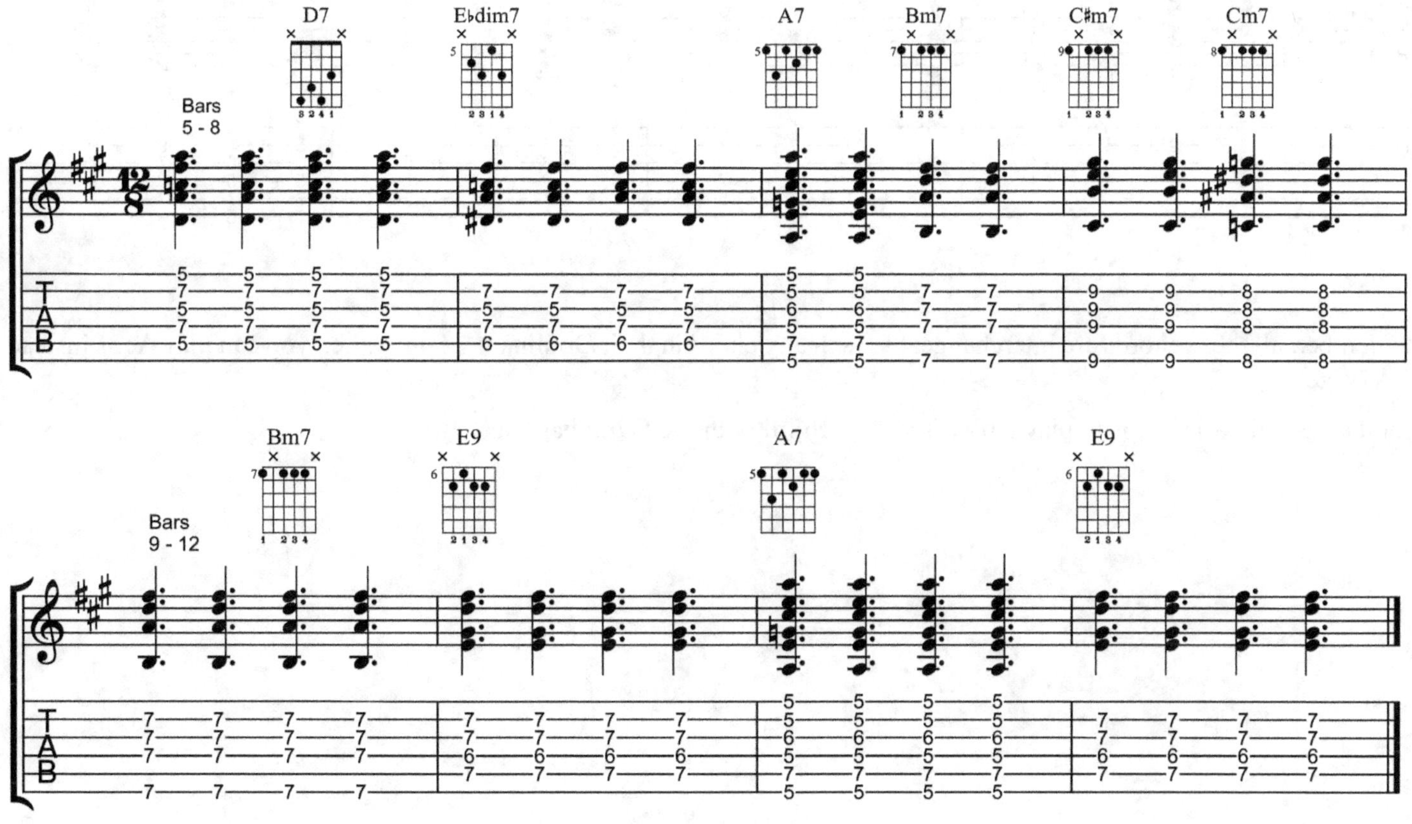

Chapter Six – Blues Turnarounds

The final four-bar section of a 12-bar blues is called the *turnaround* because it is designed to 'turn the song around' back to the beginning of the chord sequence. This is where most of the musical tension in a blues exists, both harmonically and melodically. You will find that *altered* chords are often used in the turnaround section and the *harmonic rhythm* (chord frequency) increases.

To remind yourself of the final four bars of a standard blues, look at the following notation.

Example 6a:

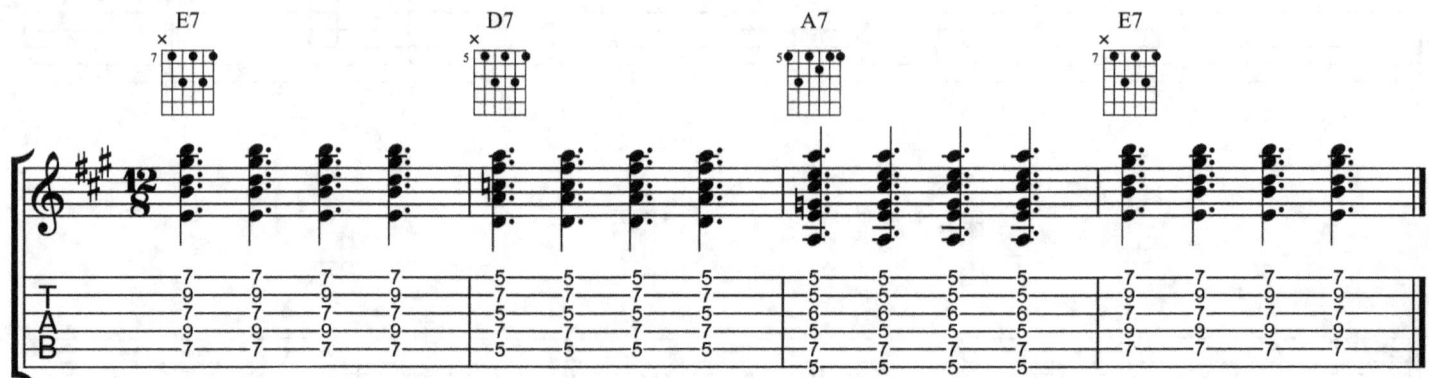

A common variation is to add the subdominant (IV) and tonic (I) chords to the final two-bar section:

Example 6b:

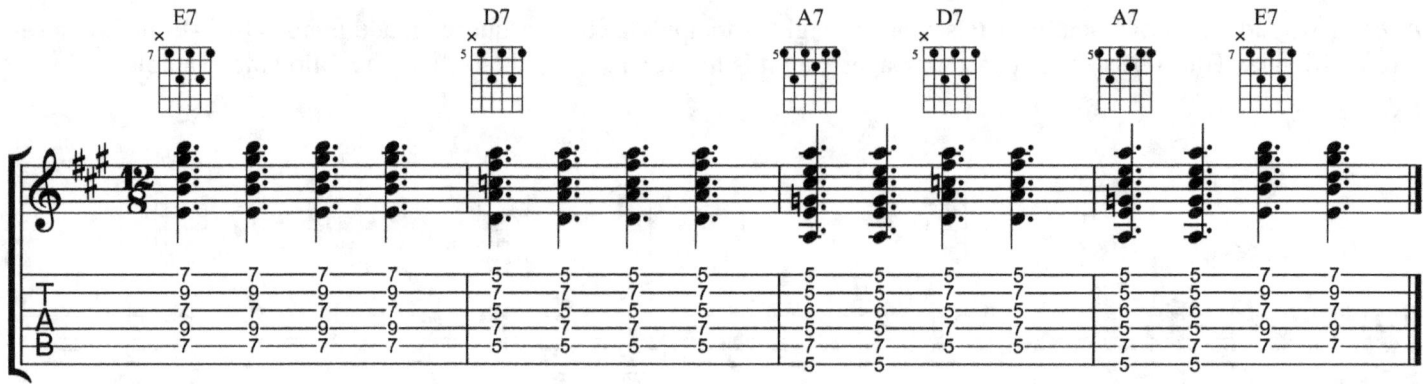

Remember, all these chords are interchangeable with any chord in their Dominant 7 family, i.e., you can play A13s instead of A7s etc.

Another useful variation is to play a bVI (F or F9) chord with the D7 in bar ten.

Example 6c:

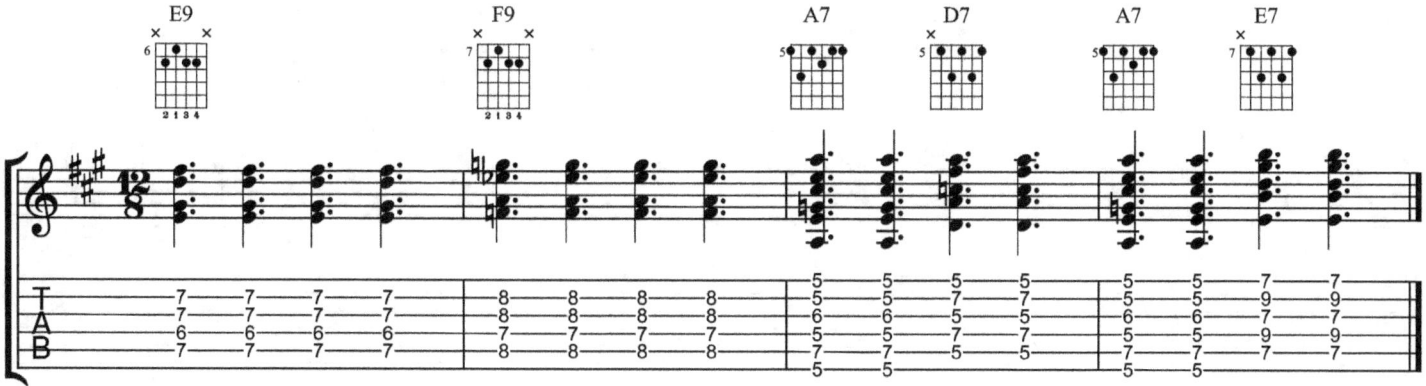

Before looking at the next chord progression go back and remind yourself of example 5e.

When we use chords VI and II in bars eight and nine it is common to repeat the chords from bars eight to ten at double the frequency in the final two bars of the form.

Example 6d:

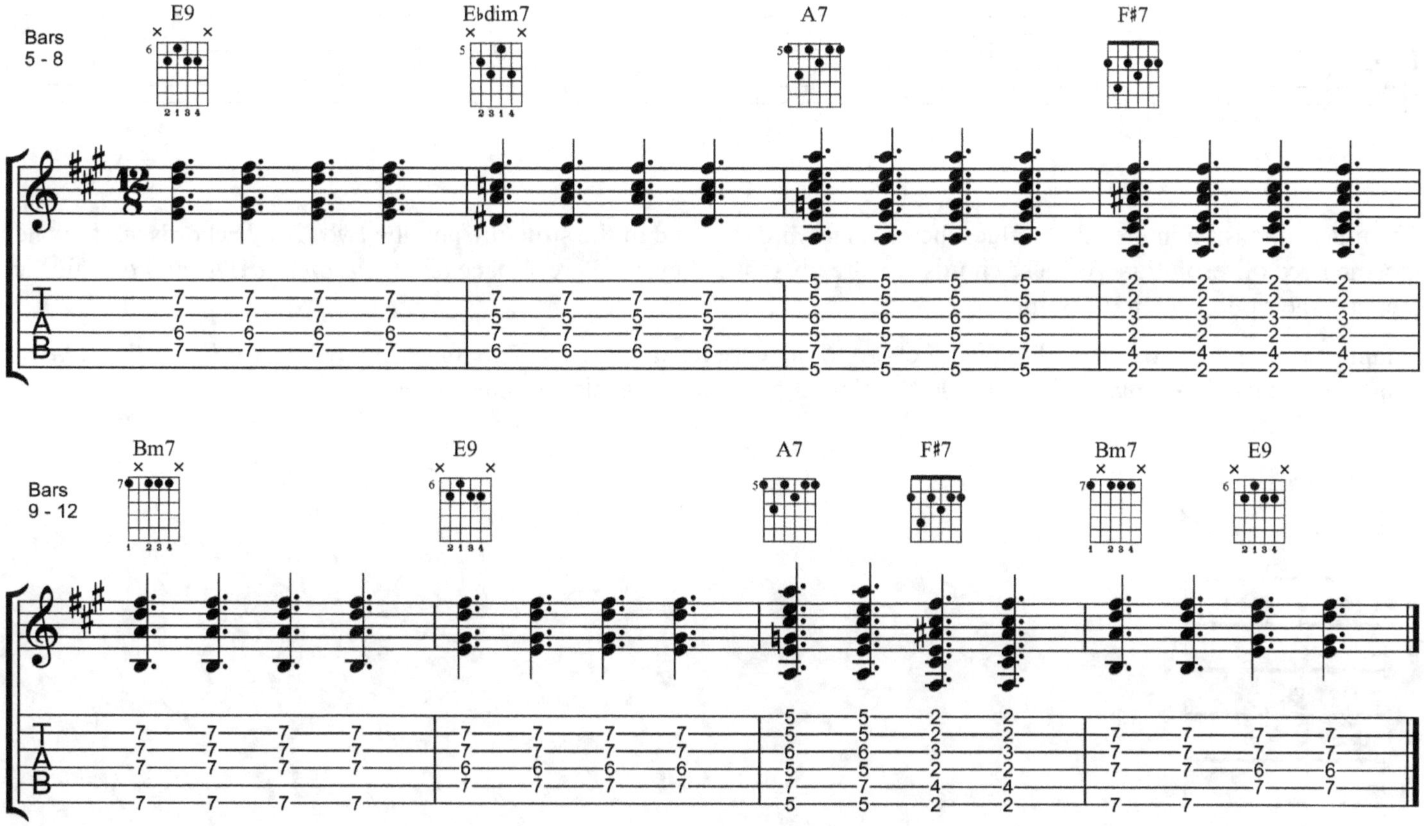

The previous progression is set up by the Eb diminished 7 in bar six although you are by no means obliged to play the whole turnaround if you use the diminished chord.

Example 6e:

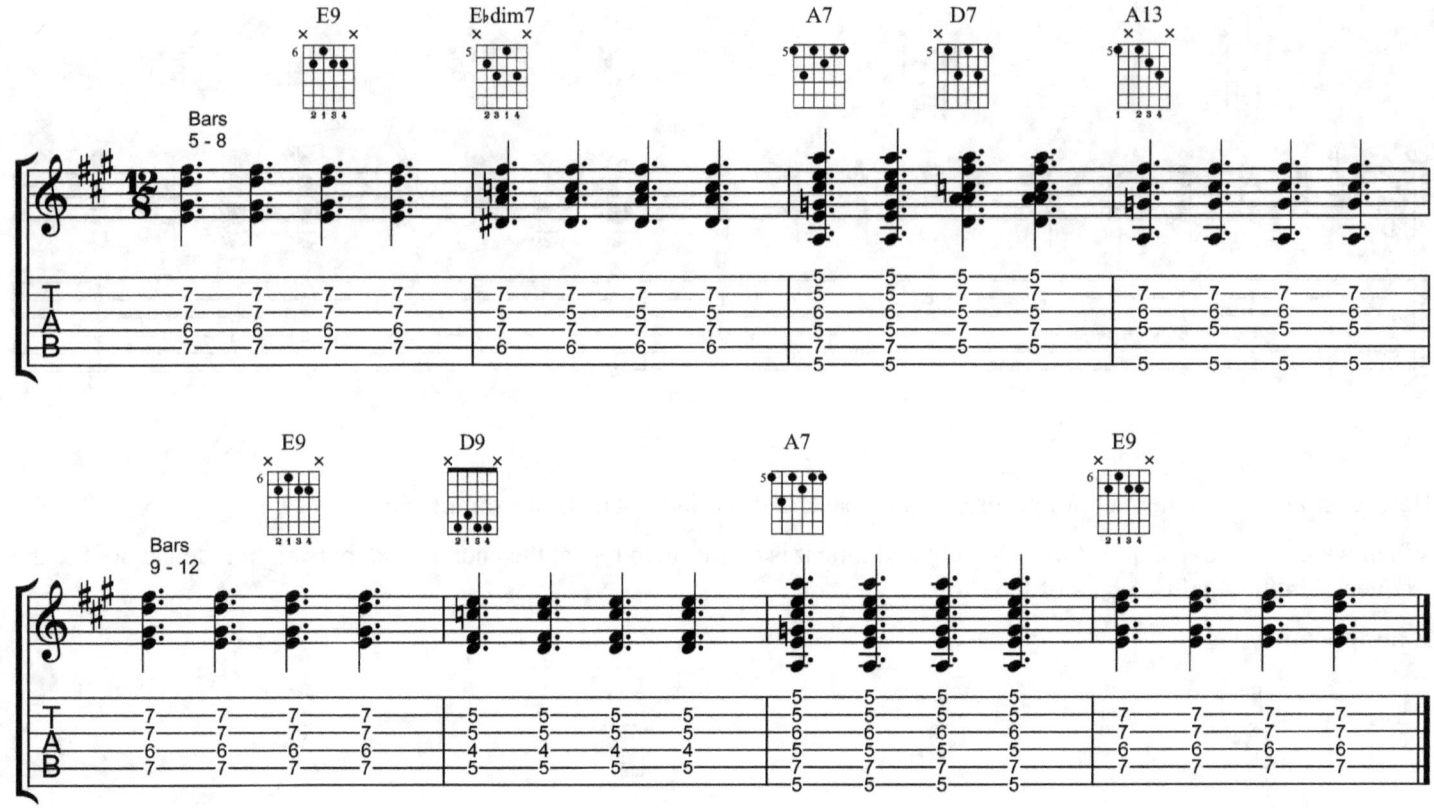

The musical tension in the 12-bar blues increases towards the end of the structure and the two E7 (V) chords are the ones most in need of resolution. As these chords are already tense, they are a great place to add *chromatic alterations* to further increase their pull back to the tonic.

A fantastic alteration we can add to the E7 chord to increase tension is a #9. You may already know E7#9 as the *Hendrix* chord that he used in songs such as Purple Haze and Foxy Lady. It is played like this on the guitar:

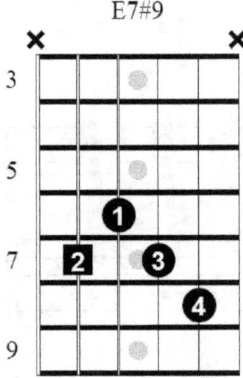

Try playing it as the final chord in the turnaround.

Example 6f:

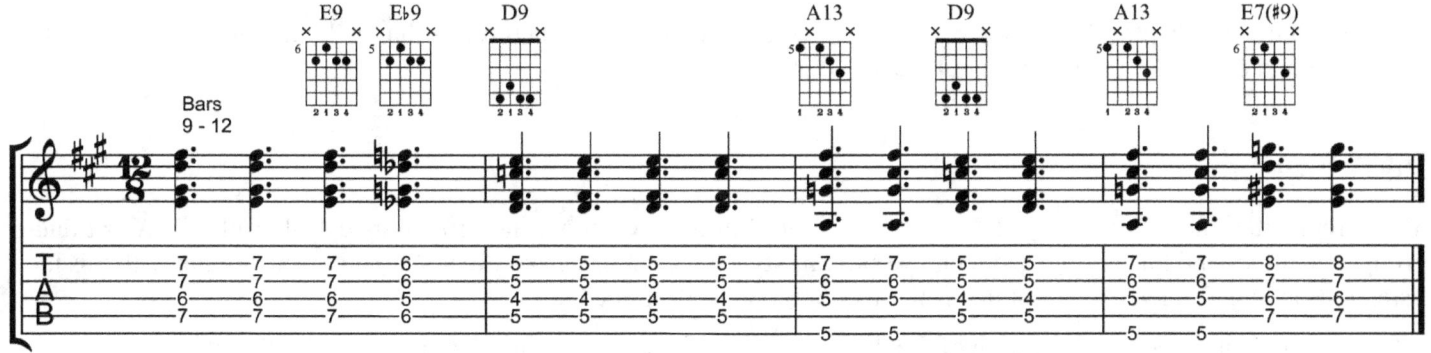

The next example is a little more 'jazzy' but I also like to use the 7#9 as a passing chord between D7 and F#7 in the following manner:

Example 6g:

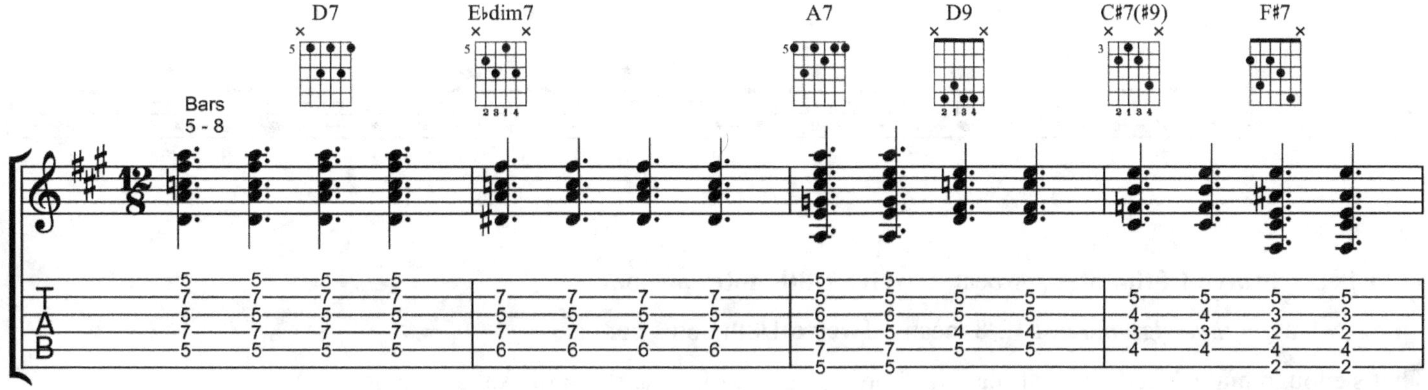

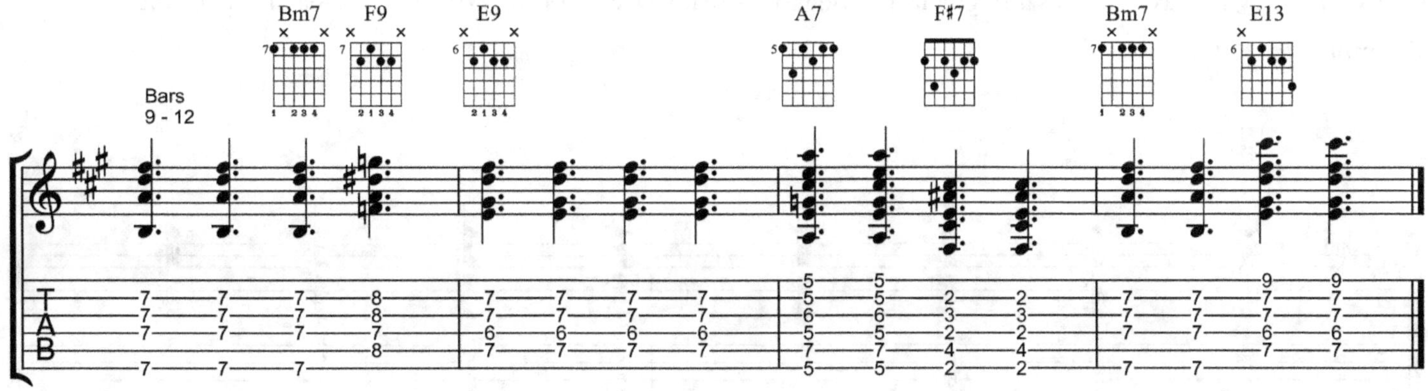

The examples in this section just scratch the surface of some more advanced jazz chord ideas but they represent some of the most common substitutions used in the 12-bar blues progression.

Chapter Seven – Rhythmic Placement with Triplet Blues

While the previous chapters have looked at harmonic ideas for the blues structure, we'll now look more closely at rhythm placement and concepts that you can apply to all your playing.

Triplet Blues

You'll remember that we count "1 2 3 1 2 3 1 2 3 1 2 3" through each bar in a triplet-style 12-bar blues. Everything is grouped in threes and this is the reason that we call this style a *triplet* feel. If you're not already comfortable with this idea, listen to Backing Track 4 and count the triplet feel out loud as described above.

As strange as it may seem at first, each of the three divisions of the beat is considered to be an 1/8th note.

There are three 1/8th notes or *quavers* per beat. Three 1/8th notes in a single beat doesn't make mathematical sense in the real world but it is an extremely important concept to understand in The Blues.

In example 7a, the top row of notes shows the main beat or pulse of the music, and the bottom row shows how the three 1/8th notes fit into each beat.

Example 7a:

Four beats x **three 1/8th notes** per beat = **twelve 1/8th notes per bar**.

This is what the *time signature* of 12/8 means: Twelve 1/8th notes per bar.

That's enough maths! Let's look at placing chords on some of these rhythmic subdivisions.

One simple way to play blues rhythm guitar that we have already covered is to strum only on each beat of the bar.

Example 7b:

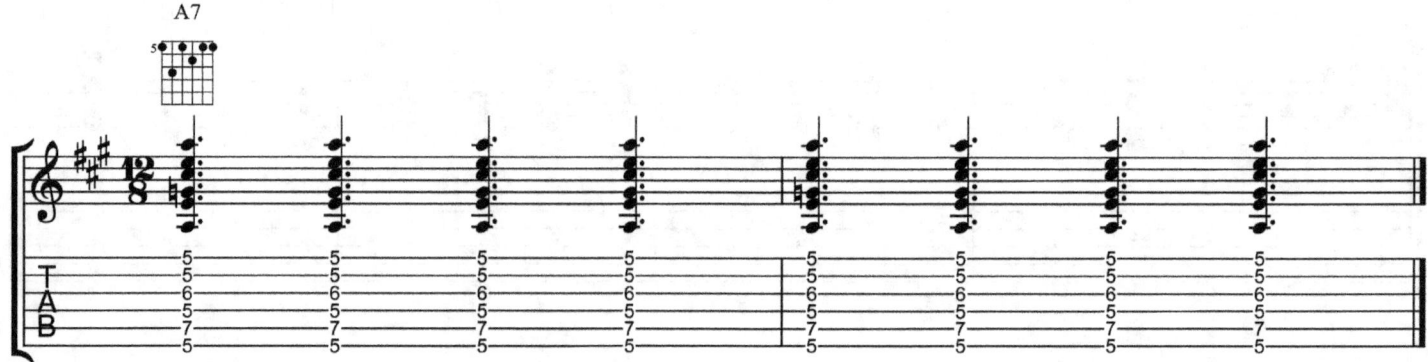

We can add more interest by playing on each of the triplet subdivisions. Use down-strokes to strum the following pattern.

Example 7c:

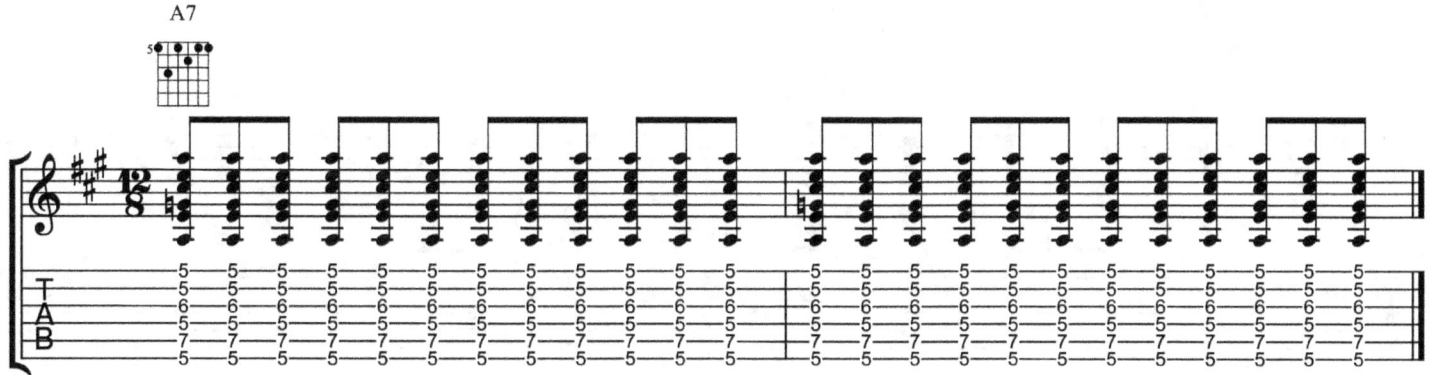

This adds more movement but it's very busy. Try playing on only the first and third triplet in each beat.

Example 7d:

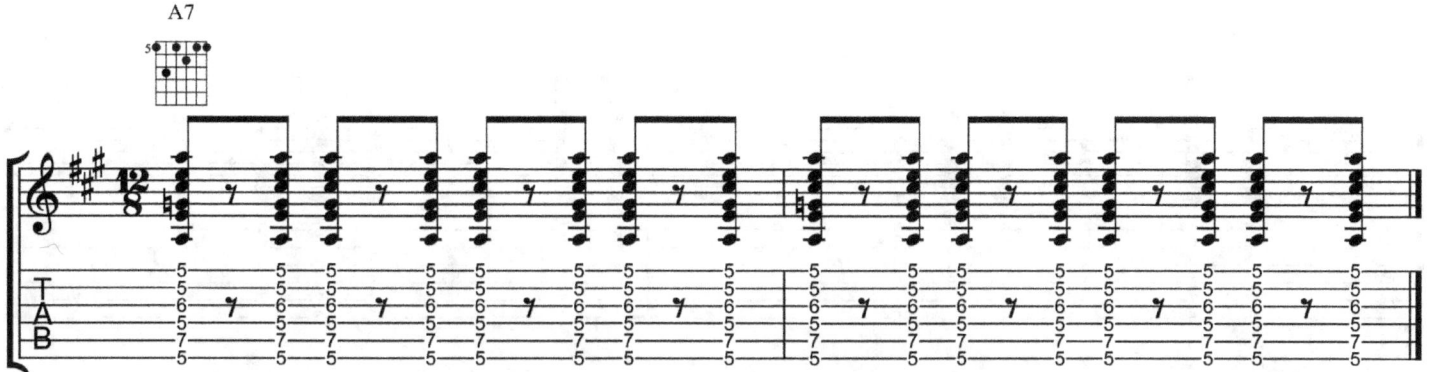

Listen to the audio example if you're not sure how to play this idea.

Personally, I feel that in most band situations it's best to leave a lot of space in the rhythm guitar part. By playing sparsely, especially at the beginning of a tune, it gives the song room to grow. Here are some patterns that use the triplet rhythms, but also leave large gaps that can be filled by other instruments.

Example 7e:

43

Example 7f

Example 7g:

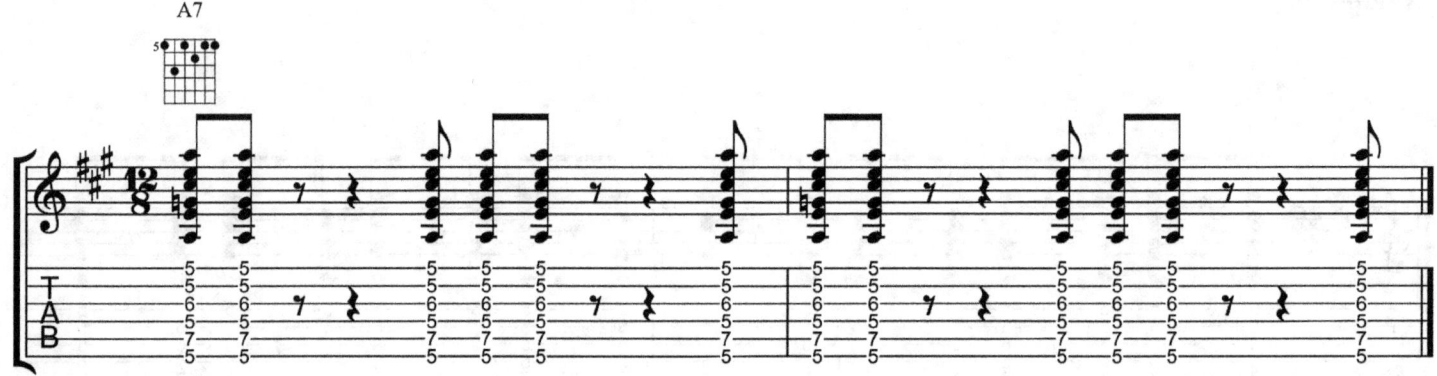

Example 7h:

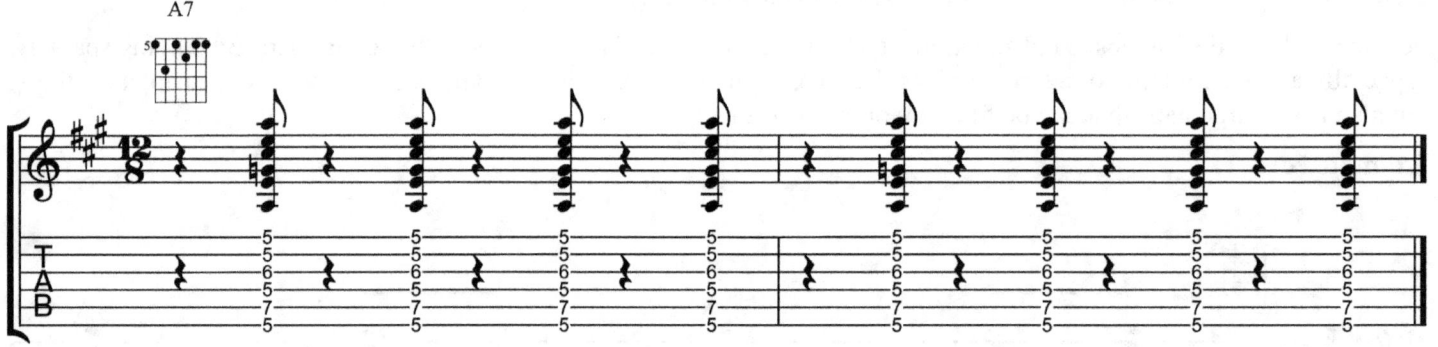

It's easy to add percussive *scratches* to the picking hand pattern. Hold the chord but release the pressure on the strings with your fretting hand while your strumming hand pattern plays a tight triplet feel. Scratched notes are notated with an 'x'.

Example 7i:

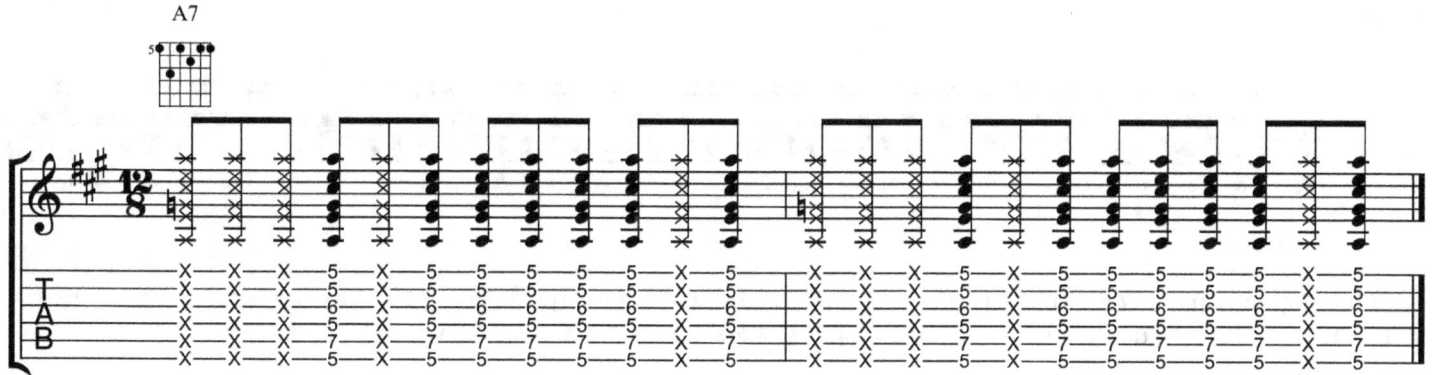

Even though I have notated the full chord, I will normally only play the highest four strings on the guitar to stay out of the way of the bass player. Try examples 7d to 7i again but this time play only the top four strings and add muted strums in some of the spaces.

Take some of these patterns through a whole 12-bar chorus. Try making your own rhythm patterns by missing out different combinations of triplets. These patterns can be as sparse or as dense as you like.

1/16th Note Subdivisions of the Beat

Each of the three 1/8th notes in the beat can be divided and split into two 1/16th notes to make a total of six subdivisions for each main pulse.

Example 7j:

The top line in this example shows the triplet divisions and the bottom line shows how each triplet can be evenly divided into two subdivisions.

Count this out loud by saying "**1**and**2**and**3**and**1**and**2**and**3**and", etc.

Strum this rhythm with muted strings in the following way:

Downupdownupdownup **Down**updownupdownup.

Accent the first down stroke of each beat and ensure you can play in time with the audio from example 7j.

Blues rhythms based on 1/16th note subdivisions create many interesting strumming patterns but it's important not to overpower the rest of the band so use discretion and space in your playing.

To keep me in time and help with my dynamics I play quiet, muted strums on *every* 1/16th note and accentuate the chords I wish to play with an unmuted chord.

To get the feel for this, play through the following example and mute every single strum.

Example 7k:

Next try to quietly play *all* the subdivisions with an A7 chord without overpowering the drums and bass. Relax your wrist and remember that you don't have to play every string. Accent each main pulse (down beat) in the bar.

Example 7l:

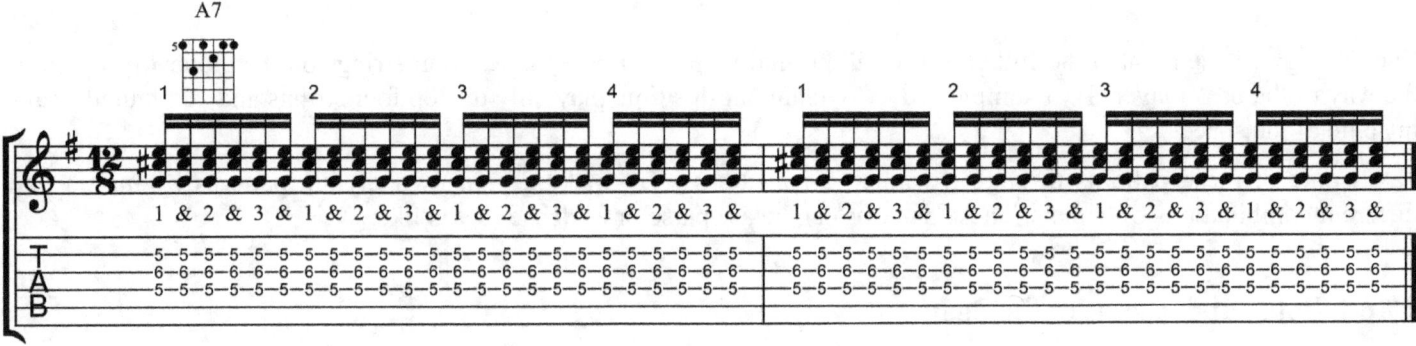

Now we will combine some 1/8th note and 1/16th note ideas. Try taking these patterns throughout the whole 12-bar progression.

Example 7m:

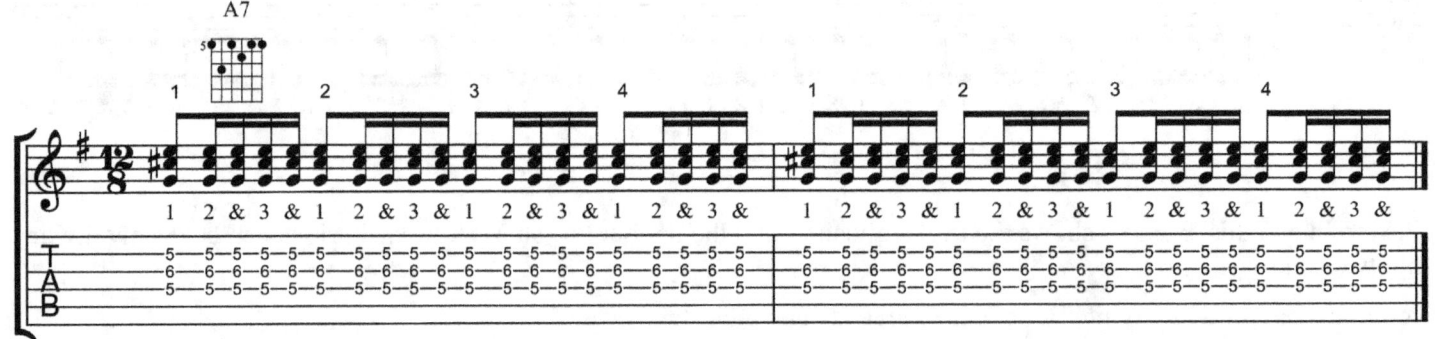

Example 7n:

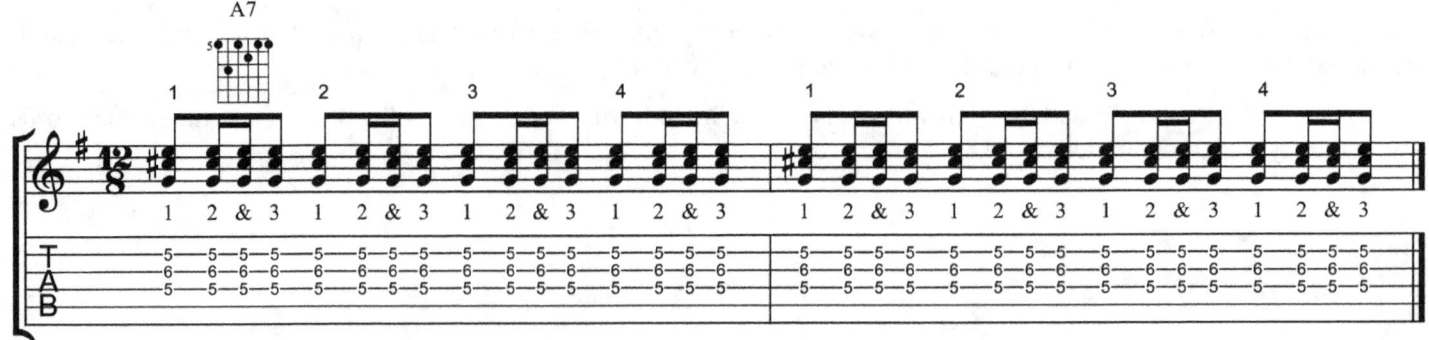

Now combine the percussive scratches with chord stabs. In the following examples, muted notes are notated with an *x*.

The first idea is quite challenging as it's very syncopated. Start slowly and gradually build up the speed when you get into the feel of the rhythm. Remember; keep your scratches light and accentuate the chord stabs.

Example 7o:

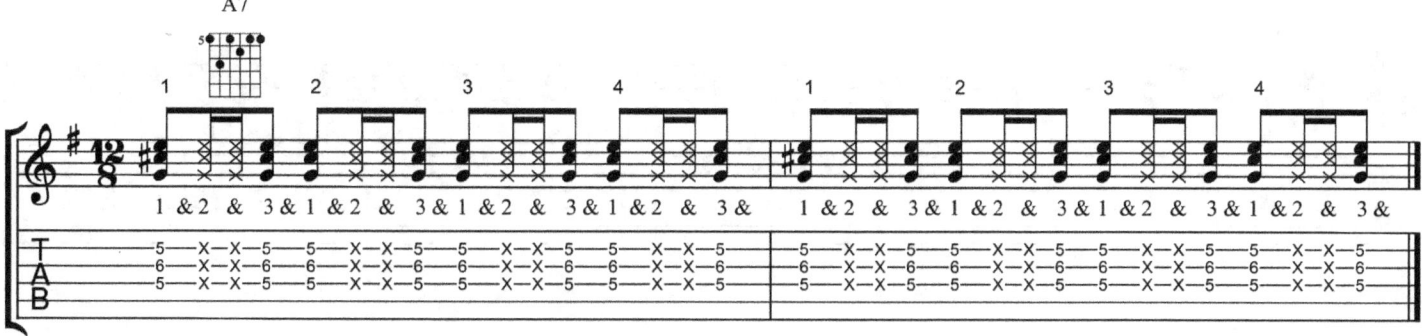

Example 7p:

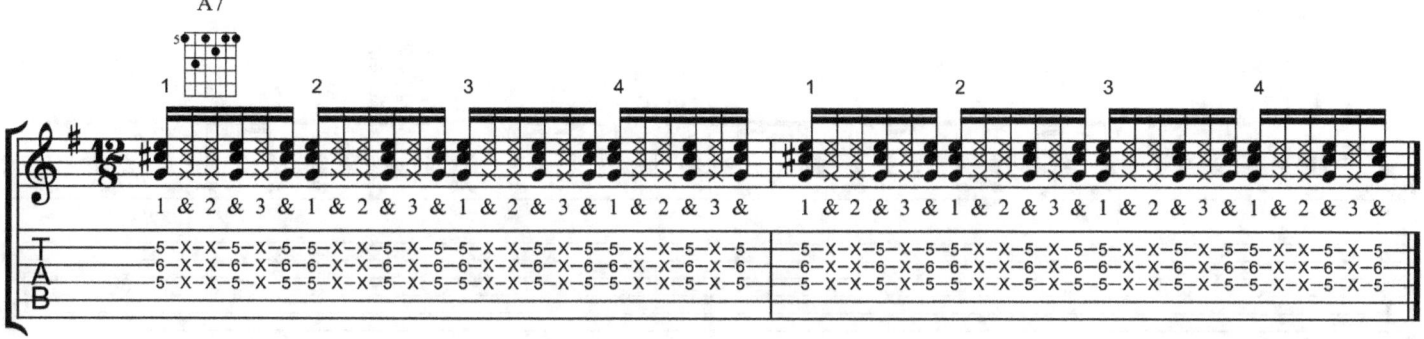

Example 7q:

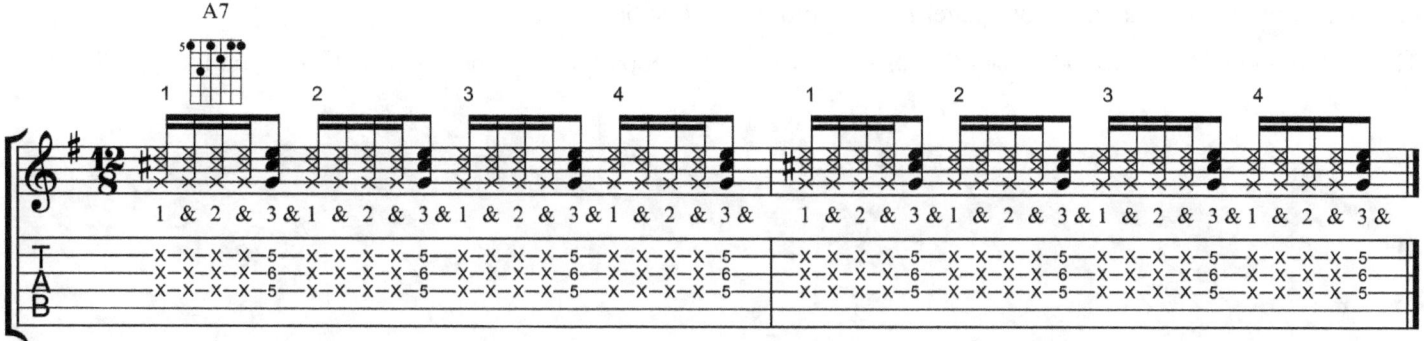

Often, we don't want to play a note *or* a scratch on a beat because sometimes the music requires silence. You can *mime* 1/16th notes in the same way you played the 1/16th note scratches. Move your strumming hand up and down in time, simply do not connect with the guitar strings. This is a great way to stay in time and develop control and placement with your strums.

Example 7r contains a 1/16th note rest in beat one. Keep your strumming hand moving throughout, but don't connect with the strings on the rests.

Example 7r:

We can still use rhythmic ideas like sliding chords from a semitone below. These create a 'sub-rhythm' against the main groove of the rhythm part.

Example 7s:

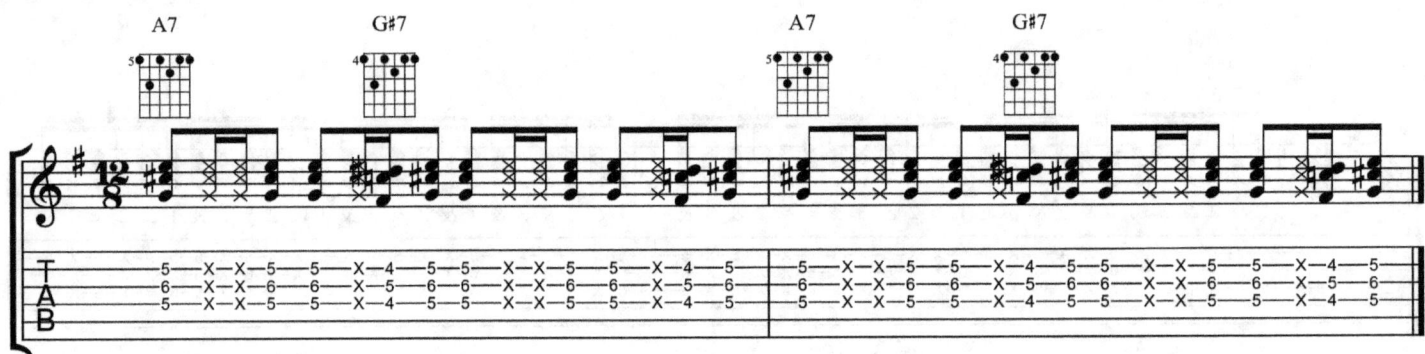

Use the strumming patterns in this chapter to play through full 12-blues progressions. Don't be afraid to alter or combine them, and don't forget that a rhythm pattern can be more than one bar long.

The best thing to do is to listen to your favourite recordings and copy the style the rhythm players you like.

Chapter Eight – Rhythmic Placement with Straight Blues

In a *straight* time feel, each beat in the bar is split into *even* subdivisions. Whereas a triplet feel is split into rhythmic groupings of three, a straight feel is split into rhythmic groupings of two and four.

In example 8a the top line of music shows the main 1/4 note (crotchet) beat of the bar and the bottom line shows how each beat is divided into two subdivisions.

Example 8a:

Look at the 4/4 time signature. If a time signature has the number 4 at the bottom then the convention is to group the subdivisions into even rhythmic divisions.

Begin by strumming on just the first beat of each bar. Although this is a similar exercise to example 7b you will find that this rhythm feels quite different when played with a straight drum groove. Remember, you don't have to play the full chord, often just the top four strings will do.

Example 8b:

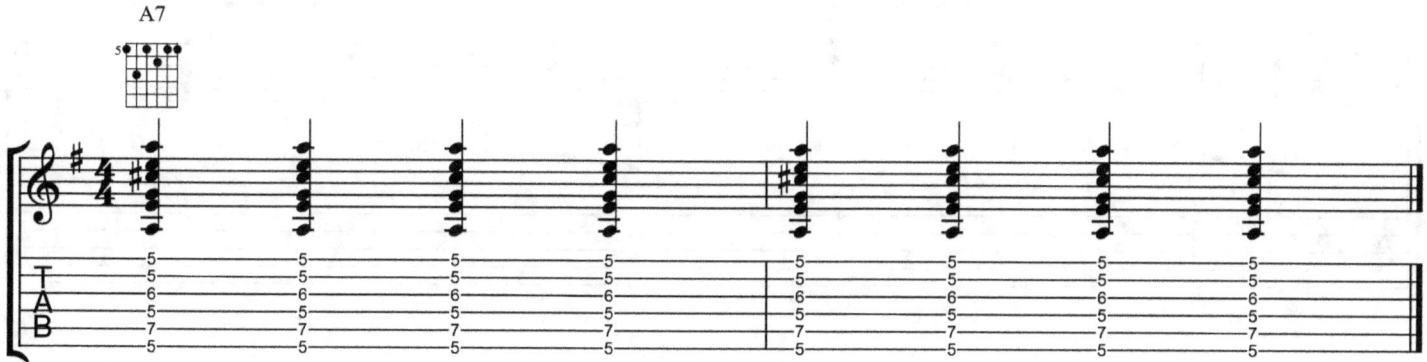

We can add more movement by playing on each 1/8th note (quaver) subdivision.

Example 8c:

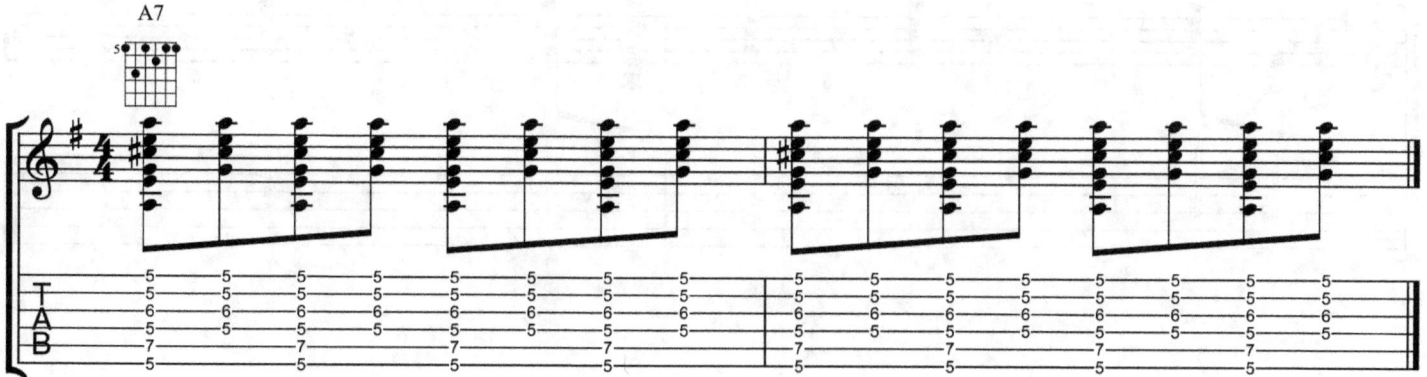

Playing on each 1/8th note can be a little too rhythmically dense, so here are some patterns that use 1/8th notes but don't include a strum on every subdivision of the beat. Take these rhythm figures through the full 12-bar blues chord sequence and play along with Backing Track 1: Straight Blues in A.

Example 8d:

Example 8e:

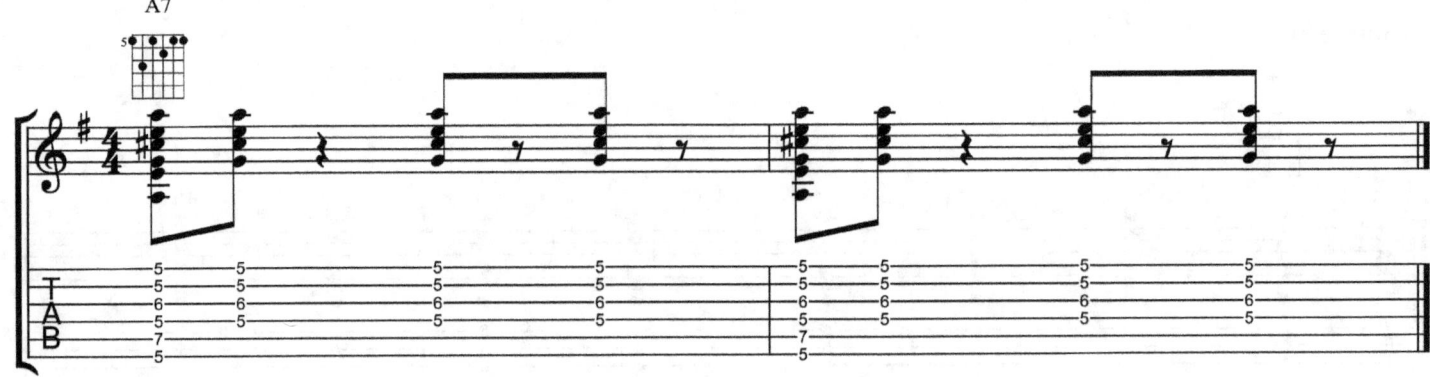

Example 8f:

Example 8g:

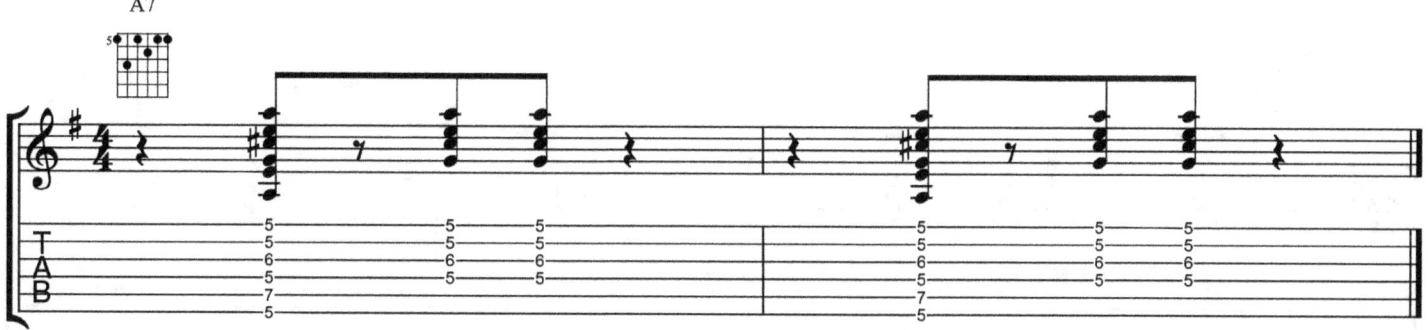

Once again, we can use scratches to add percussive rhythms to the chords and to help us stay in time. In the following examples, I split the chord so that I play the bass strings and the high strings separately.

Example 8h:

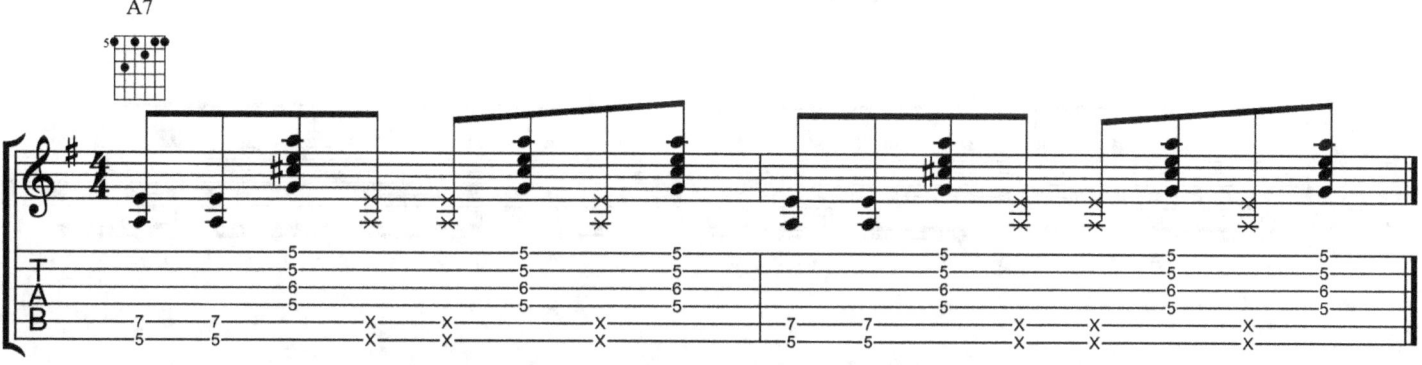

Example 8i:

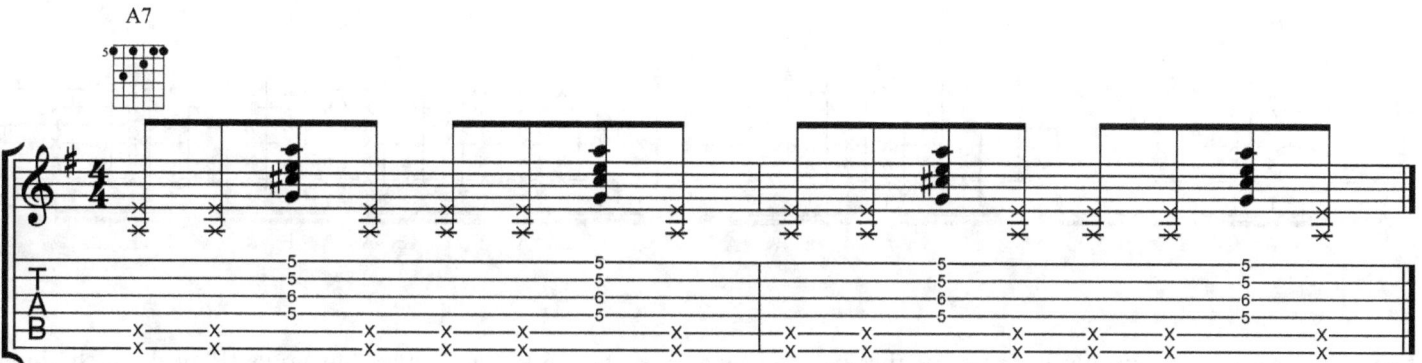

Example 8j:

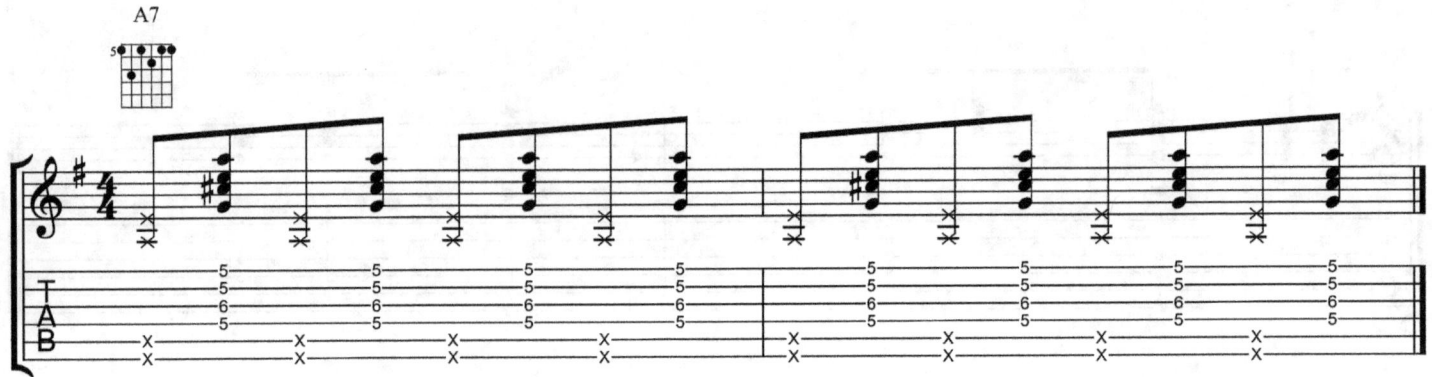

1/16th Note Subdivisions of the Beat

As with triplets, each 1/8th note can be split further into 1/16th notes.

To get a feel for this rhythm count "1 e and a 2 e and a 3 e and a 4 e and a" out loud along with Backing Track 1.

Try strumming this rhythm with muted strings. Throughout the whole bar your strumming should be

Downup down up**down**up down up

Example 8k:

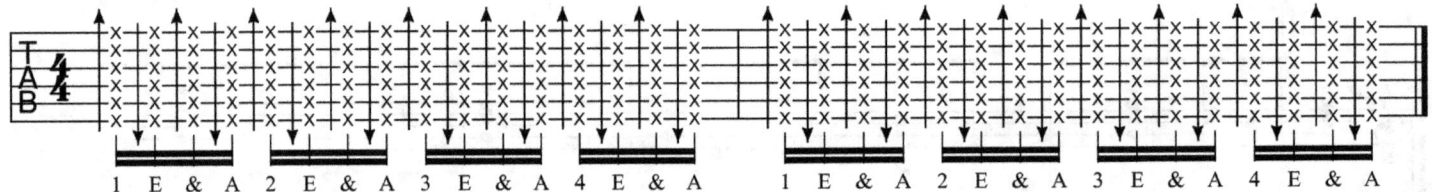

Now let's study some strumming patterns that use combinations of 1/16th notes and 1/8th notes. Play these rhythms throughout the whole 12-bar progression.

Example 8l:

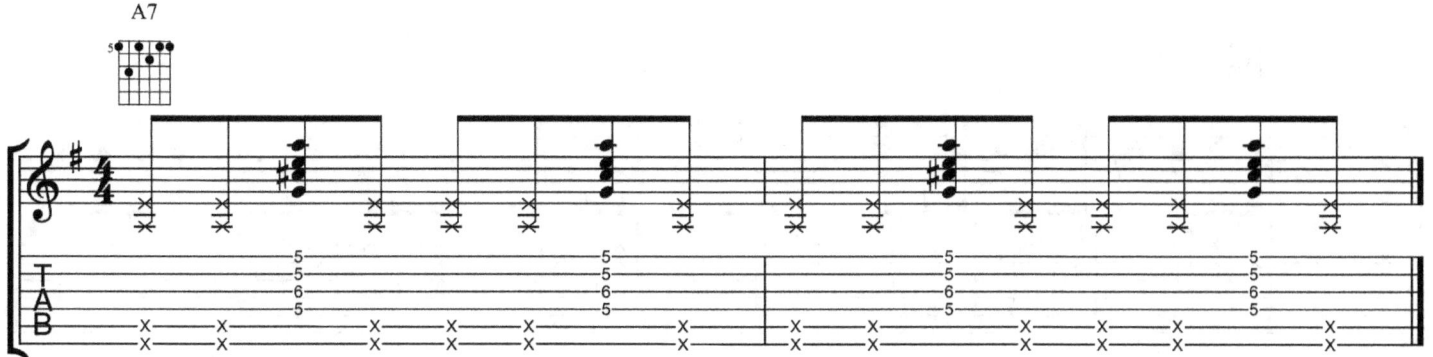

Example 8m:

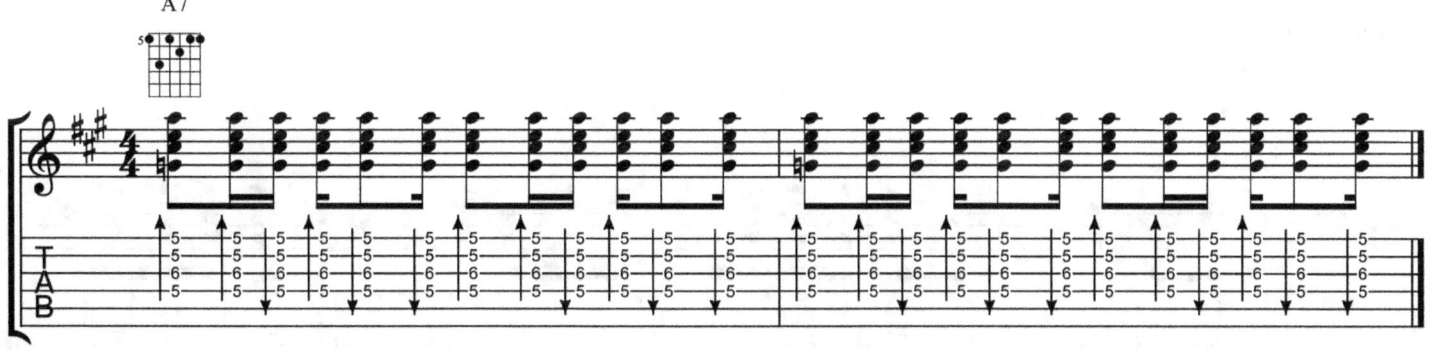

Example 8n:

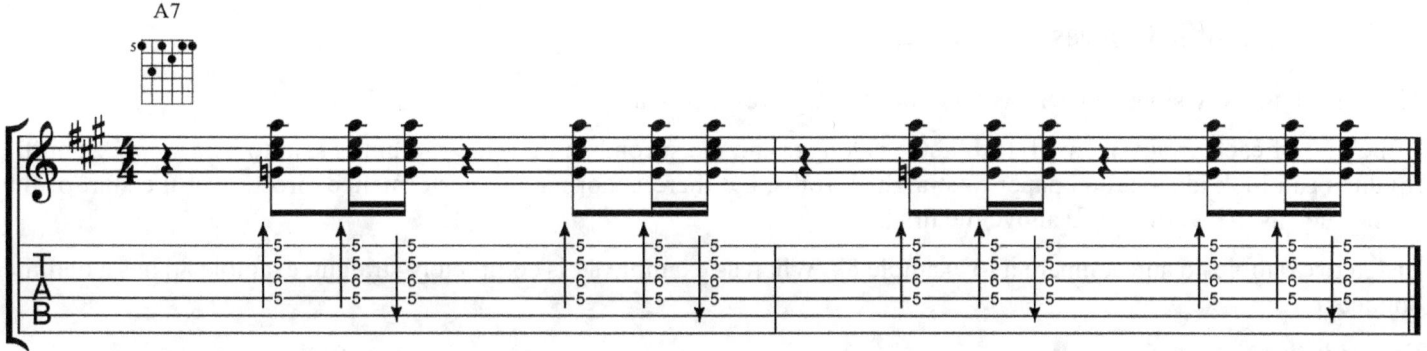

Example 8o:

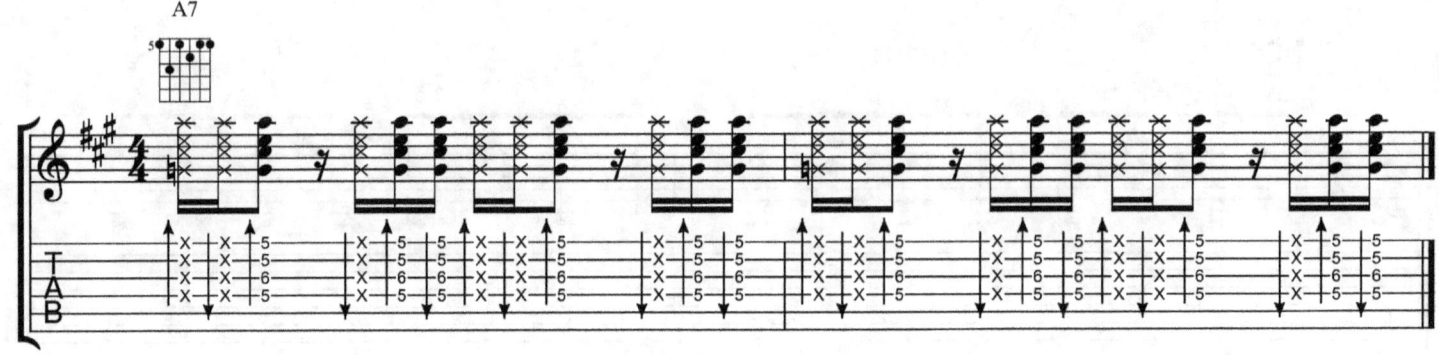

Example 8p is a bit trickier than the earlier examples. Listen carefully to the audio and keep your strumming hand moving in 1/16th notes, whether you are connecting with the strings or not.

Example 8p:

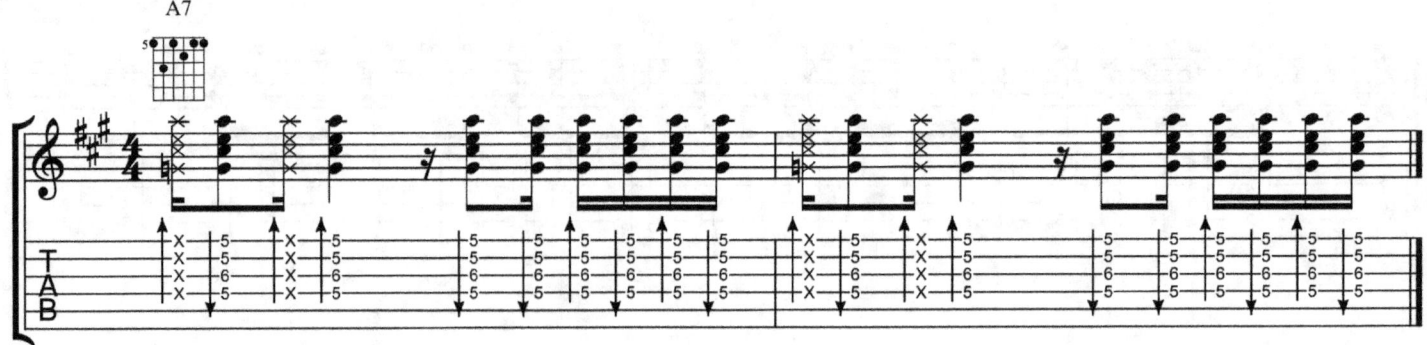

1/16th Note Shuffle Grooves

The 1/16th note divisions of each beat do not have to be evenly spaced.

If the first of each group of two 1/16th notes is longer and the second shorter, the rhythm is said to be a *shuffle*. Shuffle rhythms can look identical on paper to straight 1/16ths, but there is normally a performance direction at the start of the music such as the word *shuffle* above the first bar.

Listen to example 8q and compare it to example 8k. Whereas example 8k is completely straight, example 8q has a definite bounce to it.

Example 8q:

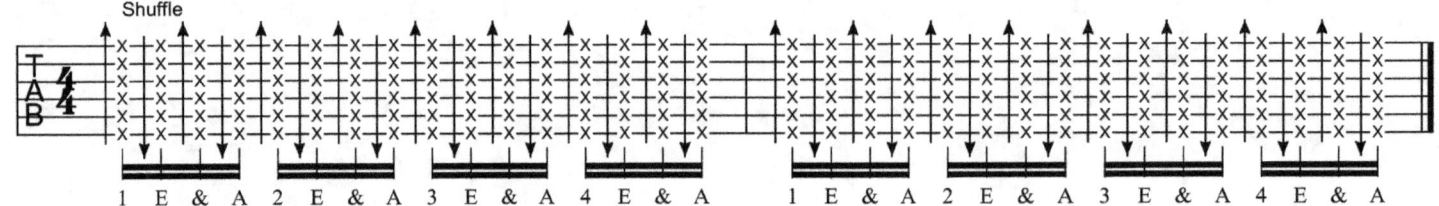

The following rhythm is the same as in exercise 8o, however this time the rhythm is played with a shuffle feel.

Example 8r:

Shuffle

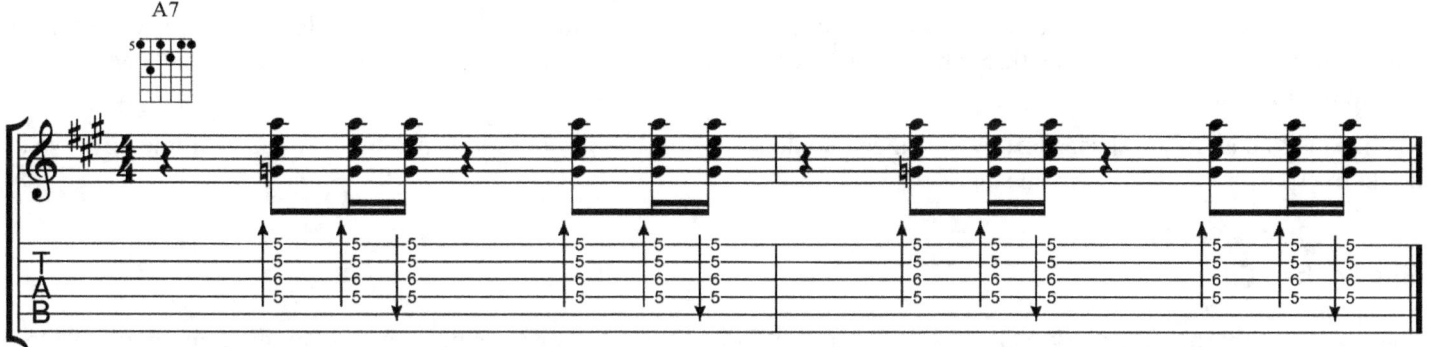

Chapter Nine – Melodic Fills between Chords

Rhythm guitar playing isn't just about playing chords; we can *decorate* the chords we play with single-note phrases to provide movement and countermelody to the singer or soloist.

The art is not to over-play, and to ensure our playing is appropriate to the music. There should always be space for the main melody of the song to shine through. In fact, overplaying and cluttering the melody is one of the easiest ways to get kicked out of a band!

The idea is to play in the spaces left by the singer, so don't try to fill every possible gap, and roll your volume down so as not to overpower everyone else on stage.

Fills on the I Chord

The following rhythm fills work well on a static I chord. This is the A7 chord in a blues in A. Play them in other keys too.

Example 9a:

Example 9b:

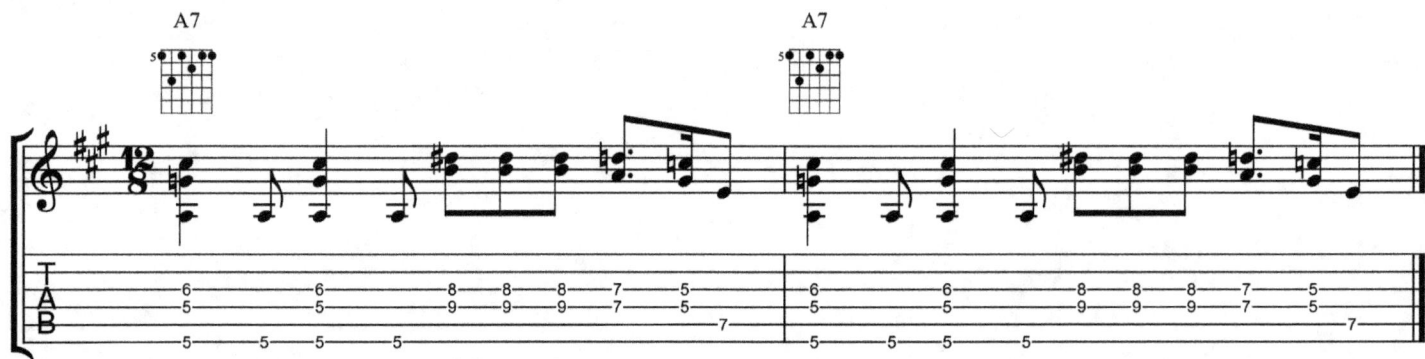

Example 9c:

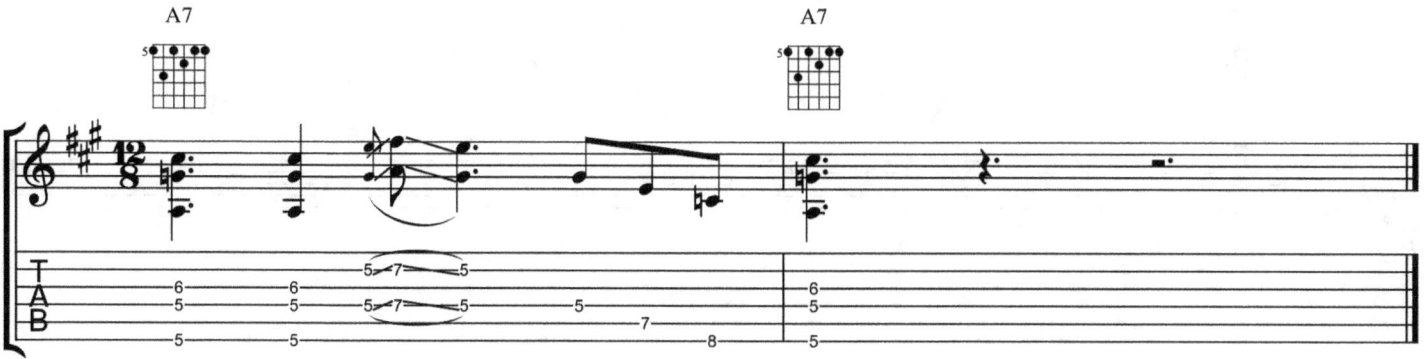

Fills on the IV Chord

These licks target important notes of the IV (D7) chord, however you can shift them all up by one tone so they work on the V (E7) chord.

Example 9d:

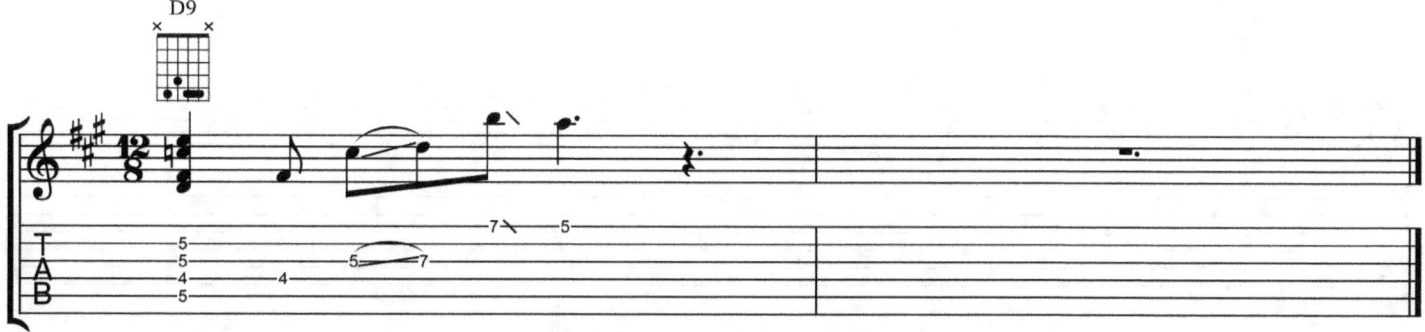

Example 9e:

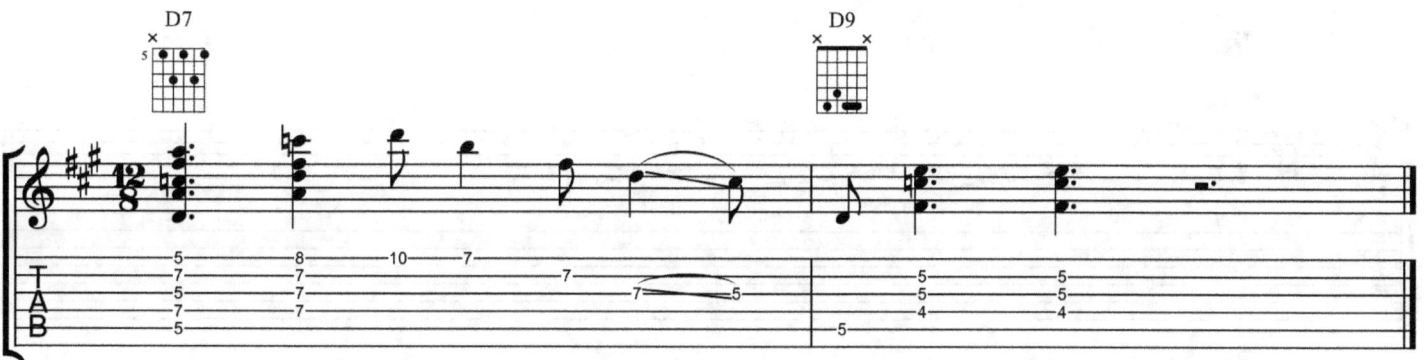

Example 9f:

Fills on the V Chord

Again, you can shift these V-chord (E7) lines *down* one tone and they work well as D7 licks.

Example 9g:

Example 9h:

Example 9i:

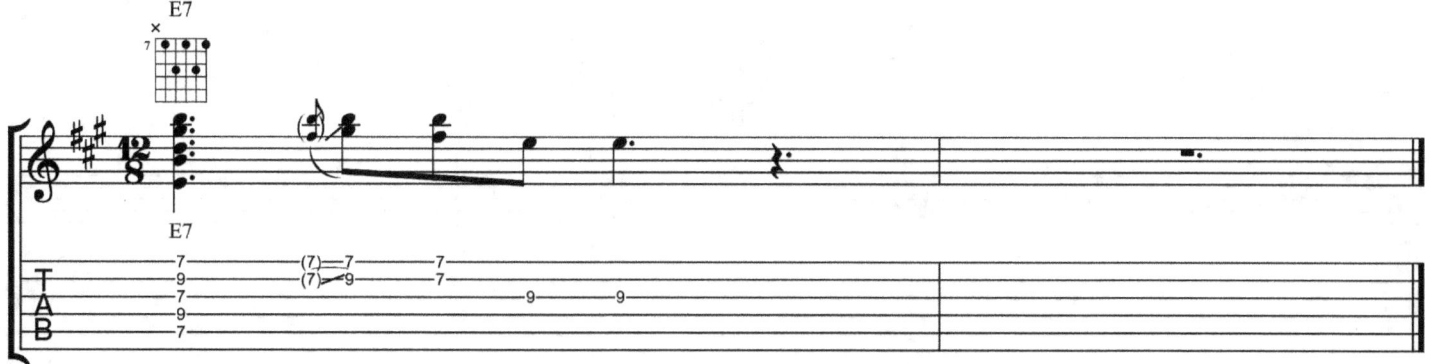

Fills Moving from Chord I to IV

The following ideas are used to target notes while moving from the I chord (A7) to the IV chord (D7).

Example 9j:

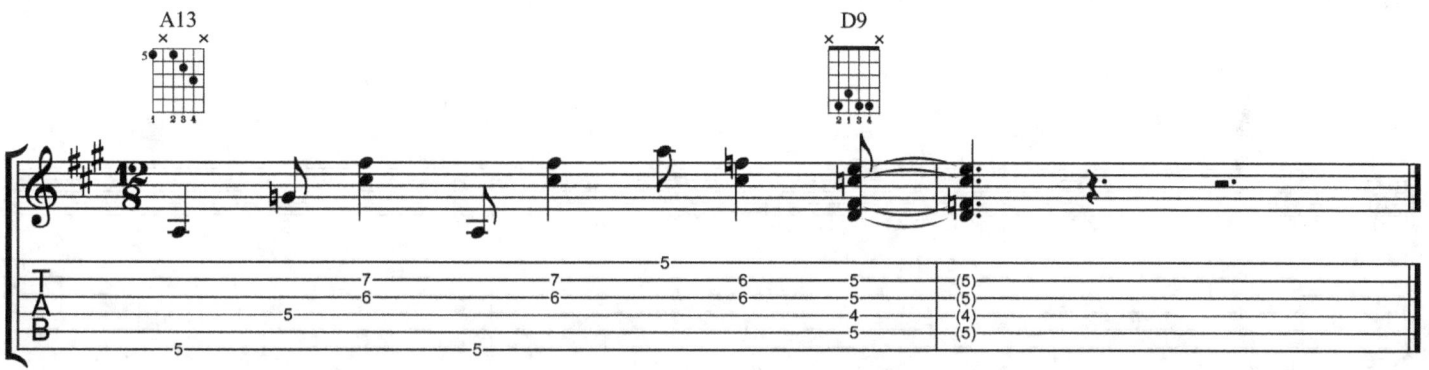

Example 9k:

Example 9l:

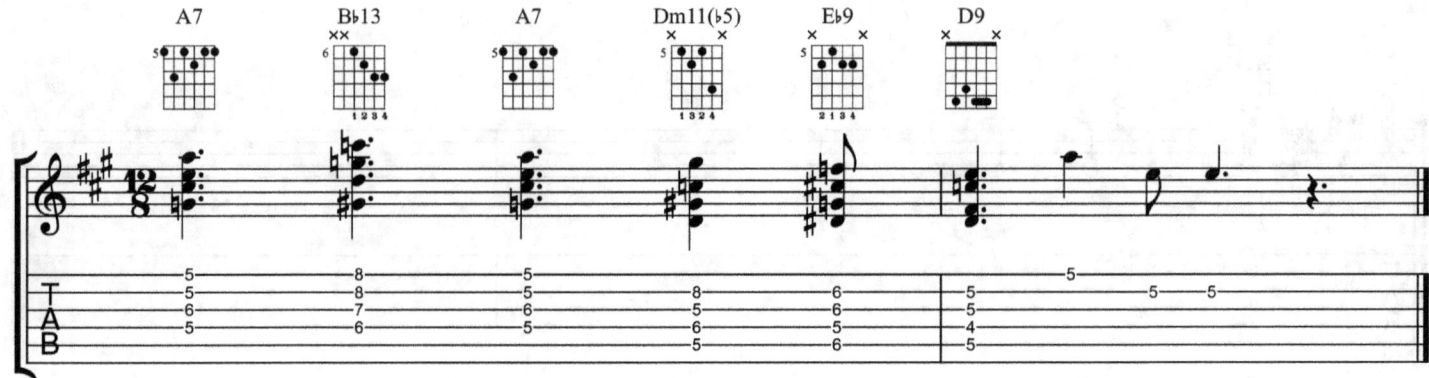

Fills Moving from Chord IV to I

These licks fill in the gaps when moving from IV (D7) back to I (A7).

Example 9m:

Example 9n:

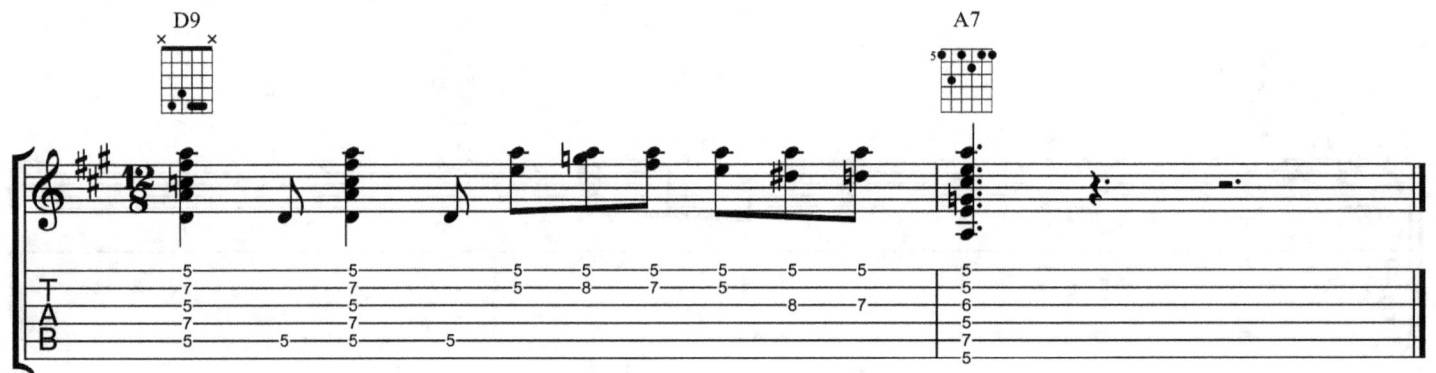

Fills Moving from Chord V to IV

The following examples add melodic interest when moving from (V) E7 to (IV) D7.

Example 9o:

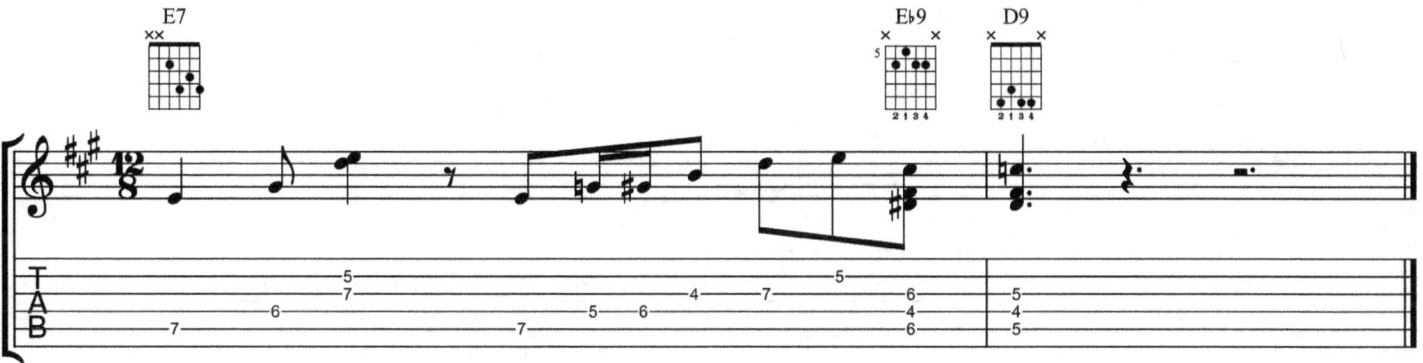

Example 9p:

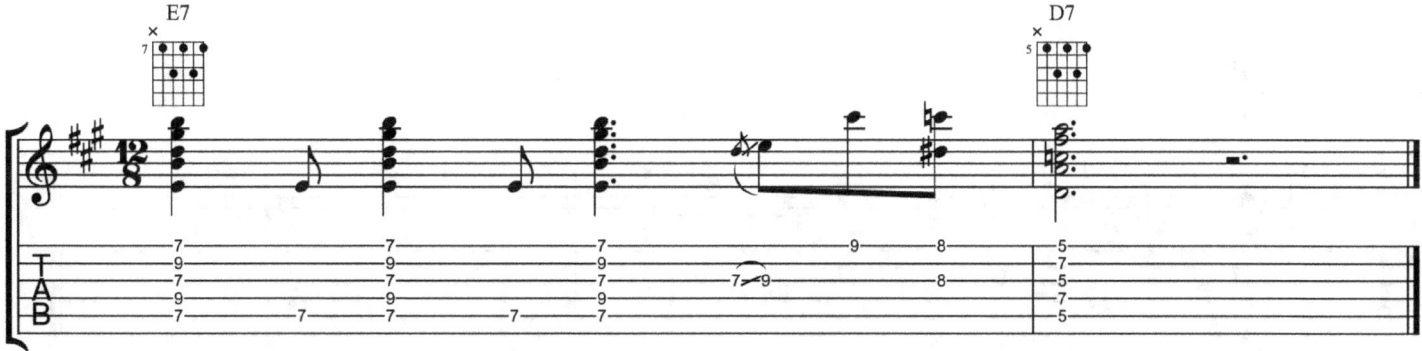

Fills Moving from Chord I to V

These fills create strong melodic voice leading when moving from chord I (A7) to the all-important V (E7) chord.

Example 9q:

Example 9r:

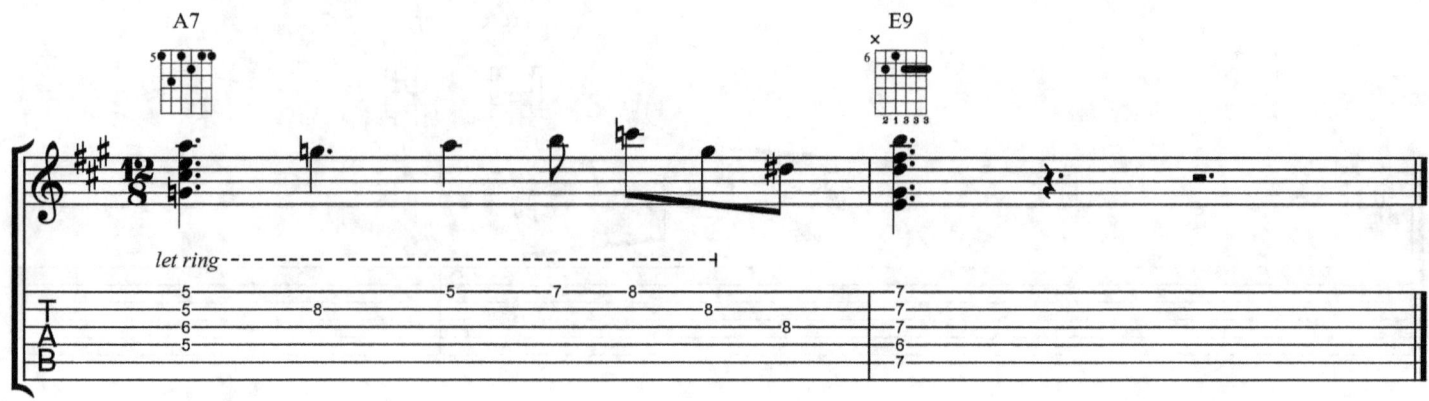

Example 9s:

The occasional melodic line leading from one chord to another or over a prolonged period on a static chord will give great contrast to a repetitive rhythm guitar part. Notice how most of the lines only occur towards the end of the bar; the crucial concept is to leave space for your singer or soloist.

Chapter Ten – Intros and Outros

Being able to begin and end a tune cleanly saves a lot of embarrassment on stage and helps to reinforce a memorable performance. Too many times I have seen under-rehearsed bands frantically looking at each other trying to find someone to take control and actually lead the tune they are playing to a satisfying conclusion. With some stock outros (and intros) you'll always be able to find a way to end a song cleanly.

Intros to many songs are often based on the final few chords or turnaround section of the song. There is a bit of a crossover in the following examples between what is considered 'lead' guitar and what is considered rhythm guitar playing but that is nothing to worry about.

Intros are extremely useful because they can always function as an outro too. It just depends on which chord you end on. For example, look at this intro in the key of A Major.

This idea is based around a descending Dominant 7th chord and ends with an E7 chord approached from a semitone above. By ending on the E7 (Dominant) chord we create the feeling that the music wants to continue by resolving back to A7.

Example 10a:

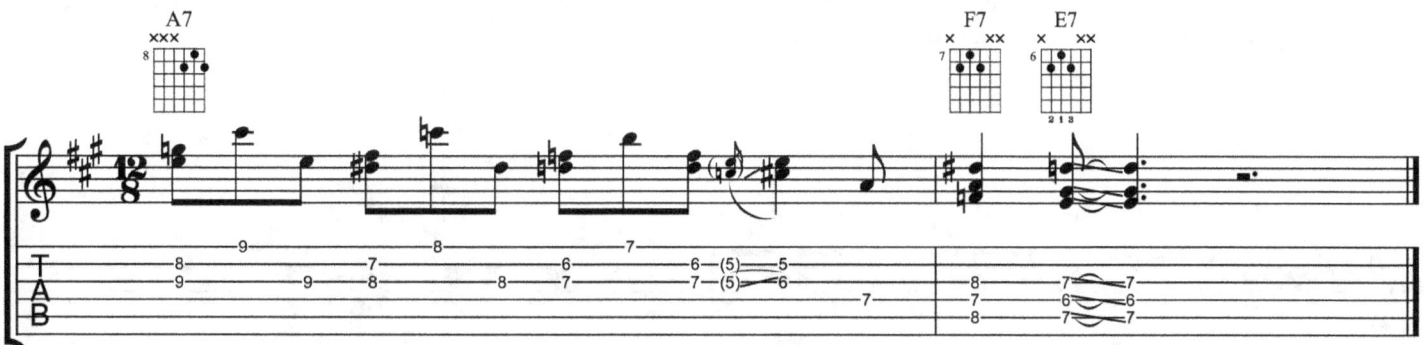

Now look at example 10b. This line begins in the same way but instead of ending on E7 as before, the line finishes on the A7 once again approached by step from above. This resolution has a certain degree of finality about it and it would be difficult to keep the music moving forward after this point.

Example 10b:

As you can hear, this is the musical equivalent of a period or full stop.

Alter all the following lines to end on A7 if you want use them as an outro instead of an intro.

The next example contains an A note *drone* as the bass line descends. The E7 is approached by a semitone from above but this time in a much lower voicing.

Example 10c:

If you end the lick with a Bb7 to A7 movement it will serve as a great final outro.

The next idea demonstrates a musical device called *contrary motion*. This is where two parts move in opposite melodic directions. Notice that the dominant chord is now approached from a semitone below.

Example 10d:

The next intro lick moves through ascending chords up to the Dominant chord E7.

Look out for a chord sequence you have seen before: The D Major becomes an E Dim7 chord before moving to the E7. This creates the chromatic bass line C#, D, Eb, E which is an extremely strong harmonic movement.

Example 10e:

Instead of an approach chord into the E7 there is a short A Mixolydian lick that leads smoothly into the change.

Next, melodic movement is created at the top of the chord by careful use of chord voicings. I would normally pick a line like this with the fingers of my picking hand.

On beats 3 and 4 there is a movement from chord IV Major (D) to chord iv Minor (Dm). This rich-sounding change is an ear-catching addition to the phrase. Try to accentuate the string which contains the melody note.

Example 10f:

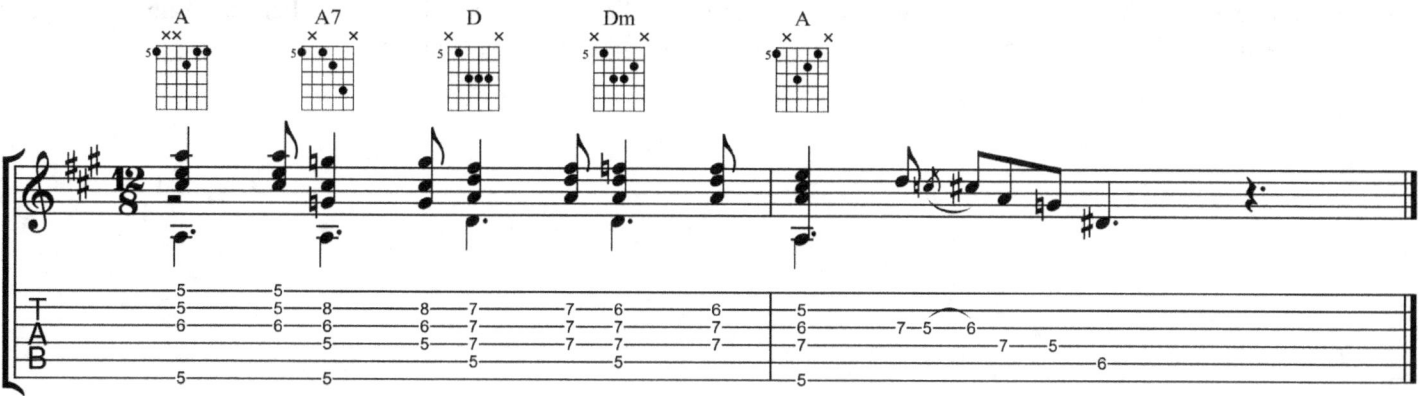

While there is no obvious E7 chord in example 10f, the lick at the end *targets* the note G# with an important *guide tone* of the chord. Targeting the G# makes the listener believe they have heard the dominant chord in its entirety, and that the song is ready to begin.

To change this intro lick into an outro lick I could simply approach an A7 by step at the end of the line.

Example 10g:

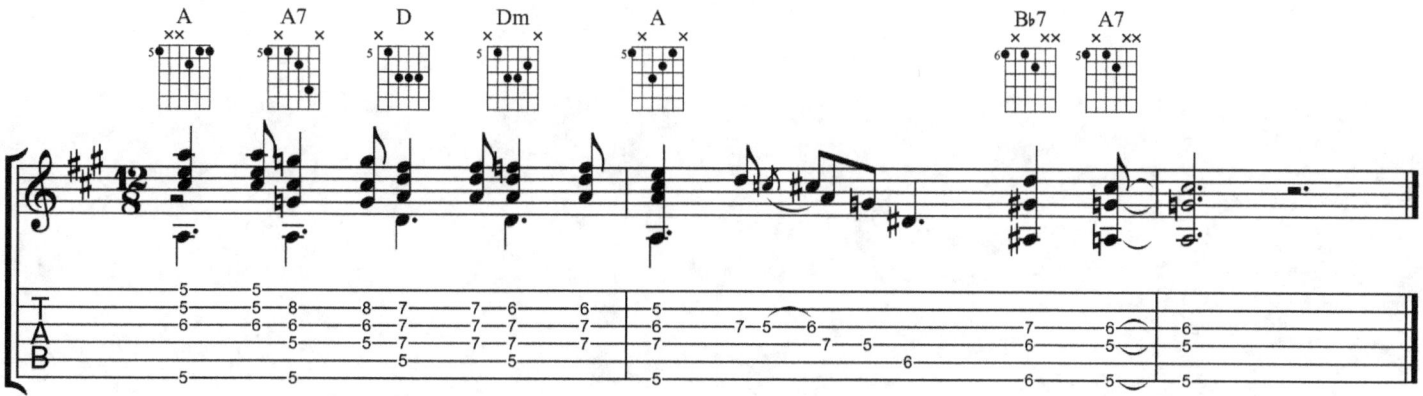

If in doubt it's hard to go wrong with this Jimi Hendrix-style ending. This example uses ascending power chords to move up to the dominant chord but ends with some big '9' chords for a rockier ending.

Example 10h:

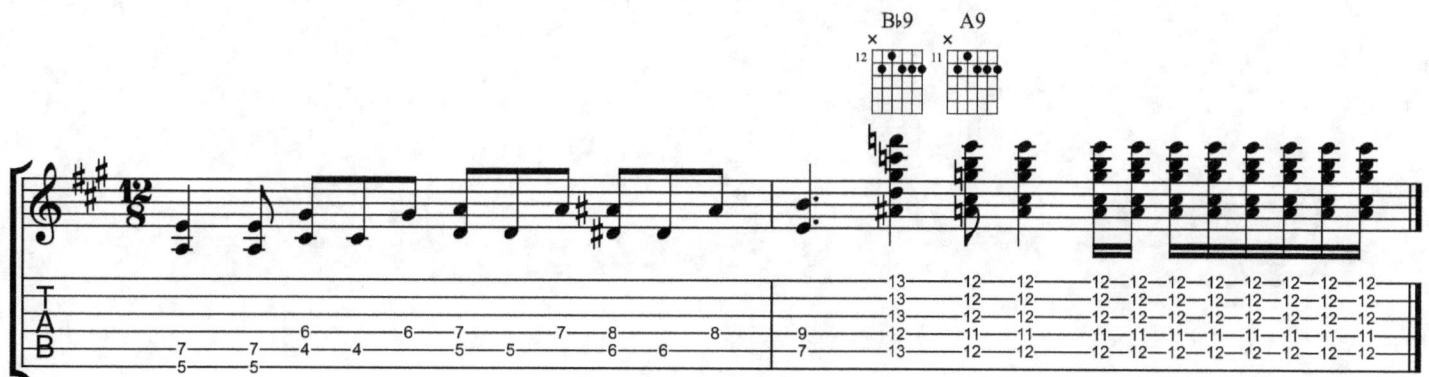

65

Convert this lick to an intro line by changing the Bb9 and Ab9 to an F9 and E9.

Clean intros and endings are an important part of a tight band performance. Always rehearse exactly what you'll play for each song before you get on stage.

There's nothing worse than a sloppy ending to a song and the audience will probably remember that, rather than your ground-breaking guitar solo. It's essential to get the basic building-blocks of the song right.

Chapter Eleven – Shell Voicings

One scenario we'll all experience in our musical career is the 'busy blues jam-night'. We could find ourselves on stage with two other guitarists, a keyboard player, a bass guitar, three singers and a flugel horn. It can be extremely tough to know what and indeed *when* to play a chord.

The rhythm section can be so crowded that it is almost impossible to play anything that enhances the music and makes the audience's experience better. If it is really that busy on stage, my best piece of advice is to not play anything at all. Playing muted, rhythmic scratches on deadened strings can work, but often it's best to leave some space. This is a legitimate musical decision and one that is often for the greater good.

You may find yourself in a band where things are quite busy but (hopefully) a little less dense. In these circumstances, I often find myself playing sparsely and using *shell voicings*, or *drop two* chords.

Shell voicings contain only the root, 3rd and b7 of a chord. They do not contain the 5th or any extensions.

The 3rd and 7th are the two notes that define the chord quality, be it Major, Minor or Dominant. No other notes are needed, not even the root. In fact, I often avoid playing the root altogether if I'm playing with a bass player.

In this section, you'll learn to play different shell voicing shapes for the chords in the 12-bar blues. They are fantastic to use rhythmically when we don't have much space in the band to play bigger chords. Shell voicings also tend to automatically create smooth voice leading between chord changes.

Here are some shell voicings for an A7 chord.

Example 11a:

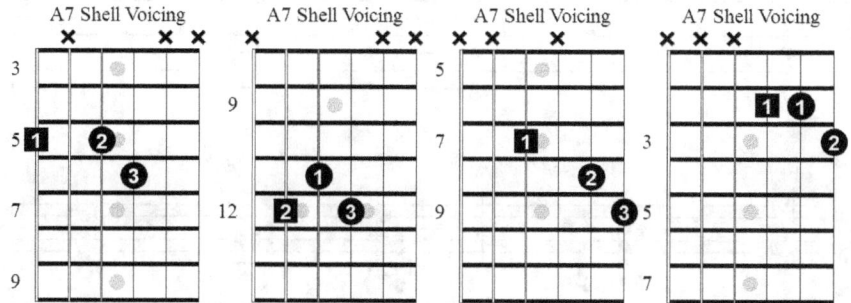

These shapes are movable so they can be treated like barre chords. For example, you could play through the chords in a blues by just using the movable shape on the 6th string.

Example 11b:

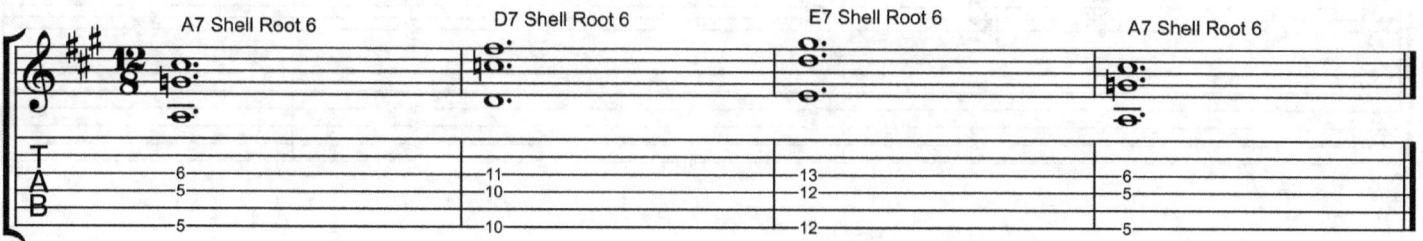

The jumps in the example above are a little large, so let's play these chords in one position on the neck.

Example 11c:

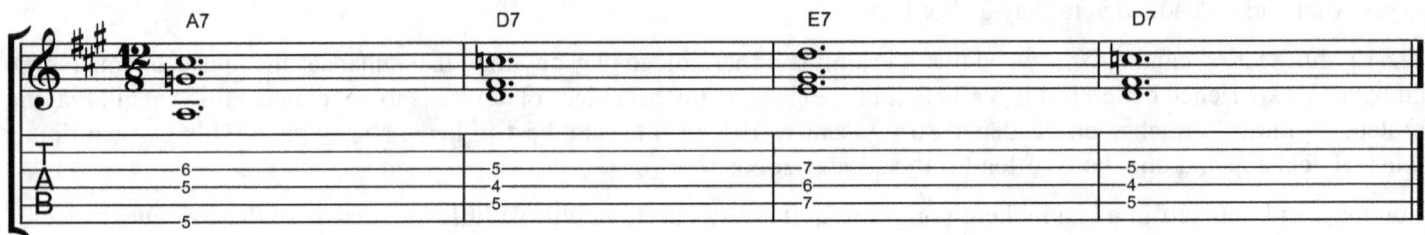

Play these chord shapes in a full blues progression and remember, all the rhythmic and approach ideas are still available. Here's just one way to navigate the 12-bar blues with shell voicings.

Example 11d:

The previous example is deliberately simple. It provides just enough movement to keep things interesting as a self-contained study although you may wish to play even less in a busy band situation.

We haven't yet explored shell voicings on higher string groups. Here's how to play the chords on the top three and four strings.

Example 11e:

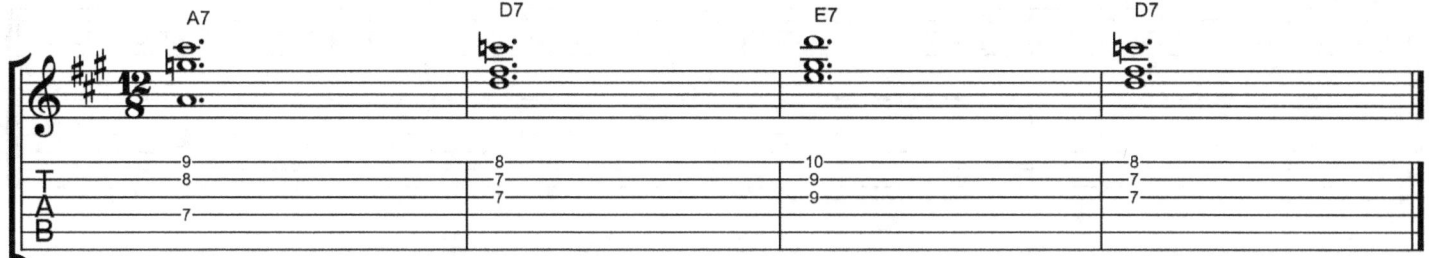

Here are the shell voicings for Bm7.

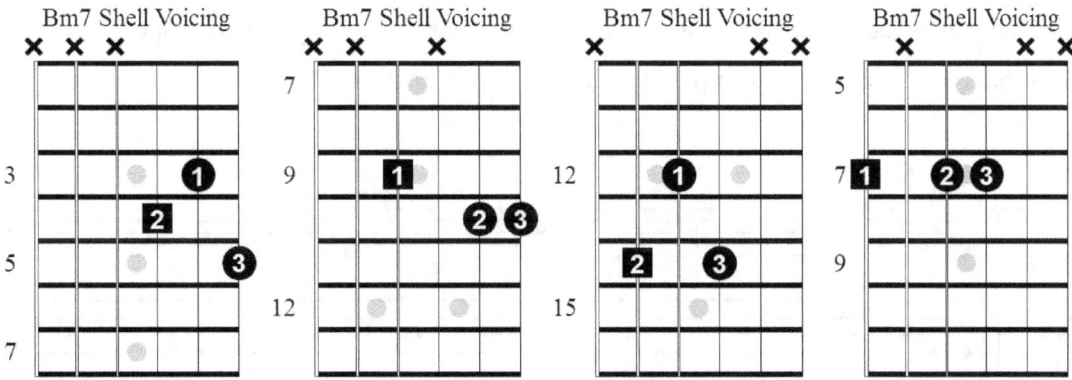

You now have all the voicings you need to play an extended blues. The next example teaches you to navigate the chords in a 12-bar blues with a 1 6 2 5 turnaround. Once the chord voicings are memorised, add in your own rhythms and approach chords to make the music personal.

Remember, the whole idea behind this approach is to keep things simple and to leave room for others to play.

Example 11f:

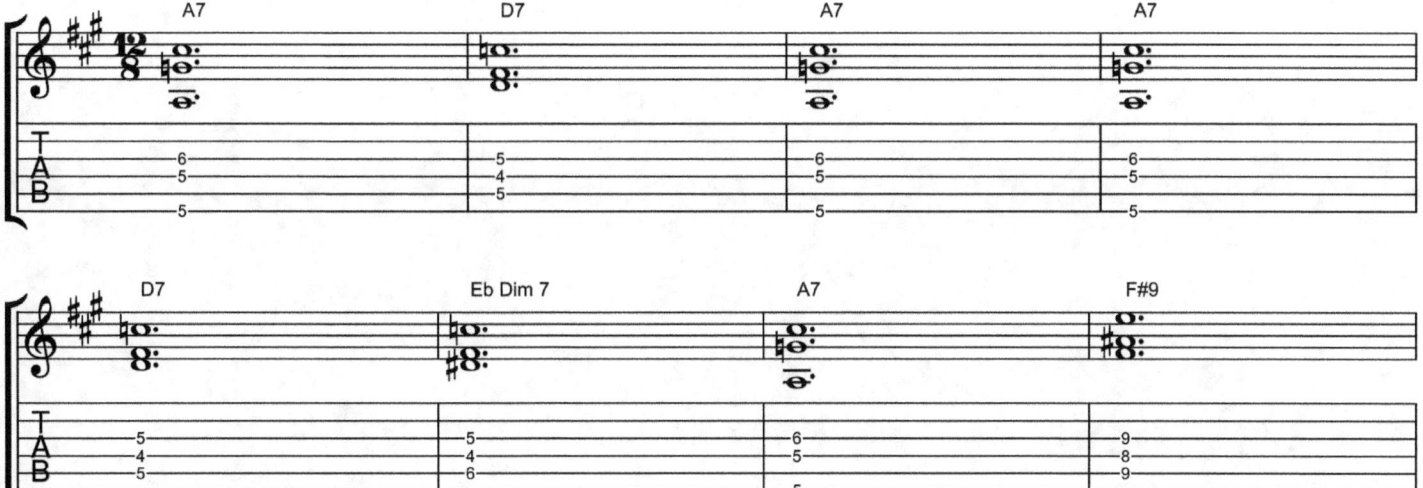

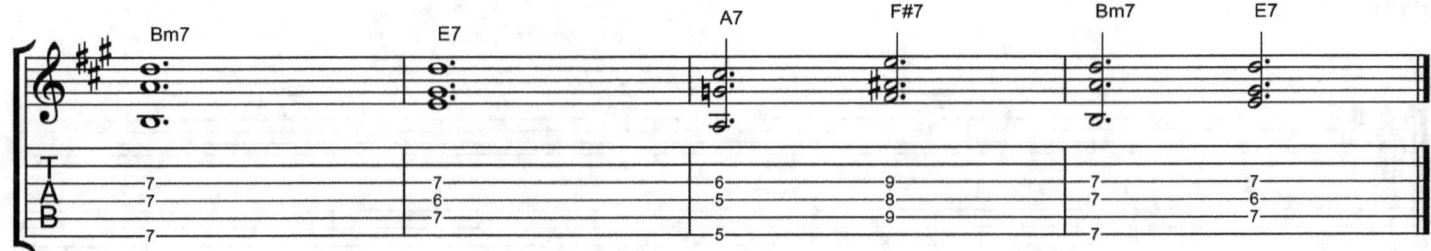

Next, try finding as many ways as you can through the changes using shell voicings on different string groups. Begin with the root of the first chord on either the 6th, 5th, 4th or 3rd string, and then try to find the closest possible voicing of the next chord to move to.

You can play just the 3rds and 7ths of each chord without including the bass notes.

This idea is useful because it teaches you to see the most important notes of the chord as closely linked shapes.

For example, here are the last four bars of the previous example played with just the 3rds and b7s:

Example 11g:

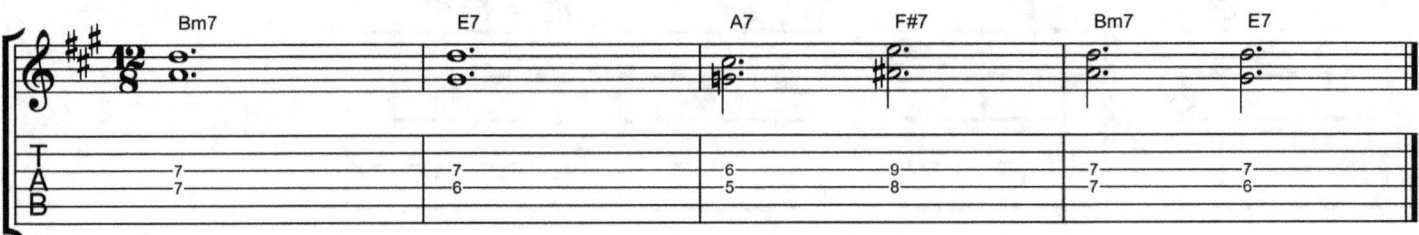

When I teach my students these movements on the guitar, it often comes as a surprise to them to see just how closely these chords are all related. These guide tones can also be used as soloing ideas to melodically outline each chord.

Spend some serious practice time working out how to play closely-voiced guide tone lines on each two-string grouping. For example, try to play through the 12-bar blues using only 3rds and 7ths on the first and second strings. Then play them on the second and third strings, the third and fourth strings, and finally fourth and fifth strings.

Chapter Twelve – Drop 2 Voicings

We have now used shell voicings to keep out of the way of a busy rhythm section and played them in low-register voicings to not crowd the range where singers and soloists play.

Drop 2 chords are another way to stay clear of dense harmony parts, but these are normally played in a *higher* register where the tone of the guitar isn't as heavy. Drop 2 chords are useful at higher tempos where we might play more percussive chord stabs rather than letting chords ring out.

Drop 2 voicings are simply an arranging technique where the second highest note in a chord is dropped by an octave. For example, here is the chord of A7 as a stacked *closed position* voicing:

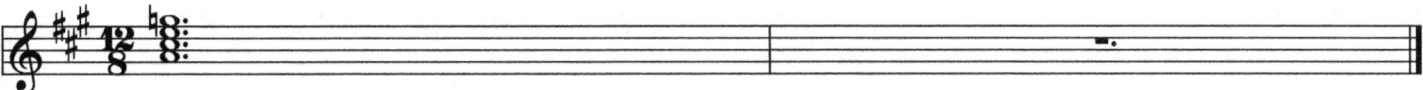

When we drop the second highest note down an octave, the chord becomes a drop 2 voicing:

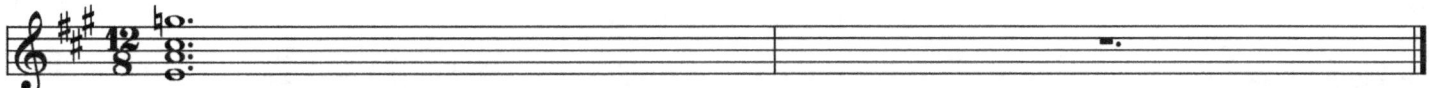

Once again, this isn't a theory book, for more information you may wish to check out my book **Drop 2 Chord Voicings for Jazz and Modern Guitar.**

It is common for drop 2 chords to be played on the top four strings, but it is a worthwhile pursuit to explore them on the middle four strings too.

Any four-note drop 2 chord can be played in any of four inversions. This gives four different ways to play each chord.

These are the four drop 2 voicings of an A7 chord arranged from the lowest position on the neck to the highest. The square dot in each chord is the root and it is only the bass note in one of the voicings.

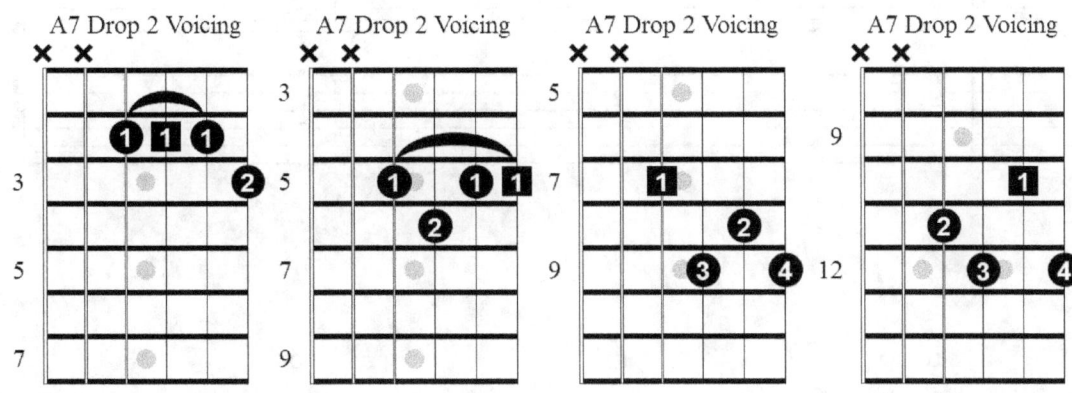

Play through all four voicings in the following way:

Example 12a:

Next, link together the chords in the 12-bar blues using the closest available shape for each chord. Beginning on each voicing of A7 in turn we quickly discover four closely related ways to play the I, IV, V progression with minimum movement.

Example 12b:

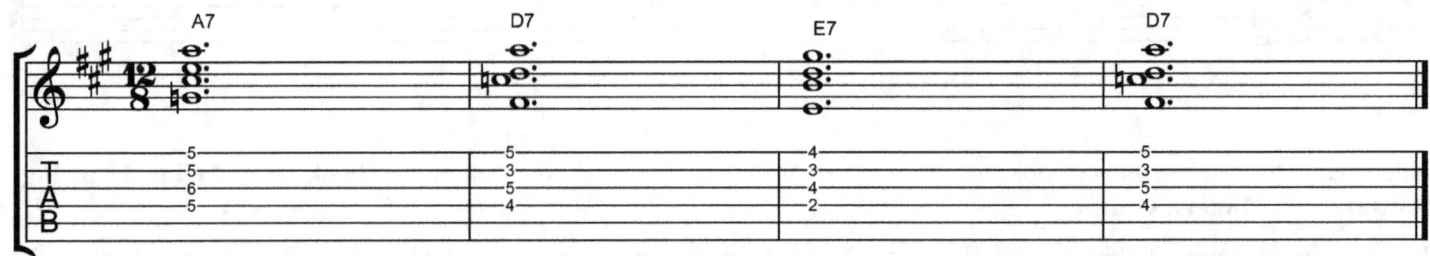

Example 12c:

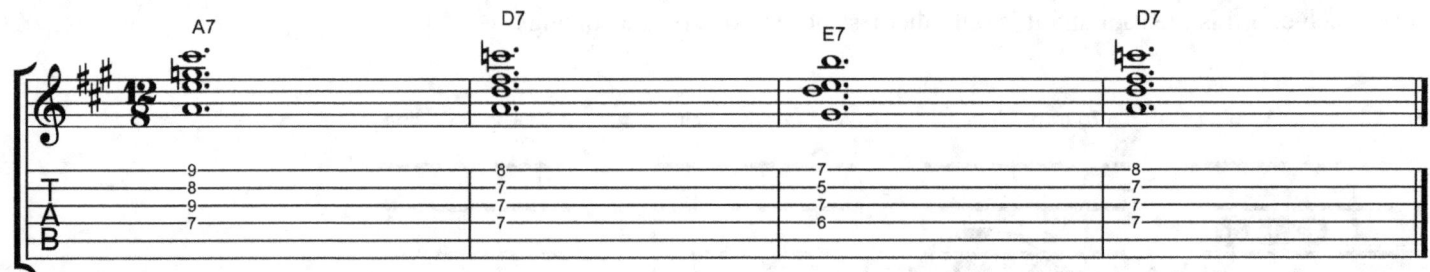

Example 12d:

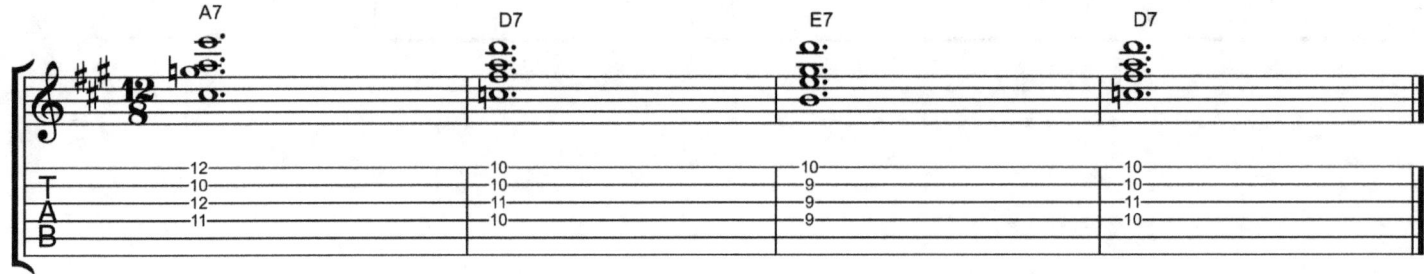

Example 12e:

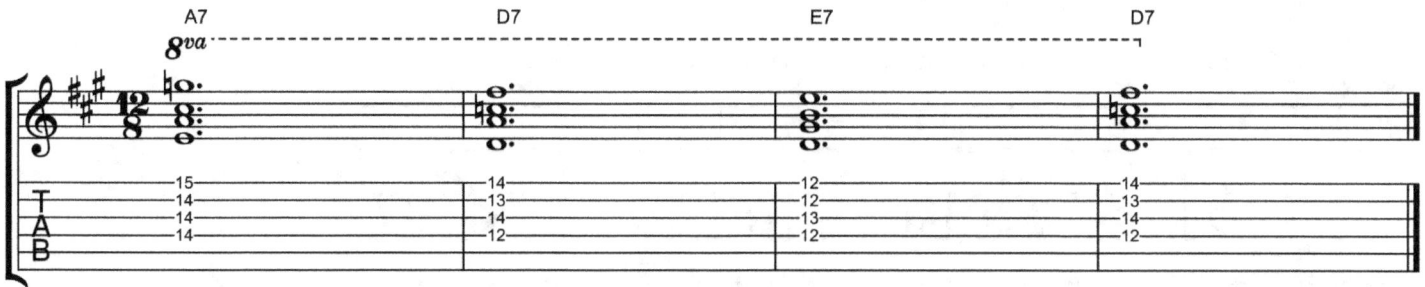

Knowing how to move between chords I, IV and V in four positions is essential, because you now have the whole neck covered. It's always possible to move to a nearby voicing when the chords change and makes for a very intelligent, smooth-sounding guitar part.

You can always use more than one chord per bar to create a melody line with the top note of each voicing.

Notice how I keep the melody flowing by approaching all the chords with stepwise chord slides from above or below to help. These ideas are totally limitless; a good grasp of drop 2 chords all over the neck is very useful for creating an interesting and *melodic* rhythm part without an overly dense chord sound.

Example 12f:

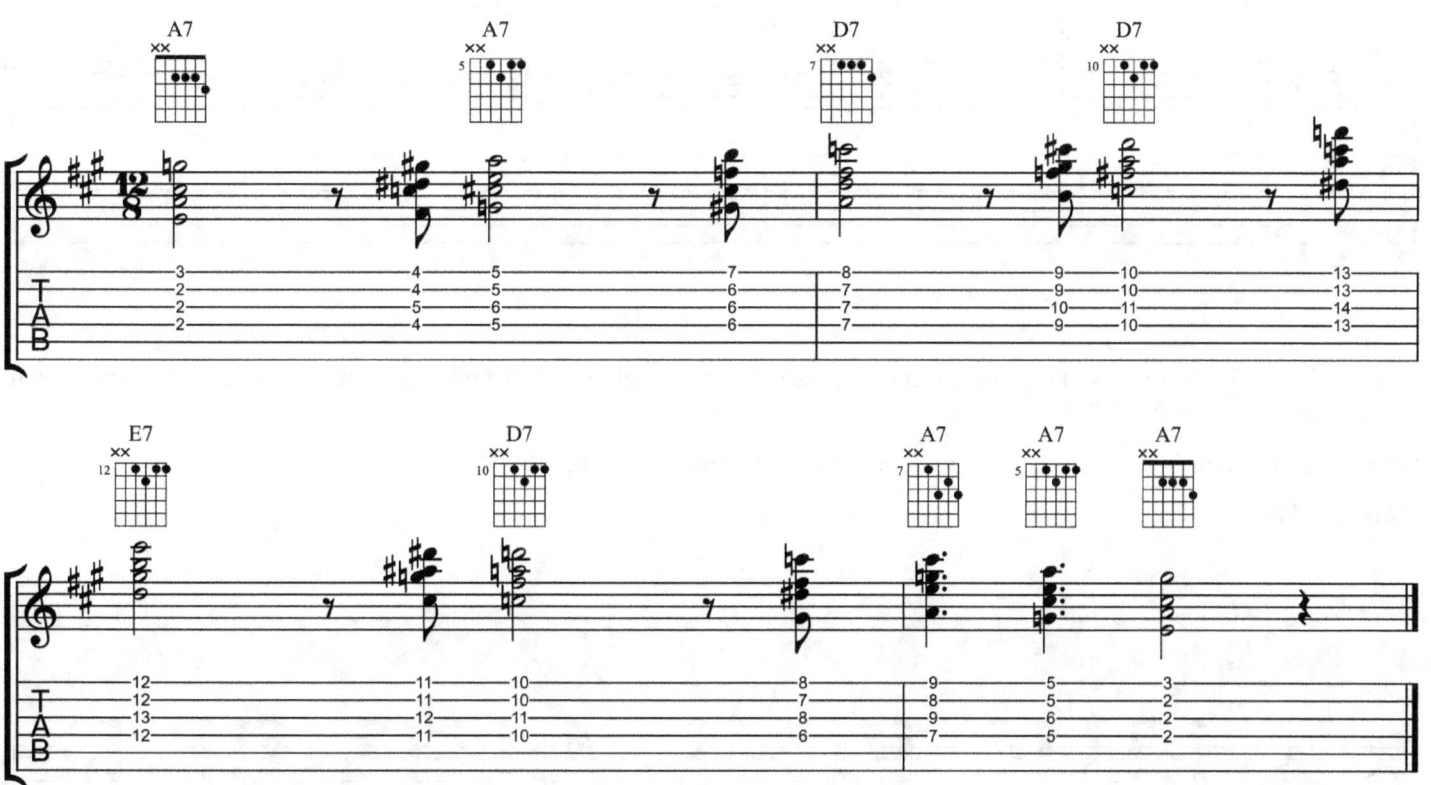

73

Add in the drop 2 voicings for the Bm7 chord and use these in the same way:

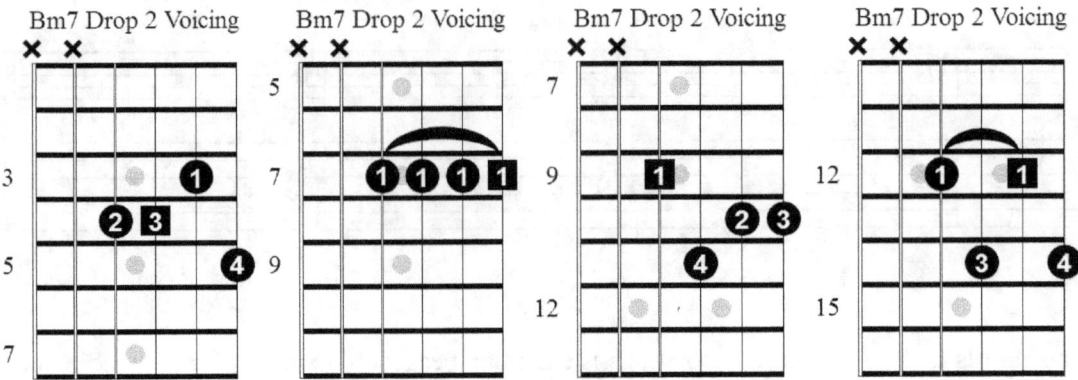

Here is one way to play the I VI II V turnaround in the key of A:

Example 12g:

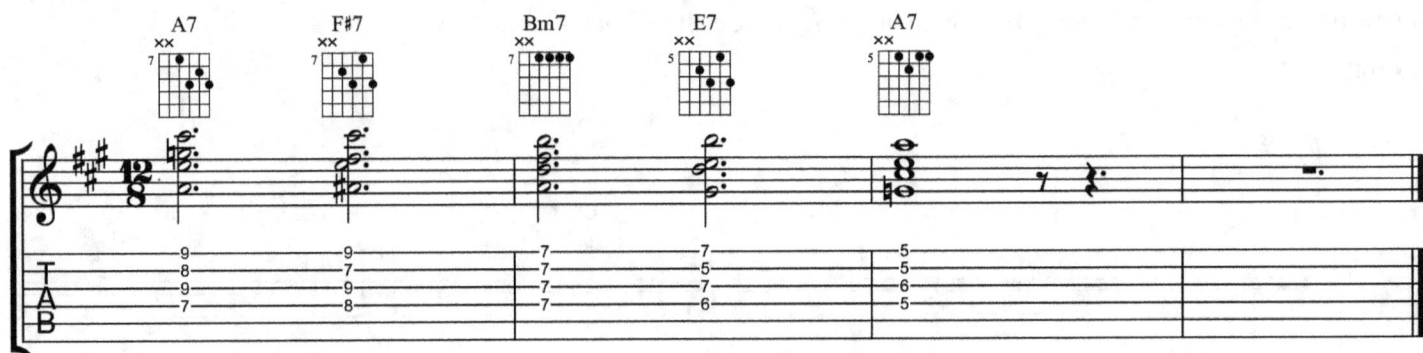

As with the earlier examples, try to find as many ways to play through this chord progression. Take it in turns to start from a different voicing of the A7 chord.

Here are some sample rhythm patterns you could use with drop 2 voicings.

Example 12h:

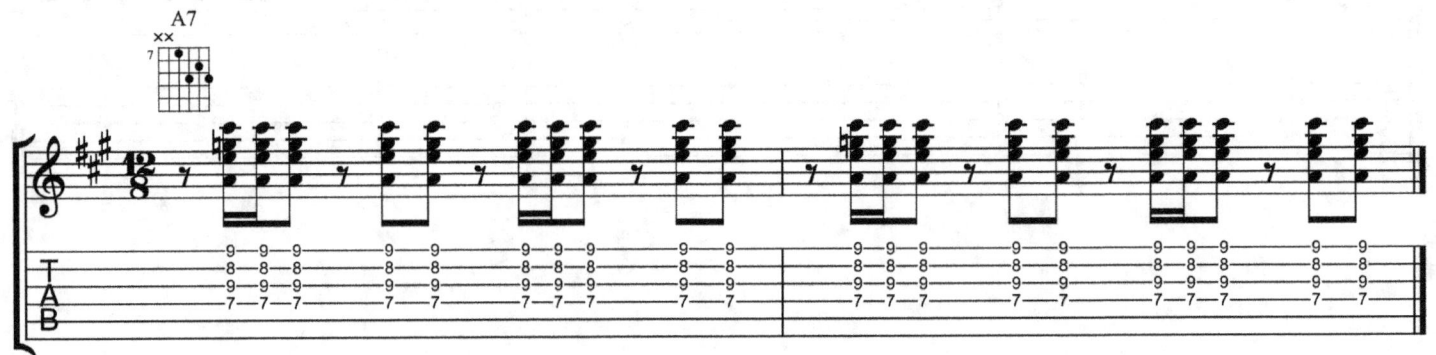

Example 12i:

Example 12j:

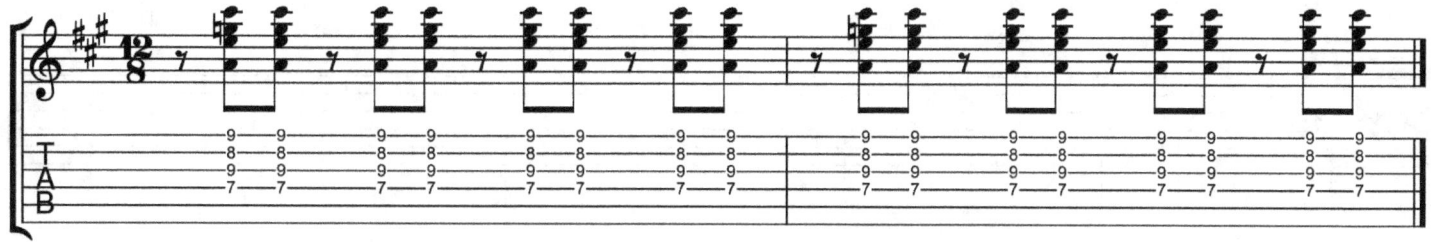

Of course, the rhythm pattern you play will depend on the groove of the song, so use your ears and lock in with the band.

Chapter Thirteen - The Minor Blues

Until now we have been mainly examining the 12-bar blues played with Dominant 7 chords. These are probably the most common type of blues chords but there is one more important blues style you should know.

The whole 12-bar progression can be based around minor chords to create a dark, sombre mood. It is acceptable to play *every* chord in this progression as a minor chord, however a Dominant V chord (E7) is often used to add tension before resolving to the tonic chord (A7).

Here is the structure for a basic Minor blues.

Example 13a:

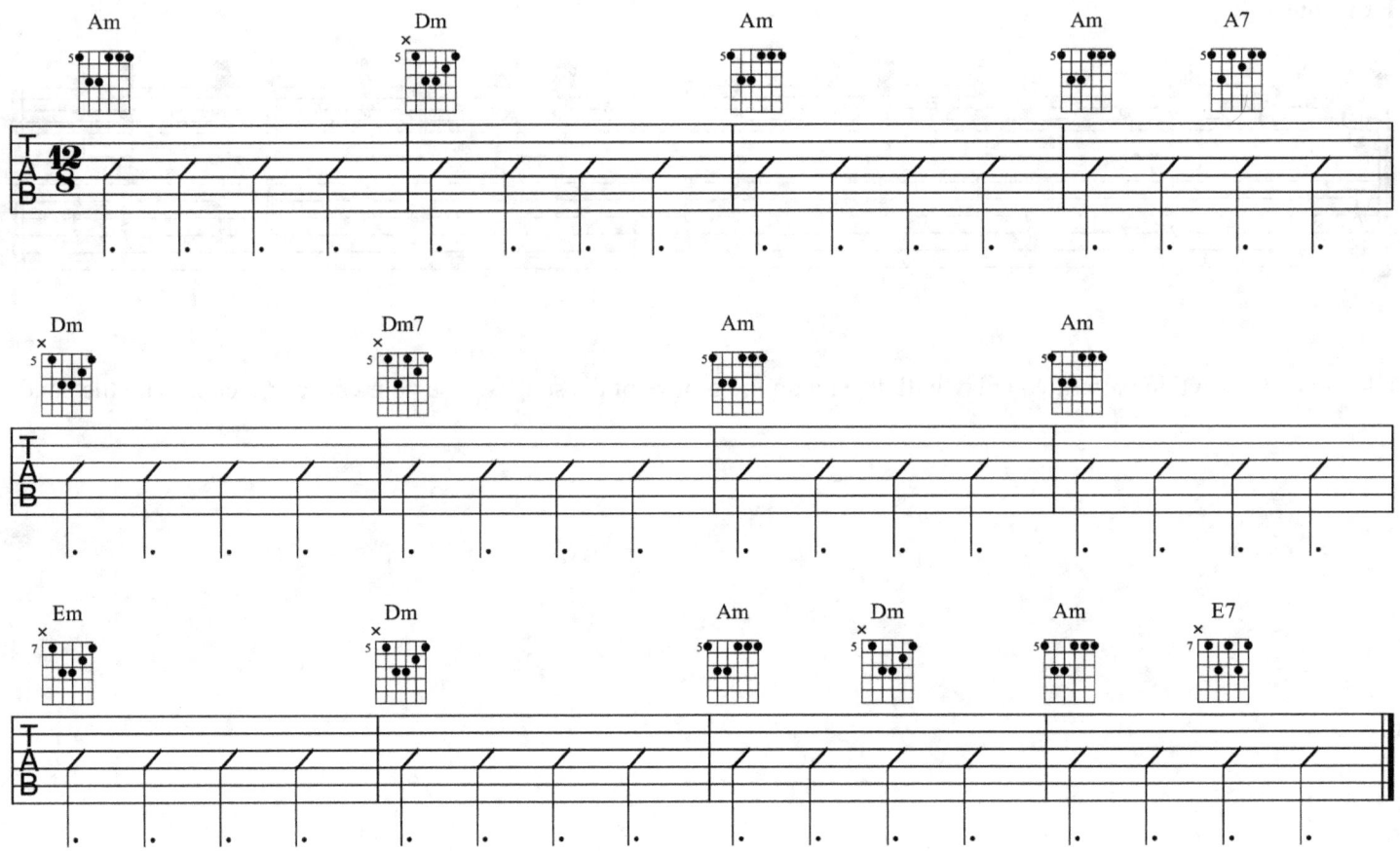

Notice how the change to A7 in bar four helps create a smooth transition into the Dm.

In bar six I use a Dm7 chord for a bit of colour, and in bar 12 I use an E7, not an Em to build the tension at the end of the turnaround.

Here's the new vocabulary you need to play the previous progression.

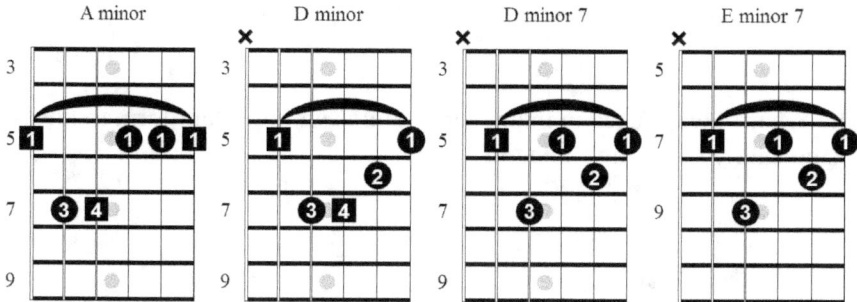

As with the dominant 7 blues there are many techniques we can use to add interest and movement to the minor blues progression. Play through the following progression and look out for examples of

- Substitutions
- Approaching chords by step
- Altered chords
- Changing from minor to dominant chords in the same bar

Example 13b:

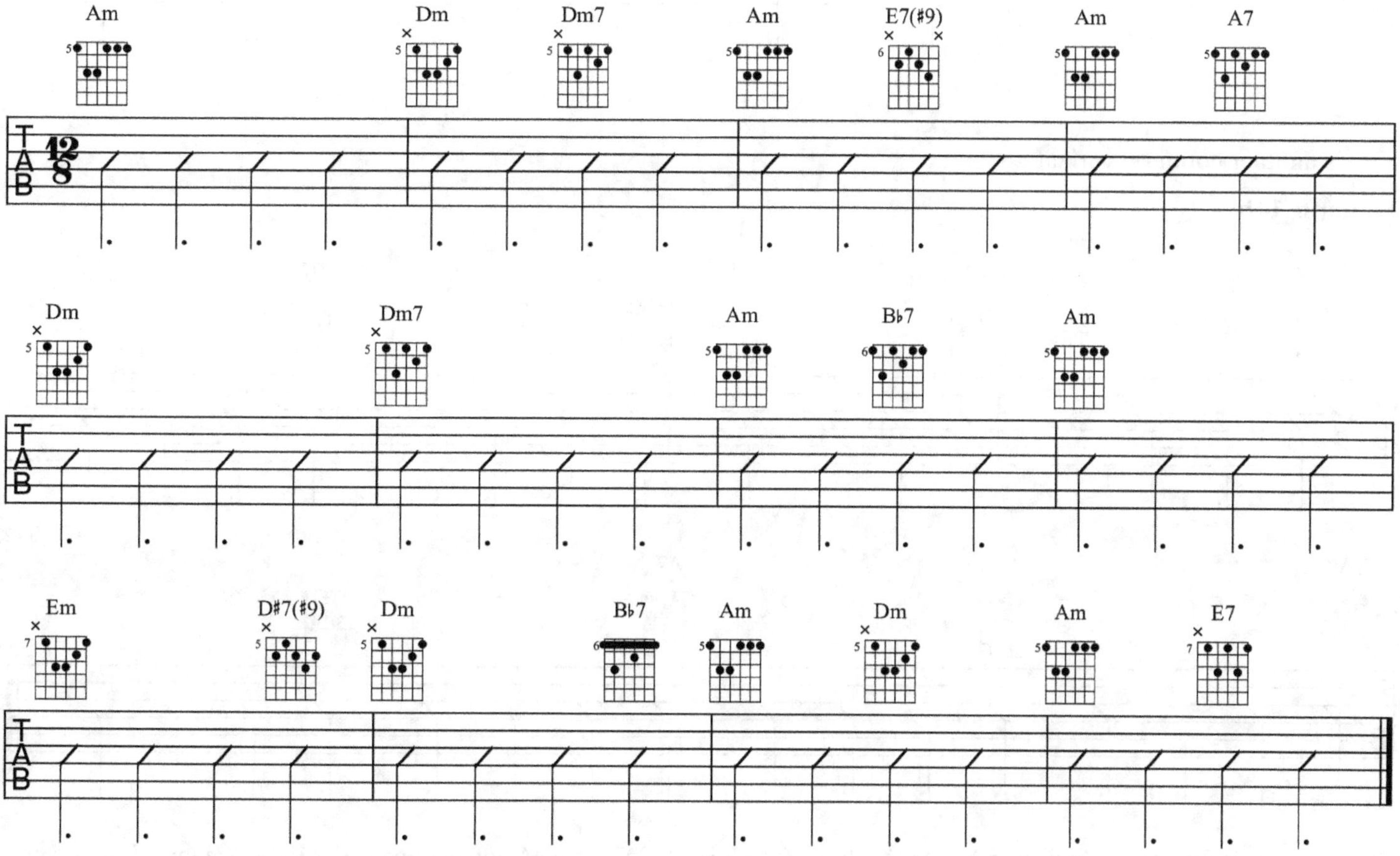

Listen to players such as Gary Moore and B.B. King as they used many variations of the Minor blues in their music.

Chapter Fourteen – Other Blues Forms

The 8-bar Blues

The 12-bar blues is not the only blues structure. The 8-bar blues is used in many songs and is an important form to know. There are many variations but the basic structure is normally something like this.

Example 14a:

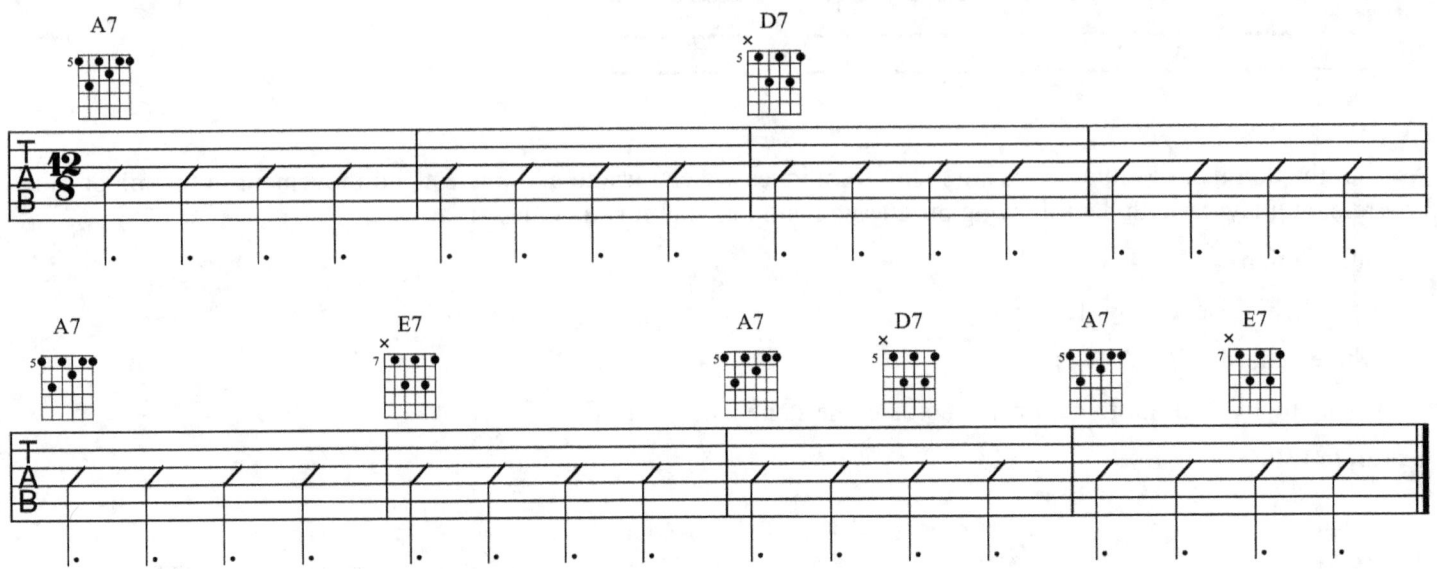

Here's another common variant:

Example 14b:

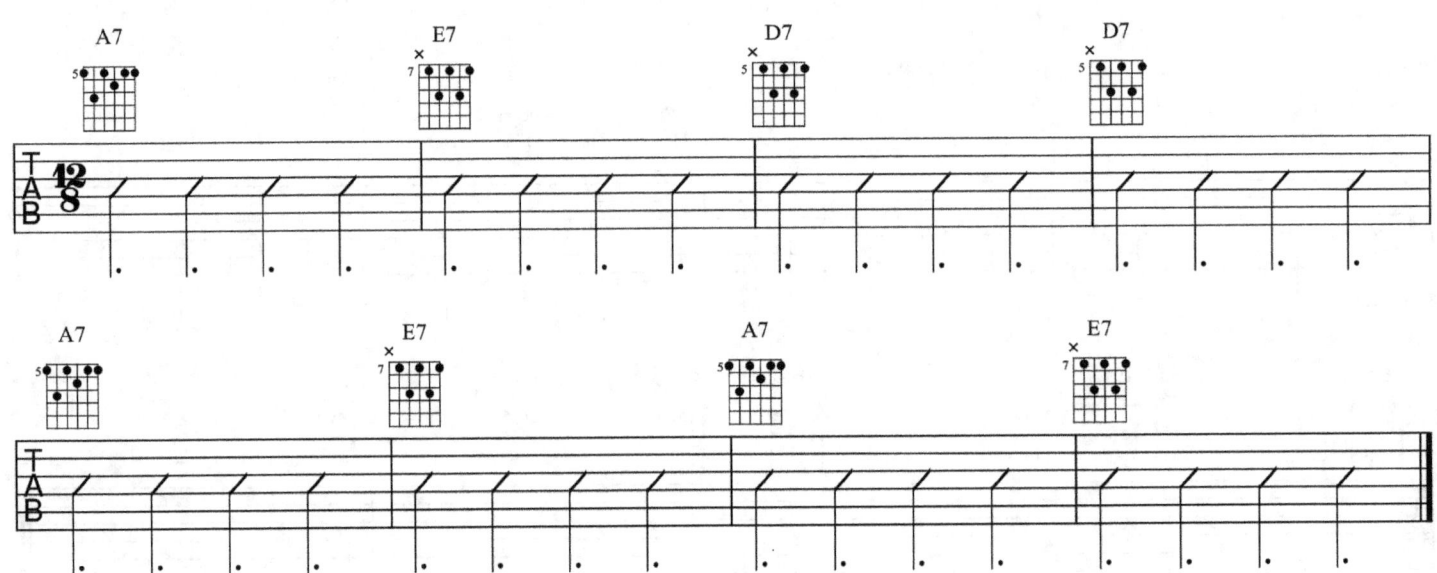

It is not uncommon to move from a Major IV chord (D Major or D7) to a Minor iv chord (D Minor or Dm7) in bar four.

Example 14c:

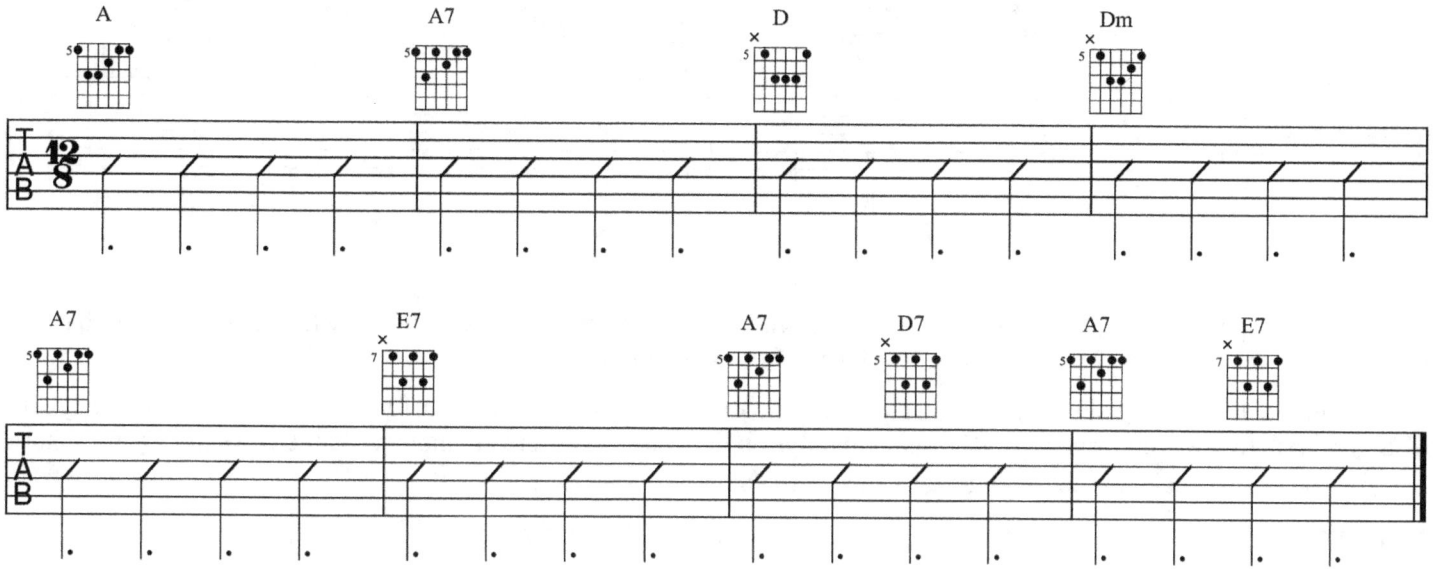

Here's chord vocabulary you need to play the previous example. Try swapping the D Minor for a D Minor 7.

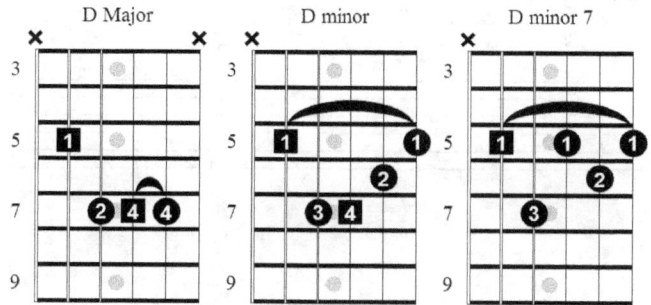

Just as we altered the chords and structure of the 12-bar blues, we can take a similar approach to playing the 8-bar form.

We can add an Eb Dim7 chord in bar four and a I VI II V turnaround in bars five and six. This time however, the VI chord (F#) is played as a minor chord instead of a dominant 7.

Example 14d:

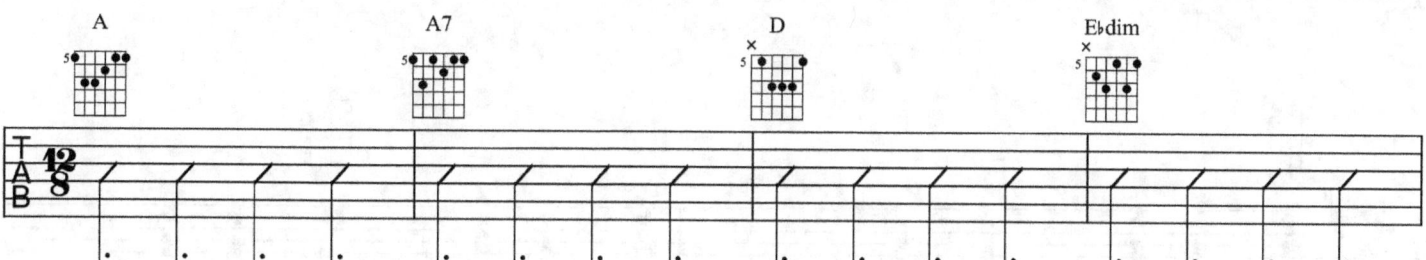

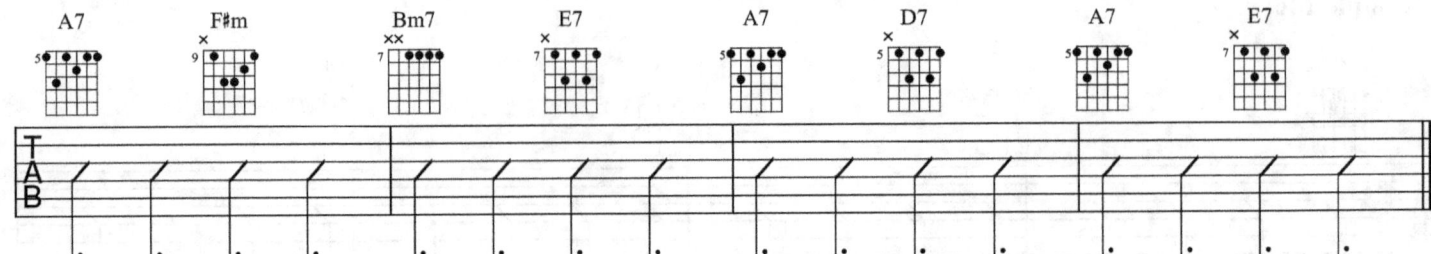

Of course, we can add in any of the harmonic ideas from the 12-bar blues too. Here is one way to add the bVI into bar six, and I've also spiced up the 7 chords with a few 9ths, 13ths, and approach chords.

The rhythm is deliberately simple so you can concentrate on mastering the new 8-bar form. Feel free to spice it up a bit. You may wish to use drop 2 chords and/or shell voicings on this tune too. There are many possible ways to vary this chord progression so don't take the following example as set in stone.

Example 14e:

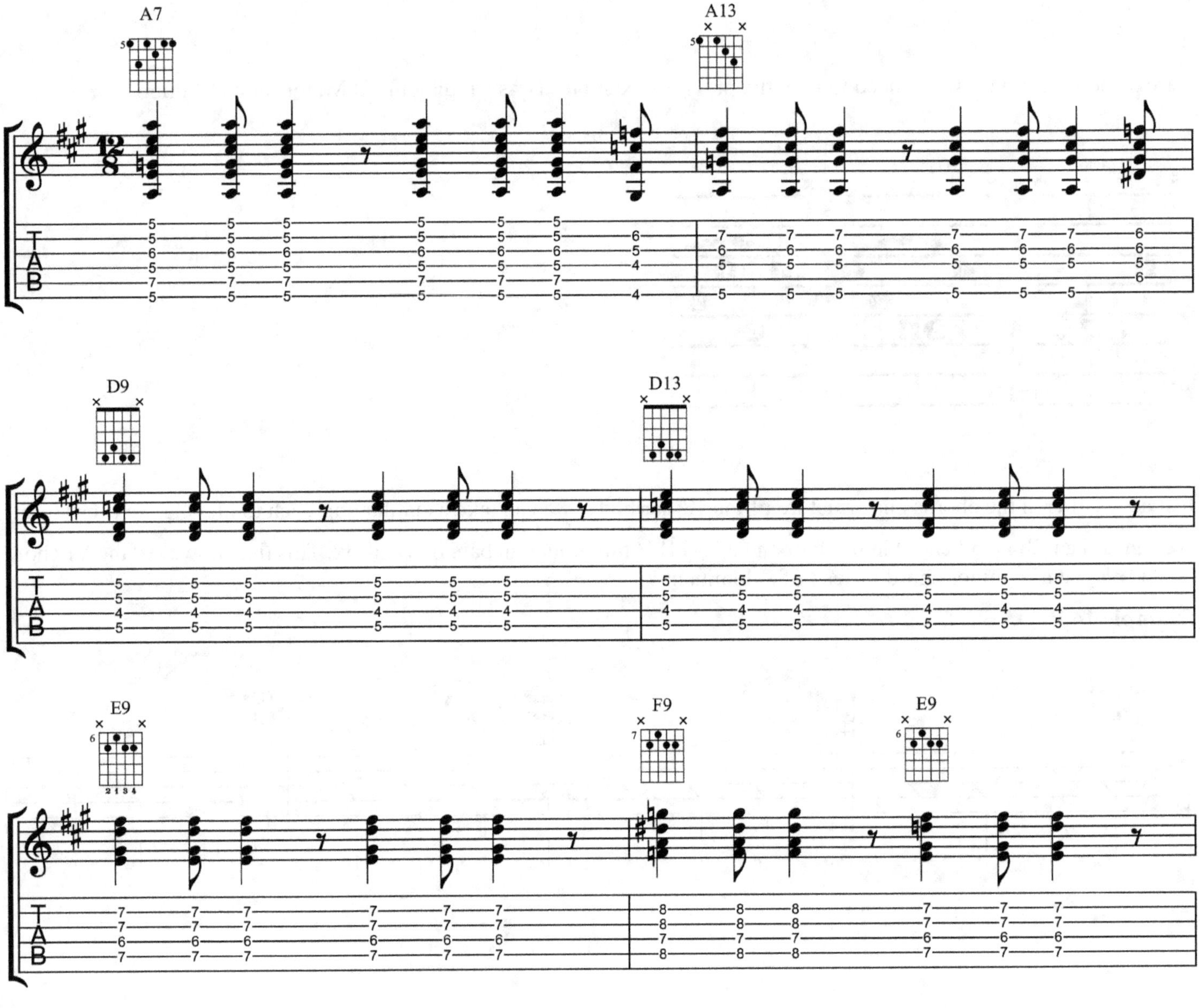

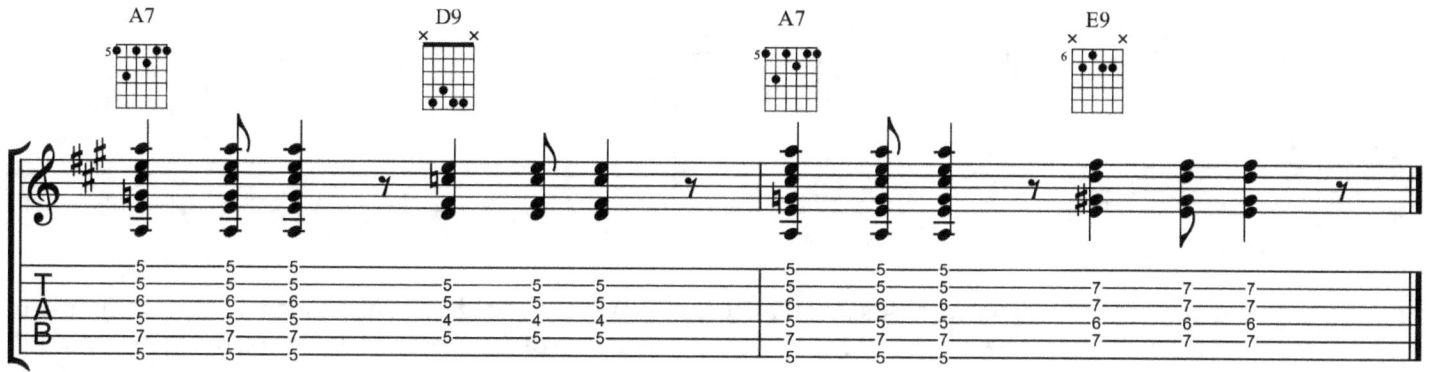

The 16-bar Blues

Another well-recognised blues form is the 16-bar blues. It is used in famous tunes such as Hoochie Coochie Man (Muddy Waters) and Oh Pretty Woman (A.C Williams).

Often the 16-bar blues is treated as a 12-bar with an extra 4-bar *tag* ending. A simple version of this is shown below.

Example 16f:

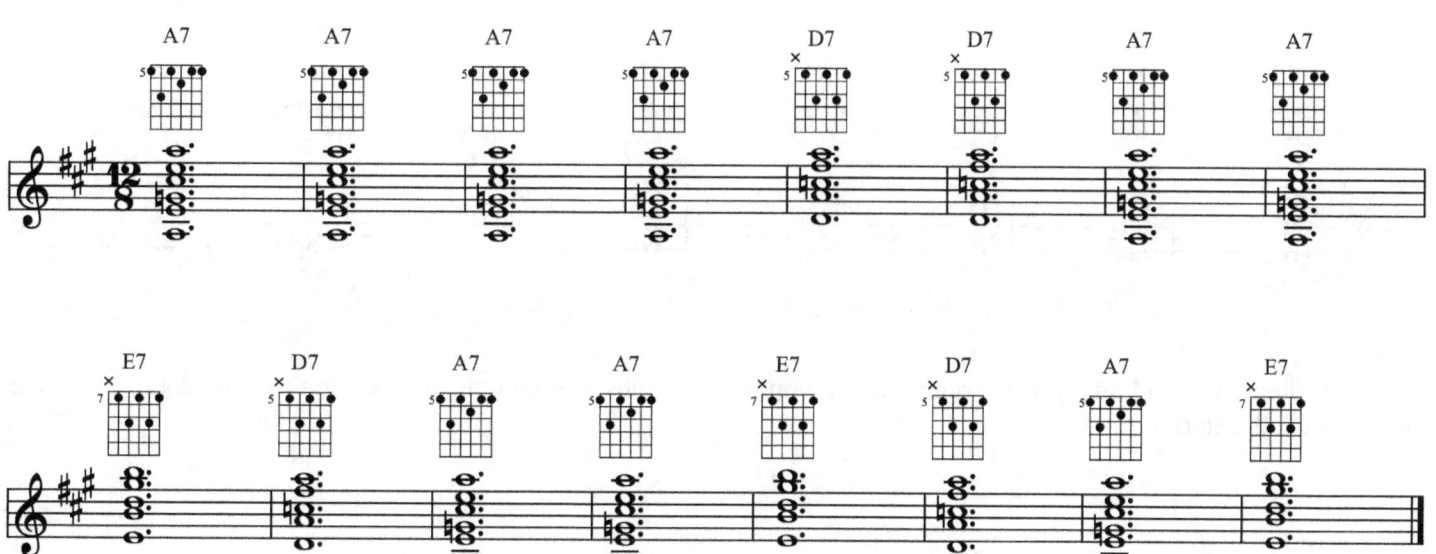

Other 16-bar forms may repeat the V to IV movement (Dominant to subdominant chords) in bars nine to fourteen.

Example 14g:

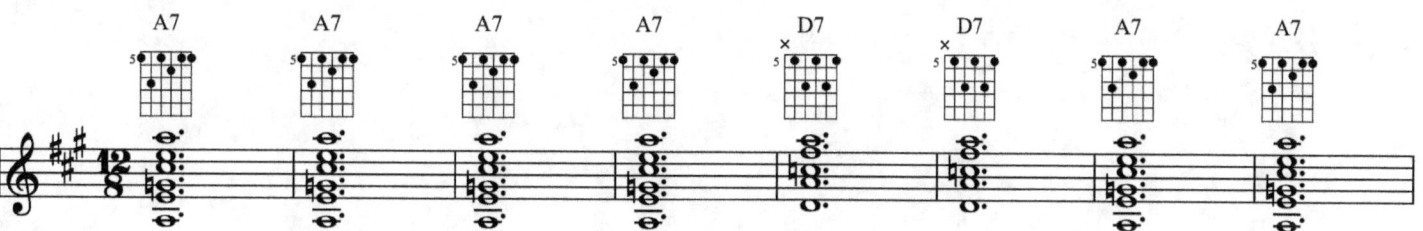

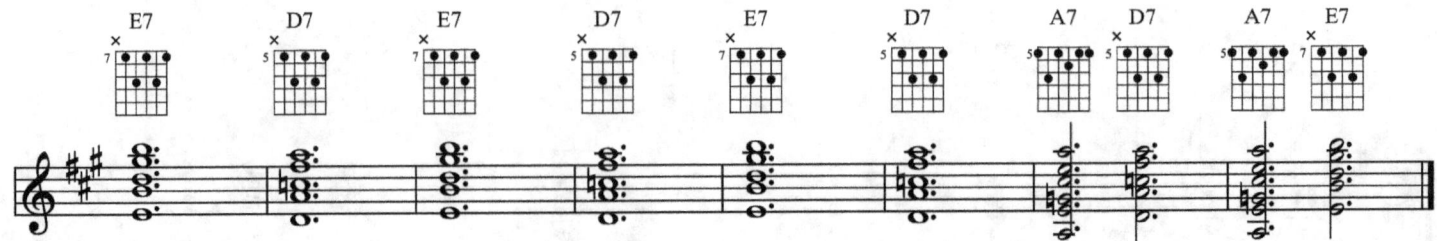

You will also find 16-bar blues sequences that stay on the I chord (A7) for eight bars. This is a great opportunity use of drop 2 chord voicings in different inversions and create a melody at the top of the chords, just like you did in example 12f.

Example 14h:

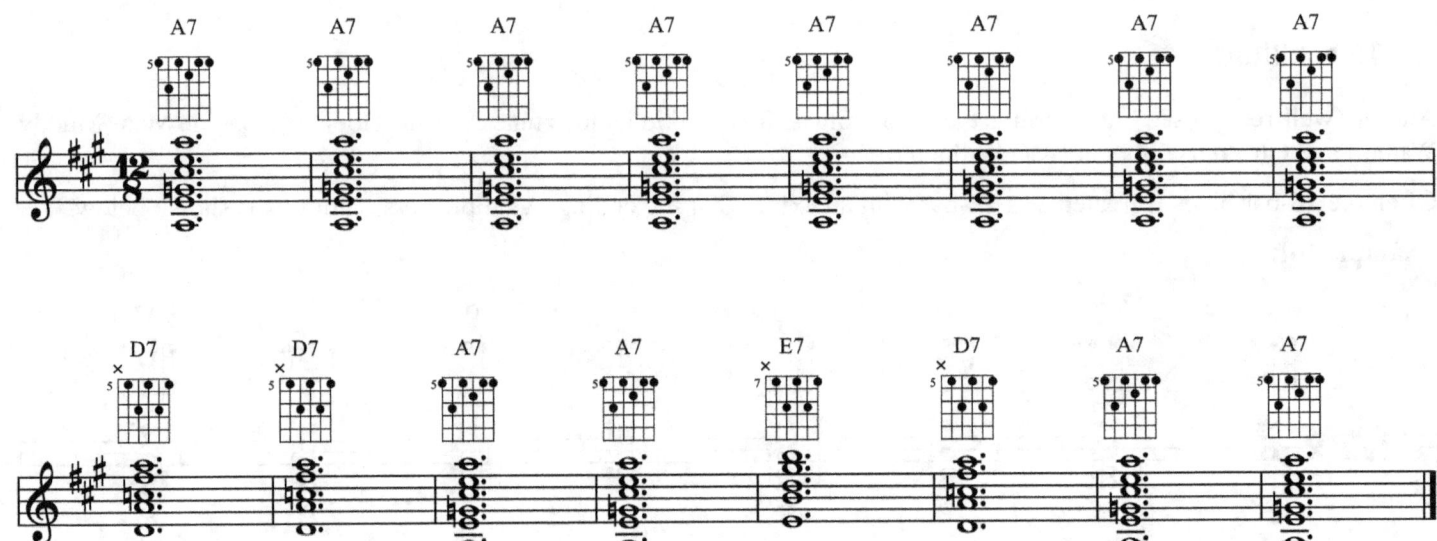

It's quite common to find this type of progression in pop or rock tunes as sometimes writers don't want a lot of harmonic movement at the start of the verse.

Chapter Fifteen – Conclusions

This book has been written to take you from the first principles of the basic 12-bar blues right through to some complex chord substitutions, rhythms and melodic fills. The emphasis has been on fitting in with the band, adding to the groove and considering what to play and what to leave out.

It is normally the case that less is more. The guitar is also a percussive instrument, so don't be afraid to fill in the gaps with rhythmic scratches, sparse chords and, if in doubt, silence. You don't have to play every chord if there is another instrument there to do it for you.

Each time you play, either in practice or in the band, record your sessions and notice what your guitar part is adding to the music. You may feel that you should play more *or* less, that you need to work more or less closely with the bass and drums, or maybe just provide the harmonic padding of playing one chord per bar.

It's OK to call a band meeting to decide exactly what and when each instrument is playing. Of course, there should always be room for spontaneity and improvisation in The Blues, but time spent in the rehearsal room building the track from the ground up can quickly revolutionise your band's sound.

In rehearsals, I normally like to begin with only the drummer playing. Next, I bring in the bass, and when they start locking together, that's when I bring in the harmonic instruments. There are no hard and fast rules but I like to get the keyboard player to play first so I can work my part around them.

Having both a guitar and keyboard in a band can be a challenge because both instruments take up so much sonic 'real estate'. Ask the keyboard player to play with just his right hand if things are getting too crowded in the guitar frequencies, or, if he is already playing higher voicings of the chords you can stick to shell voicings on the guitar.

If there are two guitarists in the band don't both play the same thing. Either sit out or arrange things so that you're using different approaches in different registers. For example, if one guitar is playing an open string riff, you may wish to play drop 2 chord pads or rhythmic staccato chops. You may want to take care of the melodic fills between chords or play the odd blues lick between the vocals, a la B.B. King. Don't overplay; save it for the solo.

If you're covering someone else's song, listen to as many different artist's recordings of it as possible. Discover what instrumentation they've used, and how they've interpreted the track in their own unique way. This process will guide you towards finding the identity you want as a musician.

I've given a list of essential listening below that should help you understand The Blues and allow you to discover your own sound. However, to give a list of definitive musicians is, quite frankly, impossible. I've tried to include specific artists and albums that you should know, but this list is by no means exhaustive so please don't send me hate mail if your favourite artist isn't here!

Don't forget, what might be considered rock music today definitely has its roots in blues. Check out bands like Led Zeppelin, Cream, Pink Floyd, The Who and AC/DC. Hear their blues influences and listen to what makes their music crossover into Rock.

For the sake of easy communication, most of the examples in this book have been written in the key of A. However, The Blues can be played in *any* key. Some of the more common keys are E, G, and C, but if there is a brass or woodwind instrument in the band you may be asked to play in Bb, Eb, Ab or Db. Any barre chord forms in this book are movable, but if a riff uses open strings you may need to be creative about using those ideas. At a pinch, you can always grab a capo.

Many blues (and indeed rock) tunes are in the key of Eb and are played with open string riffs on the guitar. This is achieved by tuning the guitar down a half step to become Eb, Ab, Db, Gb, Bb and Eb from low to high. There are a few reasons for this: Firstly, the male vocal range can be quite comfortable in that tuning but the main reason is that a Fender Stratocaster in Eb tuning with thick strings (try 11s or 13s!) and a cranked-up amp sings beautifully. Normally I keep a spare guitar tuned to Eb if I need to transcribe a solo or do a short-notice gig. Stevie Ray Vaughan and Jimi Hendrix, among many others are famous for tuning down to Eb.

Guitar tone is another important consideration. I could fill another book just talking about tone, but suffice to say that for blues rhythm guitar, depending on context, I use a clean-ish sound that starts to break up slightly when I strum a bit harder.

Try using your volume control as an extra tone control. Not enough guitarists are aware of the fun you can have with a cranked-up amp controlled by clever use of your volume knob and the many different textures that it creates.

The best piece of advice I can give anyone is to listen as much as you can to the style you wish to play. Transcribe rhythm guitar parts, even if it's just the guitarist's rhythm you focus on. Playing a different chord voicing is insignificant when compared to the benefit you get by locking into your favourite player's groove.

Have fun and good luck.

Joseph

Recommended Listening

Albert Collins - Cold Snap

Albert Collins, Robert Cray & Johnny Copeland – Showdown!

Albert King – Born Under A Bad Sign

Arthur 'Big Boy' Crudup – That's All Right Mama

Bessie Smith – The Complete Recordings, Vol. 1

Big Bill Broonzy – Trouble In Mind

Billie Holiday –Songs for Distingué Lovers

Blind Willie McTell – The Definitive Blind Willie McTell

Bo Diddley – Bo Diddley Is a Gunslinger

Buddy Guy & Junior Wells – Buddy Guy & Junior Wells Play The Blues

Bukka White – The Complete Bukka White

Charley Patton – Pony Blues

Elmore James – Shake Your Moneymaker: The Best of The Fire Sessions

Etta James – The Chess Box

Furry Lewis – Shake 'Em On Down

Gary Moore - Blues for Greeny

Howlin' Wolf – The Chess Box

Jimi Hendrix - Are You Experienced

Jimmy Reed – Blues Masters: The Very Best Of

Joe Bonamassa - Live from the Albert Hall

John Lee Hooker – Alternative Boogie: Early Studio Recordings 1948 – 1952

Johnny Winter - Johnny Winter

Leadbelly – King of the 12-String Guitar

Lightnin' Hopkins – The Complete Prestige/Bluesville Recordings

Lightnin' Slim – Rooster Blues

Lonnie Johnson – The Complete Folkways Recordings

Magic Sam – West Side Soul

Mance Lipscomb – Texas Sharecropper & Songster

Memphis Minnie – The Essential Memphis Minnie

Mississippi John Hurt – 1928 Sessions

Muddy Waters – At Newport 1960

Otis Rush – Cobra Recordings: 1956-1958

Pink Anderson – Ballad and Folksinger – Vol. 3

R.L. Burnside – Wish I Was in Heaven Sitting Down

Reverend Gary Davis – Harlem Street Singer

Robben Ford - Talk to your Daughter & Worried Life Blues

Robert Johnson – King Of the Delta Blues Singers

Skip James – The Complete Early Recordings Of Skip James – 1930

Smoky Babe – Hottest Brand Goin'

Son House – Father Of The Delta Blues: The Complete 1965 Recordings

Sonny Boy Williamson [II] – One Way Out

Stevie Ray Vaughan - Texas Flood & Couldn't Stand the Weather

T-Bone Walker - I Get So Weary

T-Bone Walker – The Complete Imperial Recordings: 1950-1954

Tommy Johnson – Canned Heat (1928-1929)

Willie Dixon – I am The Blues

There really are just too many great blues albums to mention so here's a list of the essential blues guitarists you should check out:

Albert King

B.B. King

Big Bill Broonzy

Blind William Jefferson

Bonnie Raitt

Buddy Guy

Chris Duarte

David Gilmour

Duane Allman

Eric Clapton

Freddie King

Gary Moore

Jack White

Jeff Healey

Jimi Hendrix

Jimmy Page

Joe Bonamassa

John Lee Hooker

John Mayer

Johnny Winter

Jonny Lang

Kenny Wayne Shepherd

Lead Belly

Lightnin' Hopkins

Luther Allison

Muddy Waters

Otis Rush

Peter Green

Robben Ford

Robert Cray

Robert Johnson

Rory Gallagher

Roy Buchanan

Sonny Landreth

Stevie Ray Vaughan

Sue Foley

T-Bone Walker

Wes Montgomery

I'm sure I haven't included everyone's favourites so apologies in advance!

Introduction

The second book in this series on blues guitar playing focuses on the most important ideas, musical concepts and techniques you need to develop to become a well-rounded, competent and *expressive* blues guitar soloist.

This book is not simply a list of The Hundred Greatest Blues Licks or yet another Play in the Style of…

While books like these are useful, in this book I aim to get deeper into the concepts of rhythm, phrasing, feel and melody that will take you to a new level in your playing.

The idea is not to simply teach you to play and regurgitate blues licks, I want to teach you to be in control of every note that you play. The goal is not to play one hundred different blues licks, it is to be able to play *one blues lick 100 different ways*.

If you listen very carefully to your favourite players, you will notice similar 'parent' licks reoccur throughout their solos. This is not immediately obvious, because these players are masters of manipulating their phrasing, rhythm and feel.

By thinking about your guitar solos in terms of rhythm and phrasing you will never run out of melodic ideas. You will never have to worry about forgetting your lines or being able to execute them live on stage. Your musical connection with your guitar will deepen and you will quickly develop the ability to express yourself through your guitar – rather than the all-too-common scenario of having to 'chase' licks around the fretboard.

When I introduce my private students to the concepts in this book there is often a major paradigm shift. They will start to think about solos in terms of note *placemen*t rather than just playing specific licks. Of course, melody and note choice *is* important, but when you consider we all have the same 12 notes available to us, the only logical conclusion is that it is rhythm, phrasing, dynamics and articulation that set us apart from other players.

In a blues guitar solo where you may only play 5 or 6 different pitches, it's very much a case of *when* you play, not *what* you play.

If you are looking for a book full of blues licks, don't despair! The first part of this book focuses on some of the important blues guitar basics, helping to get you into the sound of each important scale we use in the blues. In fact, there are over 100 unique blues licks contained in these pages spread over the whole neck. It's important to get the sound of the blues language into your head before you start experimenting with the rhythm and phrasing concepts outlined later in the book.

If you need more blues guitar licks, my book *The CAGED System* will teach you a complete system to learn the guitar while giving you useful blues licks to get your teeth into. I've also written a book called *100 Blues Licks for Guitar* which is a style file of the 20 most important blues guitarists.

If you've been playing a while you may wish to skip some of the introductions to scales and jump to some of the rhythm and phrasing sections. However, I would suggest that you do read the parts that you feel you might already know. There might be a little lick, trick or even a whole mental system that could make a subtle or intrinsic difference to your playing.

As always in my books, every notated example is available as a free download from **www.fundamental-changes.com/audio-downloads**. Thank you to Pete Sklaroff for recording them so musically.

I hope this book makes a positive difference to your playing. Some of the rhythmic exercises may be tricky at first, but listen to the audio examples carefully and you'll get there. These days, rhythm and phrasing are about 70% of my practise time and I wish I'd known about the ideas in this book long ago.

For a more complete introduction to the roots of the blues, check out book one of this series, *The Complete Guide to Blues Guitar Book One: Rhythm*, where I give much more background on the roots of the blues and some essential listening. If you want to add more harmonic richness to your solos and move beyond the Blues Scale, check out my book *The Complete Guide to Blues Guitar: Beyond Pentatonics*.

If you know how a 12 bar blues functions then you will get great insight into the building blocks of blues guitar soloing from this book. If not, then I suggest getting yourself familiar with this essential chord form through *The Complete Guide to Blues Guitar: Rhythm Guitar*.

As always, have fun!

Joseph Alexander

Get the Audio

The audio files for this book are available to download for free from **www.fundamental-changes.com** and the link is in the top right corner. Simply select this book title from the drop-down menu and follow the instructions to get the audio.

We recommend that you download the files directly to your computer, not to your tablet, and extract them there before adding them to your media library. You can then put them on your tablet, iPod or burn them to CD. On the download page there is a help PDF and we also provide technical support via the contact form.

Kindle / eReaders

To get the most out of this book, remember that you can double tap any image to enlarge it. Turn off 'column viewing' and hold your kindle in landscape mode.

Be Social

Twitter: @guitar_joseph

FB: FundamentalChanges InGuitar

Instagram: FundamentalChanges

For over 250 Free Guitar Lessons with Videos Check out

www.fundamental-changes.com

Chapter 1: Blues Guitar Soloing Basics

The melodic language of blues originates from the spirituals, work songs and field hollers sung by African-Americans in the era of captivity, and in the years that followed emancipation. As a result, the blues is rich in African-American rhythm, harmony, melody and phrasing. An important melodic structure that has a strong link to this time is the performance of *call and response*, or *antiphony*, where a single musical *question* is sung and then *answered* by different voices.

When musicologists transcribed and incorporated the early blues melodies into traditional Western musical thinking (classical theory), they found that many of the them were formed from just five notes. The term Pentatonic refers to a scale that uses five notes to divide up the octave.

Pent = five

Tonic = tones

In addition to this Minor Pentatonic scale, they noticed that singers also often used their voices to slide and bend from one note smoothly into another. If you're reading on an eReader check out this incredible, short clip of an **early gospel choir**. If not, search for "Early African American Spiritual Gospel Choir" uploaded by *Patterickcoati*.

This music may be from a different age, but hearing the roots of the blues sound helps us to understand the language of the music that we play today. This is why our scale choice, use of bending, vibrato and slides are so important. These sounds are the essence of the blues and form the basis of virtually all modern music.

The Minor Pentatonic Scale

We will begin by breaking down the language of the blues into a simple alphabet: The Minor Pentatonic scale. In the key of A, we can play the Minor Pentatonic scale as follows:

Example 1a:

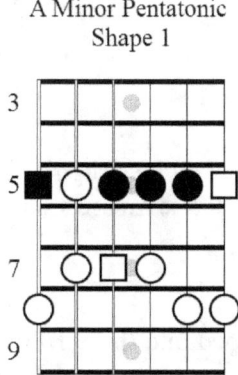

The coloured or dark notes in the scale diagram form a minor 7 chord. It is a good idea to learn a chord shape in conjunction with every scale shape to aid your memory. Throughout this book, every scale shape will have a chord shown within it. Think of it as an anchor to help you organise your thinking.

This first shape (there are five to eventually learn) of the Minor Pentatonic scale is one of the most common shapes used by guitarists. It is the melodic starting point for thousands of guitarists learning to solo and you may already be familiar with it. We will of course progress beyond this shape and access other areas of the guitar neck, but for now learn this pattern thoroughly.

Begin by playing this scale shape ascending and descending and try out these melodic patterns to get the sound of the scale into your ears.

Example 1b:

Example 1c:

Just as learning a new alphabet does not automatically allow us to speak a foreign language, you may well be struggling to hear The Blues by playing these exercises. After all, these are just some scale patterns. What we need to learn are some actual phrases and an idea of the *structure* of the language to learn how it functions.

Most blues is played in *triplet* time. In other words we can count: **1 2 3 1 2 3 1 2 3 1 2 3**

This is known as 12/8 time as there are twelve 1/8th notes in each bar. Each of the four beats is grouped into three 1/8th notes.

Playing the Pentatonic scale with this triplet feel automatically sounds a little more blusey.

Example 1d:

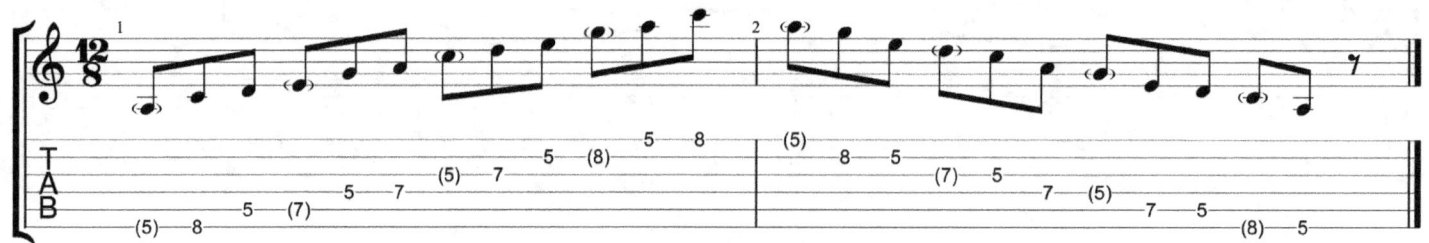

Give a slight accent to the first of each group of three notes (shown in brackets).

Play the Minor Pentatonic scale with this triplet feel over backing track one. You will begin to hear your playing become a little bluesier.

Simple Minor Pentatonic Blues Guitar Licks

Playing a scale straight up and down is little more than reciting an alphabet. However, these *letters* can be arranged into short *words* and *phrases* which make sense to the listener. Play through the following examples and try them with backing track one.

Example 1e:

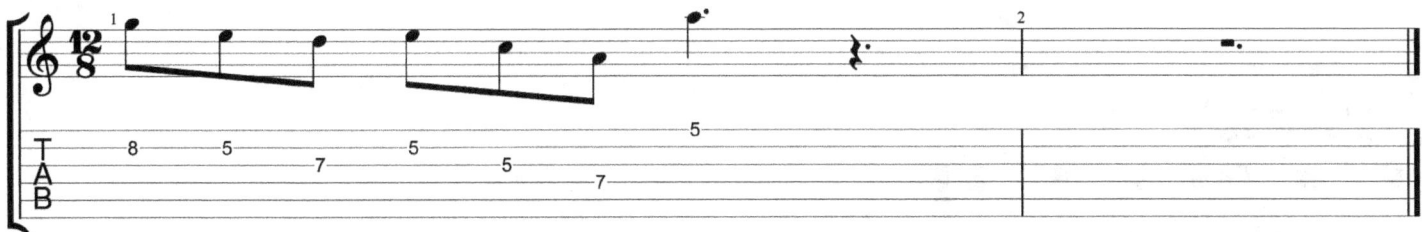

Example 1f:

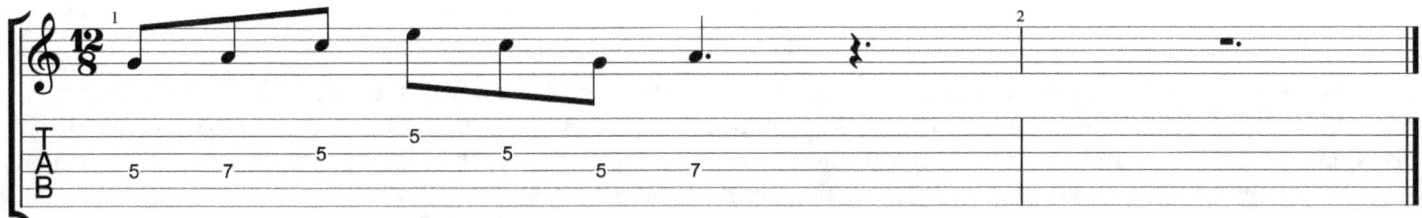

Example 1g:

These first few examples contain nothing in the way of phrasing marks, bends, slides or any of the other subtleties that we use to make the music vocal and alive. They are simply some strong melodic lines that get you into the ballpark of the blues language, and by playing them you will start to train your ears and fingers to find melodic shapes on the fretboard.

Introducing Bends

Let's look at how we can bend notes to mimic the sound of a vocalist. Blues bends are one of the most important techniques we can use to play authentic-sounding blues on the guitar.

The chords played in the rhythm guitar part of a blues are normally Dominant 7. These chords contain a *major 3rd* which gives them a major or *happy* sound.

The scale we just used to create melodic lines is the *Minor Pentatonic* scale. It contains a b3 (flat three) interval which defines its minor or *sad* sound. The difference between the notes in the Dominant 7 chord and the Minor Pentatonic scale can be seen clearly on the guitar:

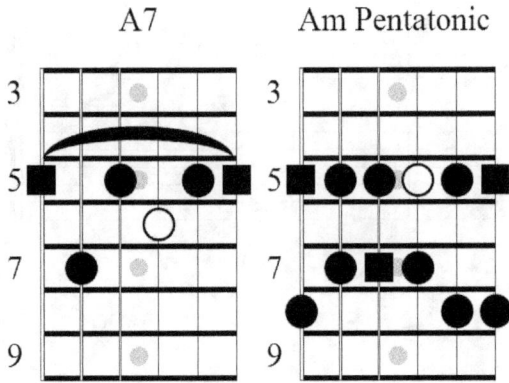

Look at the note on the 3rd string, 6th fret in the A7 diagram. This note is different from the note in the A Minor Pentatonic scale on the 3rd string *5th* fret. These two notes, a semitone apart (C# and C) will clash and many musicians would say this is undesirable. It certainly isn't the greatest sound if you continuously play the minor 3rd over the Dominant chord and don't manipulate it. You can hear a b3 against the major 3rd here.

Example 1h:

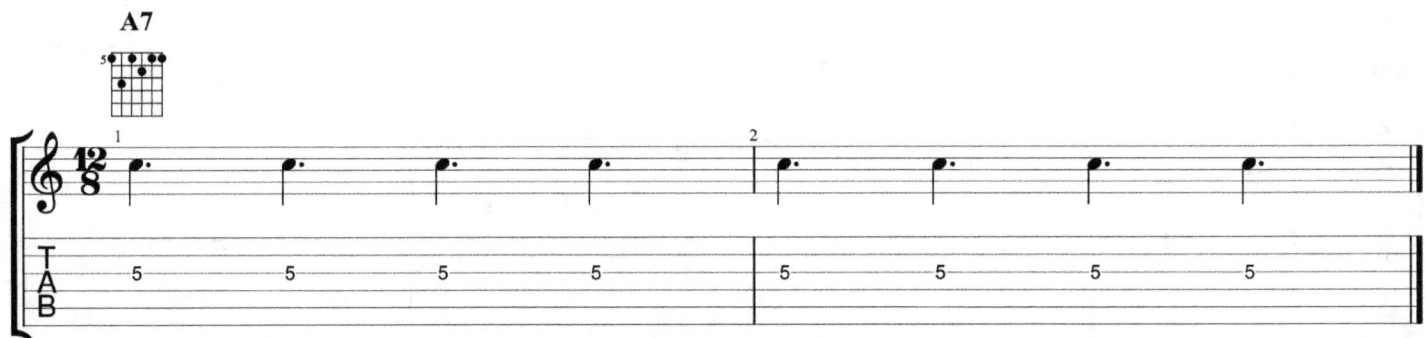

I'm sure you can hear that this isn't the greatest sound in the world!

The trick is to give the minor 3rd (C) a little bend up towards the major 3rd (C#).

Use your 1st finger to bend the string towards the floor slightly raising its pitch. I normally put my thumb on the top of the fretboard to provide strength, leverage and support.

While this isn't a technique book, I have included some useful bending intonation exercises in Appendix A.

When we add bends to the previous exercise we start to catch a glimpse of the blues guitar sound. Don't worry if you don't have the strength to bend all the way to C# with your first finger. Often, we don't bend the C all the way to C# anyway. You can have a lot of fun had seeing how many different *microtones* you can find between the b3 and major 3.

Listen carefully to exercise 1i. This demonstrates the minor 3rd being bent all the way up to the major 3rd.

Example 1i:

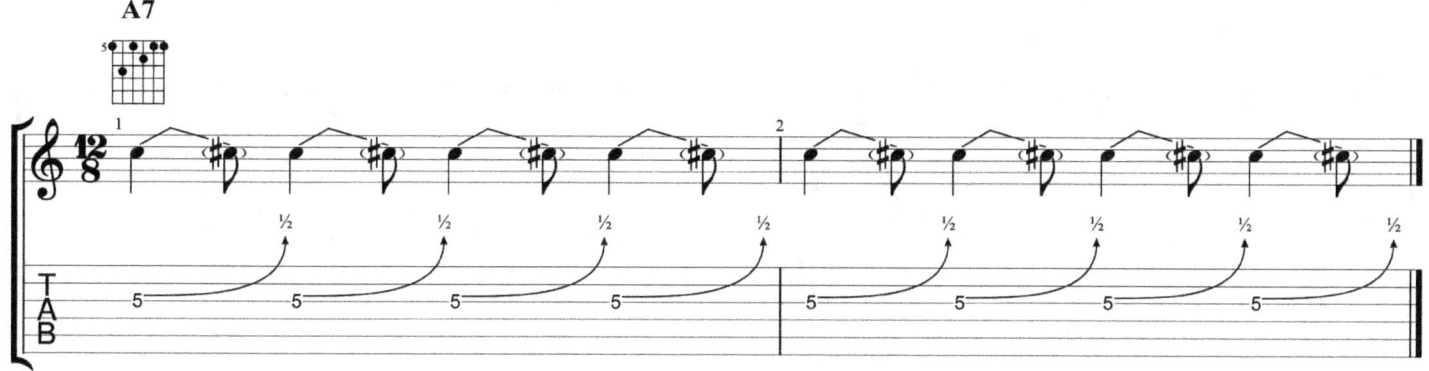

Now compare example 1i with example 1j where we don't necessarily make it all the way to C#.

Example 1j:

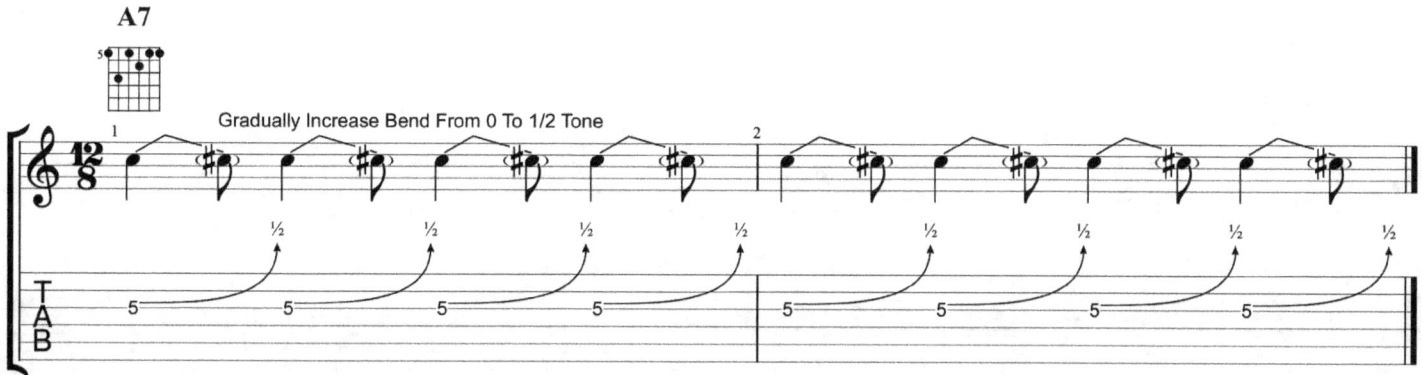

We will talk much more about this kind of nuance in a later chapter, but for now just be aware that you can just give the minor 3rd a little nudge towards major 3rd territory. Slightly bending a note in this way is called a *curl*.

There are some other common bends that occur in blues guitar. Let's look at them before incorporating them into some useful blues licks.

We can bend from the 4th of the A Minor Pentatonic scale (D) to either the b5 (Eb) or the natural 5 (E).

The b5 note (Eb) is called the *blues note* as it is extremely common in the blues sound. In fact, there is even a scale called the Blues Scale which you will learn later. It is simply the Minor Pentatonic scale with the addition of the b5 note.

Practise the bend from the 4th to the b5th (semitone bend) and then bend from the 4th to the natural 5th (whole tone bend). Use your 3rd finger to bend the D note and support the 3rd finger with your 1st and 2nd fingers added on the string behind it for extra strength. Aim to get it absolutely in tune with the recorded audio examples.

Example 1k (a and b):

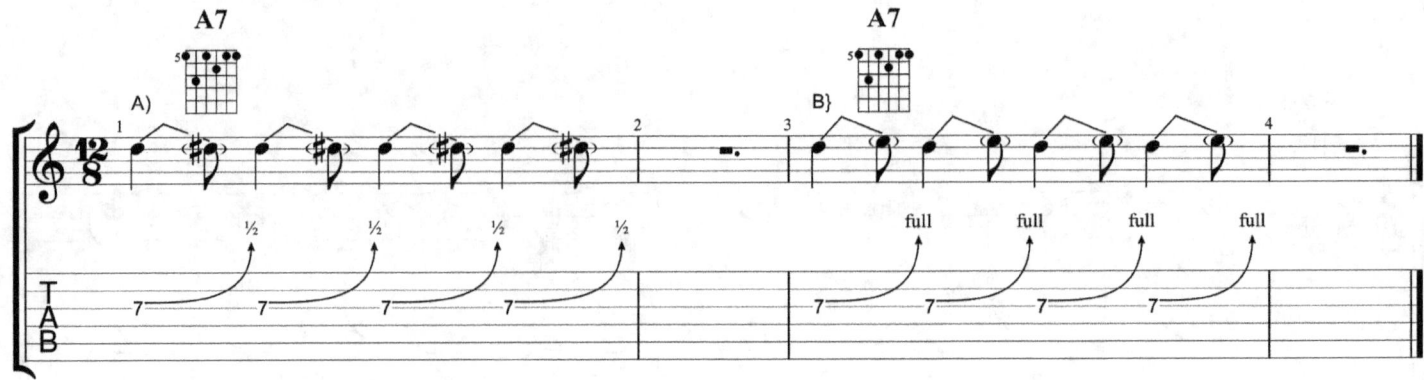

Another common bend is from the b7 (G) to the root (A). Play this bend with your 3rd finger and then your 4th finger. Again, support the bend by placing your spare fingers on the string behind the bent note to help with strength, accuracy and control.

Example 1l:

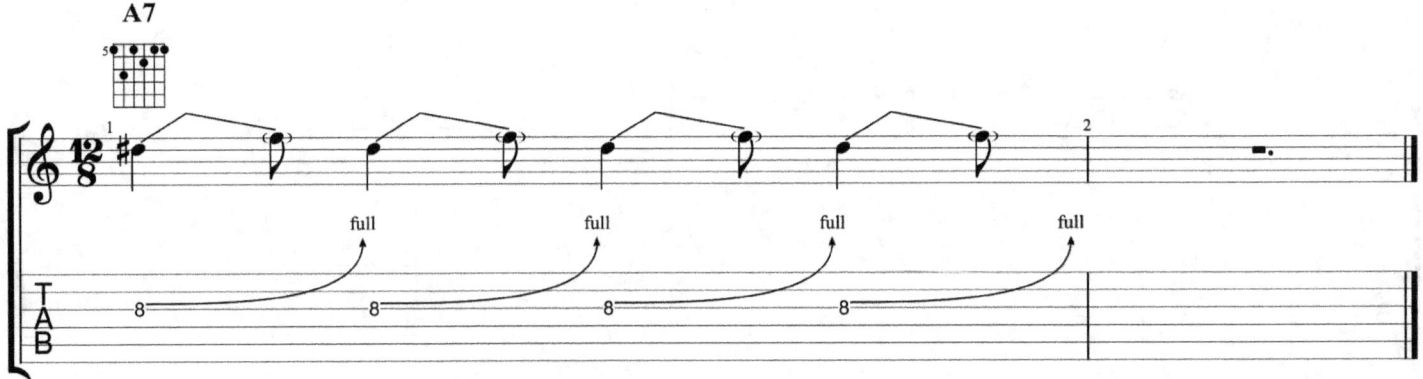

Work hard to develop your accuracy. The root of the scale is such a strong note and an inaccurate bend here will sound terrible. Practise the exercises in Appendix A.

There are other places in this scale where bends are effective. Experiment by working through the scale and bend each note in turn. Try this over backing track one.

Let's incorporate these bends into useful blues guitar licks.

Using Bends in Blues Licks

These Minor Pentatonic lines are rhythmically simple and teach you to incorporate bends into your solos. Remember to *always* support the bent note with any spare fingers and listen carefully to ensure your bend is in tune.

There are many different ways to phrase a bend: slow, fast, immediate, delayed or gradual. We will discuss these ideas when we study *phrasing* in Chapter Three. For now, just try to match the phrasing on the audio track.

Examples 1m - 1p:

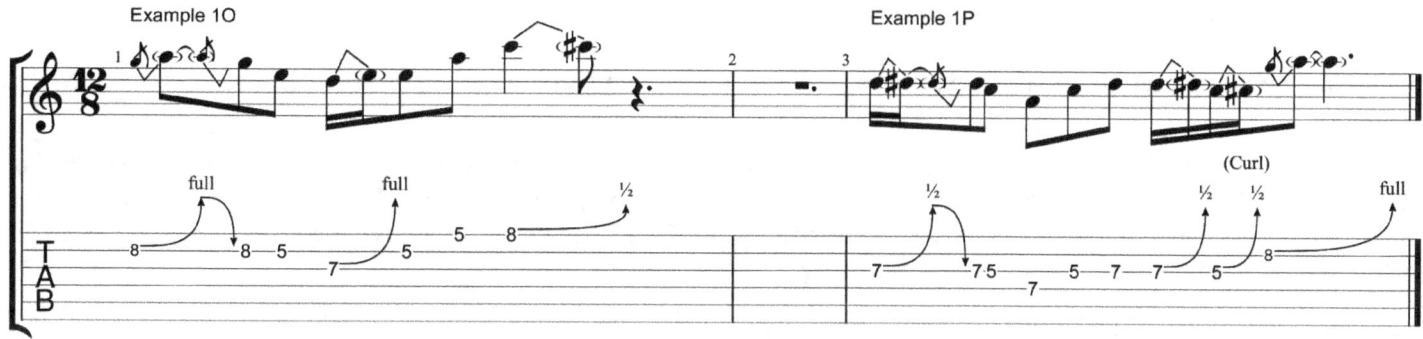

Keep a strict '1 2 3 1 2 3' feel to these lines at first. Learn them by syncing your playing to the recorded audio examples before playing them against backing track one. Once you have learnt them thoroughly don't worry about sticking to the exact timings written here; make the licks personal by varying the rhythms and phrase lengths. Chapter Three will teach you many ideas about how you can alter licks to suit your own taste and feel.

By adding bends, the Pentatonic scale comes alive with bluesy melodic possibilities. Bent notes are an intrinsic and vital part of the blues sound and without them we're often left just playing scales.

Sliding in and out of Blues Licks

Continuing with the theme of mimicking the human voice, let's think for a minute about how our bodies create a vocal sound. Say the syllable 'huh' out loud. Pay careful attention to the way the first 'H' is formed in your throat and larynx. Can you hear and feel the 'breathy' noise in your throat before your vocal folds engage and the Huh noise catches in your throat?

This little breathy lead-in to a vocal sound can be replicated on a guitar by sliding into the first note of a phrase. A diagonal line before the start of a phrase shows that you should play a slide. However, in practice it will rarely be notated, so you should always get into the habit of sliding into each lick.

Example 1q is played without the slide, whereas example 1r is preceded by a grace-note slide into the first note of the phrase. Use your third finger to play this slide, so you are in position to execute the rest of this lick.

Examples 1q and 1r:

Which line do you prefer? In my opinion, the second line has a much more vocal quality and contains more energy and flow.

In example 1r I began the slide from the 3rd fret, however the starting point of the slide isn't that important. Try starting the slide from the 1st fret or the 6th fret. Try moving your finger slowly or quickly up the neck too. You can get some interesting results by simply playing the slide in different ways. If you slide slowly, you will need to begin the movement earlier to hit the target note on the first beat of the bar.

If you're feeling brave, try adding a grace-note slide to the final note in the phrase. You'll have to be quick, but this is a great way to emphasise the melodic leap in the melody. It is also possible to slide into a note from *above* in the same way.

Listen carefully to the next example where I slide into the D note at the start of the line. This is a little more difficult but gives great results. As before, the priority is to ensure that the first note of the phrase falls in time on the first beat of the bar.

Example 1s:

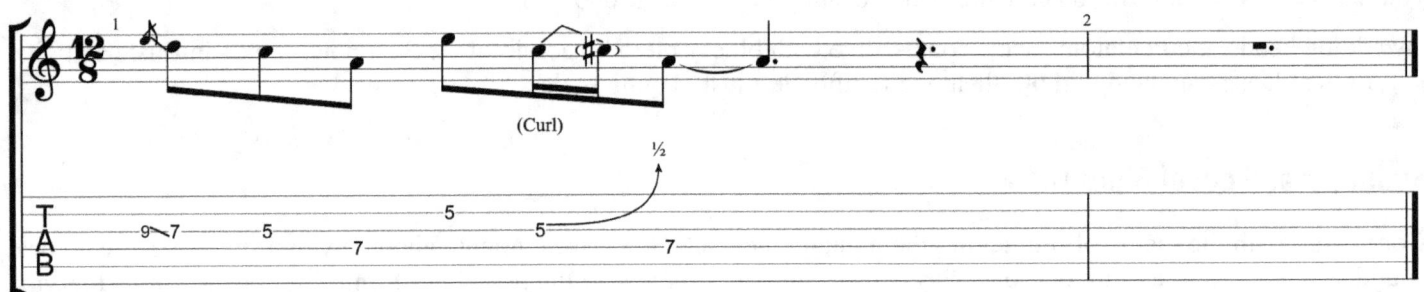

Try sliding from different distances into the first note of the phrase.

Now let's combine a descending slide with an ascending slide using the previous example. In example 1t, I slide into the second half of the phrase from a semitone below, hinting at the b5 blues note described earlier.

Example 1t:

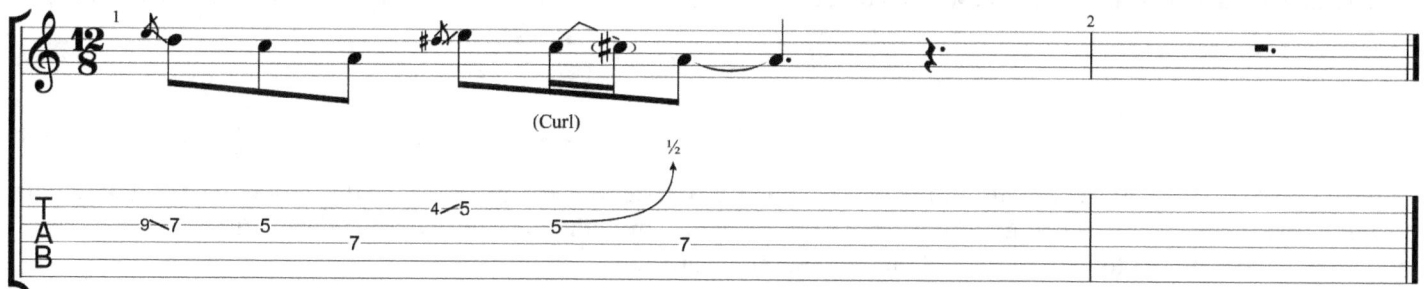

Often these slides are not notated as they are difficult to define musically. However, you should get into the habit of playing them often.

Let's return to the analogy of speaking for a moment.

Our voice does not die away the instant that our mouth closes. There is always going to be natural decay in our environment. Say 'Huh' out loud again and listen carefully to the end of the note. It can be difficult to hear but there will be some natural reverberation (echo) to your voice as the sound bounces off the surfaces around you. As the sound gets absorbed by these surfaces it loses energy and fades away.

Imagine that you are in a large, empty concert hall. How would your 'Huh' sound now? Singers normally enhance this type of decay and add *vibrato* to their voices with their diaphragms. To play guitar with the emotive qualities of a singer it is important we learn to recreate this on the guitar.

We can break this decay of sound down into two distinct parts: *sliding out of phrases* and *vibrato*.

Let's start with the easier of the two areas: sliding out of phrases. This technique is unsurprisingly the exact opposite of sliding into notes. We simply add a descending slide to the final note of the phrase.

Here is example 1t again, but this time with a slide added at the end.

Example 1u:

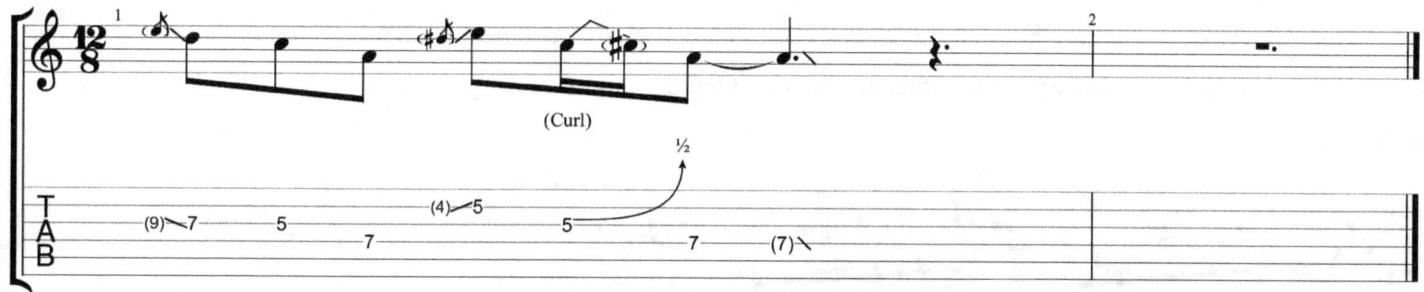

Notice that there is no indication of where you should finish this slide. I often end up around the 1st fret but there are no hard and fast rules. To end the descending movement, practise releasing your finger pressure as you come to the end of the slide, but don't let your finger lose contact with the guitar string. This will prevent the open string ringing.

Once again, you have some exciting creative options here. How long are you going to let that final note ring before you slide out of it? How quickly are you going to slide away from the note? Slide too slowly and you may hear the individual frets sound as you move; too quickly and you risk sounding jerky and uncontrolled.

Use the licks that you learnt earlier and practise sliding in and out of them. Make up short phrases using the Minor Pentatonic scale and try to keep your fretting hand moving in a circular fashion as you slide in and out of each line. Use big, small, fast and slow slides and add them to the middle of phrases both ascending *and* descending.

Use subtlety and grace, and then really go overboard by sliding into or out of *every* note. Don't worry about playing in time! With enough experimenting, you will make these techniques your own and develop your own unique voice in blues guitar.

Vibrato

Now we move on to the more difficult of the two techniques we use to end a phrase: *vibrato*. Vibrato is a technique that most guitarists never stop practising. It takes time to develop the strength, control, rhythm and subtlety it requires to play good vibrato, so it is best to get started early in your soloing career.

Vibrato is essentially adding 'wobble' to the end of each phrase. It is an extremely vocal quality and in my opinion it is one of the main factors that separates an OK guitarist from a great one.

To add vibrato to a note we move the string quickly up and down in a series of fast bends. The further we bend the note the wider and more pronounced the vibrato will be.

Listen to example 1v. First, the note C is held for two beats before a small, subtle vibrato is added to the end of the note. Next, the note is held for two beats but a wider, more obvious vibrato is added.

Example 1v:

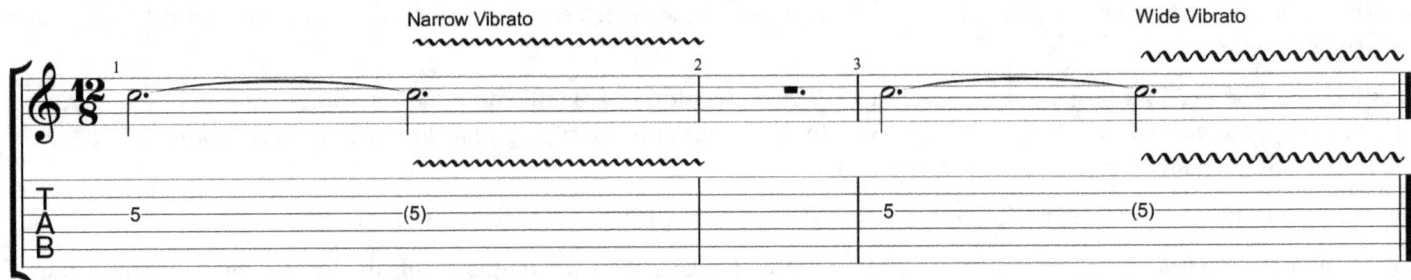

The technique for executing controlled vibrato can be tricky so the exercises are included in Appendix B. The basic idea is to try to play the vibrato with the *side* of the fingertip rather than the point.

By adding even narrow, subtle vibrato to the end of a phrase the melody becomes much more lyrical.

Here is the same phrase as example 1u, with soft vibrato added to the end of the phrase.

Example 1w:

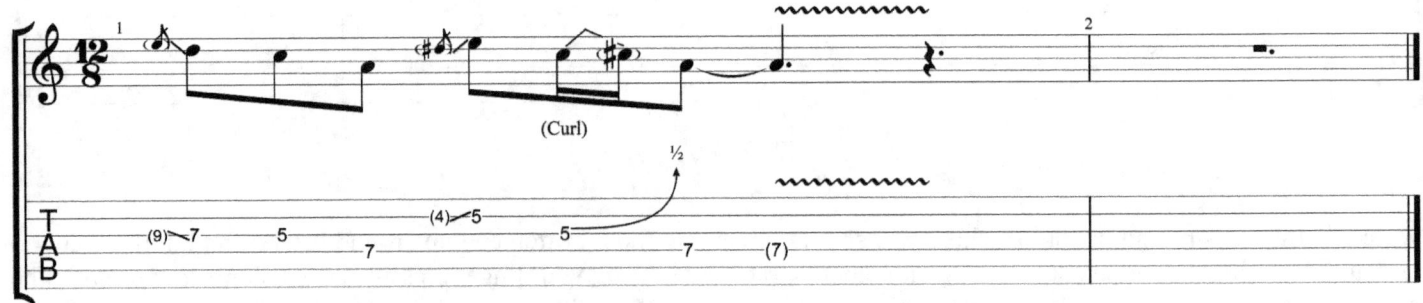

Let's add the slide-off on the last note and the phrase is complete.

Example 1x:

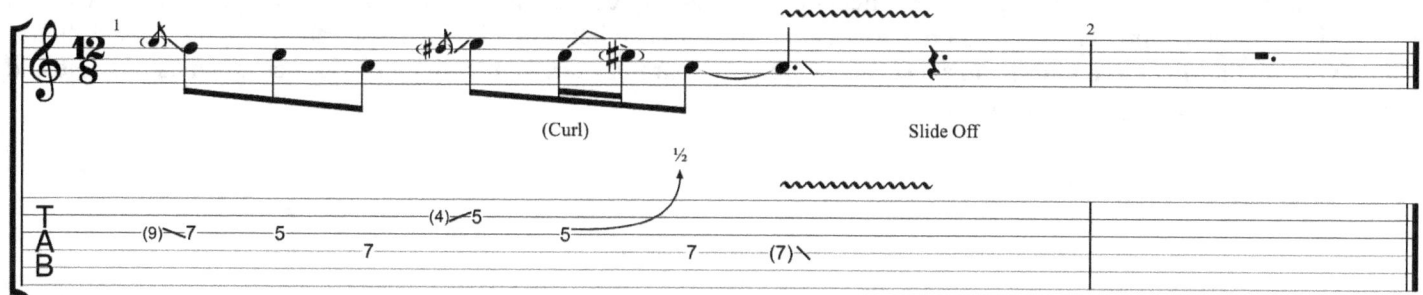

To see how much these small techniques affect the music, play the phrase above first with no expressive techniques and then play it with all the articulations added. I'm sure you'll agree that the difference is enormous. Try it yourself with backing track one.

Example 1y:

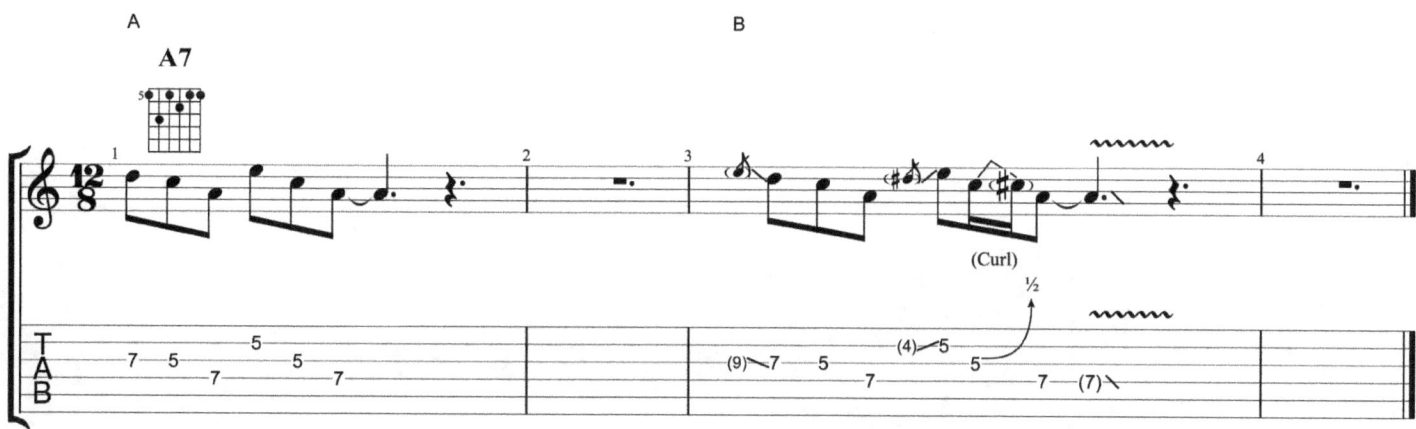

Sliding and vibrato aren't just for the start and end of phrases – you should use them in the middle of blues licks too.

Listen carefully to the audio to hear the nuances in this next phrase. The starting points for the slides (in brackets) are only suggestions, so use whatever distance feels right to make the line flow. Try this line out with the slow blues backing track and combine it with the other licks in this chapter to make a short solo.

Example 1z:

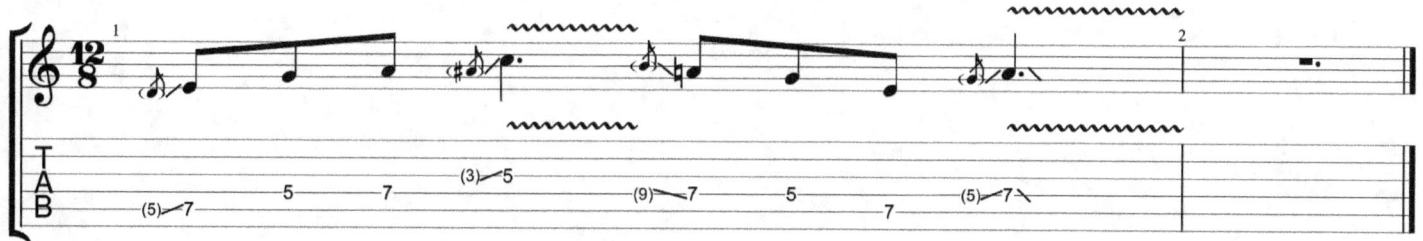

99

Work through Appendix B to help develop the control of your vibrato, and for more a more detailed approach check out my book **Complete Technique for Modern Guitar.**

It may seem like I'm over emphasising the concept of articulation, especially so early in the book, but the truth is that these techniques and approaches to just a few notes are the difference between playing scales and playing music. Practise adding varying the slides and vibrato on every phrase that you learn. Experiment with these ideas as much as possible and you will *quickly* develop your own voice.

Chapter 2: Rhythmic Divisions

I have spoken about how all musicians have access to the same twelve notes, but it is *how* and *when* we play them that set us apart from one another. If we don't want to be a blues soloist who just regurgitates lick after lick, it is imperative to learn to control the rhythmic phrasing of our playing.

When we can manipulate and alter our rhythmic phrasing at will, we can stop learning the basics of the language and begin to tell our own story. In this chapter, we will refresh the basic building blocks of rhythm and learn how we can use them to create structure to develop our melodic content.

1/8th notes in 12/8

So far, the examples and licks have all been simple in terms of their rhythmic content. Now you can learn how to manipulate these basic rhythms to generate an almost infinite number of different blues phrases.

I mentioned that most blues tunes are written in the time signature of 12/8. Let's look at exactly what this means.

In simple terms, 12/8 time tells us that there are *four beats in each bar* and each of the four beats is *divided into three subdivisions*. This can be seen in the following diagram.

Example 2a:

Listen to backing track one and count out loud "**one** and a **two** and a **three** and a **four** and a" throughout. Play an ascending A Minor Pentatonic scale in time with the track and accent the first of each group of three notes. If you're not sure how this feels, listen to example 1d.

Because there are three 1/8th notes in each beat of the bar, 12/8 is often referred to as a *triplet* feel. This is extremely important to understand because when we're soloing we normally want to 'lock in' with the rest of the band.

As each main beat of a 12/8 bar contains *three* 1/8th notes, a single beat of music in 12/8 is written as a *dotted* 1/4 note. This is shown in the example above. To get a feel for this beat division, play this lick that combines dotted 1/4 notes with 1/8th notes.

Example 2b:

First focus only on rhythmic accuracy, but then try to repeat the example adding in the slides, curls and vibrato you studied in the previous chapter.

Most of the licks in Chapter One used this combination of 1/4 notes and 1/8th notes to create short phrases, but what happens if we want to change gear and play a little faster?

1/16th notes in 12/8

To access a new, faster rhythmic level we can split each 1/8th note into two and double the amount of notes in each bar. We have now accessed the *1/16th note* rhythmic level.

Example 2c:

Notice that the *1st*, *3rd* and *5th* 1/16th notes in each beat line up perfectly with the 1/8th note above it.

Try ascending and descending the Minor Pentatonic scale using this subdivision.

Example 2d:

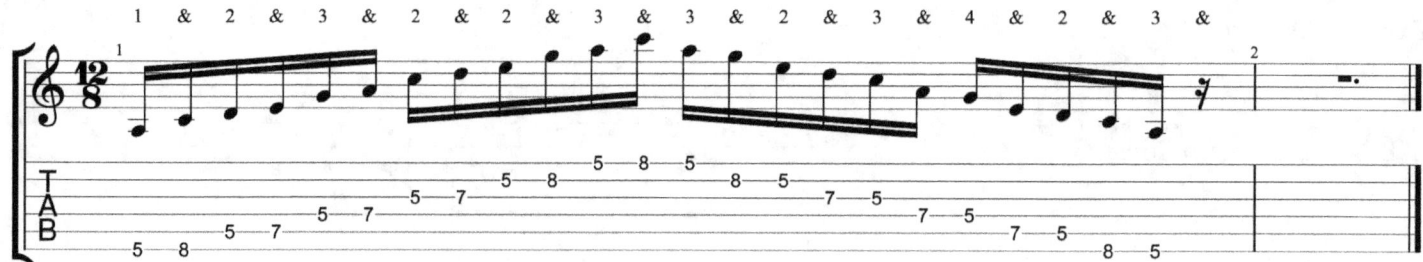

A very useful way to practise this kind of note division is to set your metronome very fast and hear the click as the 1/8th note division. Using your metronome in this way means that every *three* clicks is one beat.

Set your metronome to 180 bpm (beats per minute). As the click is playing the 1/8th notes this is equivalent to the tempo being 60 bpm. On each click count out loud, "**One** and a **Two** and a **Three** and a **Four** and a".

Practise moving between one bar of 1/8th notes and one bar of 1/16th notes with the metronome. Start by repeating just one note, but move on to either playing the full Pentatonic scale or short melodies. Don't worry too much about playing the following notes exactly as written – the exercise is all about switching between 1/8th and 1/16th notes.

Example 2e:

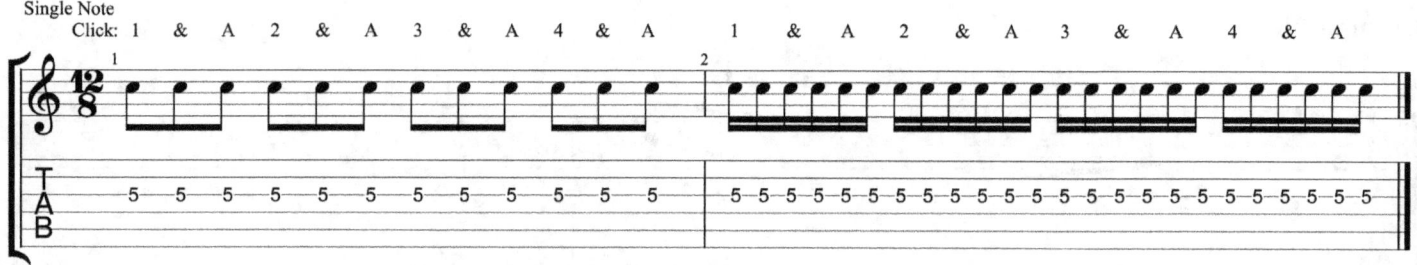

Example 2f:

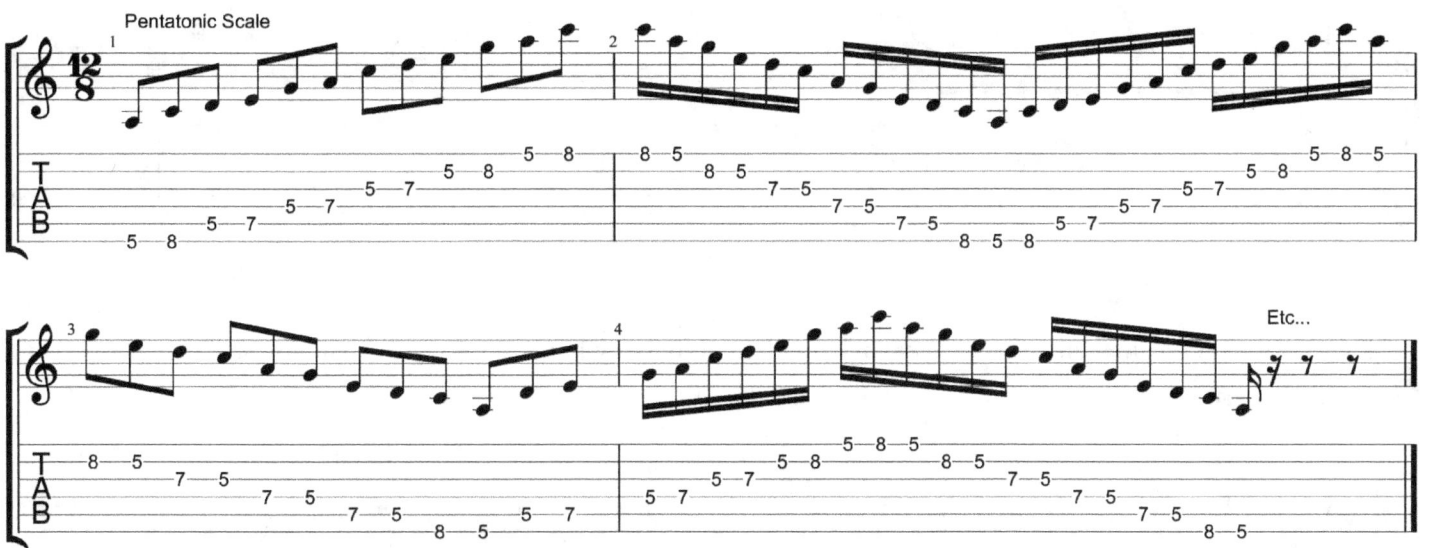

Now change between 1/8th and 1/16ths every beat. Once again, don't worry about *which* notes you are playing, just make sure you are changing rhythmic divisions every beat. Let your fingers go for a walk around the Pentatonic scale and get used to changing gear in this way.

Example 2g:

If these divisions are too fast, reduce the metronome speed to 150. Remember, the metronome is clicking the 1/8th notes, *not the beat* as you may be used to. The real tempo is three times slower than the metronome speed. 180 bpm = 60 bpm and 150 bpm = 50 bpm.

Creating Melodies by Using Rhythmic Structures

Although the previous exercises may not have felt bluesy to you, the next few ideas will put these rhythmic exercises into a musical context and show you that it is easy to construct your own unique blues phrases.

Once you can switch accurately between 1/8th notes and 1/16th notes, it is time to start combining these rhythmic subdivisions in the space of just one beat.

In the following rhythm, the first two divisions of beat one are 1/8th notes and the last division is two 1/16th notes. I finish the phrase with a 1/4 note on beat two to give the rhythm a sense of completion. Play the rhythm for two full choruses with backing track one. This may be a little harder than you imagine because it requires discipline not to meander off and start varying the rhythm of the phrase.

Example 2h:

Next, try creating a few melodic phrases that stick *precisely* to this rhythm. Here are some examples:

Example 2i (a-d):

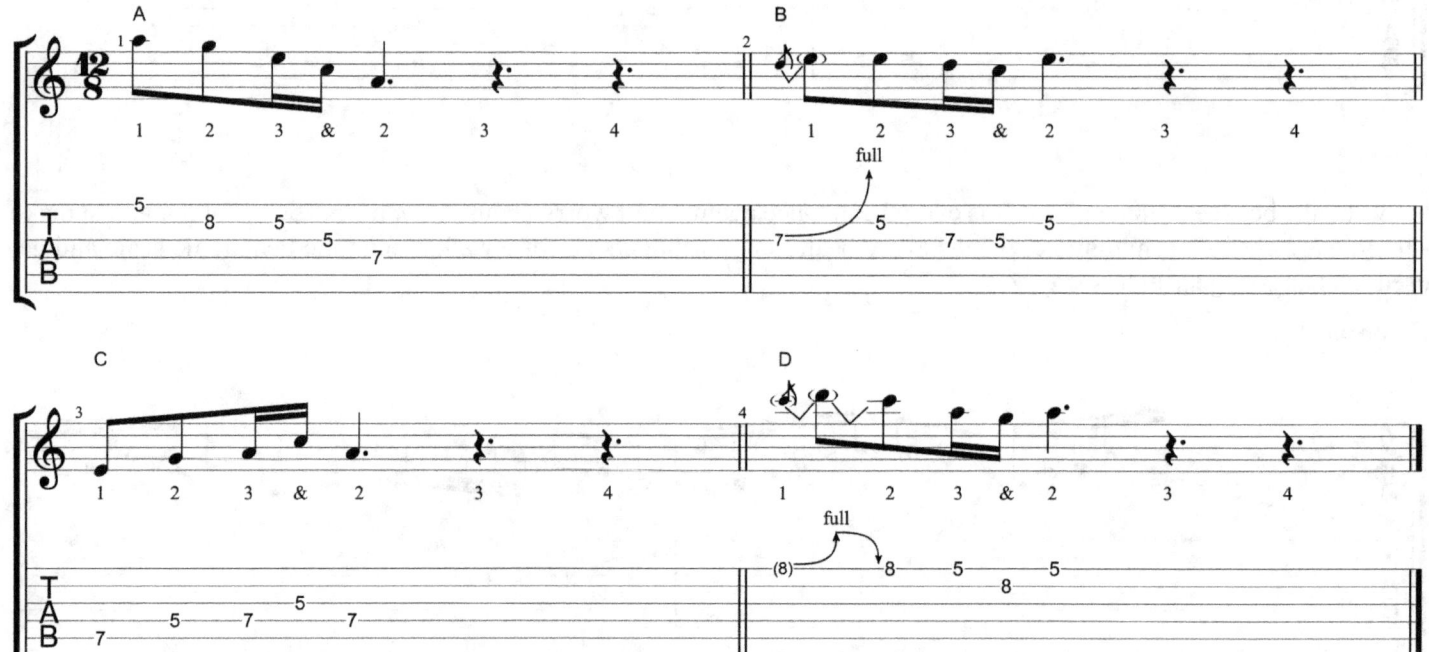

Notice that they all start on beat one of the bar, end on beat two and are identical to the rhythm shown above. Although these licks are here to get you started, the real goal is for you to use the A Minor Pentatonic scale to create *your own* lines that stick precisely to this rhythm.

When you have developed a feel for this rhythm by using the licks above, I want you to improvise a solo over backing track one using *only* the rhythm of the phrase, but altering the melody of the notes each time.

Use the A Minor Pentatonic scale as your source of melody, but *do not deviate from this rhythm*. This is a lot harder than you may think as the impulse to 'noodle' answering phrases in the gaps is quite strong.

Begin your phrase on beat one of each bar and *do not play in the gaps!* Spend a decent amount of time on this exercise until you're confident you can stay controlled and accurate while making phrases with this technique.

Example 2j is not notated here, but shows how this exercise should sound.

The previous examples were formed by doubling the note frequency on the 3rd division of the beat. i.e., we played two 1/16th notes instead of one 1/8th note.

We can play two 1/16th notes in place of any of the 1/8th notes in a beat. For example, the rhythm could be played as shown in example 2k (a) which would give us phrases like examples 2k (b-d).

Don't forget to freely add in the slides and vibrato we discussed in Chapter One to make these lines sound vocal and musical. **Example 2k (a-d):**

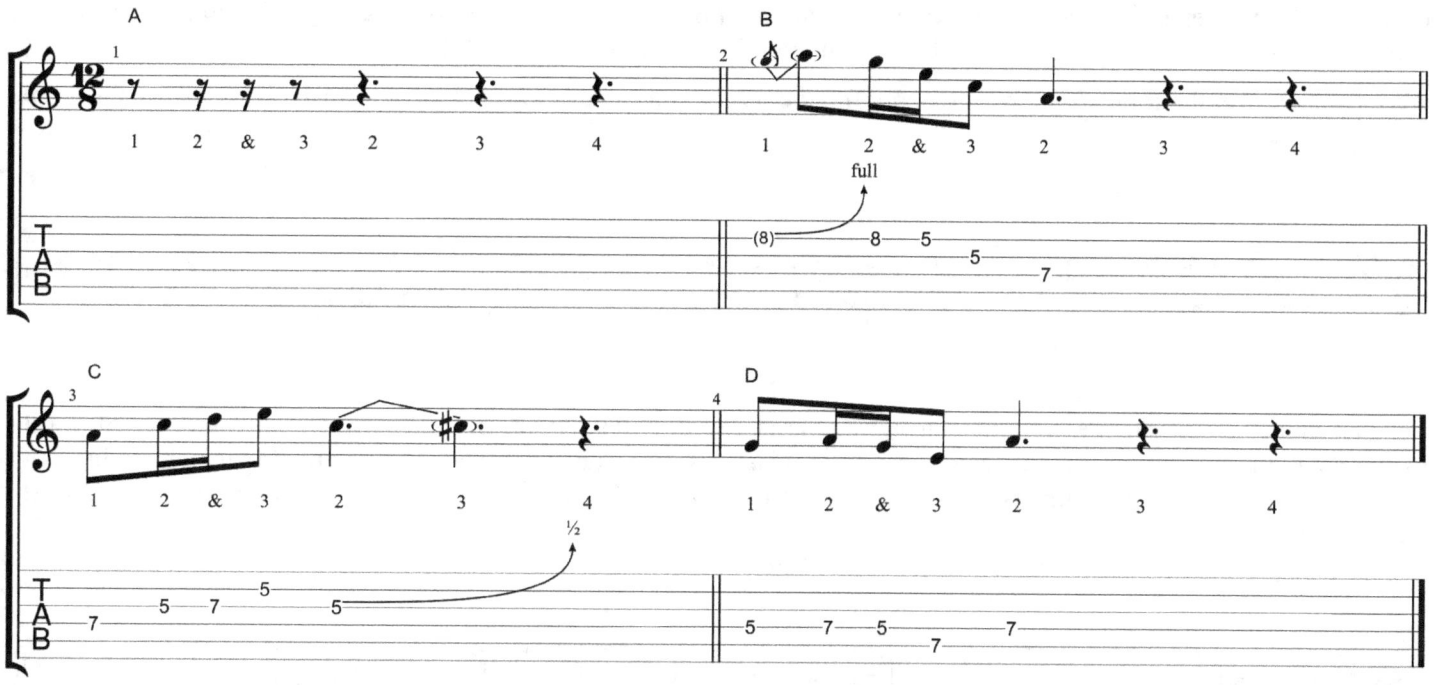

Now try improvising a 12-bar blues solo with the Minor Pentatonic scale but stick rigidly to the rhythmic structure above.

When you're comfortable with the previous rhythm, try doubling the *first* division of the beat as shown in **example 2l (a-d)**. Then try improvising one more solo using this set rhythmic pattern.

Example 2l (a-d):

When you create blues solos by sticking to one of the rhythmic patterns given above, you should start to notice a new melodic *strength* start to develop in your playing.

Your ears will easily latch on to the structure of the rhythmic pattern and you will find that it hardly matters which Pentatonic notes you use; everything you play will sound *musically linked,* like lines from one big story. These rhythmic ideas are a bit too repetitive and we will soon elaborate on this concept, but I hope you are beginning to see the value of approaching your solos from a primarily rhythmic point of view – at least for a while.

We have looked at the following three rhythmic fragments and practised using each one exclusively throughout a simple blues guitar solo.

Let's try taking each structure in turn and using it to create short phrases twice in each bar. Your solo may sound similar to example 2m, however this is just one of my improvisations. You can spend many hours creating new melodies with just one of these rhythmic fragments. Remember to use all the articulations from Chapter One to colour the lines and help make them melodic.

Example 2m:

Play some full 12 bar solos using each of the rhythmic fragments in example 2l. Stick strictly to just one or two phrases in each bar. Next, try mixing two rhythmic structures together. You can start with just one phrase per bar and then move on to two phrases per bar. For example,

Example 2n (a-b):

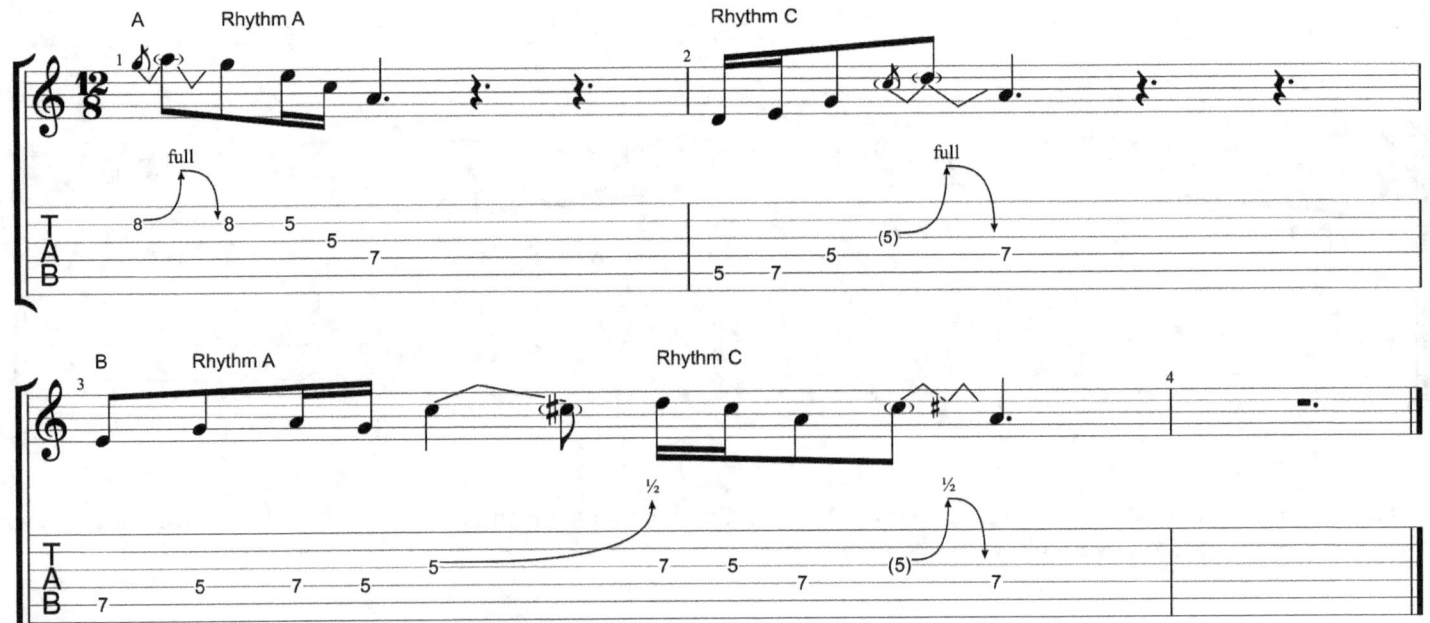

By combining rhythmic combinations in this way we start to develop the important *call and response* phrasing mentioned at the beginning of Chapter One.

Spend time in your practice session combining the three different rhythmic fragments and varying the frequency at which you play them. By doing this you will *internalise* the rhythms and they will become an unconscious part of your melodic improvisational approach.

Further Rhythms

So far, we have split just one of the three subdivisions of the beat into 1/16th notes. We can create many further permutations by splitting *two* of the divisions into 1/16ths. Here are the possibilities:

Example 2o:

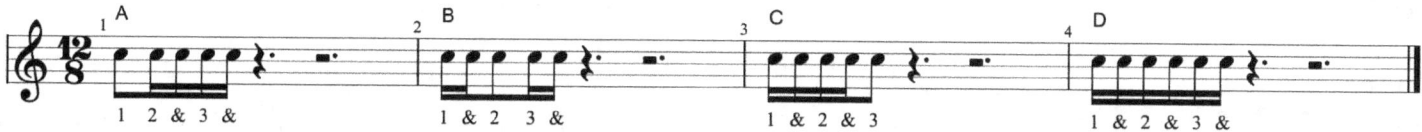

We covered rhythm D in example 2d so we won't study it again here.

Here are two phrases for each of the rhythms A, B and C:

Example 2p (a-f):

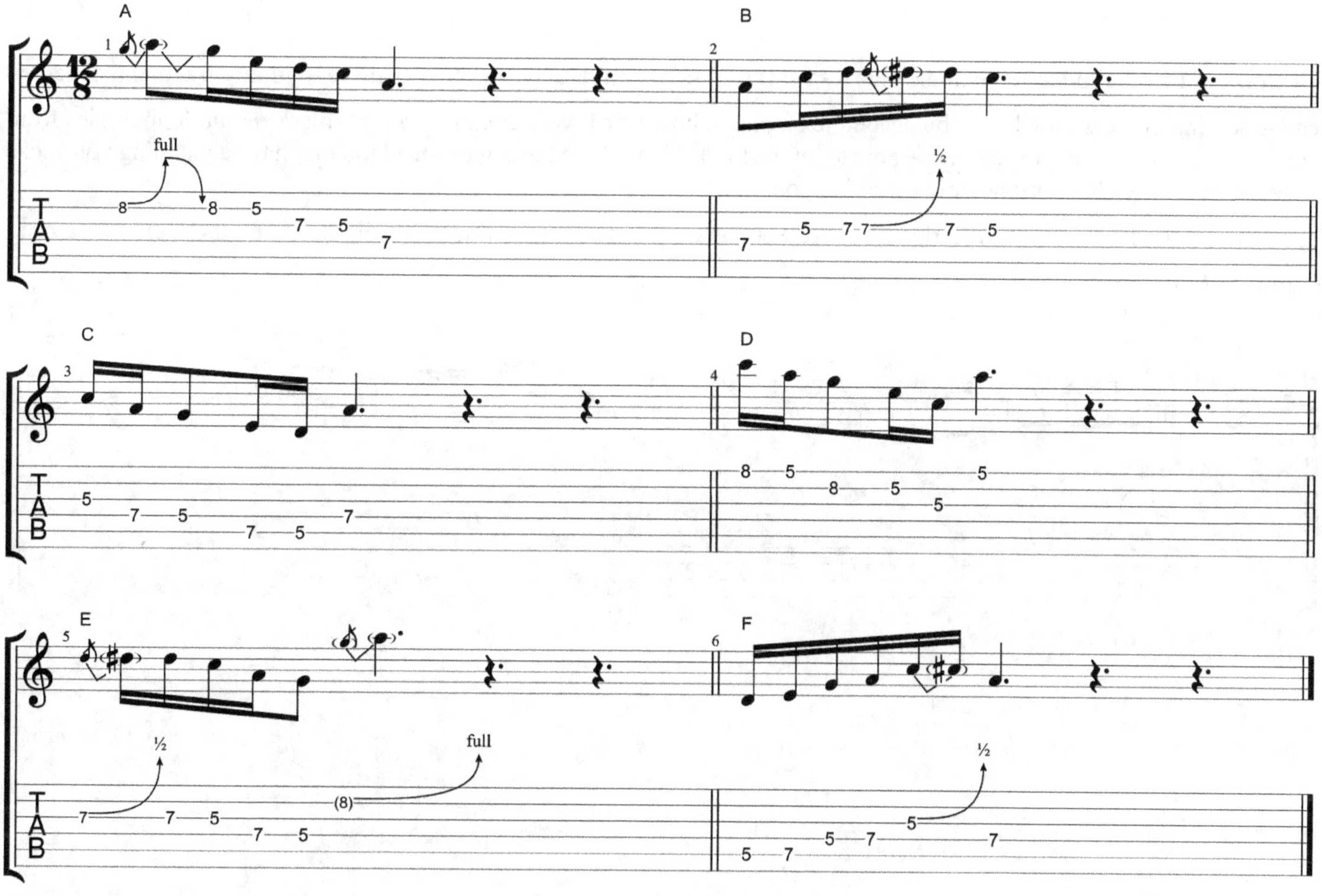

These melodic phrases are just here to help you to hear the rhythms in example 2o. Come up with as many of your own melodies as you can. Then practise using just one of them and soloing *exclusively* with it over backing track one. Begin by playing each rhythm just once in a bar, then twice in a bar.

When you feel you've exhausted all the possibilities,[1] combine two of the rhythms from example 2o in the same way.

Finally, combine all three rhythms in your solo by first playing one phrase per bar, then two phrases per bar.

Building Longer Lines

Let's briefly recap all the rhythms we have covered in this chapter.

When we want to build longer melodic phrases we can simply combine two or more of these rhythmic fragments together.

The following process may look a bit academic on paper, however if you take the time to isolate and build melodies from each rhythmic fragment, you should be able to jump straight in without having to spend too much time planning your licks in this way. Always let your melodic ear guide you.

Let's try combining rhythm F with rhythm B. To help us get a sense of resolution we will again end the phrase on a beat.

Example 2q (a-b):

---

1. You haven't!

How about combining rhythms C and G?

Example 2r:

Why not try rhythms H and C together?

Example 2s:

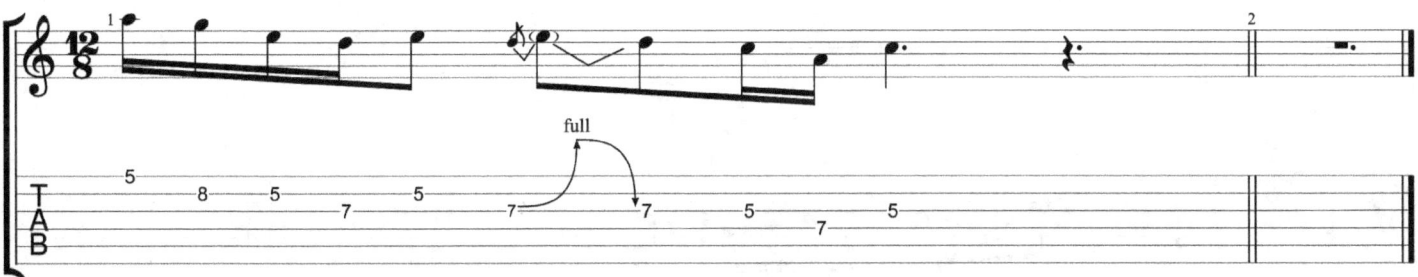

We have covered just nine common rhythms, yet these give us over 80 possibilities to combine them into unique two-beat phrases. When you consider you can play *any* note on *any* rhythmic division, the melodic possibilities are almost infinite; especially when you can make longer phrases by simply adding another rhythm.

The lesson here is that many of the phrases you hear and create are formed from just these nine basic chunks of rhythm.

To speak a language unconsciously you must first start to hear and understand some of its fundamental building blocks. When these rhythms are all internalised into your melodic consciousness, you won't even think about what you're playing any more. Rhythm and pitch will naturally combine into strong, structured melodic solos.

Silence

We have discovered many possible permutations of rhythms that can be used to build interesting, unique phrases in our solos. However, one important factor we haven't considered yet is silence. Using *rests* (beats of silence) allows us to get creative with melodic phrasing by simply missing out a few notes.

Here are the main rest values to be aware of when playing in 12/8. The rests are written along the top with their corresponding note values written below.

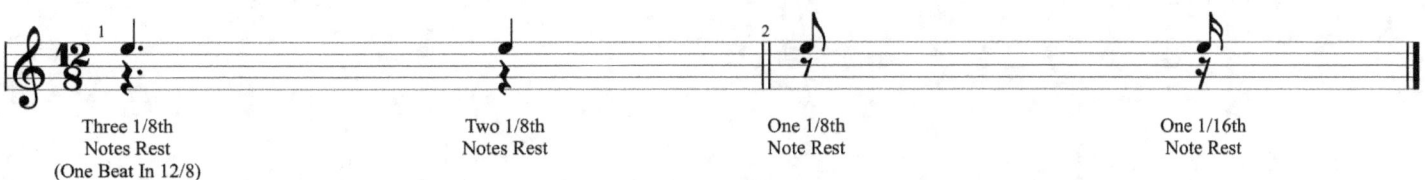

Three 1/8th Notes Rest (One Beat In 12/8)   Two 1/8th Notes Rest   One 1/8th Note Rest   One 1/16th Note Rest

Using example 2s as a workhorse, let's explore what happens when we use these rests on the first beat of the bar.

Example 2t (a - f):

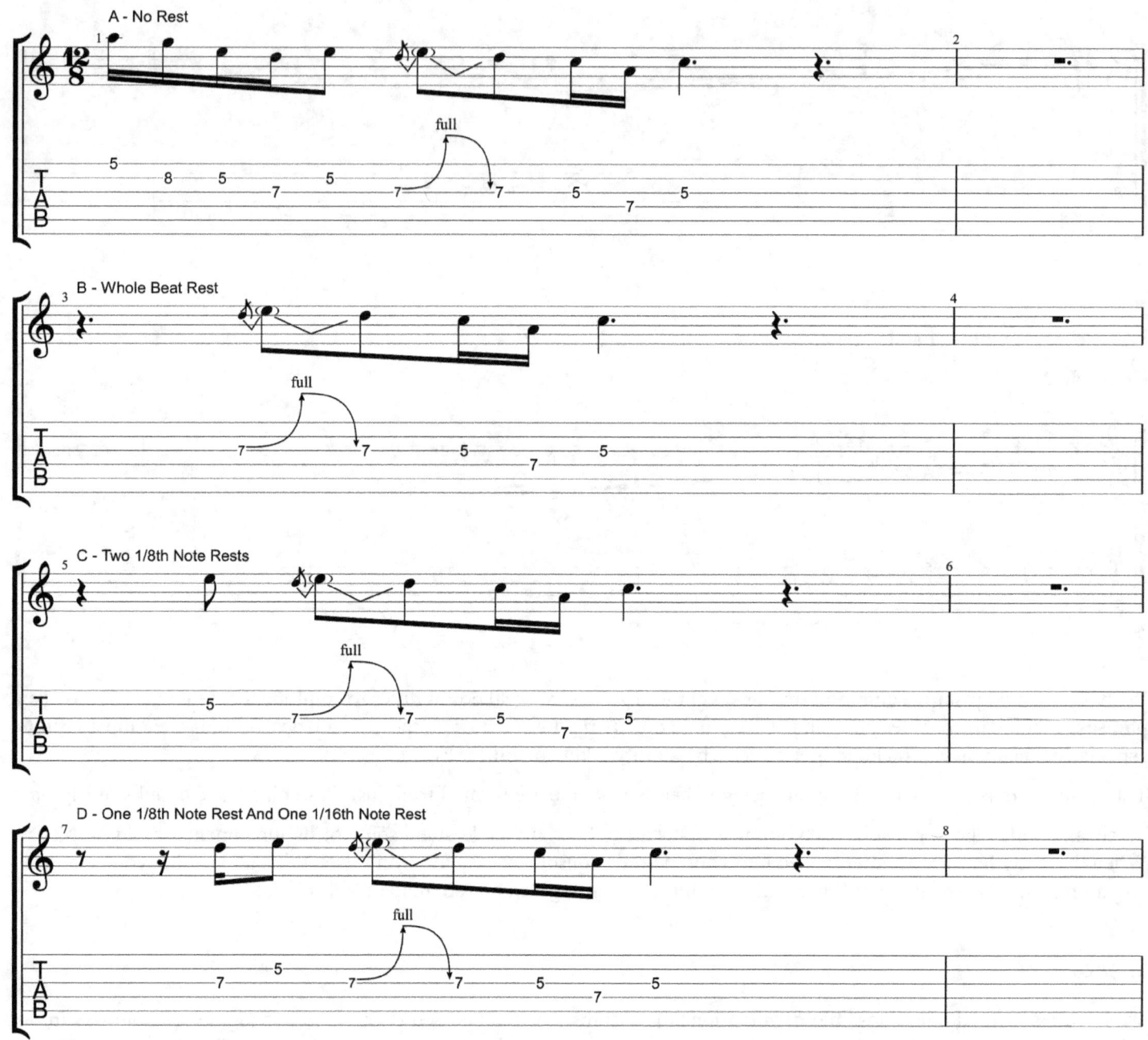

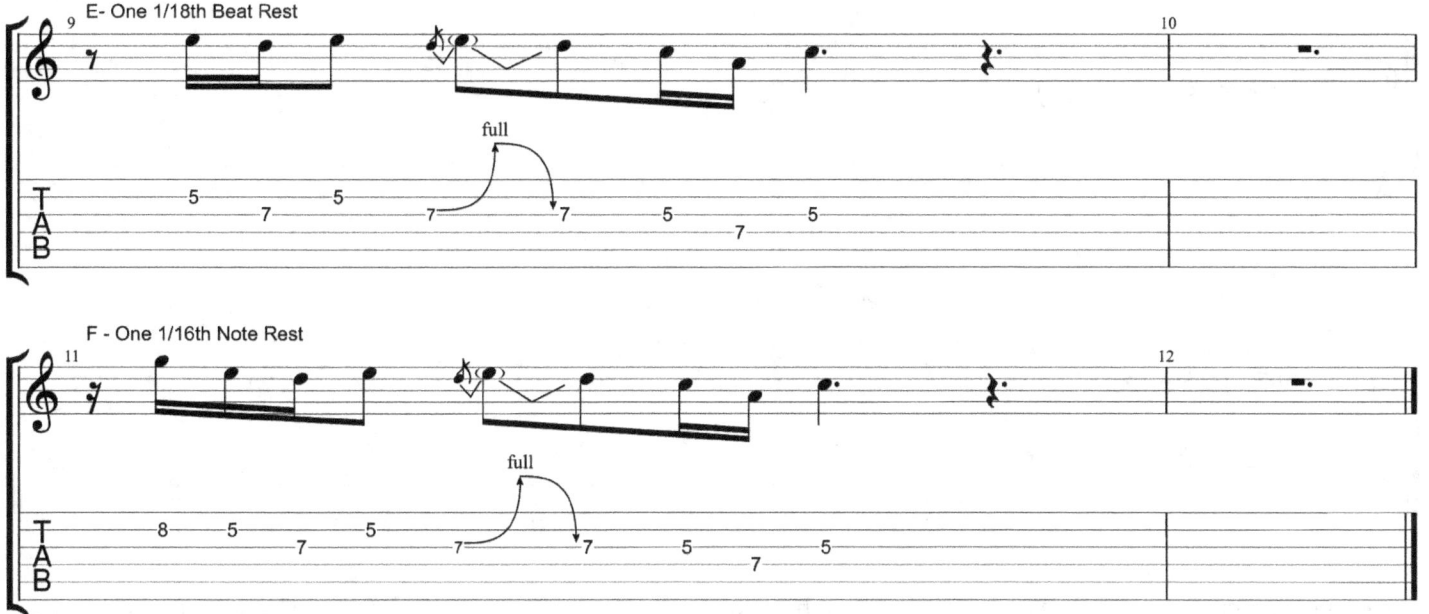

As I'm sure you can hear, playing a rest instead of a pitch opens up an abundance of melodic options.

We can place rests at *any* point in the bar we choose. It can be placed on any main beat (Beat 1, 2, 3 or 4) and/or on any subdivision of any beat. If I was to go into every possible permutation I would fill many hundreds of pages, so here I will give you some useful ideas to explore in your practice sessions.

Begin by using the same approach as on examples 2t (a - f) but apply each rest value to the second beat of the bar. You will not be able to use some of the 1/16th note rests because the second beat is comprised mainly of 1/8th notes.

Here are a few ideas to get you started. Make them sound vocal by adding in slides and vibrato as soon as you're confident with the rhythms.

Example 2u (a - d):

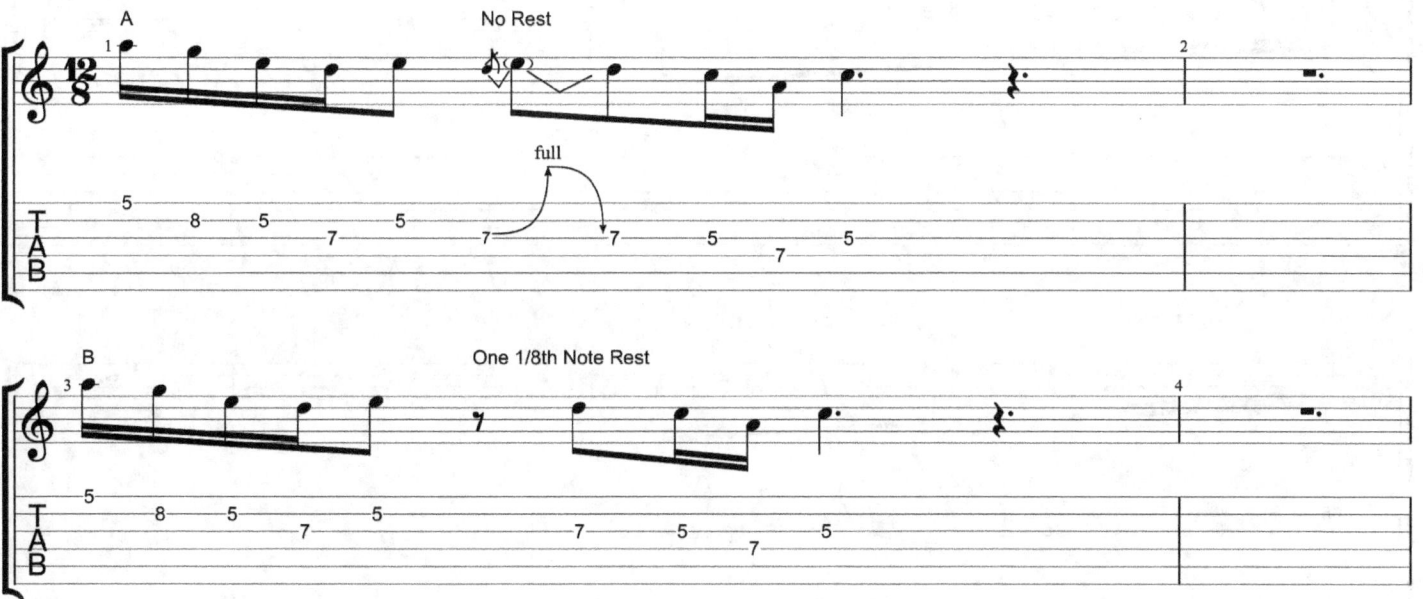

The previous four examples used rests on the start of beat two. However, rests can be added to the subdivisions of the beat. Here are some examples that use rests in the *middle* of beat two.

Example 2v (a - c):

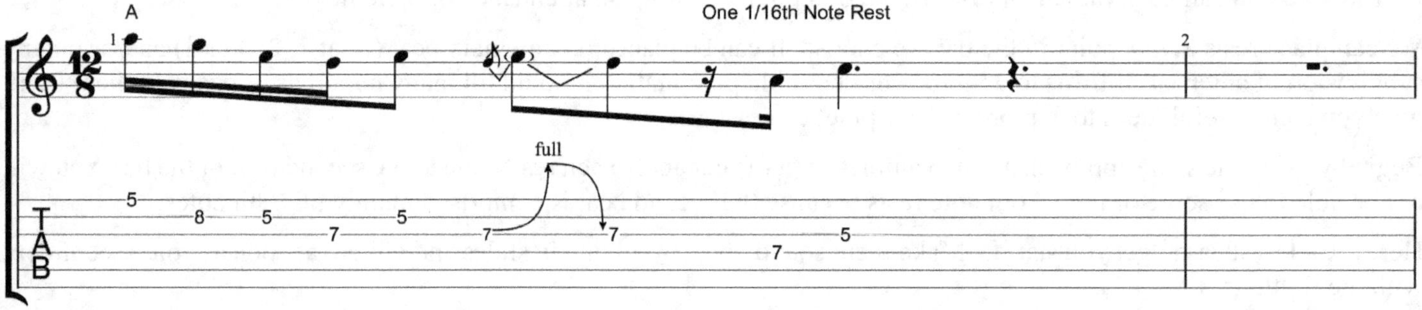

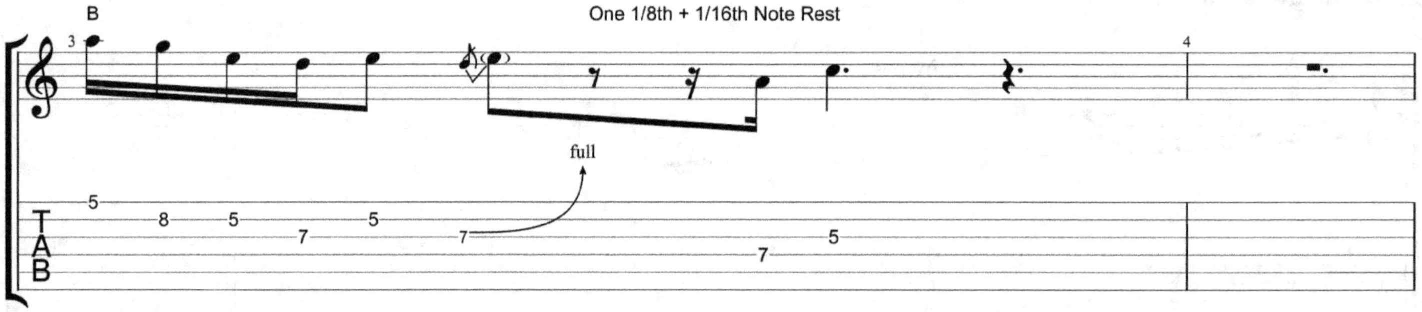

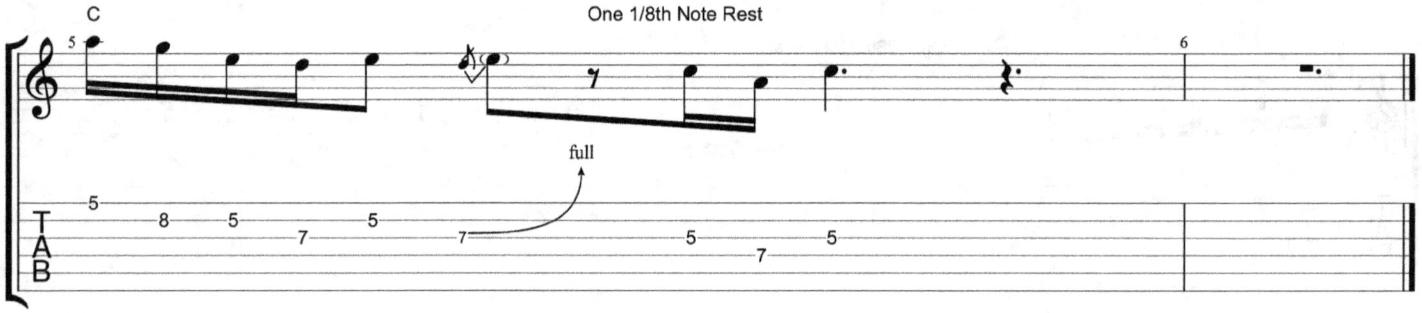

112

Feel free to let the note preceding a rest ring into the gap if you like the sound of it. Try each example with and without the note ringing to create very different effects.

Try adding rests to *both* beat one *and* beat two.

Example 2w (a - c):

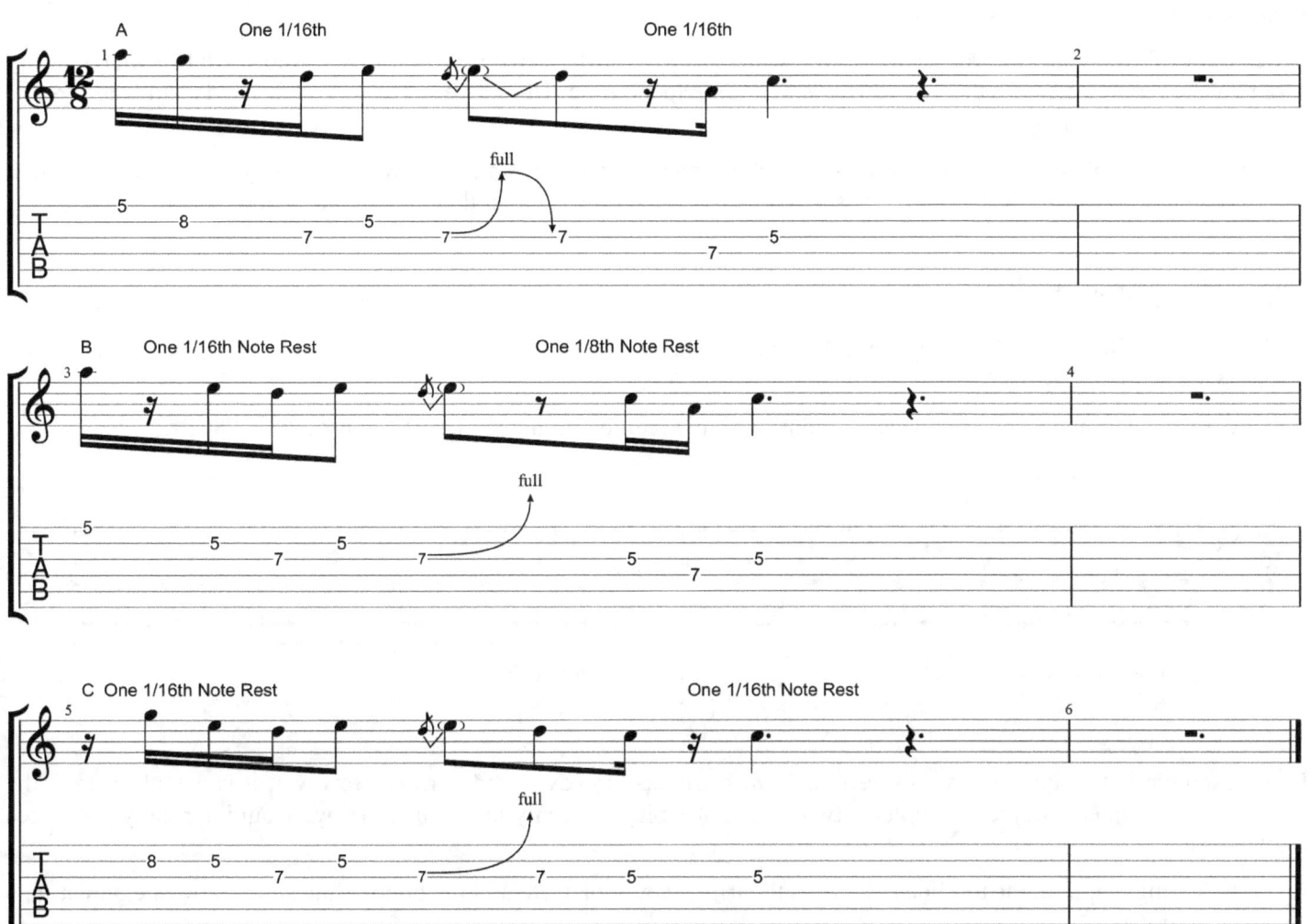

Including rests and held notes gives us massive scope to vary our melodies and avoid beginning every lick on the down beat.

The final lick shown above demonstrates this idea. It begins on the second 1/16th beat of the bar and creates an interesting *syncopated* effect in the melody line.

I wouldn't go as far as to say, "Never begin your licks on the beat", however developing the ability to start from *any* 1/16th note subdivision of *any* beat will greatly free up your melodic and expressive ability by helping you control the placement of every note. We will study this idea of note placement in detail in Chapter Three.

To bring all these ideas into the practice room, begin by taking any two-beat lick from this chapter, for example 2q, and arbitrarily add rests to different places in the lick. Begin by adding one rest, then two and maybe even three rests. You can choose the rest values, either one 1/16th, one 1/8th, two 1/8ths or three 1/8ths. Remember, you can often directly follow/ combine a 1/8th rest with a 1/16th rest and vice versa.

Do this with a few of the licks in the book and then try constructing your own from the lists of rhythms.

The point of this exercise is not to see how far you can push the envelope in terms of crazy, disjunct blues phrases (unless those sounds appeal to you). The point is to develop your melodic awareness to encompass rests and breaks in melodic phrases unconsciously. These exercises are a little on the academic side, but in order for you to feel the music, it must first be deconstructed before being rebuilt.

In this section, we have looked at building short lines which last just one or two beats. When you're ready, extend them to last for three or more beats.

Listen to the players that you like. Stevie Ray Vaughan, Jimi Hendrix, Robben Ford, Larry Carlton, Joe Bonamassa, Gary Moore and everyone else use these rhythms *all the time*. Spend time without your guitar in your hands and listen for the *spaces* in their longer runs.

Soon you will be able to stop constructing lines in this way and just let the music flow. Whenever you get stuck in a rut it can be a great idea to simply choose a few set rhythms, add the notes and let them feed your melodic creativity.

Duplets (2 against 3 feel)

You may be familiar with playing *triplets*. To play a triplet in 4/4 time we simply play three 1/8th notes in the time it normally takes to play two 1/8th notes.

Playing triplet 1/8th notes in 4/4 creates a similar rhythmic feel to playing straight 1/8th notes in 12/8.

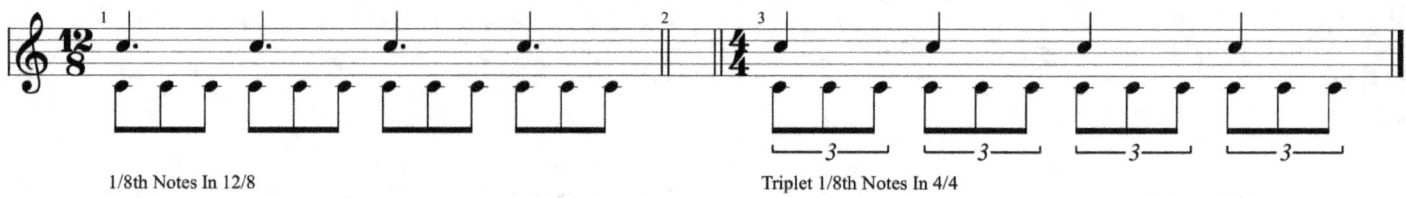

Every example in this book so far has been in 12/8 so triplets already sound normal. However, it is useful to study the 'opposite' of a triplet: a *duplet*. A duplet is two 1/8th notes played evenly in the time that we would normally play three 1/8th notes:

In the following diagram, the top line represents the triplet count of 12/8, and the bottom line shows how the duplet falls against the triplet.

Play along with the audio example to internalise its rhythm. These rhythms can be difficult to perform accurately at first, especially at a slow tempo. Try using backing track two or three (medium and fast speeds) when you practise this idea.

Example 3a:

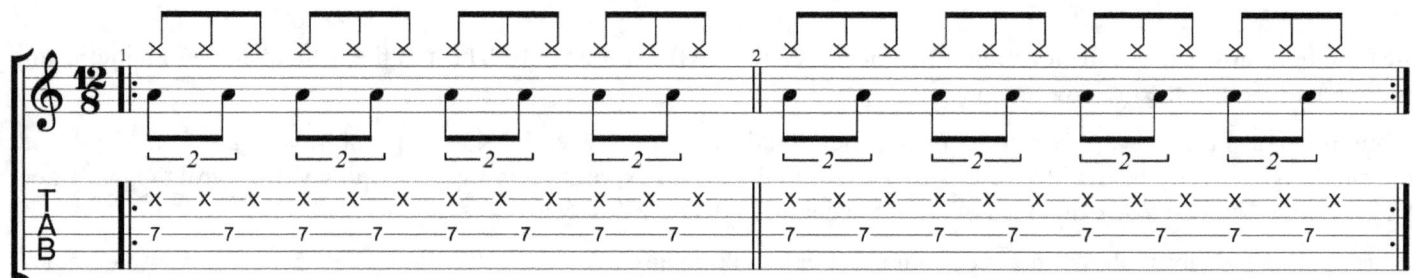

One trick I use to stay in time is to 'zone out' of the triplet feel played by the hi-hats in the drum part and focus closely on the bass drum and the snare drum, which mark each main pulse in the bar. I *always* tap my foot with these drums and then count out loud "one and two and three and four and…" It makes it a lot easier to divide the beat in two by removing the distraction of the hi-hats.

Once you have this feel clear in your mind, try playing an ascending A Minor Pentatonic scale using duplets against backing track one:

Example 3b:

While these duplets are useful, it is useful to practise 'doubling up' the 1/8th note duplets into 1/16th notes. These are a more common rhythmic division in a 12/8 blues.

1/16th notes played *4 against 3* look like this on paper:

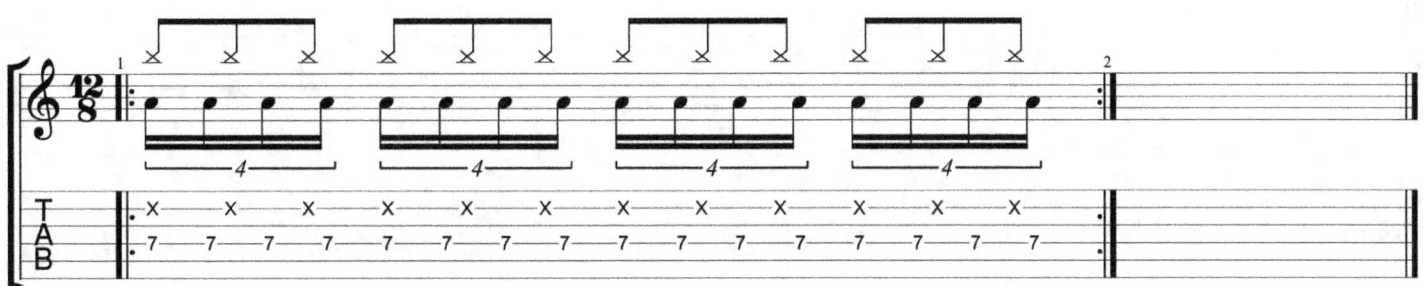

Practise this idea in the same way as described for the duplets. Focus on the kick and snare drum and try to ignore the hi-hats. Duplet 1/16th notes are easier to hear and play than duplet 1/8ths.

Again, play the Pentatonic scale ascending and descending in this rhythm against the triplet backing track.

Example 3c:

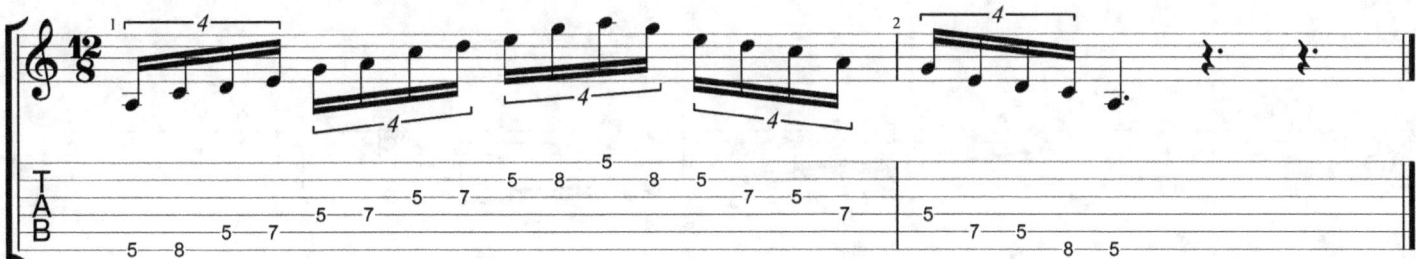

115

Practise moving between a normal triplet feel and the 1/16th note duplets:

Example 3d:

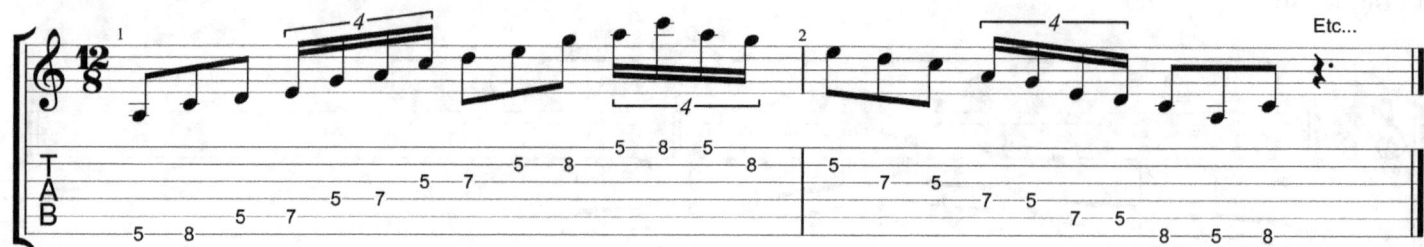

Next, learn these lines which combine both normal and duplet notes. Play along with the audio examples and be careful to match the phrasing exactly.

Example 3e:

Example 3f:

Example 3g:

In example 3g, notice how I use notes of decreasing value to give the effect of speeding up throughout the lick. The rhythmic tension of the duplet 1/16th notes is resolved by the normal 1/16ths in bar two.

These examples are just the tip of the iceberg, but it is often how your favourite players get that 'straining against the beat' feel, and is an important way to create rhythmic, as opposed to melodic, tension.

Another reminder! On the page, these licks are simply written as ink on paper. If I was to include every little slide, curl, vibrato and other nuance in my playing they would become very difficult to read. A large part of your practise should be to make these lines come alive with expressive techniques.

Chapter 3: Rhythmic Displacement

In Chapter Two we examined how to insert silence into a blues lick with a rest. This rest could either create a rhythmic 'hole' in the lick, or it could 'delete' the first couple of notes and make it seem like it was starting later.

In this chapter we will look at how to move a whole phrase across the different beats of the bar and discover the interesting, musical effects this creates.

Displacement on the Beat

We will begin as always with a simple example. Here is a six-note phrase that begins on beat one of the bar.

Example 3h:

Play this line over backing track one and be sure to begin it accurately on beat one.

Let's move this line one beat to the right and begin on beat two.

Example 3i:

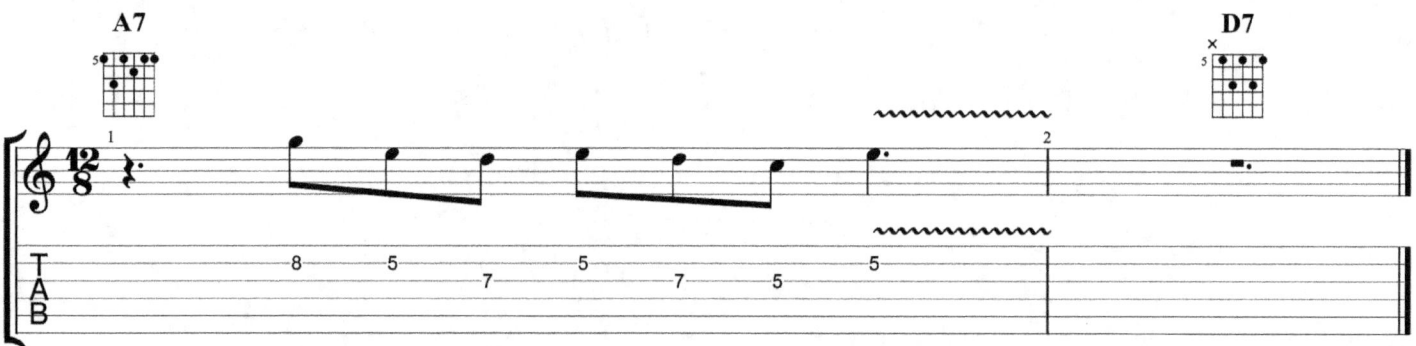

Ensure you are definitely playing example 3i on beat *two* of the bar. When I teach this concept to private students I have them count out loud "One Two Three Four One" before beginning to play on beat two. This helps to help them develop acute awareness of the point in the bar at which they place the lick. Listen carefully to the audio example as this is a crucial concept to grasp.

Example 3i taught you a musical idea called *rhythmic displacement*. We took a single phrase and *displaced* it so it began later in the bar. By beginning a lick one beat later we leave a rhythmic 'breath' at the start of the bar and make our phrasing less predictable.

You may not notice at first but you are subtly altering the musical *effect* this simple lick has on your listener. Different notes fall at different points in the bar giving a subtly altered flavour to the line. This is an easy way to reuse material without it being completely obvious. Moreover, learning to play from any point in the bar is an essential step towards mastering your timing, rhythm and phrasing.

Let's see what happens if we move this phrase another beat to the right and begin playing on beat *three*. Again, count in before playing the line. Begin counting in the preceding bar and say out loud "One Two Three Four One Two" and then start the lick on beat three.

Example 3j:

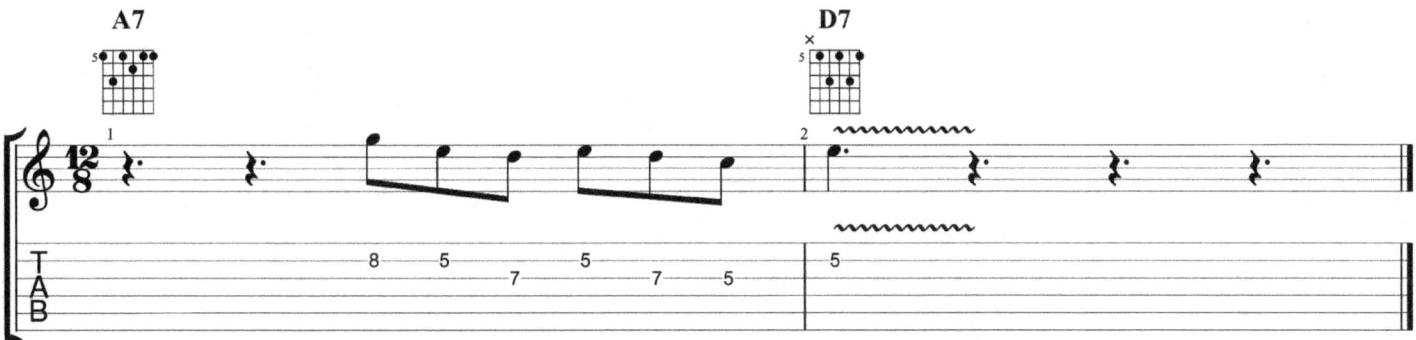

On one level, this is great practise for controlling your phrasing. How often have you actually been *aware* of when/where in the bar you are starting your line? This kind of heightened consciousness can be revolutionary in your playing.

On another, more profound level, something very interesting has happened to the way this phrase *feels* musically. By starting on beat three in this way the final note (E) no longer falls on the A7 chord in bar one; it falls on the D7 chord in bar two. The note (E) is now heard in a different *context* from before because the harmony has changed beneath it. It's like placing a painting in a different location. How you feel about the artwork will be influenced by its surroundings.

You may know that when the note E falls on the A7 it functions as the 'stable' 5th of the chord, however when it falls on a D7 chord, as above, the E is heard as the slightly 'tense' 9th in the scale of D. The best way to hear and understand this effect is to simply listen to the lick in context.

Listen again to example 3i and then immediately listen to example 3j. Can you hear the subtle difference in the 'meaning' of the phrase?

This is an important and common way to recycle your melodic material (licks). The line in 3i sounds completely different than the line in 3j and it is very hard for the listener to consciously distinguish their similarities, even when they're played right next to each other! In fact, the listener subconsciously hears that these phrases are linked in some way and gets the feeling that the music is well constructed.

Let's try the lick beginning on beat four. Remember to count out loud to ensure your accuracy.

Example 3k:

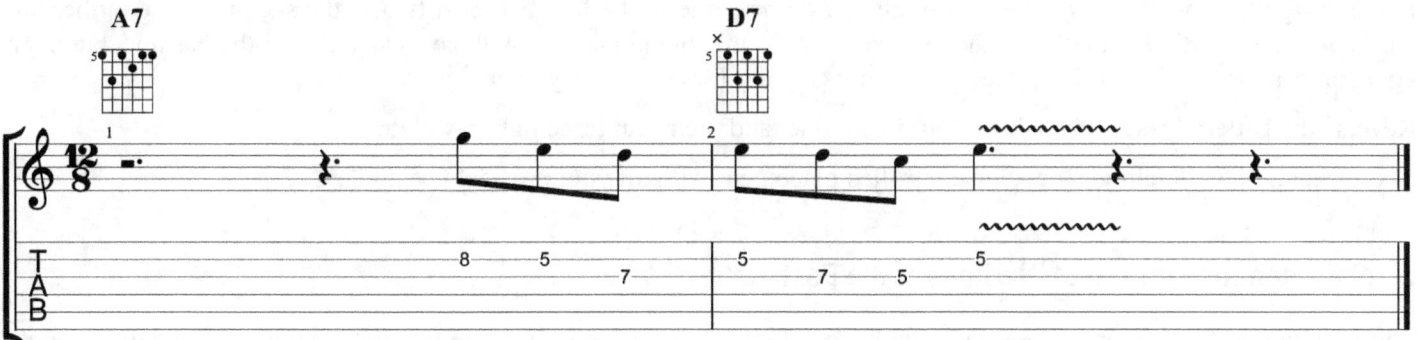

This time, the line sounds very different as more than half of the notes fall on the D7 chord.

Of course, the harmony/chords in a blues tune does not change *every* bar, however, if you time your licks to overlap a bar line when the chord *does* change you will create some very musical results.

Here is a full 12-bar blues progression chord chart. Use it to locate areas where you can play the six-note lick in the second half of the bar to cross the bar line and 'hit' a chord change. Listen carefully to the effect this creates.

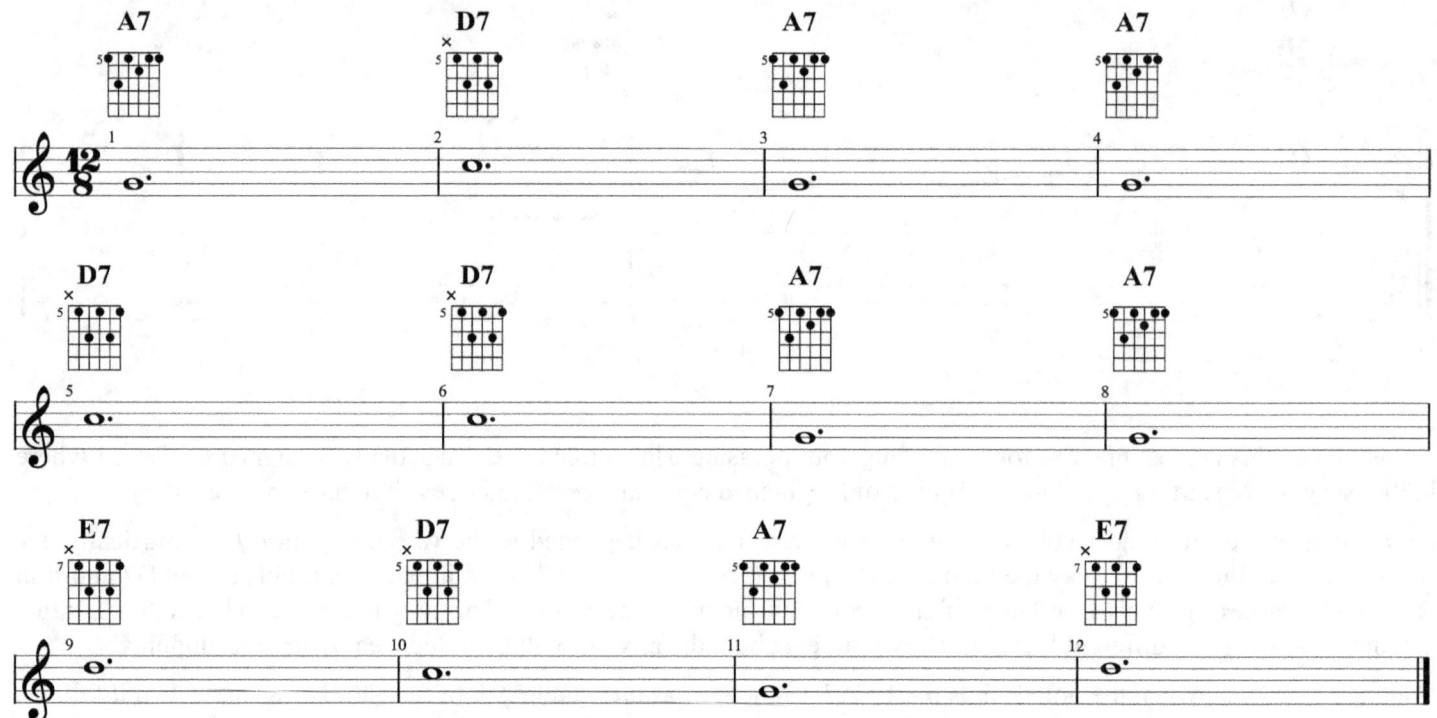

Play the following exercises with backing track one to develop your control of rhythmic development.

Take a short blues lick that is 4 or 5 notes long; something like *example 2i (b)*.

Play the lick (and *only* the lick!) just on beat one of each bar for a **full 12 bar chorus**.

Next, use the same lick but beginning each time on beat *two* of each bar.

Now begin the same line on beat three of each bar. A line longer than two beats will now start to cross the bar line.

Begin on beat four of the bar. Remember to repeat each exercise for a *whole chorus*.

Play through a complete chorus but begin the line on beat one in the first bar, beat two in the second, three in the third and four in the fourth. Don't play in the fifth bar because the line in bar four will have carried over the bar line, but begin again on beat one in the sixth bar. Keep this process going for as long as you can.

Reverse the pattern by starting on beat four in bar one, and then beat three in bar two etc.

These exercises will help you develop controlled placement with all your musical vocabulary.

Displacement by 1/8th Note Divisions of the Beat

The following section is one of my favourite lessons to teach. This lesson is often where the student suddenly 'gets' the whole concept of musical placement and understands why we *don't* need ten thousand licks to play creative, emotive, and effective blues solos. I've seen these ideas completely transform many students' playing in minutes, often with astonishing results.

In the previous section, we looked at how we could take a musical phrase and displace it to begin later in the bar by moving it *one beat* at a time. Now we will study how to take a phrase and rhythmically displace it by *one 1/8th note* each time.

By displacing a lick by an 1/8th note we *completely* change its musical effect. This means we can easily manipulate licks to make them sound and feel completely different.

We will begin with a short, 1/8th note phrase like this.

Example 3l:

Play this along with backing track one and *count out loud* each 1/8th note division. As you play say "One two three one two three one two three one two three."

Let's rhythmically displace this phrase one 1/8th note to the right. Listen to the profound effect this displacement has on the melody.

Example 3m:

It helps a great deal to count out loud as you play these examples. As you practise more and more, they will become second nature and you will not need to count.

There are two reasons that example 3m sounds so different from example 3l. Firstly, as we discussed previously, the individual pitches fall at slightly different times in the bar and this will subtly alter their flavour. However, there is another more intrinsic reason for their difference.

Certain beats in a bar of music are subtly accented to create musical feel and momentum. These accented beats vary from style to style, and from time signature to time signature. The precise accents are hard to pin down, but as a rule, the down beats (beats one, two three and four) in modern music are strong with beats two and four being more accented than beats one and three.

In addition, the first and third 1/8th notes of a 12/8 blues are often given a slight natural accent too.

By simply displacing the lick by one 1/8th note, different parts of the phrase fall on different strong or accented parts of the bar.

Using rhythmic displacement in this way will completely disguise a repeated lick because your audience will hear different notes (scale intervals) falling on different parts (rhythmic accents) of the bar. They may consciously or unconsciously hear the same melodic *shape*, but unless they are musically trained they will not spot a rhythmic displacement unless you make it extremely obvious. Even then they'll only spot it if you play the displacement directly after the initial line.

Now play this phrase onto the third 1/8th note of beat one.

Example 3n:

Make sure you count the 1/8th notes to ensure you start the lick at the correct point.

Again, the phrase *feels* completely different. Instead of being a line that is based around the first beat of the bar, it has become focused on the second and third beats. In this version, the accents fall on the second and final notes of the lick, making it almost unrecognisable from the original phrase.

Of course, we can continue to move this line one 1/8th note to the right each time to create multiple altered phrases. Things start to become quite interesting when the displacement crosses the bar line. We can achieve this by beginning the lick on the second 1/8th note of beat three.

Example 3o:

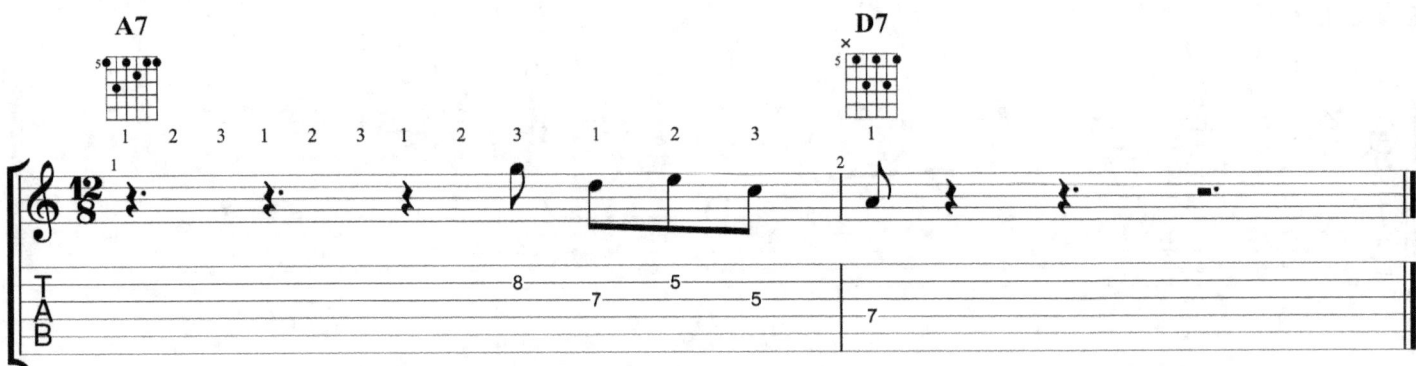

As with example 3j earlier, you can hear that the final note of example 3o now 'functions' differently from example 3n. The final note now falls on the D7 chord and creates a huge difference in its melodic effect.

We can start this line at any point from beat four and cross the bar line by a few notes. Learn the following examples to understand how to move a displaced lick further across the bar line.

Example 3p (a):

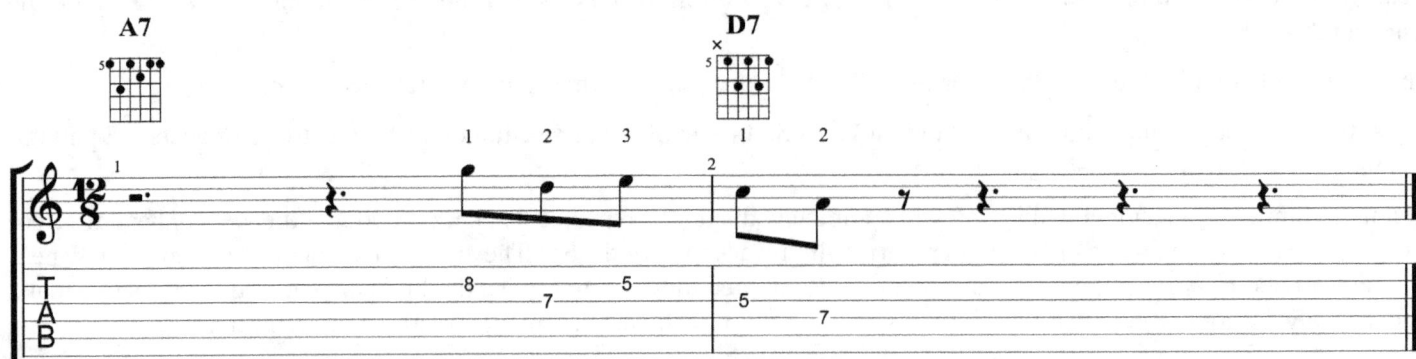

Example 3p (b):

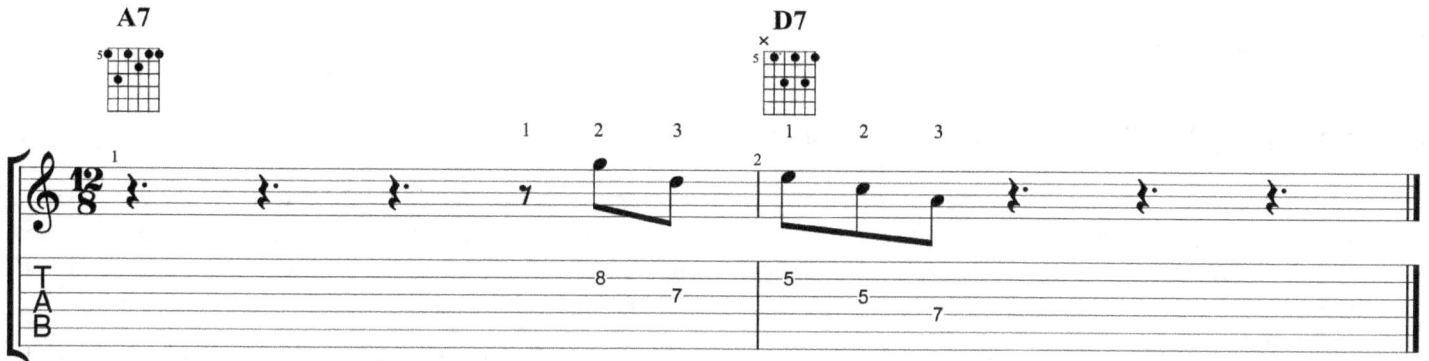

Example 3p (c):

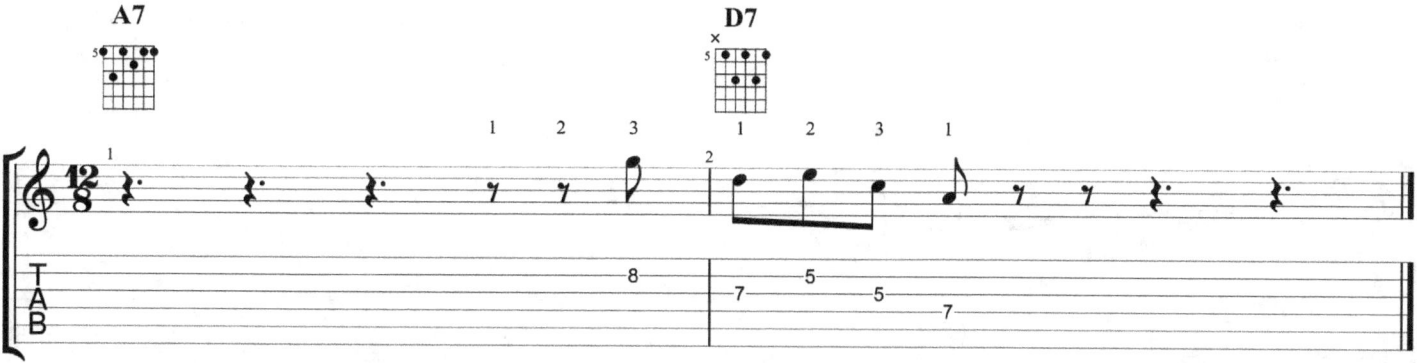

These three lines all feel unique even though we are playing the same sequence of notes. The key to unlocking this powerful technique is to be totally in control of where you begin your line.

To practise this idea:

1. Choose a short line based around 1/8th notes; something like example 2k b, c or d.
2. Play through one chorus beginning this line on the first 1/8th note of bar one.
3. Repeat this lick on the second chorus but begin on the *second* 1/8th note of beat one.
4. Now begin the line on the *third* 1/8th note of beat one.
5. Keep moving the line one 1/8th note to the right until you reach the third 1/8th note of beat four.
6. Try playing a few choruses and shift the line one 1/8th note to the right *each bar*.

If you struggle playing a whole phrase at first, begin by placing a single note or muted strum at the designated place in the bar. This will quickly develop your rhythmic awareness.

Important 'Big Picture' Point!

These rhythmic techniques above are not only essential when learning great phrasing, there is another major benefit to practising in this way.

The best model for creating memorable and melodic blues solos is the 'call and response' structure which goes right back to the field hollers and spirituals I mentioned in Chapter One.

Imagine that the phrases you have worked on are the questions in that model. If you create a few subtly different questions from just one phrase, you give yourself the opportunity to let your creativity flow and answer these questions in many ways.

By phrasing a question lick in different ways you will spontaneously generate hundreds of possible, individual and unique answers.

We will study the question and answer concept much more deeply in Chapter Four.

Displacement by 1/16th Note Divisions of the Beat

Displacing a phrase by a 1/16th note is harder than displacing by a 1/8th or whole beat. However, when you have mastered this level of precision your rhythmic perception will rocket into uncharted territory and you will be able to begin the same lick at twenty-four different points in the bar. Don't panic though; we have already covered twelve of them in the previous two sections!

When displacing a phrase by a 1/16th note, any line that begins with an 1/8th note will be fairly tricky to play at first. It's worth working some careful practise though and we will come to that later. For now, let's look at a line that begins with some 1/16th notes.

Example 3q:

You know the process by now, so let's displace this phrase by one 1/16th note to the right:

Example 3r:

Play this first displacement through a whole chorus of 12 bar blues.

The other permutations for 1/6th note displacement on beat one are as follows:

Example 3s (a):

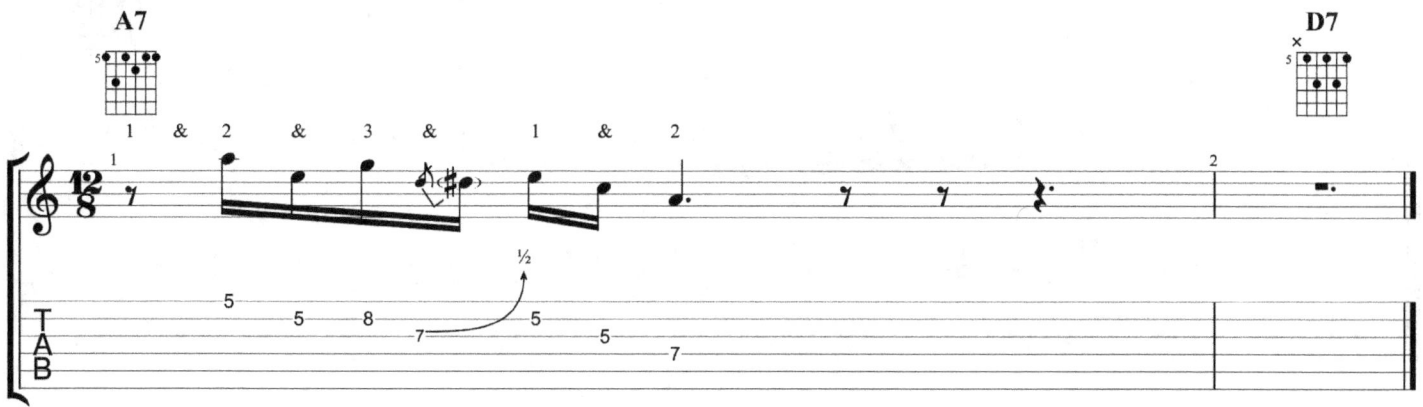

Example 3s (b):

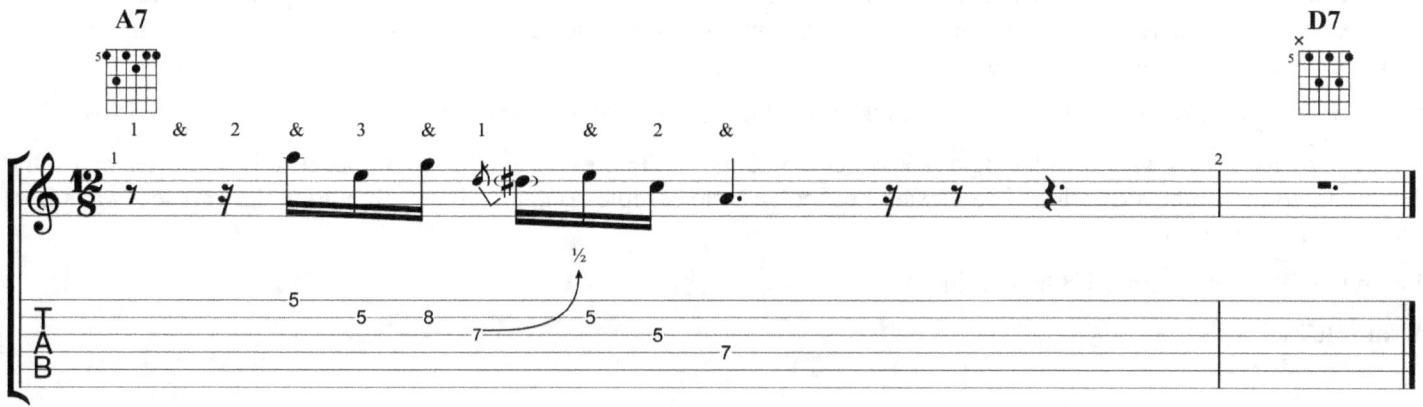

Example 3s (c):

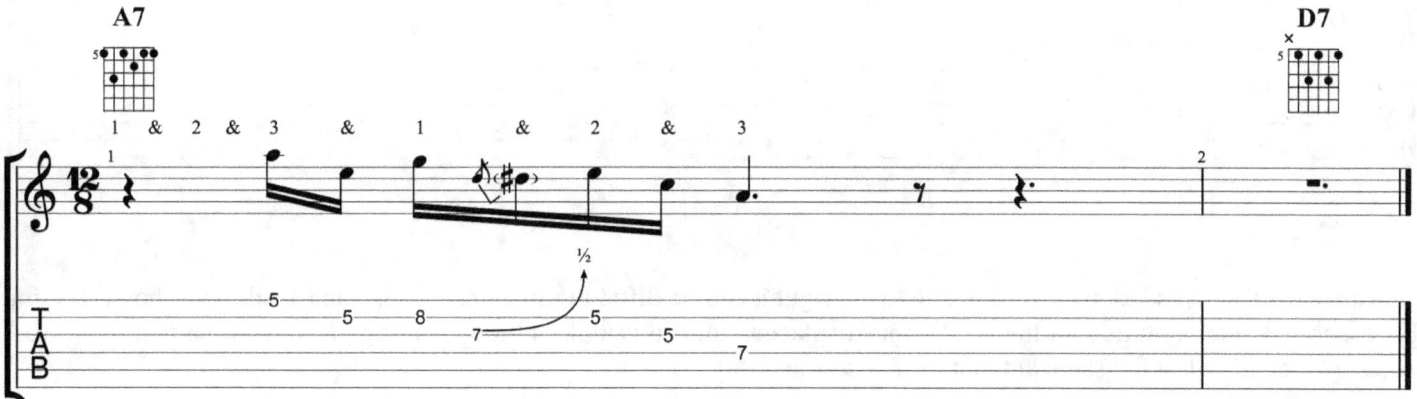

Example 3s (d):

Keep moving the lick back by one 1/16th note in each successive chorus. Notice how placing the line on beat four and playing the lick over the chord change completely alters its sound.

Displacements with 1/16ths are harder than displacements with 1/8ths, so take your time and pay careful attention to the audio examples to make sure you are getting it right. You will find some harder than others, so note down the ones you struggle with and keep working on them.

Come up with your own 1/16th note licks and then displace them using the same process.

A complication arises when displacing a lick which contains 1/8th notes by a 1/16th note because it will often cause the 1/8th note to cross a beat division. These examples look a little complex on paper but each note in the phrase always lasts the same amount of time.

Learn the following simple 1/8th note line.

Example 3t:

When we displace this lick by a 1/16th note to the right it can be difficult to feel how long each 1/8th note should last for. Here is the 'correct' notation for the 1/16th note displacement. If this looks a little daunting just remember that two 1/16th notes tied together last the same amount of time as one 1/8th note.

Example 3u:

You may wish to see the lick like this:

Although according to standard musical convention this notation is incorrect, it does make it easier to read and the previous two examples do sound identical.

When learning to internalise the feel of lines like this, the secret lies in what your foot is doing. Try the following steps learn to displace 1/8th notes by a 1/16th note.

Without a metronome, tap your foot three times per beat. Your foot is now tapping the 1/8th note pulse. Each note in the previous example will fall directly *between* the foot taps. Count "one and two and three and" as your foot goes *down up down up down up.* You should play a note every time your foot is in the up position and you say the word "and".

As this starts to become natural, set your metronome to 150 bpm (beats per minute). The click is now the 1/8th notes you were tapping. Repeat the previous paragraph but with the metronome ticking.

Now set your metronome to 50bpm and keep your foot tapping three 1/8th notes per click (just as you were before). Repeat the previous exercise.

Finally, play this lick along with backing track one. As your ears and internal clock start to process this advanced use of time and rhythmic placement, your phrasing will start to feel more natural.

This is one of those 'brick wall' exercises which, when students start to grasp it, their musical ability improves dramatically. Don't forget, this kind of placement can be applied to any musical style. Working on these skills will reap huge benefits in all your playing and your perception of time and space *within* the beat will increase dramatically.

The problem with any brick wall exercise like this is that you can only knock out a few bricks at a time, and sometimes it will feel like the mortar isn't even crumbling. The secret is to keep returning to the wall regularly and steadily chip away at it.

These exercises feel uncomfortable to everyone at first, but it's only by working outside our comfort zones that we practise effectively. We feel uncomfortable because our brain is working hard to process the mental and physical aspects of our playing. Take a lot of breaks; much of the brain's processing is done in the 'down time' away from the guitar. Ten-minute bursts of practise work great.

Another 'Big Picture' Observation

The exercises in this chapter don't just teach you a specific kind of rhythmic displacement. The big picture is that you learn to begin at any point in the bar with any note value. These exercises may seem academic and cerebral right now, but soon you can forget about specific displacements and just play. You will quickly find that you've developed the ability to consistently play when and where you like in the bar.

This level of rhythmic freedom is one of the ultimate goals in music. To be truly expressive in our playing, the ability to place a note anywhere is surely an essential ability.

These are the exercises that helped me master my phrasing. My students who practise them diligently are the ones who quickly reach a higher level of musical expression. Isn't that more appealing than using your practise time to run scales?

Let's continue with the displacement of the previous lick across the bar. When the beginning of the line falls on the 1/8th note you will find it easy. When it falls on the 1/16th note it will be more difficult.

Example 3v:

Continue with this 1/16th note displacement in the same way as in previous examples. Pay careful attention to beats three and four when the lick will start to cross the bar line as some very interesting things start to occur.

Repeat the 1/16th note displacement exercises with other licks that begin with 1/8th notes.

The main use of all these displacements is to get more out of a single guitar lick. By disguising our vocabulary, playing it over different chord changes and starting a lick on different subdivisions of the beat, we can create thousands of subtle variations on a theme that all sound unique and fresh to the listener. We can cover great melodic ground with just a few simple licks.

Remember: It's better to learn to play one lick in one hundred different ways than it is to learn one hundred different licks.

This heightened level of rhythmic perception frees us from regurgitating and 'chasing' licks around the fretboard. We can now create and genuinely improvise our solos with an individual freedom not available to 'lick' players. When you learn a new lick, you will instantly be able to manipulate it in different ways to disguise its origins and make it unique to you.

Finally, let's explore the effect of displacement over more harmonically dense passages of music. When the chords are changing more quickly, displacement of a melodic phrase becomes more effective as you will continually place different notes over different chords in the harmony/rhythm guitar part.

The final four bars of the blues are a great opportunity to practise this idea:

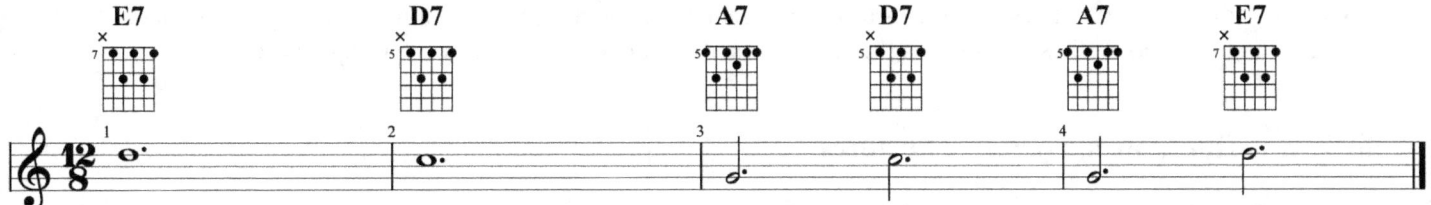

Take simple phrases and displace them so they cross the bar lines at different points in the progression. You will be amazed at how different each lick can sound.

This is all fantastic ear training. When you create new sounds you like, you will remember them and eventually they will flow freely when you improvise for real at the gig.

Chapter 4: Developing Lines and Creativity

The ideas in this chapter all centre around the concept of creativity and how we can reach deep within ourselves to develop a personal and individual style. These exercises transcend genre and can be applied to almost any style of music. There are no right or wrong answers in these lessons as this chapter is about developing your own unique voice.

Creativity with Question and Answer Structures

In the blues, great importance is placed on phrase structure and keeping a musical dialogue running between each successive line. The easiest way to explain this dialogue is by the phrase 'call and response'. In the early spiritual music I referenced in the introduction this is easy to hear. The first phrase is a *call* and sets up the *response*. This structure continues throughout the whole piece of music.

For a slightly more up-to-date and 'guitarry' example, listen to the guitar solo in Stevie Ray Vaughan's *Lenny*. The whole thing is packed with this call and response idea. Even though both the call and the response are both played on the same instrument there are echoes of the early gospel blues phrasing structure. B.B. King is another great exponent of this idea.

Practising call and response by yourself can be a little challenging, so it might help to work on the following ideas with a musician friend.

In this first set of exercises I will give you a set lick as a question. It will be your job to provide an answering phrase.

Get very familiar with the following lick. This is going to be your *question* phrase and will form a repeating figure throughout a 12-bar blues. Notice that it begins on beat two of the bar.

Example 4a:

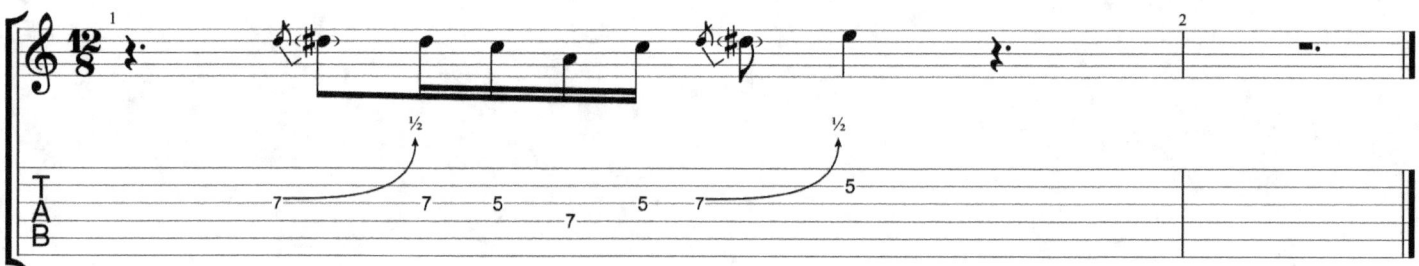

The first exercise is to play this lick in each alternate bar (one, three, five, etc.) and improvise your *own* answering phrase in bars two, four, six, etc.

The 'scheme' of your solo will look like this:

You may improvise any answering phrase you wish. There are no wrong answers. The only rule is that you must be ready to play the question phrase when it reoccurs in the next bar.

Here is one of the infinite number of possibilities that I came up with.

Example 4b:

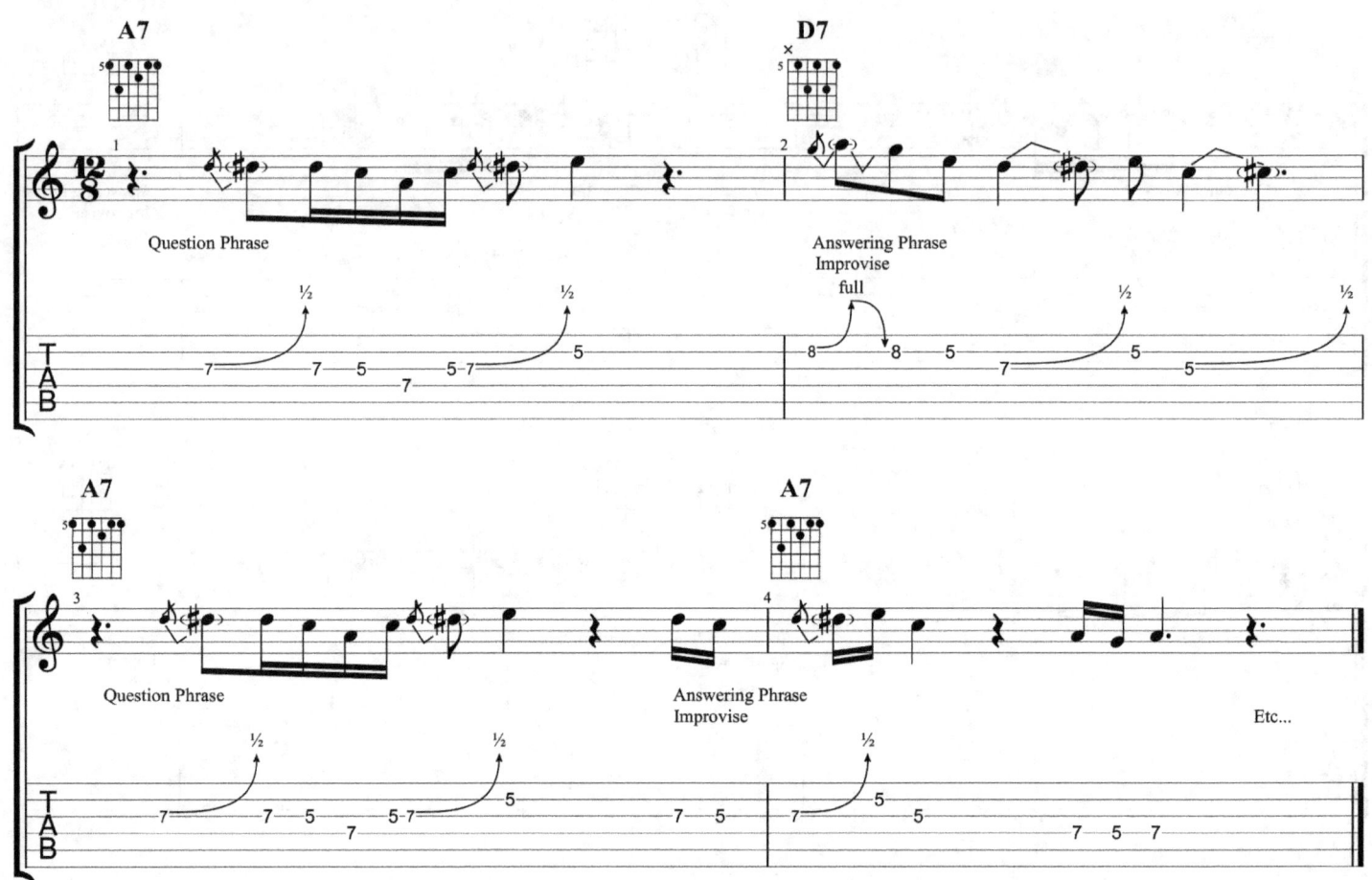

Play as many choruses of blues as you can and find multiple answers to the same question.

By having to answer the same question in many ways you will force yourself to get more creative in your answers. You will start to see your solo as one story full of connected dialogue, rather than a series of short unrelated ideas.

Even in this seemingly restrictive exercise I am still really giving you free rein to answer the question as you please. I allow you to feel what should come next, with very few limitations.

In one sense, this is good because it helps you develop your own voice on the guitar, however in another sense, this freedom is a little restrictive as a learning exercise because I'm not forcing you to play outside your comfort zone.

I have been fortunate enough to have had some exceptional guitar teachers, and one sentence from Shaun Baxter has always stuck with me: "It's a paradox, but the more you limit yourself, the more creative you are forced to become."

If I sat you in a restaurant, you're not going to have to think too much about how to feed yourself, but if I dropped you in a desert you would have to quickly get creative about finding your next meal. You may do things that you never thought you were capable of to find sustenance. I firmly believe that if we are to find creative new ways to speak on our instruments, we must isolate one small creative aspect at a time and try to exhaust its possibilities before moving on.

Creativity by Limiting Rhythm

Let's look at some ways we can force ourselves to play something new within the above question and answer structure. The first thing we do is play the answering phrase with *exactly* the same rhythm as the question. This requires strict discipline and quickly shows when our fingers, not our ears, are in control of the guitar.

Example 4c:

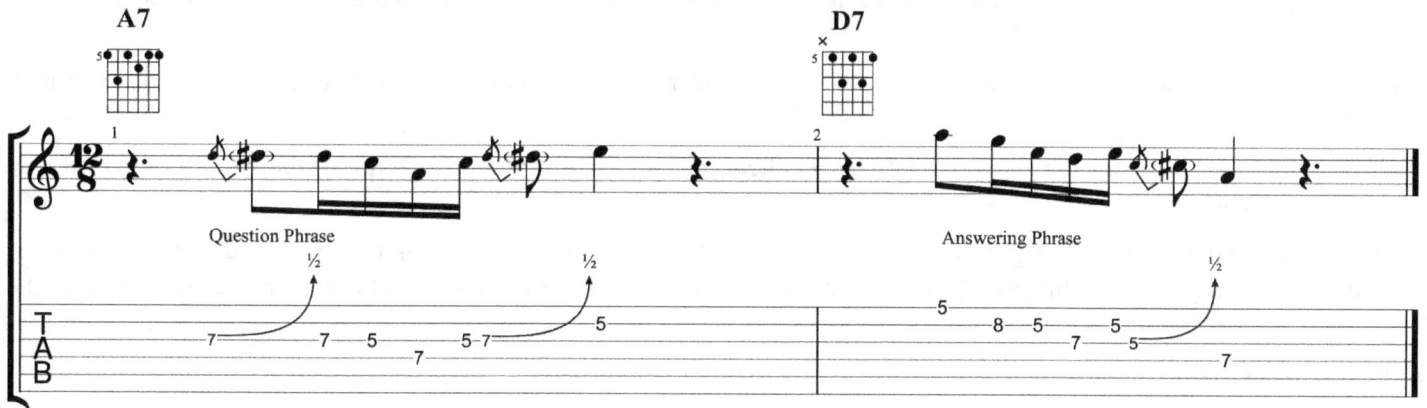

Obviously this is just one possible answering phrase, but you should play through many choruses of the blues and answer the question using the same rhythm played with different melodies.

Next, how about using the same rhythm for the answer but displacing it earlier or later by one or more 1/18th notes? The next example shows an answer that is one 1/8th note early.

Example 4d:

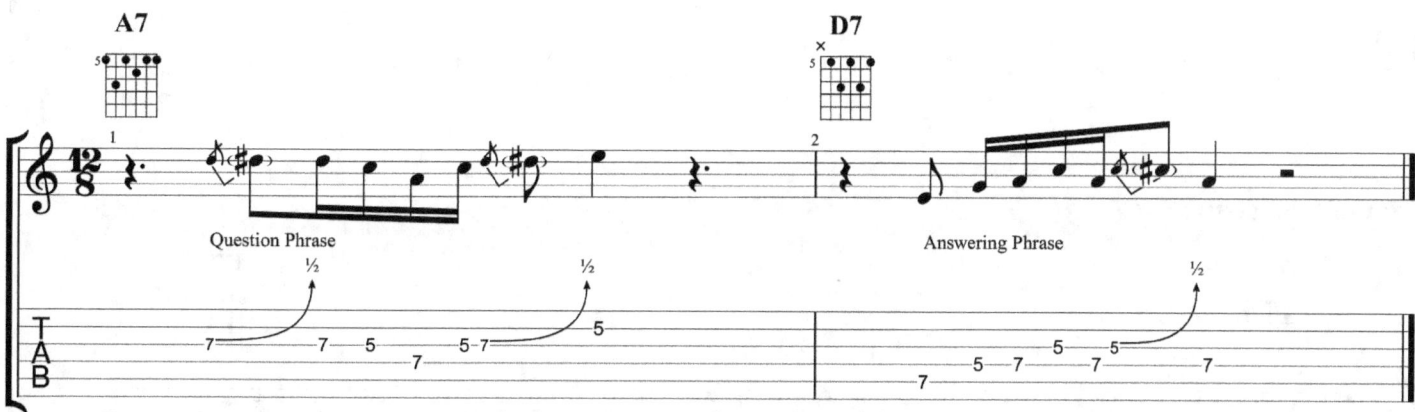

Here is an example where the same rhythm is used starting one 1/8th note later. As you can see, the rhythm is identical but it starts one 1/8th note later and uses different notes.

Example 4e:

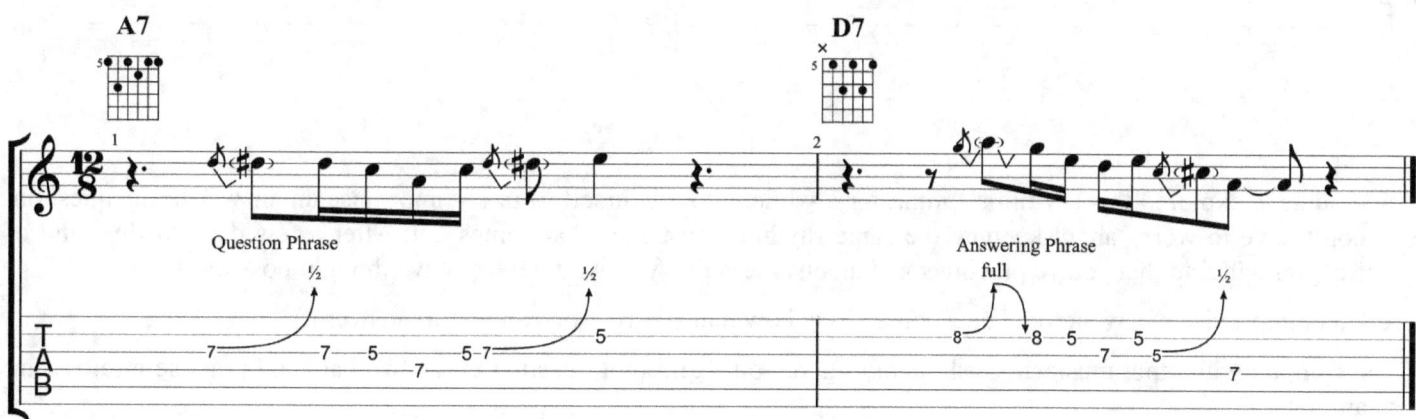

See if you can find ten unique answering phrases that begin on beat two, then ten beginning an 1/8th note early, and finally ten beginning an 1/8th note late. This is difficult, it will force you to create new music on the spot. It will get easier over time.

When you feel you have exhausted all the possibilities, try starting your answering phrase two 1/8ths earlier and later while keeping to the same rhythm.

If I were to write out even just a few possible answers here for each displacement I would fill the whole book so it's up to you to get creative.

Do you remember how displacing a lick completely alters the phrase's 'meaning' and inspires a different answering phrase? When you get tired of the previous exercises, move the question phrase one 1/8th note earlier or later and see how this affects your answer.

Example 4f: (Early)

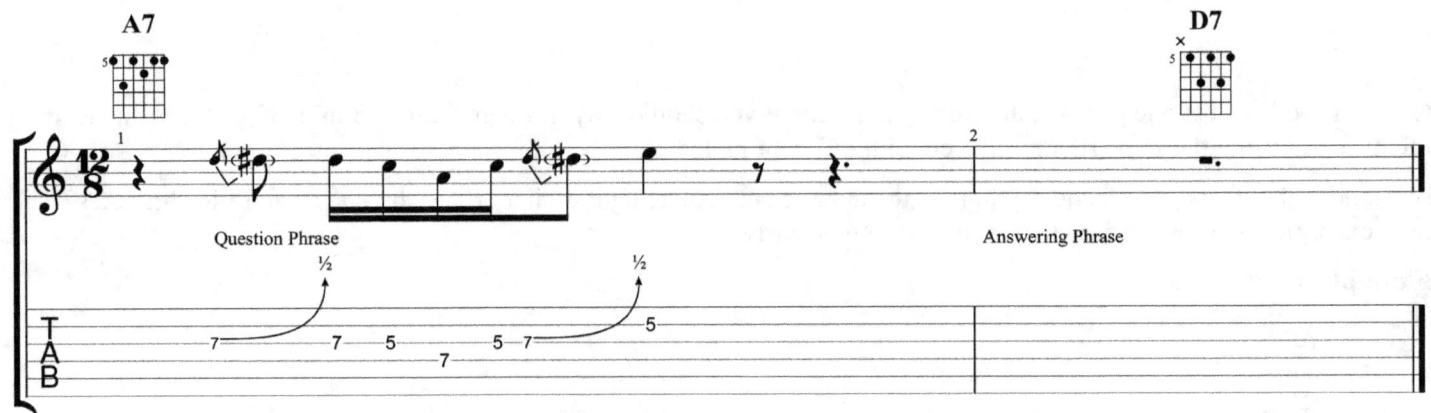

Example 4g: (Late)

Now you have explored this rhythmic format for a while, allow yourself to freely improvise an answer to the question. You don't have to worry about keeping the same rhythm – just see what comes out. After a few days of this kind of practise, you will find that you're playing spontaneous ideas that you would never have thought possible.

Every day improvise a new melodic question and see how many ways you can find to answer it.

If you can jam with other musicians, ask them to give you a different question every two bars and practise improvising new answers.

Creativity by Limiting Range

Sticking to just one rhythm is not the only way to get creative when improvising. How about simply limiting the musical *range* that we use when we solo?

In the following exercise, you are only allowed to use these four notes in your answer:

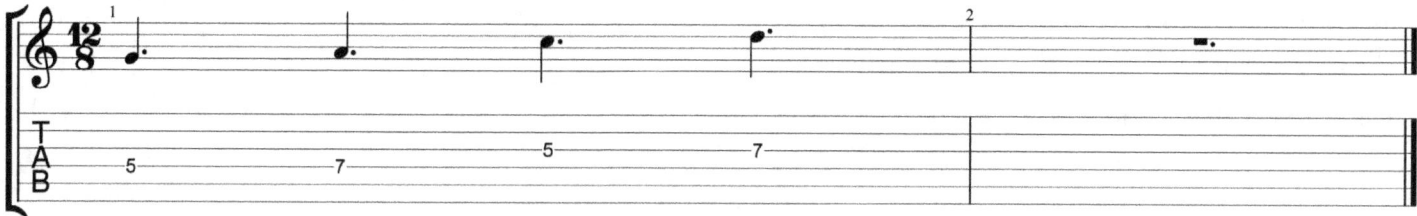

Start by brain-storming all the techniques you can use to make these four come alive. My list includes, but is not limited to:

Rhythm

Play fast (high density of notes)

Play slow (low density of notes)

Short burst of fast notes surrounded by long rests

Long bursts of fast notes surrounded by rests

Stick to one rhythm and alter the melody

Stick to one sequence of notes and alter the rhythm

Play duplets or 4 against 3 feel

Play different rhythms on one note

Play different rhythms on one note while gradually bending it

Beginning and Ending Notes

Sliding into notes (beginning and during phrases)

Sliding out of notes (after and during phrases)

Slide in/out slowly, slide in quickly, slide from below, slide from above

Slide to an open string

Slide up and off the neck very quickly

Wide Vibrato

Narrow Vibrato

Narrow Vibrato *becoming* wide vibrato and vice versa

Vibrato before sliding out of a phrase

(Go to Appendix B for vibrato technique exercises).

Bending

Focus on semitone bends

Focus on tone bends

Focus on one-and-a-half tone bends

Bend *very* slowly

Bend quickly

See how many 'in-between' (microtone) notes you can find by bending very gradually from one note to another

Repeatedly pick slowly during a bend

Repeatedly pick quickly during a bend

Pre-bend – bend the note to pitch *before* picking it and then release

Bend a note up but don't release the pitch

Bend a note up but 'kill' it with the picking hand

Bend a note up and then release the bend quickly / slowly

Bend repeatedly from one pitch to another

Double-stop bends (bend two notes simultaneously)

(Check out Appendix A for more information on bending technique).

Duration/Frequency

Play for one beat

Play for two beats

Etc.

Play only one note

Play only two notes

Etc

Play long full notes

Play short staccato notes

Only play on beat one/two etc.

Pick Angle

Angle the pick sharply against the strings

Angle the pick flat against the strings

Change the pick angle *during* the phrase

Alter Picking Dynamics (more on this later)

Pick every note
Pick hard
Pick soft

Pick near the bridge
Pick near the neck
Move pick from the bridge towards the deck *during* the phrase

Get louder / quieter during a phrase

Articulation

Play legato
Pick everything
Only use Hammer-Ons and Pull-Offs

Pick the first note of a phrase and play the rest legato (Hammer-ons and Pull-offs)
Pick the first two notes of a phrase and play the rest legato.
Etc.

Play double-stops (two notes at the same time)

Add as many ideas as you can to these lists.

While I feel a bit guilty for simply listing ideas for you to experiment with, I feel there is significant benefit to be had by picking just one of these concepts each day and seeing how much mileage you can gain from it.

Take your chosen idea and stick to *only* the four notes given above. Find as many ways as you can to apply that idea musically. This is difficult at first, but if you stick with it you will force yourself to be creative within the confines of the exercise.

If you do it for long enough you will find new ways to approach melodic soloing and these ideas will easily transfer themselves to the full licks and lines that you already know.

Finally, make sure you apply these ideas *musically*. Play whole solos focusing on just one or two of the listed approaches. By using these ideas in a realistic context, you will internalise them and they will quickly become an integral part of your playing.

Remember our premise: We all have the same twelve notes. It is how and when we play them that set us apart from one another. It is easy to hear the players who have worked on expressive exercises like this and those who haven't.

Exercises that focus on creativity are always going to be a little bit 'out there', and I certainly don't want to get too existential. However, the more you put into practising these ideas, the deeper you will look inside yourself and the more personal your music will become. After a while, your 'borrowed' licks won't sound borrowed: You'll be playing them in your own way.

So do you want to be unique and instantly recognisable, or do you want to be just another clone?

Asking the Question

We have taken a detailed look at how to answer a set musical question with an improvised phrase. This is a great exercise and helps you to dig deep within yourself rhythmically, melodically and expressively.

However, advanced musicians think ahead about phrases that are yet to be played. It is not uncommon to be thinking at least two phrases ahead and to have a kind of planned outline or scheme for the solo.

This may be hard to comprehend at first, but it is possible to learn to project what you'll be doing a couple of bars in the future. Rather than thinking of this like a complex game of chess, imagine yourself as an artist who is making a very early, rough sketch of the location of objects in a landscape painting. Things may move around later and there may be no detail yet, but there is definitely an overarching scheme of what the picture will become.

The difficult part is how to get away from the *now* and to start conceptualising the *then*. We need to learn to think ahead.

The best exercise I have seen to encourage this kind of musical forethought it to reverse the question and answer exercise. We will work with a set answering phrase but try to create as many ways as we can to set it up with a new question. This means we are forced to imagine/hear in our head the phrase that is going to come after our next line and thus develop our forward-thinking ability.

Learn the following lick:

Example 4h:

This will be our answering phrase throughout the next section. Look at the following soloing scheme.

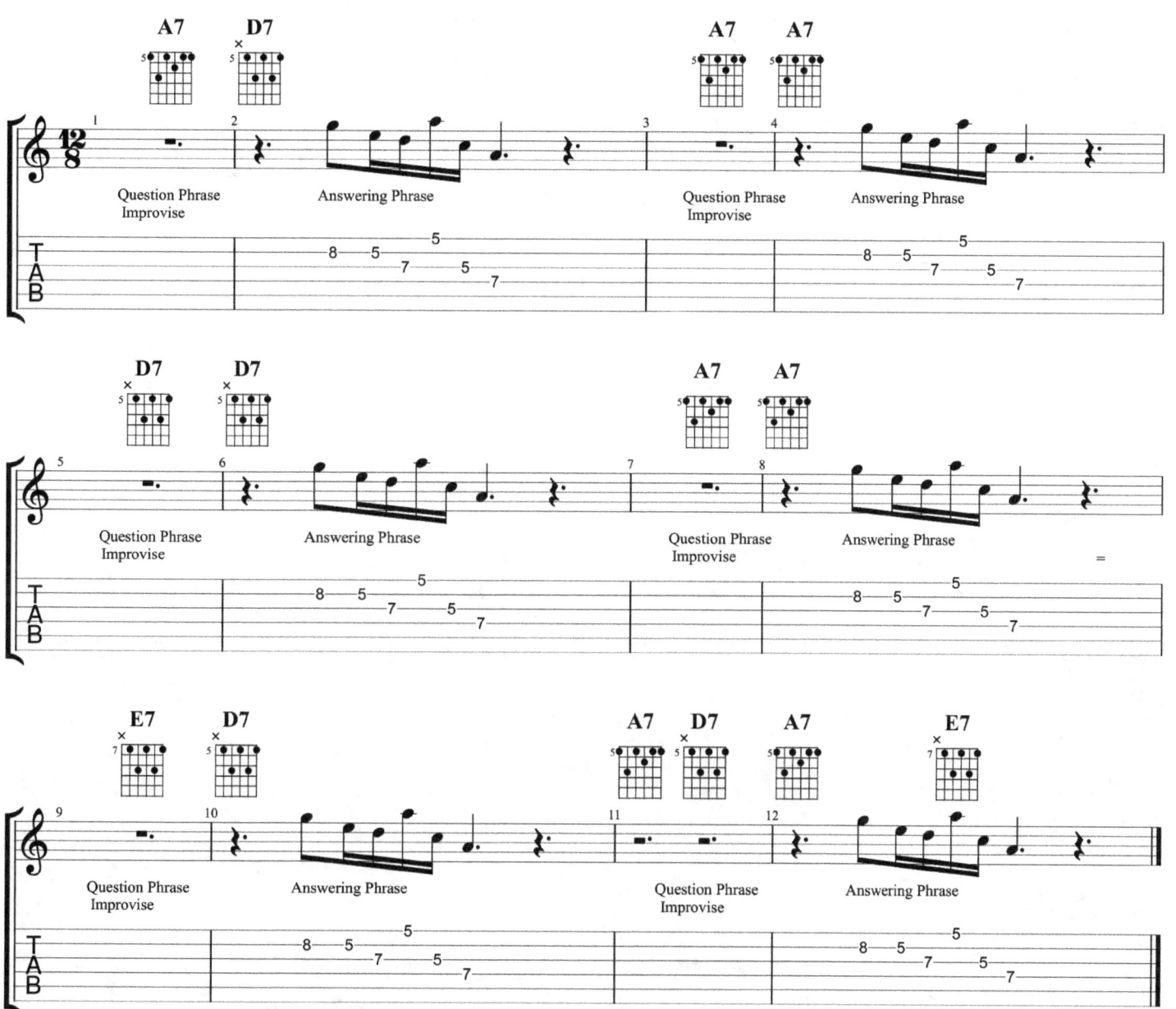

Your job is to set up the answering lick by spontaneously improvising a new question in bars one, three and five etc.

This is harder than you may think, because the answer should always be relevant and in some way musically linked to the question.

Try to keep the rhythm and placement of the answering phrase in your head just before and during your question phrase. If you're conscious of where you're going, you will find it easier to 'blend' your question and answer into one cohesive musical statement.

Don't be too strict about the *placement* of the answering phrase. Try to keep is rigid, but if you feel you should play it a bit earlier or later, go ahead.

This freedom is helpful to ease you into the exercise, but when you're more confident try to force yourself to keep the answering lick in the predefined place.

Here are just a couple of ways that I could approach the exercise.

Example 4i:

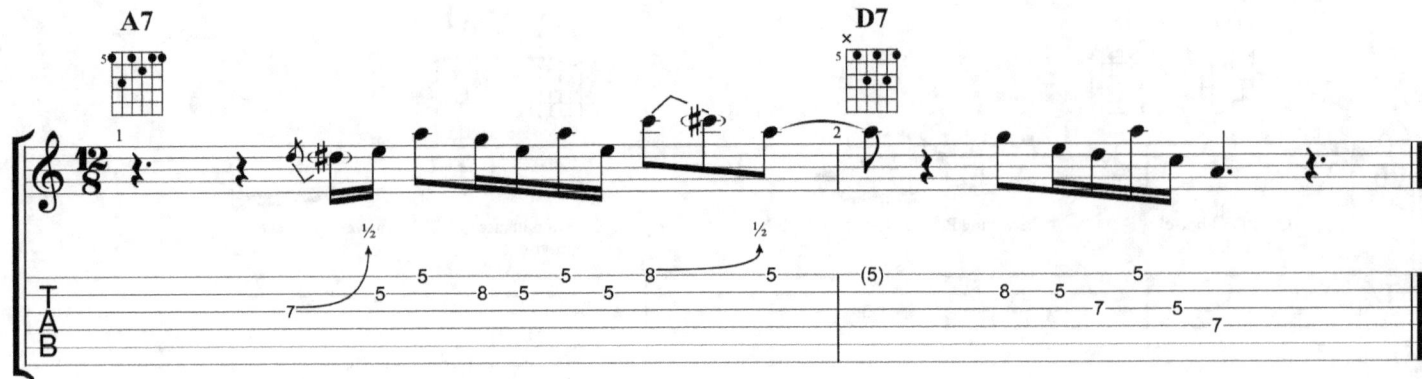

Example 4j:

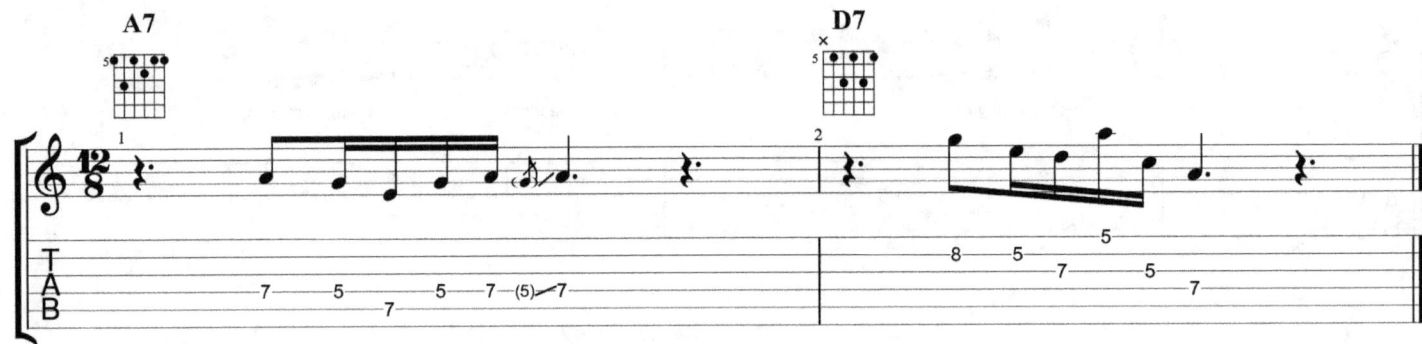

Example 4k:

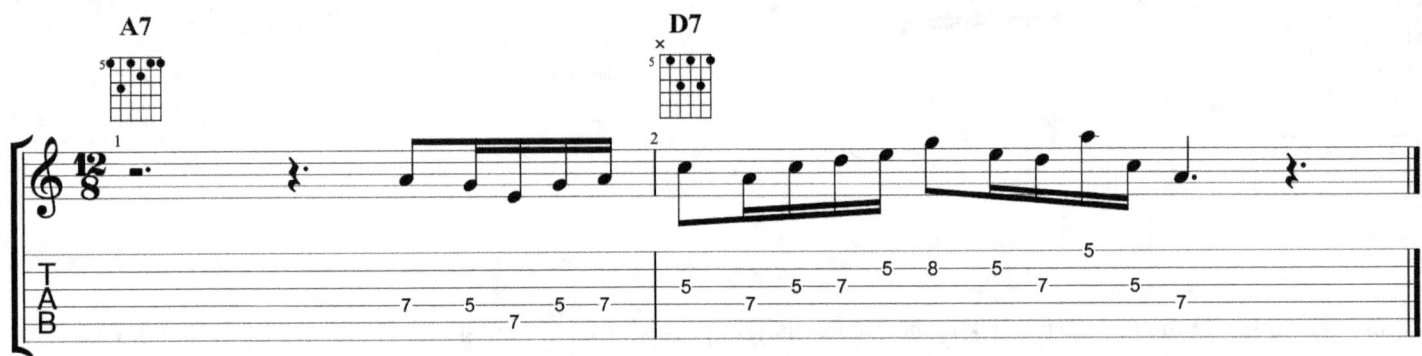

In exercise 4i, my approach was to try to create two rhythmically distinct yet symbiotic phrases that functioned as the traditional question and answer phrasing structure. Notice that my question phrase tends to ascend in pitch while the answer generally descends. This is common practice, and a good starting point on which to model your practice.

Exercise 4j is slightly different. I purposely use the rhythmic structure of my answering phrase in my question. This approach will normally develop a strong link between the question and answer licks.

Finally, in exercise 4k I take a different approach and blend the question phrase into the answer using a short rhythmic sequence. This idea is much harder to work on, but it does quickly give great benefits.

Come up with your own answering phrases and do this exercise every day. Remember, the overall goal is to mentally hear the line you will be playing *after* the one you are playing now. This type of forward thinking helps you strongly structure your solo, and take your audience on a journey by developing a melodic pathway throughout the whole solo.

Developing a Melodic Line

This exercise is one of my favourites to give students who struggle to develop a single melodic idea throughout a solo. It requires quite a lot of concentration but will quickly improve your ability to build a strong melodic thread.

The exercise sounds simple on paper, but in fact it takes a lot of discipline and patience to master.

Take a short, fixed rhythm and use it to improvise a melodic line

Play the rhythm once-per-bar for three bars, varying the melody each time

In the fourth bar, play the rhythm again, however this time freely develop the rhythm

Use the rhythm you created at the end of bar four as the set rhythm for the next three bars

Repeat

The secret to making this exercise work is to keep the rhythms short and uncomplicated. It is much easier to see this concept on paper than it is to explain in words.

Example 4l:

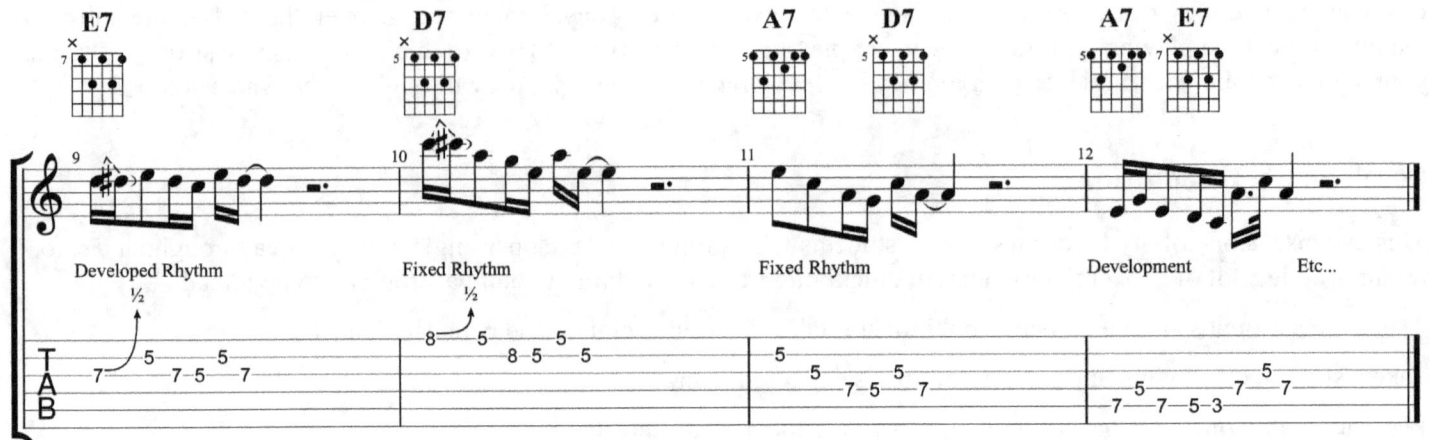

I begin with a simple phrase – just a couple of notes – and then repeat that rhythm for the first three bars. In bar four I trust my ear and allow myself to slightly develop the idea. A small variation is much better than a big one here.

The tricky bit is to remember the last couple of notes you played in bar four. Take the rhythm of the notes in bar four and play a new short phrase with that rhythm in bar five. Once you have your new, developed rhythm, stick with it and repeat the process.

Compare bar 12 to bar 1. These lines are very different, but we have arrived at the complexity in bar 12 through a natural, *organic* process.

Unfortunately, the music notation doesn't do justice to the exercise here. The rhythm in bar 9 is identical to the one in bar 8, however the bend is notated by tying two 1/16th notes together which looks a little misleading.

For a really masterful demonstration of rhythmic development, one of the best pieces of music you can listen to is the first movement of **Beethoven's Fifth Symphony in C Minor.**

While not strictly the blues, you can easily hear how he develops a four-note phrase into one of the most important pieces of music ever written. Listen to how the phrase develops rhythmically throughout the piece and changes with subtle and not-so-subtle use of orchestration and dynamics. It's the perfect lesson in creating something massive out of the smallest of rhythmic fragments.

A bluesier example of all the techniques in this chapter, including the rhythmic development ideas in this section, is **Lucille by B.B. King**.

There's an extremely strong question and answer theme running throughout the song, especially in the longer solos, but if you listen attentively you can clearly hear how he rhythmically develops his melody from one phrase to the next.

At this point people often say, "Yes, but he just feels it. He probably never even thought about it like this."

I'm sure they're right, however if we are to learn to develop as musicians, we often need to break down the unconscious skills of talented musicians into tangible, learnable chunks and work on them as exercises before they eventually become 'I'm just feeling it' to us too.

Imagine you were going to learn a magic trick from an illusionist. They would be an inadequate teacher if they just said, "It's magic!"

The previous example revolves around developing awareness as a musician. You must be in control of your playing for it to work, and you need to consciously remember the rhythm you played previously. It's a fantastic exercise to help you move away from just noodling on the guitar, and start working towards being in control of what you play.

Tonal Variation with Phrasing

Earlier, I quickly gave you some ideas about how to change your tone by varying the angle of your pick. I think this is one of the most criminally overlooked areas of guitar playing and not enough attention is given to the thousands of subtle variations you can give to a phrase just by simply using your pick.

"If you go to see a professional orchestra, it is possible that the lead violinist is playing a £1,200,000 Stradivarius. The bow, just the stick and horse hair they are using can cost upwards of £60,000.

As guitarists, we use a $0.50 piece of plastic.

Virtually every single tone you create on the guitar starts with the pick, so it follows that we have a lot of work to do to get as much good tone out of our plectrum as possible."

(from *Complete Technique for Modern Guitar*)

Here's a simple demonstration. Compare these two identical lines. The first is played with a pick held lightly at a normal angle; the second is played *hard and aggressively* with the pick angled almost at 90 degrees to the strings.

They are both played with the pick located between the neck and the middle pickup and both examples are played with the same amp settings and pickup selection. There is a dramatic difference between the two lines with a couple of noticeable things happening.

Example 4m:

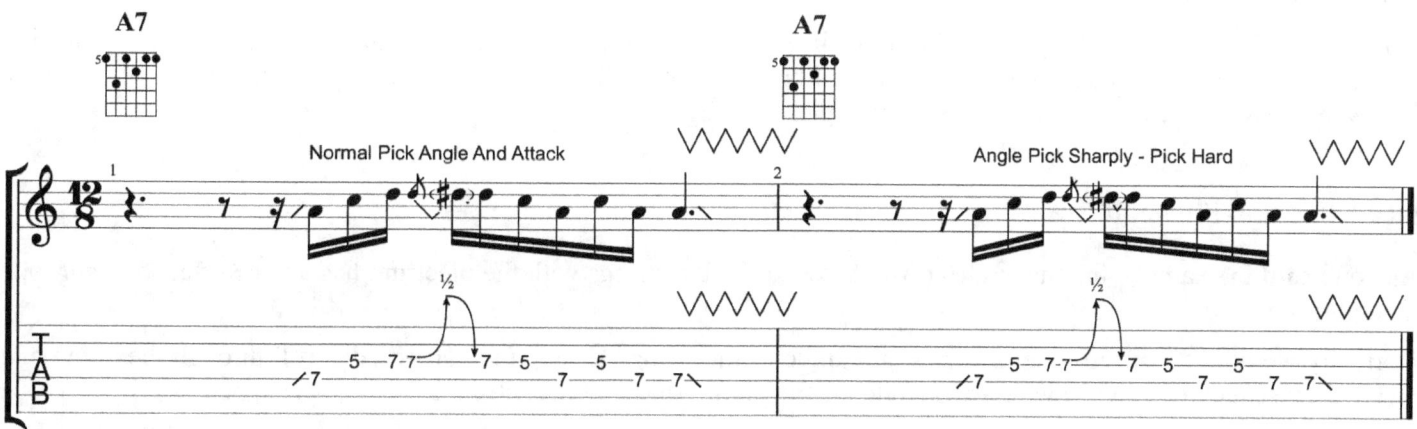

Forget the pick angle for a second. When you pick harder, you send more of the guitar signal to the amp. This results in being able to use less gain to achieve an overdriven tone. This is how you create that clean, slightly-broken-up sound that's perfect for blues.

I would never say pick hard *all* the time, but in general I find that most guitarists don't practise picking hard. So much is written about finding a consistent, even picking technique that colour and tonal possibilities are often forgotten.

Try picking extremely hard in a few practise sessions. Really overdo it. You might find that you're not able to play some of the licks that you thought you knew. If this is the case, relearn them with much harder picking. By just relearning a few of your licks in this way you will find it much easier to access all the tonal colours and possibilities that can be achieved by playing harder.

Here is a simple exercise to help you with your picking attack. Begin by playing softly and see how many different volumes you can find between soft and loud.

Example 4n:

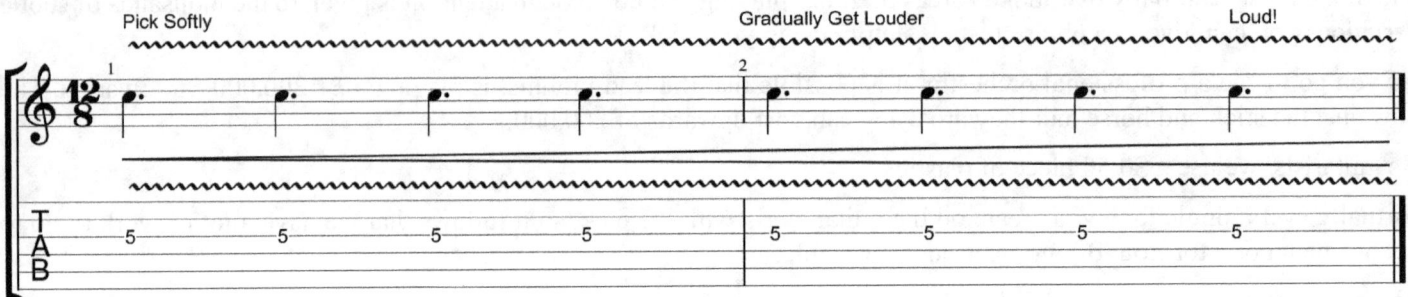

If you use a decent amplifier, then you should be able to set it so that when you play softly your sound is clean, but when you increase the power of your attack it starts to break up and distort.

As I'm sure you can imagine, the tonal possibilities are immense.

Another thing you will find is that when playing with different picking dynamics you will phrase your lines differently. You will alter rhythms and stumble across new ways to phrase your lines.

Play a few licks with the picking approach shown in example 4n. Gradually pick harder throughout the lick. Try picking hard to begin with and gradually get softer. You could play the whole lick quietly and accentuate a couple of notes, or play loudly and leave some holes in the lick when you pick very lightly.

Pick Angle and Phrasing

As you heard in example 4m, the angle at which you strike the strings with the plectrum has a huge effect on your tone (and phrasing) too.

Normally we hold the plectrum at a very slight angle to the strings to help the curved edge roll through the string and create a consistent tone. When we start to angle the pick more sharply to the string a few things happen.

The tone of the guitar changes dramatically, but it becomes much harder to physically move the plectrum through the strings to create a note.

You might find that because it is more difficult to push the pick through the strings, the note you create is very slightly delayed from when you were expecting to hear it.

In essence, you have started to play slightly behind the beat. It's not necessarily the most controlled way to practise the important skill of behind-the-beat playing, but it can be a great way to access this difficult rhythmic technique easily.

Compare these two lines. Not only does the tone change considerably, the notes in the second line fall very slightly behind the beat.

Example 4o:

Behind-the-beat playing is an extremely desirable skill, and this method of angling the pick is a great way to fake it until you make it. This is not the way to build a consistent, controllable behind-the-beat feel, but if you change the angle of your pick during a melodic line you will create some interesting phrasing variations.

Practise changing your pick angle throughout a guitar lick that you know extremely well. Listen to the way the following lick pushes and pulls against the beat as I vary my pick angle.

Example 4p:

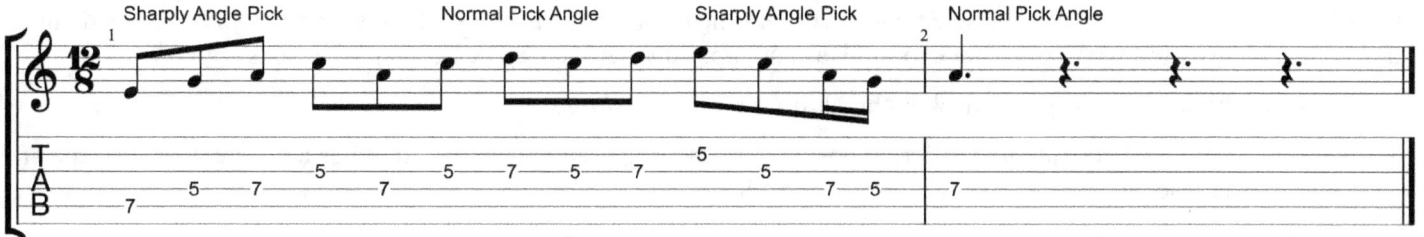

An equally effective way to alter your tone is to alter where you pick the guitar. Pick near the bridge, near the neck or anywhere in-between.

Play the above lick with different pick placement. Playing near the bridge will give you a thin, harsh tone which will soften off as you move towards the neck. Try varying your pick position from forward to back as you play.

We can combine all three techniques in this section:

Play Hard / Play Soft

Normal Pick Angle / Sharp Pick Angle

Pick Near the Bridge / Pick Near the Neck

This means that the right hand can be constantly evolving – fluidly changing between any of the permutations. This variance in attack creates a vocal, three dimensional aspect to our sound and continually changes the amplifier's reaction to our playing.

Suddenly our playing becomes more than just notes; there is a new human dynamic, full of nuance and personality. There are subtle textural differences in each note and our playing becomes personal and unique.

Time spent working on varying your picking approach will set you head and shoulders above the crowd.

Chapter 5: Range and Other Positions on the Neck

So far, we have concentrated on a small range of notes in just one area of the guitar. I can already imagine the negative reviews coming in on Amazon![2] However, as you know, by limiting the number of notes we play, we can focus deeply on the *hows* and the *whens* of our phrasing and not get bogged down in note choice.

In this chapter, we will look at how to expand our phrasing ideas all over the fretboard.

The great news is that if you have worked hard at the concepts in this book, it is easy to apply these techniques to other areas of the neck. In fact, if you have spent considerable time on these ideas you will have started to *internalise* them on a deep musical level and won't even have to think about applying them to new scale shapes or licks anymore.

Most guitarists think about the guitar neck by breaking it up into *positions*.

It is common to split the neck into five different positions of the same scale. Each position has a different scale shape and we normally call these 'shape one', 'shape two', 'shape three', etc.

The scale shape we have been using so far is A Minor Pentatonic shape one:

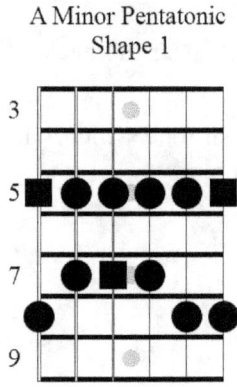

We will now explore the four other shapes of the A Minor Pentatonic scale, look at some useful vocabulary for each one, discuss their advantages and disadvantages and finally look at how we can join them up to form runs that ascend and descend the entire neck.

---

2. Yep! As I edit this book for the second edition, there's already one person who didn't read this far and wrote a bad review on Amazon.

A Minor Pentatonic Shape Two

Shape two is one of the most commonly used soloing positions. You may have heard the phrase, "The B.B. box". This refers to the notes on the top two or three strings of shape two. It is certainly true that B.B. King used this position frequently in his playing and a lot of blues phrases and vocabulary can be found there.

Example 5a:

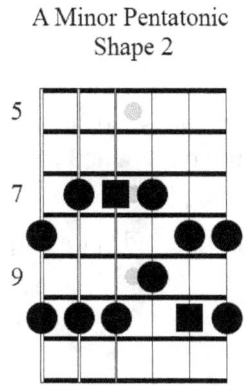

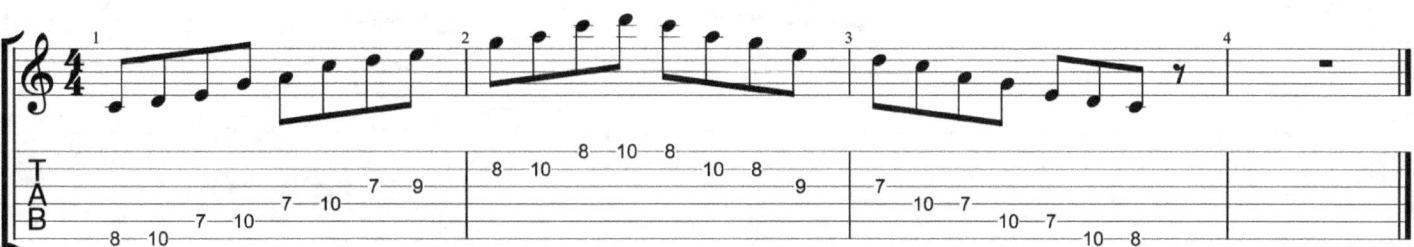

In this kind of fretboard positional system, shape one interlocks with shape two, which in turn interlocks with shape three, etc. You can see this by comparing the higher notes on each string in shape one with the lower notes on each string in shape two. They fit together like a jigsaw.

Also, despite having a completely different scale shape, most of the note pitches in shape two are identical to those in shape one. In fact, shape two only extends the range of the Minor Pentatonic scale by one tone on the top string. In other words, the highest note in A Minor Pentatonic shape one is a C (8th fret) and the shape two is a D (10th fret). It's good to remember this when we get obsessed with learning a scale all over the fretboard.

If we're playing mostly the same notes, and extending the range of the scale by just one tone, you may be asking, what's the point is in learning all these new shapes?

The answer is that different fingering patterns lend themselves more easily to different licks, phrases and vocabulary.

When playing different shapes of the Minor Pentatonic scale, the intervals (root, b3, 4, 5, and b7) are in different physical locations on the neck. This means it is easier to bend or manipulate intervals that you may not have had access to in other shapes.

Guitar tone is also a consideration. The same pitch played low down on the 3rd will sound very different high up on the 4th string. For example, listen to the tone of a C note played on the 3rd string compared to the tone of the same C played on the 4th string.

Example 5b:

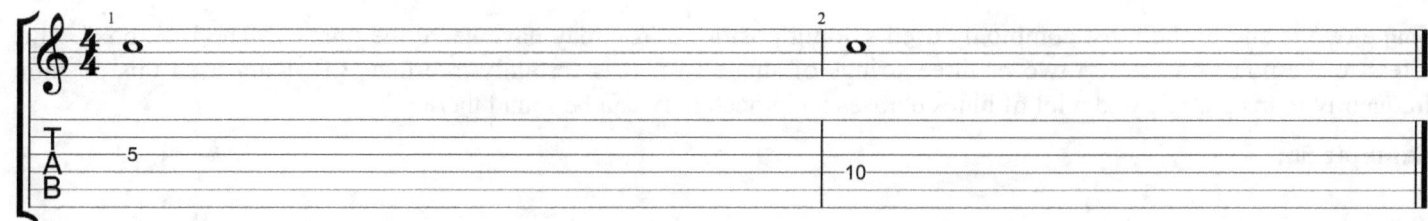

I'm sure you can hear the difference in tone here, however subtle it may be. This is one of the reasons we use different shapes – an identical phrase will take on a different tone and phrasing when we use a different fingering pattern and play it on different strings.

It is these kinds of subtleties that set us apart as individual players. When combined with the rhythm and phrasing techniques in the previous chapters they really help to create unique and personal soloing.

Here are some short, typical phrases that often occur in shape two of the Minor Pentatonic scale.

Example 5c:

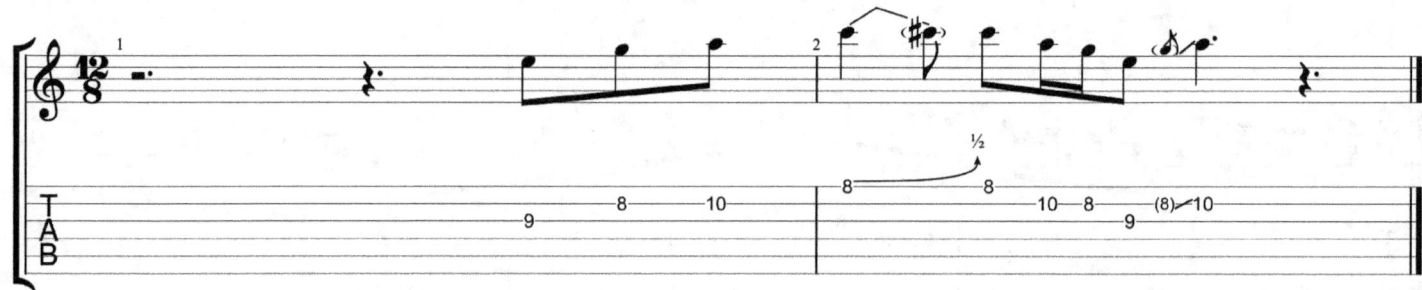

Example 5d:

Example 5e:

Example 5e uses *the Blues Scale*. This scale is covered in more detail in *The Complete Guide to Playing Blues Guitar Part Three: Beyond Pentatonics*.

Pick some of your favourite phrasing ideas from earlier in the book and spend as much time as you can discovering your own ideas in this new position.

Finally, if you want to get into using these shapes as quickly as possible, *transcribe* (steal!) ideas from your favourite players. If you use the phrasing techniques from this book, no one will ever know where they came from!

I mentioned earlier that shape one and shape two interlock. It is common to change position between them using slides. Here are a few ways to ascend from shape one into shape two.

Example 5f (a):

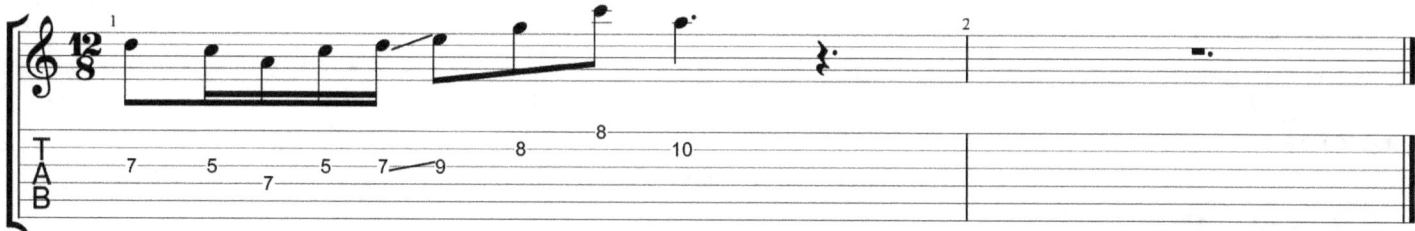

Example 5f (b):

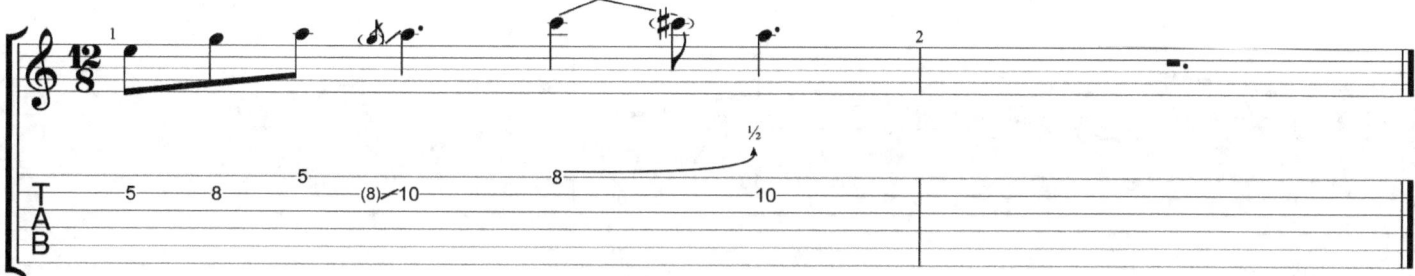

Example 5f (c):

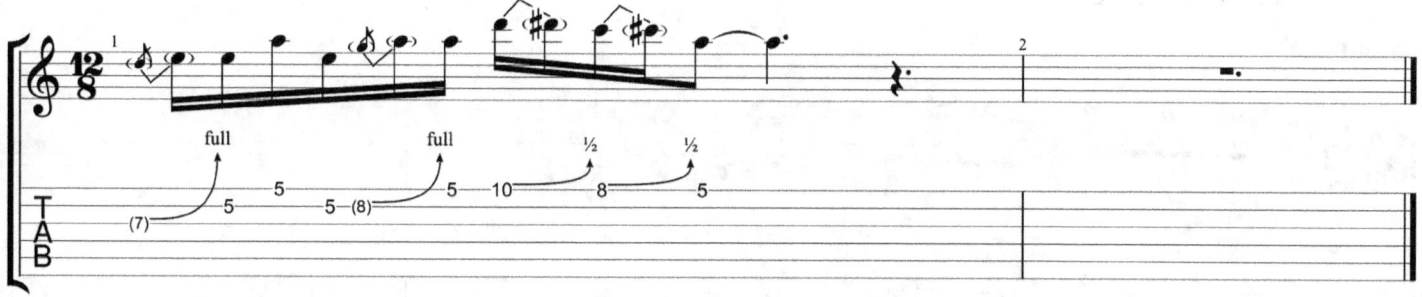

These are just a few ideas to get you going. See how many different melodic lines you can find while moving between shapes.

Practise these shapes in other keys to get used to playing them in different areas on the guitar neck. Find some slow blues backing tracks and practise moving between shape one and two in different keys.

A Minor Pentatonic Shape Three

Shape three is one of my favourite Pentatonic shapes to explore. I enjoy experimenting with the simple pattern on the bottom three strings and exploring the opportunities for bending notes on the top three strings.

Shape three is slightly less common to use when soloing but don't let that put you off. The fingering pattern can help us access some wonderful and unique phrasing opportunities.

Example 5g:

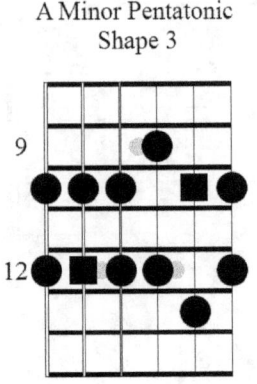

Here are a few sample licks to help you explore the scale. Work to create your own shape three licks and vocabulary by using the concepts in this book.

Example 5h:

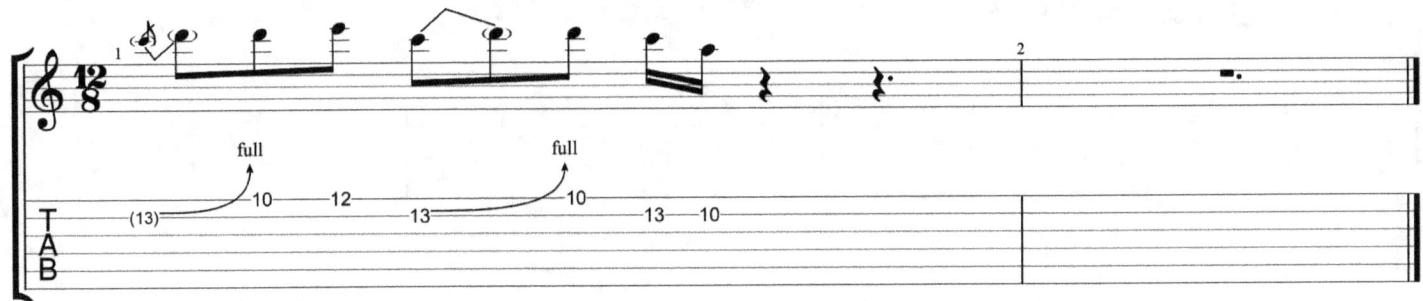

Example 5i:

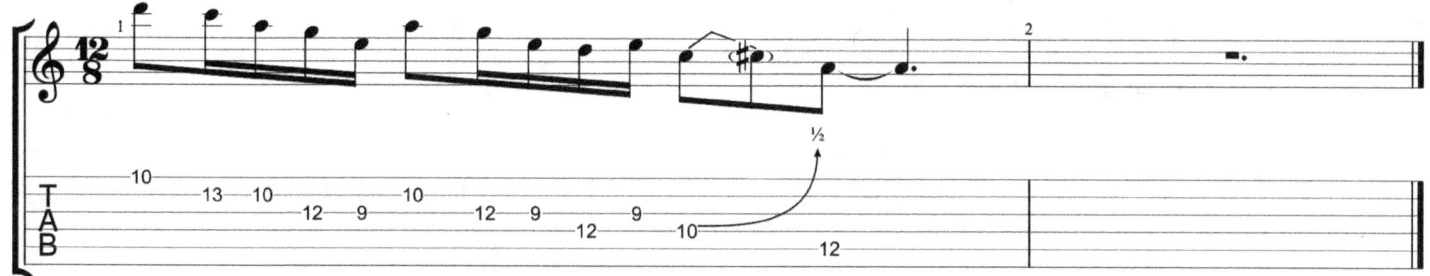

Example 5j:

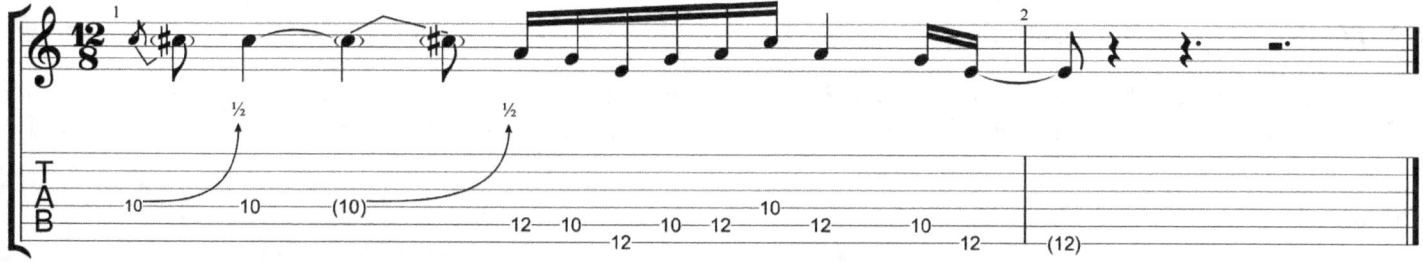

Try the following ideas to help you move seamlessly from position two into position three:

Example 5k (a):

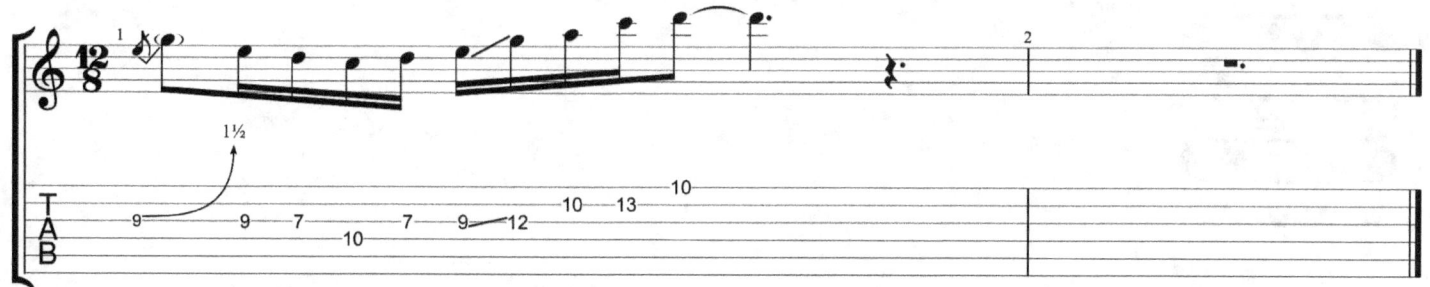

Example 5k (b):

(Blues Scale)

Example 5k (c):

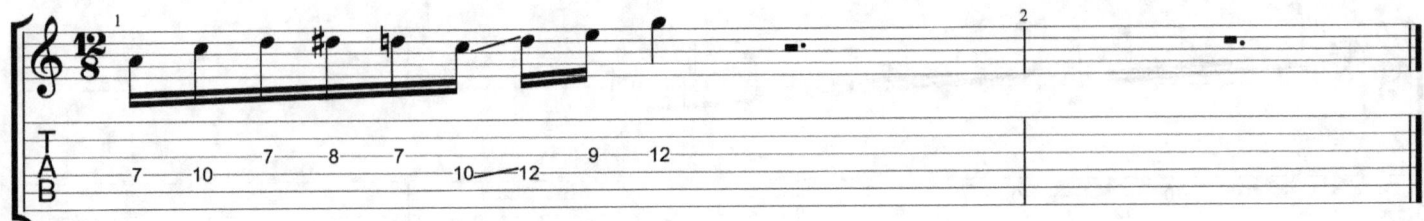

(Blues Scale)

Try linking up some lines that move from shape one via shape two into shape three.

A Minor Pentatonic Shape Four

Shape four is a frequently used position of the Minor Pentatonic scale. It shares many features with shape one but the different pattern caused by the tuning idiosyncrasies of the guitar helps us to access some new sounds. *Unison bends* are common here.

Example 5l:

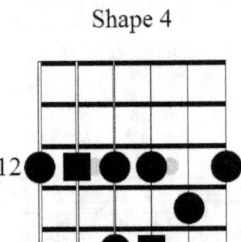

A Minor Pentatonic
Shape 4

Here are some useful licks based around shape four.

Example 5m:

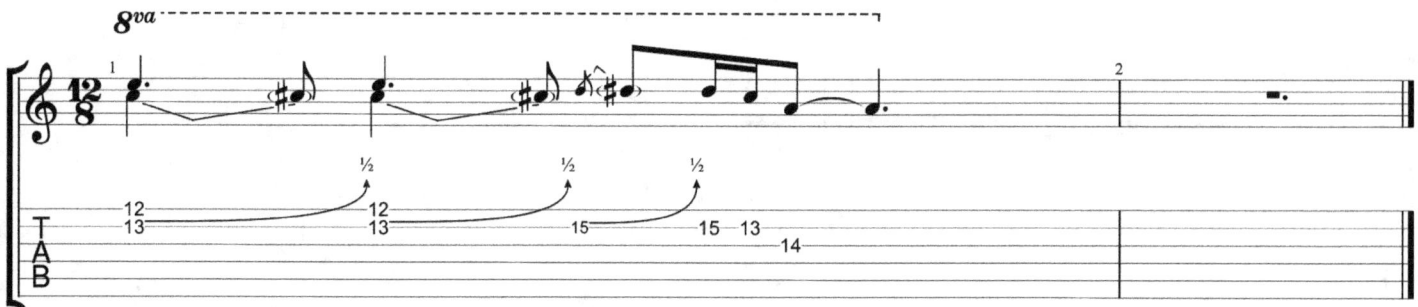

Example 5n:

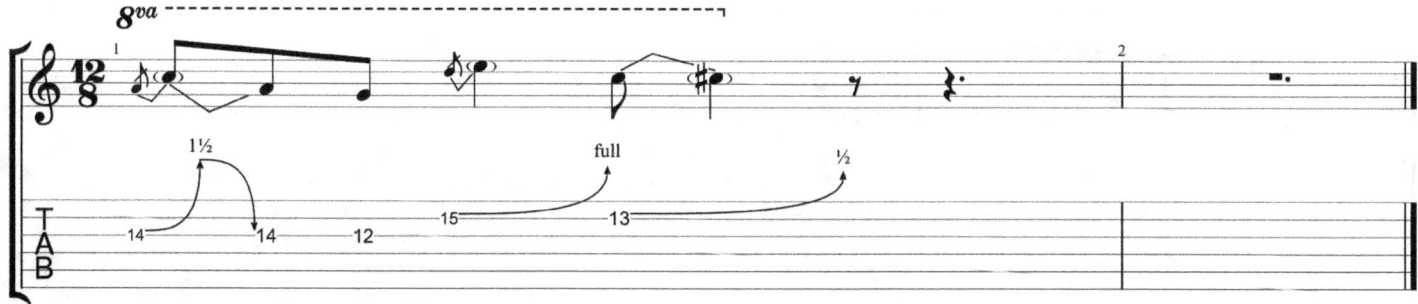

Example 5o:

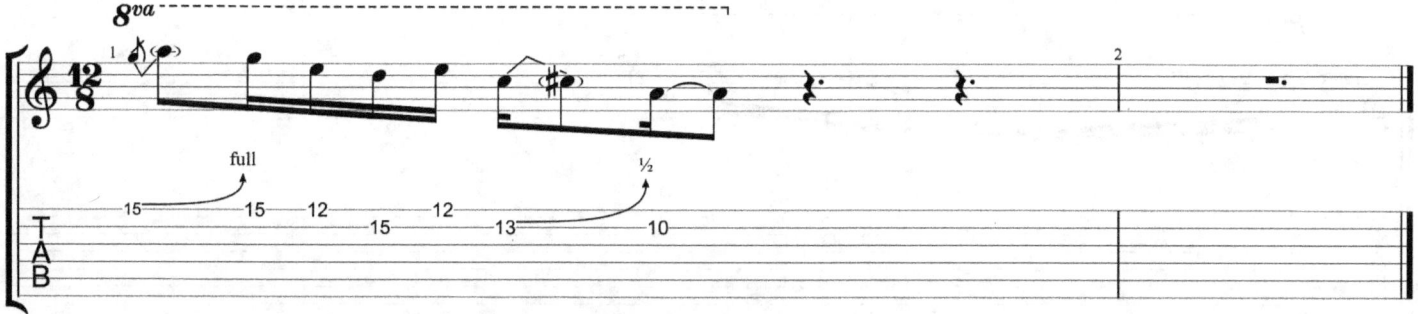

When we use shape four in the key of A, we start to reach the upper range of the guitar. Try this shape in different positions on the fretboard to hear how these licks sound in different keys.

Here are some ways to position shift from shape three into shape four using slides.

Example 5p (a):

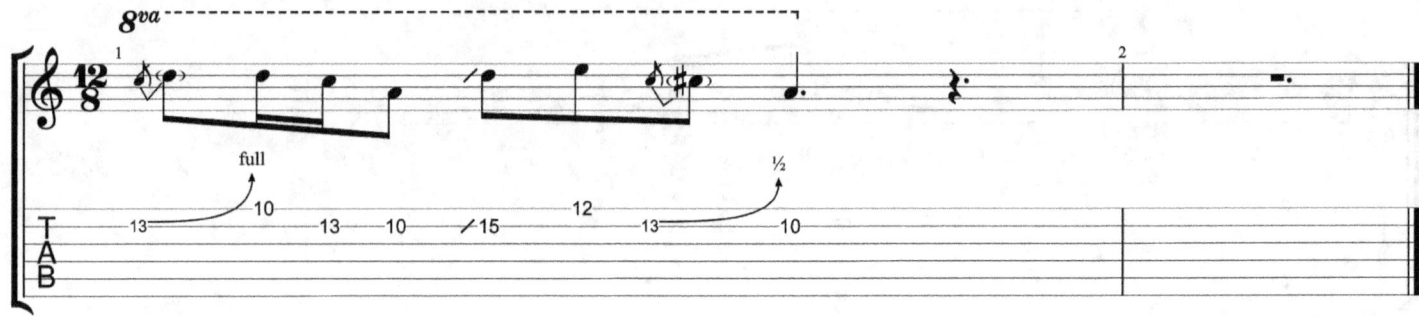

Example 5p (b):

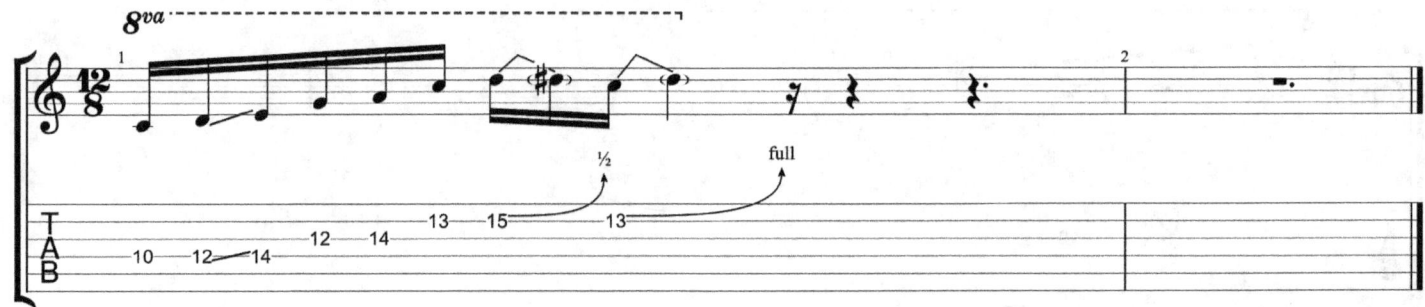

Example 5p (c):

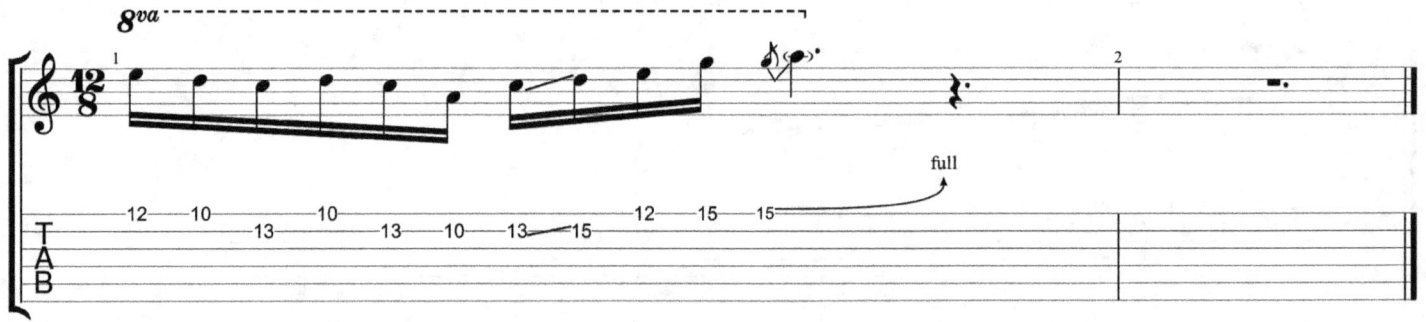

Shape four is my favourite scale shape to use when soloing. There is a lot of milage to be had, so try using it exclusively for a week. You'll be amazed how many blues licks it contains.

A Minor Pentatonic Shape Five

Shape five is an interesting position. In my opinion it can be a little harder to use because the best notes to bend tend to fall on weak fingers. On the flip side, there are good opportunities for some big tone-and-a-half bends so with a little perseverance you should be able to get some useful results. One common approach is to slide down into shape five *from* shape one to add some bass notes.

As we are reaching the top of the guitar now I have written the scale out in both the lower and higher octaves. Learn to use the scale in both positions and transpose it to other keys.

Example 5q (a):

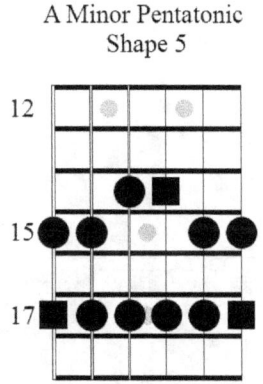

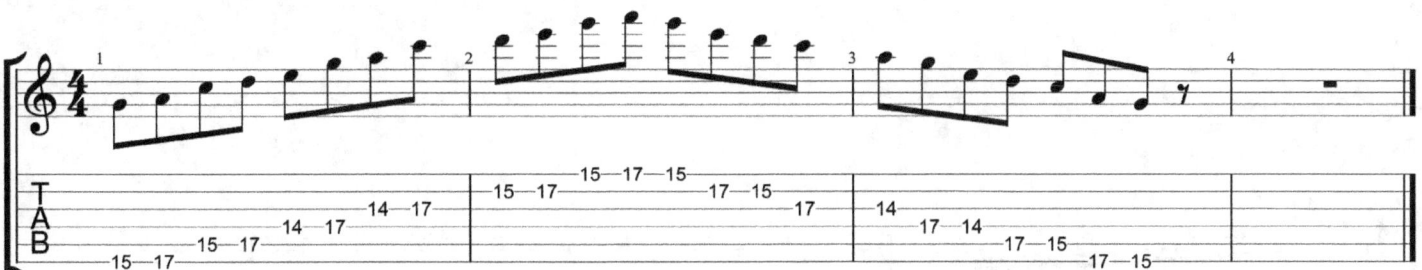

Example 5q (b):

Here are a few 'shortcut' licks to help you find some useful applications of this scale shape.

Example 5r:

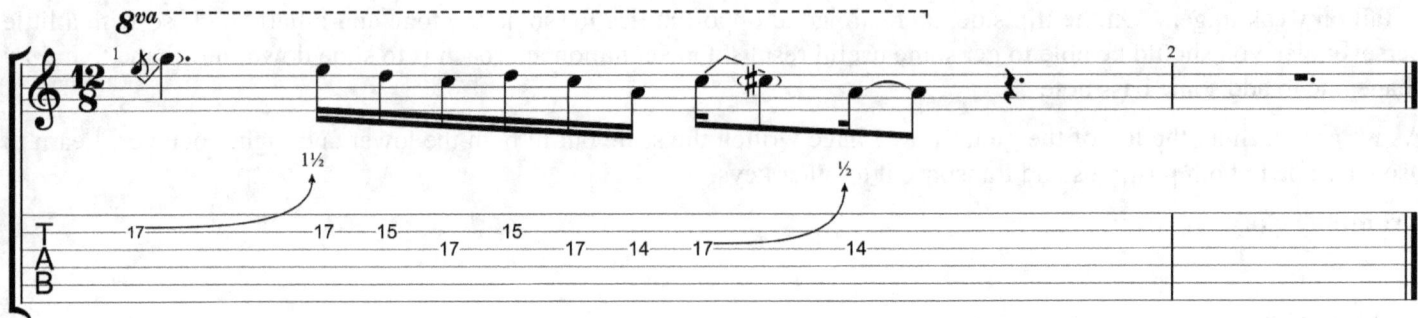

Example 5s:

Example 5t:

The following licks show a few methods of moving from shape four into shape five:

Example 5u (a):

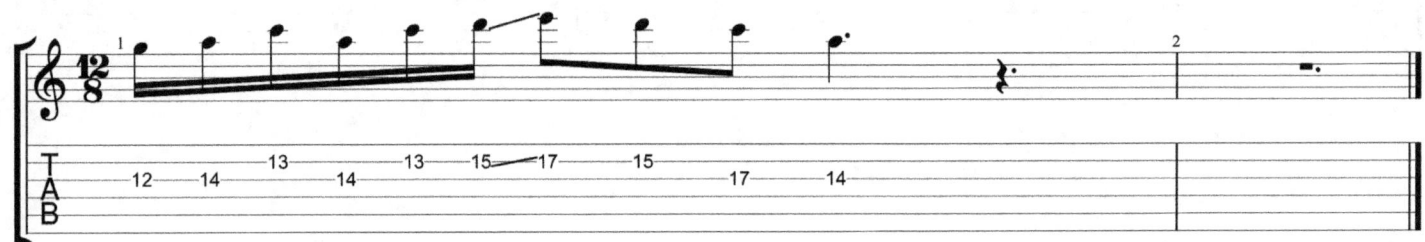

Example 5u (b):

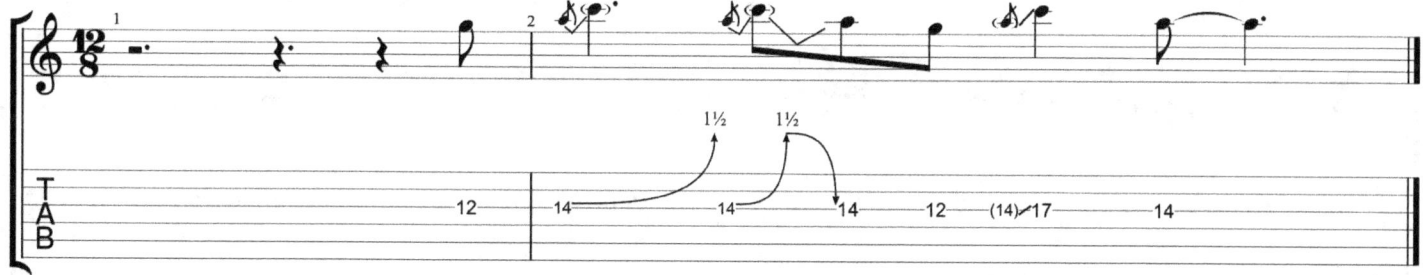

Example 5u (c):

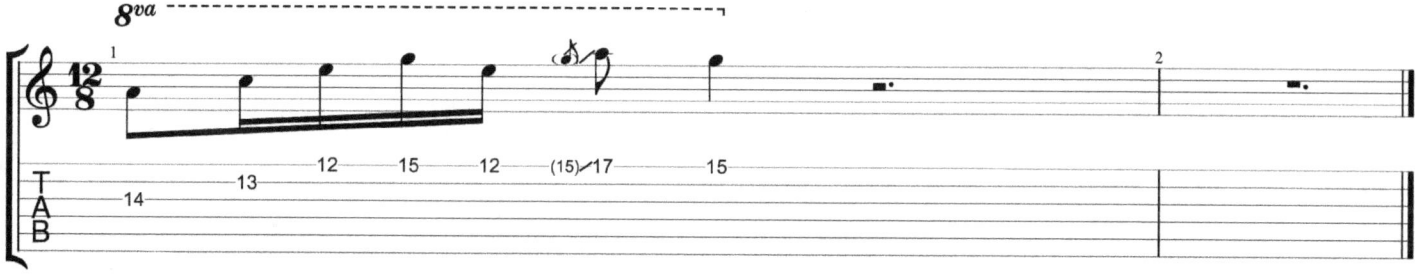

Linking Minor Pentatonic Shapes

We will now look at some ideas to link all the Pentatonic shapes together, from the bottom of the neck to the top. These are just a few possibilities, so spend some time seeing how many ways you can find to move between them all.

Example 5v:

Example 5w:

Example 5x:

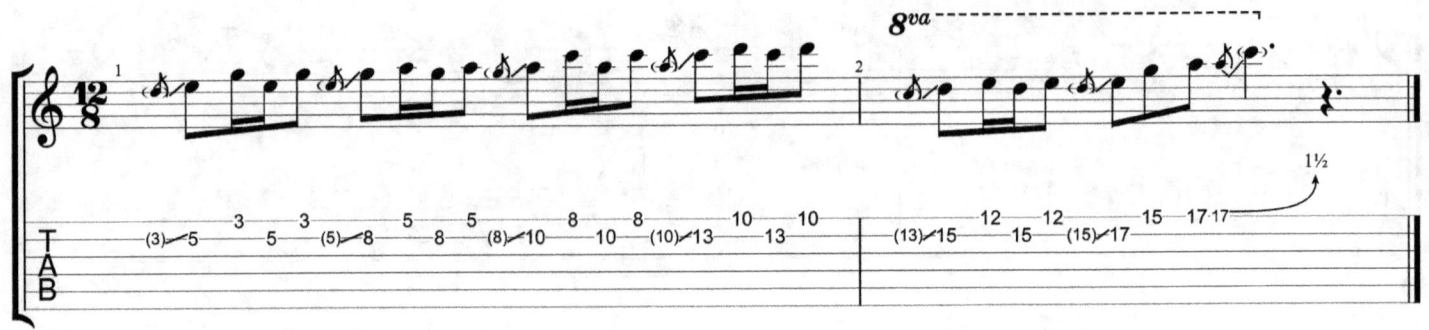

Conclusions

This deliberately set out *not* to be a lick book. Even though there are hundreds of examples of blues vocabulary on these pages, they are all formed by experimenting with specific rhythmic, melodic and phrasing techniques.

I have tried to teach you the skills you need to develop to *transcend* the need for licks, so that when you solo you are able to play the lines that you conceptualise and *feel* inside your head. This kind of control is what people have when 'the music flows through them'… there is no barrier between the music in their minds and what they can play on their instrument.

This level of freedom on your instrument is difficult to attain, but it's one of the most worthwhile pursuits in music. To have a melody appear in your head and to instantly play it as you hear it is an incredible feeling.

Learning this freedom is a circular process. The more you study rhythm and phrasing (and of course scale choice and hitting chord changes, which will all be covered in book three), the more your ears will awaken to thousands of new melodic possibilities. In most languages, you can't add a word to your own vocabulary unless you have heard or read it somewhere before. Our advantage is that focused practise of rhythm, phrasing and creativity will help you to invent your own words.

I have given you the tools to create your own dialect within the established language of the blues. If you work on just one concept for long enough you will always discover a new and personal way to play it. When you have studied three or four concepts they will naturally combine to generate exponential possibilities.

I'm not discounting learning licks. To improve our written language and vocabulary we read the works of other authors and the same applies in music. The quickest way to sound like Jimi Hendrix is to transcribe and learn Jimi Hendrix's music. All I'm saying is that if we choose to learn his ideas, we should try to make them our own through personal interpretation and phrasing.

I hope that you have enjoyed this book and see it as a fresh approach to melodic soloing. The ideas contained here don't just apply to the blues – they are applicable to any form of music. Please take them and run with them.

Joseph

www.fundamental-changes.com

If you enjoyed this book, please review it on Amazon.

Appendix A – Bending in Tune

The following exercises are all taken from my book *Complete Technique for Modern Guitar*.

Bending

Bending notes with perfect intonation is one skill that really sets the professionals apart from amateurs. Other than good rhythm, perfect intonation is the highest priority I give my students when they start playing guitar solos, because nothing ruins a solo more than an out-of-tune bend.

It is vital to learn to bend accurately with each finger, and your 2nd, 3rd and 4th fingers should be capable of executing up to a *one-and-a-half tone* bend.

To bend a note on the guitar you should always support the bending finger with any spare fingers below it. In other words, if you are bending a note on the 3rd string, 7th fret with your 3rd finger, your 2nd finger (if not also your 1st) should also be on the string to give strength and control.

The idea behind all these bending exercises is to play a reference note, descend the string a few frets and then bend perfectly back up to the reference. Treat this as an aural exercise; you are listening for the bent note to sound exactly like the reference pitch.

Try the following three exercises using different fingers on each bend. Repeat each line four times. The first time bend with your 1st finger, then your 2nd etc. When you are on line three, don't worry about bending with your 1st finger.

Begin the exercises by bending very slowly to pitch. This will give you time to *hear* if you are in tune. It also develops control and strength in the fretting hand fingers. Then, gradually speed up the rate at which you bend to the target note. If you can hit it perfectly with an immediate, fast bend you know you've got it right.

Example 6a:

Example 6b:

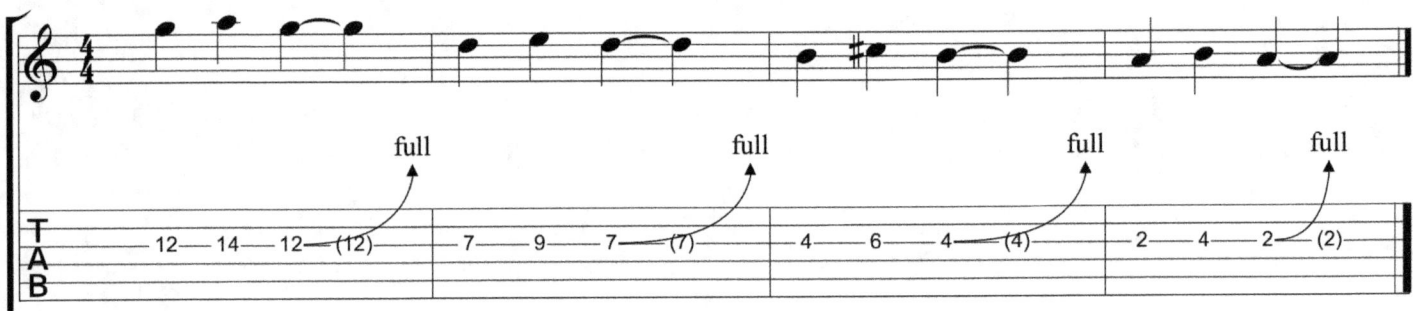

Example 6c:

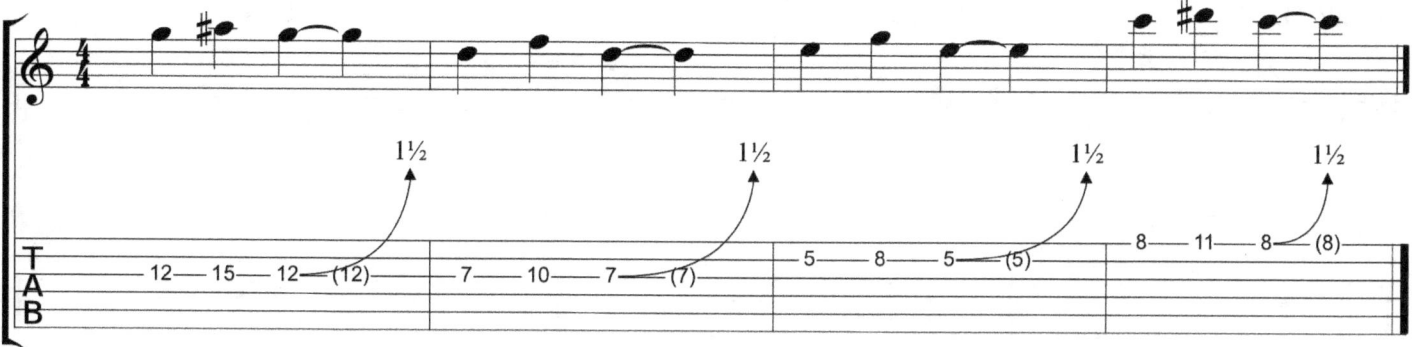

Pre-bends

A pre-bend is essentially a bend in reverse. You bend the note to the desired pitch before picking it and releasing the bend. Pre-bends are notated like this:

Example 6d:

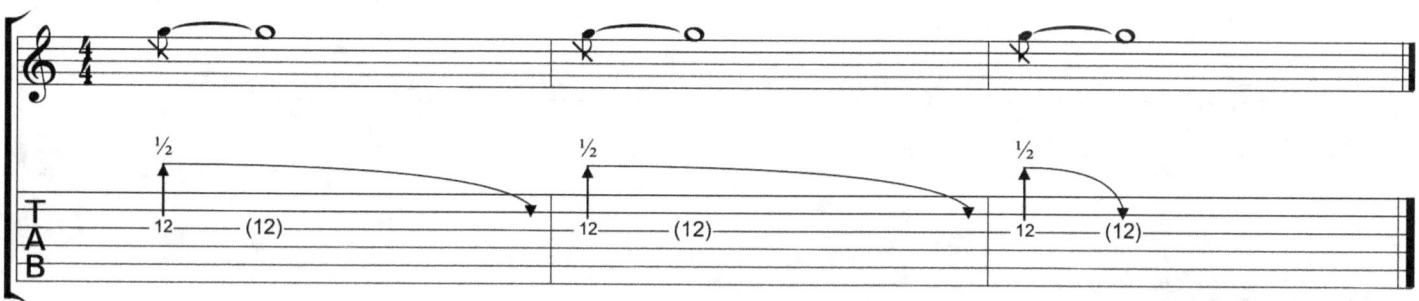

To practise this expressive technique, go back through exercises 6a – c and modify them to include pre-bends in the following way. Do this with all fingers over all bend distances.

Example 6e:

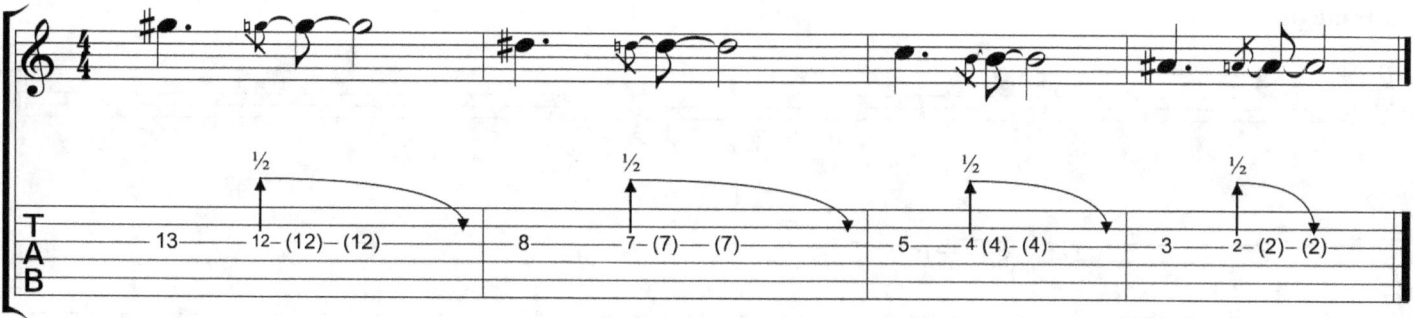

Unison Bends

Unison bends are when you play two notes together on adjacent strings. The higher note is not bent, while the lower note is bent to sound identical to the higher one. Jimi Hendrix and Jimmy Page both made great use of this technique.

These bends are quite difficult to execute on a Floyd Rose tremolo and will always be slightly out of tune due to the nature of the mechanism, but with a bit of vibrato, intonation errors can be covered slightly.

A unison bend is notated in this way:

Example 6f:

Example 6g:

Double-Stop Bends

A double-stop is simply playing two notes at the same time. A double-stop bend is when you bend both notes. It is a common technique in blues and rock guitar playing.

To execute a double-stop bend, lay your finger flat across both notes with your fingernail pointing towards you. To bend the notes, rotate your wrist in the same manner as vibrato, but only do it once, slowly as you pick both strings.

Example 6h:

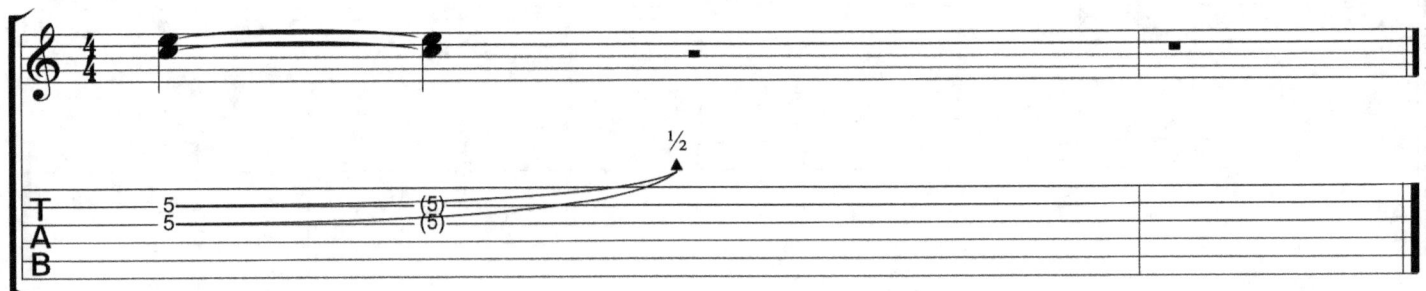

Try these all over the neck.

Appendix B – Vibrato

Vibrato is one of the most important expressive effects. It gives your phrases a vocal quality and makes your music sing. There are many types, but here we will focus on just two: *axial* and *radial*.

Axial vibrato is when you quickly and repeatedly pull the string slightly sharp, *parallel* to the guitar string.

Radial vibrato is more like string bending; your wrist moves in a direction perpendicular to the guitar string, using a finger as a pivot on the underside of the neck. This is more difficult, but it does give beautiful results.

Axial Vibrato

To perform axial vibrato, press firmly on a fretted note and, making sure your wrist is soft, quickly move your wrist backwards and forwards parallel to the neck of the guitar. Often, your thumb will momentarily release from the back of the neck to help with the speed of the wrist movement. This movement, combined with the pressure you place with your fingertip, repeatedly pulls the string slightly sharp before releasing.

Axial vibrato is an easy technique to give life and dynamics to your music whenever there is a longer, sustained note. It is a subtle effect, and it is important to practise it with every finger of the fretting hand. It is much harder to produce good vibrato with the 4th finger than the 1st.

Here is an exercise to develop good axial vibrato:

Example 6i:

Try removing your thumb from the back of the guitar neck to allow your wrist to move quickly and evenly backwards and forwards. This technique isn't right for everyone, but removing the thumb works for a lot of players.

Practise moving from slow to fast and back to slow vibrato for added effect. Try the above example in different areas of the guitar neck and on different strings. Each feels different and requires different types of control.

Add this vibrato to any licks you know. Take into account the tempo and groove of the song; you might want to sync your vibrato to 1/8th, 1/16th or 1/32 notes.

Radial Vibrato

Radial vibrato is a more difficult technique and creates *much* wider vibrato which can often be up to a tone wide. Some guitarists go as far as to add vibrato which is a tone and a half wide when playing hard rock and fusion.

With radial vibrato we must greatly alter the position of the hand on the guitar neck so that we can *bend* the desired note up and down quickly. This involves using the *outside* part of the finger on the string, (so that your fingernail points straight down the neck towards you), and using the first finger as a lever or *pivot* against the underside of the neck to aid quick, repeated bends.

If you imagine your wrist turning a door knob, or the Queen of England waving, you will get the idea.

Radial vibrato is an individual technique which tends to be unique to each guitarist, however I will describe the method by which I get the best results. You may want to alter the following steps which apply to vibrato on the *1st* finger as you see fit. The ultimate goal is to achieve the ability to execute *tone wide* vibrato with *each* finger of the fretting hand.

1. Play and hold the desired note. Try playing the 7th fret on the 3rd string with your 1st finger.
2. Roll your wrist *away* from you, so instead of playing the note with the tip of the 1st finger you are playing on its side. Pushing your elbow out away from you will help with this.
3. The nail of your first finger should now be pointing straight down the string towards you.
4. Push your 1st finger up, into the underside of the neck. It should connect with the neck just below the knuckle closest to your palm.
5. Let your thumb creep over the top of the neck and relax your wrist, so your unused fingers fall and fan out slightly.
6. Using your already-placed 1st finger as a pivot, turn your wrist *away* from you to bend the string down towards the floor, pulling it slightly sharp.
7. Relax the pressure in your wrist and hand to let the string release back to its starting position.
8. Repeat this as many times as you can.

At first you won't move the string far and it may become sore on the side of your finger quite quickly. When this happens take a break.

As you get stronger and your skin becomes tougher, you will be able to move the string further and more quickly. The key to all this is to always use the *side* of the finger, and always have a pivoting finger under the neck.

I like to build redundancy into my playing, so I spend time practising bending the string much further than I would ever realistically use. If you can work your way up to a tone-and-a-half vibrato then you're doing well. In my playing, I normally aim for a semi-tone.

The following examples will help you develop vibrato strength, depth and speed on all fingers.

Example 6j:

Example 6k:

Example 6l:

Example 6m:

It is difficult and unusual to place the 4th finger on its side in the same manner as the other fingers. You should still roll it slightly, but use your other fingers placed on the string behind to add strength and support.

Vibrato is a difficult technique that may take longer to develop than the other skills in this book. Try to spend five minutes every day working on your depth, speed and coordination with each finger. Try the ideas in this section over different string groupings, and in different positions on the guitar. Vibrato is much more difficult towards the lower frets.

165

Introduction

I originally intended for this series to be just two books, the first focusing on blues guitar rhythm and the second focusing on soloing. I'm extremely proud of both books, however there were some things that I didn't have room to cover in enough detail:

1. Different scales and approaches you can use for soloing
2. How to articulate or target chord changes in your solos to give depth, interest and emotion to your melodies

Scale Choice

The soloing concepts in Book Two were all about rhythm and phrasing. First and foremost, I believe that rhythm and feel are much more important in authentic blues soloing than scale choice. This is because even if we know every possible scale that could be used, they won't sound good if played with poor rhythm, phrasing and feel.

However, once we can play solos with great feel, then a detailed knowledge of scale choice options and their unique colours is essential if we are to be truly expressive.

There are many different scales that can be used over a 12-bar blues. Some can be used over the whole progression and some sound better when played over just one or two chords.

We will study the most common scales in turn and learn their theory and application, with many useful licks given for each one. The main thing to discover is the sound of the scales. Each one brings different colours and inflection to our music, and subtly alters the mood of our solos.

We end up with a wide variety of soloing possibilities, so to help internalise and organise this information I have included a set of soloing schemes suggesting useful scale applications and licks for each section of the blues progression.

Chord Articulation (Note Targeting)

Have you ever wondered how the great blues guitar players always seem to hit exactly the right note at exactly the right time? You know, that one note in a solo that made you go "Ahhhh!"?

The secret to this seemingly magical technique is to *target* specific notes exactly when the chords change.

The targeted note is often (but not always) an important arpeggio tone in the new chord, and by playing it at a specific time it outlines part of the underlying chord progression of the solo.

If overdone, our lines can start to sound a bit jazzy, but used with subtlety and discretion we can play emotive and articulate solos over any chord progression.

Often, amateur blues guitarists drape the whole blues chord progression with the tonic Minor Pentatonic scale, but in this book you will learn that by changing just one or two notes in our solos we can give a profound new level of depth to our music.

When the concept of target note articulation is combined with interesting scale choices, we start to play more meaningful, emotional and melodically interesting solos. Then, combine these approaches with all the rhythm and phrasing techniques from Book Two and you'll be well on your way to mastering blues guitar soloing.

Chord articulation is the most immediate and effective way to bring new life and soul into a solo. By becoming aware of just a few melodic possibilities that are presented as the chords change, we can make a profound and emotive melodic difference to our solos. It doesn't take much work to alter just one or two notes in your solo to highlight the harmony and create your own little moments of magic.

The ideas contained here are the icing on the cake. They should be used with subtlety and at specific times to draw the listener's attention to certain notes and to create different feelings. When overused they can make a solo sound contrived and pre-planned.

It is likely that over 80% your blues soloing will still be Minor Pentatonic/Blues scale-based because these scales form the traditional vocabulary of the blues. However, with restrained use of the melodic techniques here, you will quickly progress far beyond your current ability.

Remember, rhythm, phrasing and feel always comes first. If you haven't checked out Book Two in this series yet I highly recommend doing so, as it focuses exclusively on those skills.

Have fun and good luck!

Joseph

Get the Audio

The audio files for this book are available to download for free from **www.fundamental-changes.com** and the link is in the top right corner. Simply select this book title from the drop-down menu and follow the instructions to get the audio.

We recommend that you download the files directly to your computer, not to your tablet, and extract them there before adding them to your media library. You can then put them on your tablet, iPod or burn them to CD. On the download page there is a help PDF and we also provide technical support via the contact form.

Kindle / eReaders

To get the most out of this book, remember that you can double tap any image to enlarge it. Turn off 'column viewing' and hold your kindle in landscape mode.

Be Social

Twitter: **@guitar_joseph**

FB: **FundamentalChangesInGuitar**

Instagram: **FundamentalChanges**

For over 250 Free Guitar Lessons with Videos Check out

www.fundamental-changes.com

Part One - Chord Articulation: Playing the Changes
Chapter One: Outlining the Chord I to Chord IV Movement

Many people solo over the 12-bar blues progression exclusively with the Minor Pentatonic scale. In this book, we will pay much more attention to the notes contained in each individual chord of the progression and adjust our soloing approach slightly for each one. By targeting specific notes in each chord, we break free from Minor Pentatonic playing and bring emotion, articulation and some great-sounding note choices to our solos.

We will begin by examining the first significant chord change in the blues progression. This chord change is from chord I (A7) to chord IV (D7) and occurs in bar five.

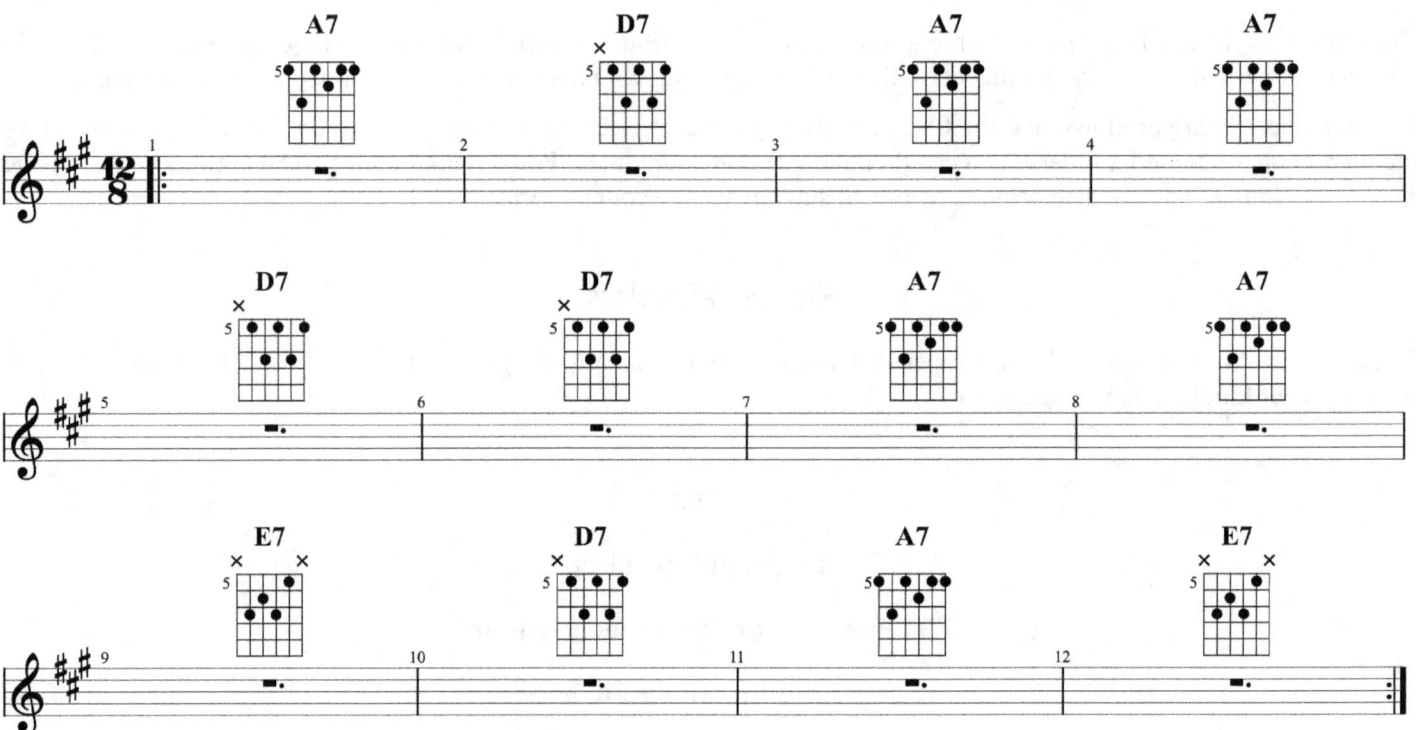

Although there is sometimes a change from A7 to D7 in the first two bars of the blues, the point where the listener first really *feels* the change to the IV chord (D7) is in bar five.

Let's look at the actual notes contained in the chords of A7 and D7, and more specifically how these notes move when the chords change. By targeting the notes that change between the two chords, we can find new, effective melody notes to use in our solos.

This concept can be seen in the following diagram:

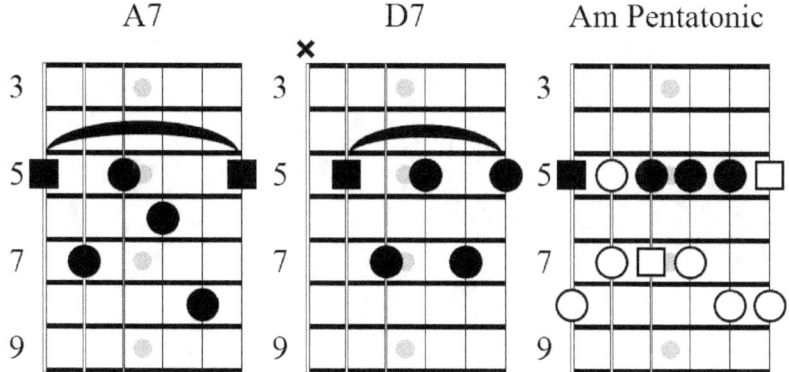

Compare the notes in the A7 diagram to the ones in D7. Pay particular attention to the following:

1. In the A7 chord, the note played on the 3rd string, 6th fret (C#) *descends* by a semitone to become C on the 5th fret in the D7 chord.
2. In the A7 chord, the note on the 2nd string, 8th fret (G) descends by a semitone to the 7th fret in the D7 chord (F#).
3. In the Minor Pentatonic diagram, notice that it does not contain the F# note mentioned in point 2.

The notes that change between A7 and D7 are called *guide tones*, and they are the secret to melodically outlining this chord change in a solo.

I like to keep theory to a minimum, but for a broader understanding of this subject it is important to know that guide tones are the 3rd and 7th intervals of any chord. The 3rd and 7th are the notes that define the chord name and character. They are even more important than the root note when it comes to describing the chord.

To outline, or *describe* a chord in a solo we can always play some of its arpeggio notes (an arpeggio is simply the notes of a chord played one at a time), but the most powerful and descriptive notes to target are always the 3rd and 7th.

The strongest notes to target in A7 are the C# and the G (3 and b7).

Interval	Root	3	5	b7
Note	A	C#	E	G

The strongest notes to target in D7 are F# and C

Interval	Root	3	5	b7
Note	D	F#	A	C

What we're most interested in is how the individual notes move when the chord changes from A7 to D7.

When playing a blues solo, until now you have probably only used the A Minor Pentatonic scale to solo over the D7 chord. There is nothing wrong with that, but let's take a deeper look and compare the notes of the D7 chord to the notes of the A Minor Pentatonic scale:

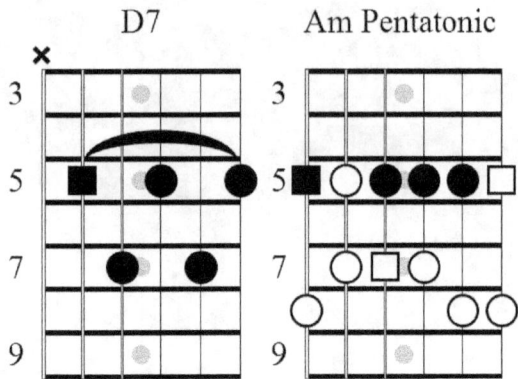

Look at the notes on the 2nd (B) string. You can see that the D7 chord contains the important F# note on the 7th fret and that it is not contained in the Minor Pentatonic scale. Instead, the Minor Pentatonic contains a note on the 2nd string, 8th fret instead (G). Remember that the note G is the b7 guide tone of A7.

The F# (3rd of the D7 chord) is an important guide tone in the chord of D7 (it is the 3rd) and helps define the D7 sound.

To outline the chord of D7 in our solo, simply target the F# guide tone as the A7 chord changes to D7.

The b7 note G in the A7 chord falls by a semitone to target the F# as the chord changes to D7. By targeting that changing note in the solo melody, we outline the chord change.

Listen first, and then play the following line along with backing track one. Notice how the final note in bar three descends by a semitone to land on (target) the F# and how this note choice highlights and strengthens the D7 sound.

Example 1a:

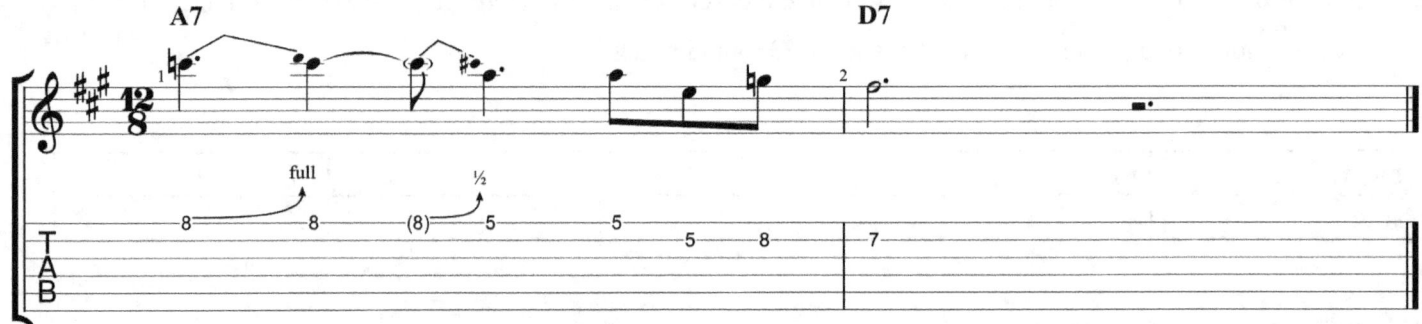

This kind of melodic movement is so strong that you can force your listener to hear the chord change when there is no band or backing track playing. Try playing the previous lick unaccompanied and see if your ears hear the chord change.

Targeting guide tones is a powerful tool and by learning how to use this technique on any chord change we can play emotive, articulate solos.

The reason this sounds so strong is because until this point we have not heard the note F# in the melody.

As long as we hit the 3rd of D7 just as the chord changes, we can target it in any way we like. Let's target the 3rd of the D7 chord with a slide from below.

Example 1b:

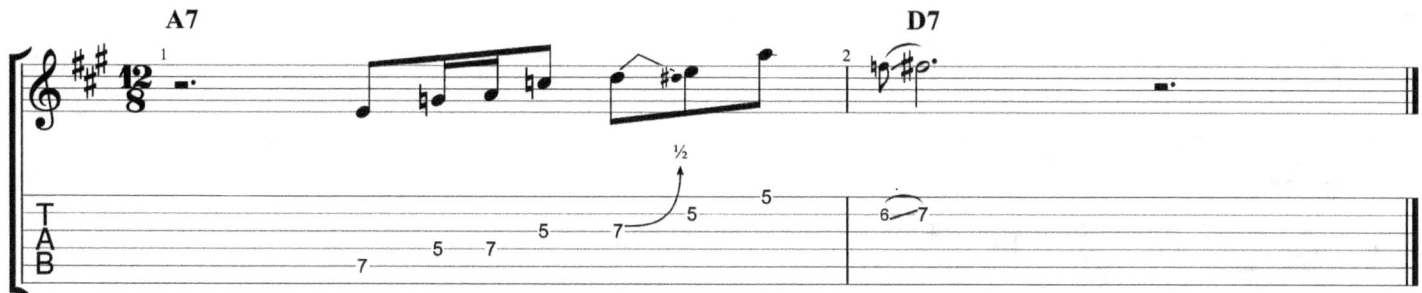

Here are a few more lines to help you target the 3rd of the D7 (F#) on the 2nd string:

Example 1c:

In example 1d I delay hitting the F# until later in the bar. This is bit more subtle than playing the guide tone on the first beat of the bar.

Example 1d:

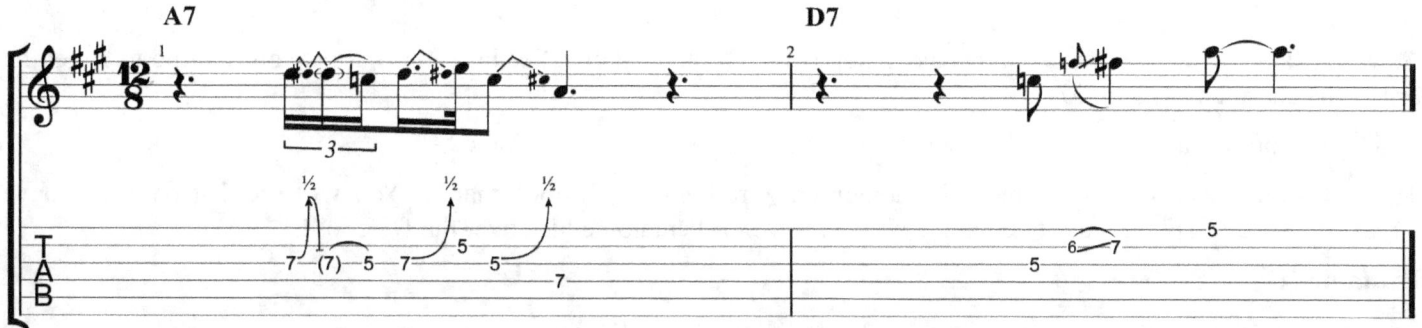

The 3rd of D7 can also be targeted in the lower octave. This is a little harder to see but if we examine the arpeggios of A7 and D7 it becomes clearer.

An arpeggio is simply the notes of a chord played in sequence. Here are the arpeggios for A7 and D7:

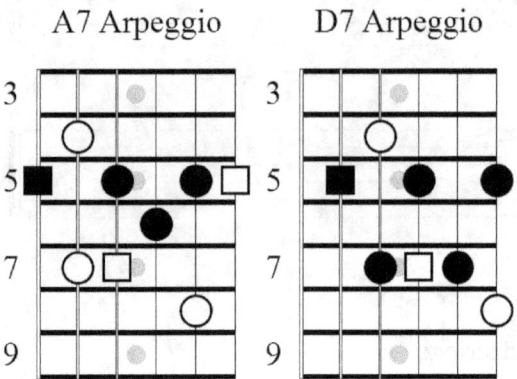

In the A7 chord look at the note G on the 4th string, 5th fret. Notice how it falls to the F# 4th string, 4th fret in the D7 chord. This is the same movement we played before, just in a lower octave.

Here is a simple idea to highlight this change in the lower octave:

Example 1e:

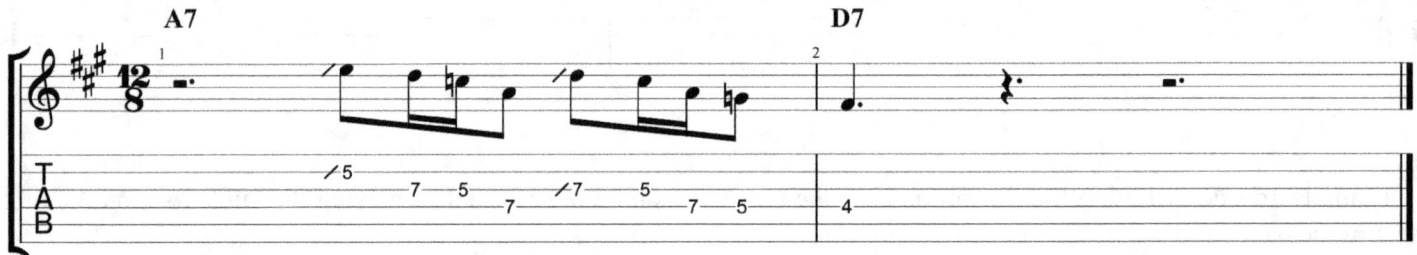

As with example 1a, example 1e targets the major 3rd of D7 on beat one. See how many ways you can find to target the 3rd as the chord changes to D7.

Ending the melody as soon as you hit a target note sounds a bit obvious and forced.

The following ideas build some melodic momentum throughout the chord change. You will see that once you have targeted the 3rd of D7 it is easy to continue with an A Minor Pentatonic idea over the D7 chord.

Example 1f:

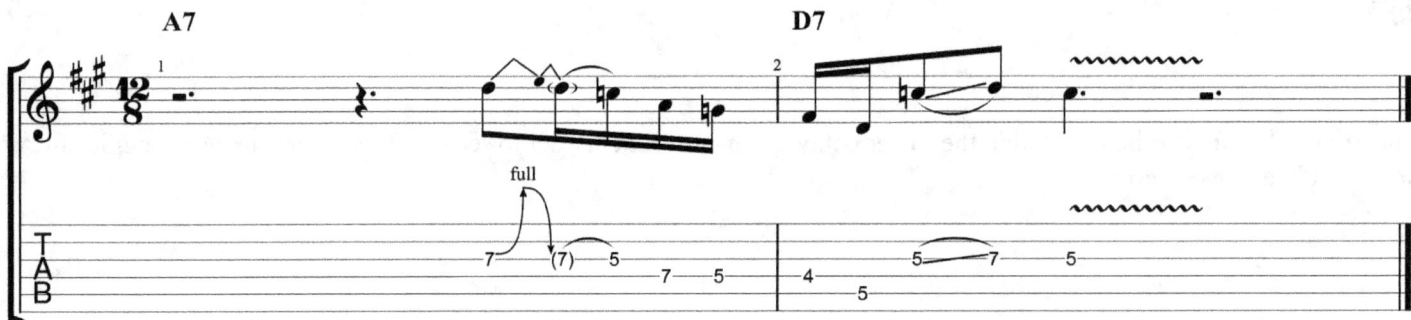

Example 1g:

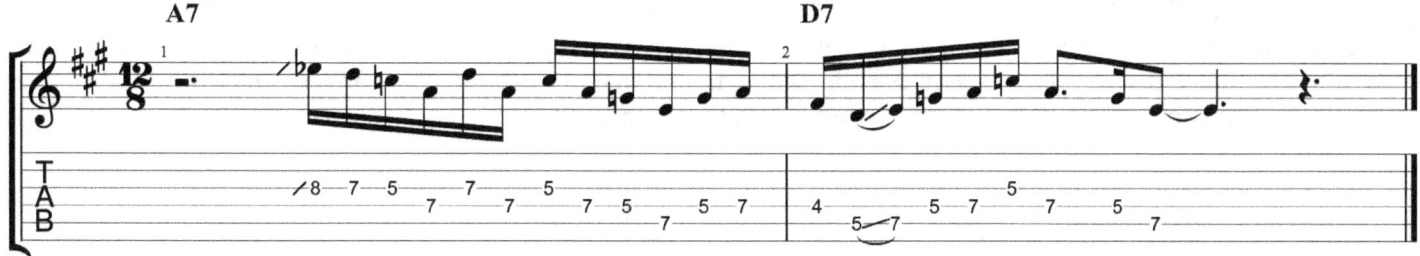

In example 1h I bend the minor 3rd of D7 (F) up a semitone towards the F#.

You could view this idea as playing *D Minor Pentatonic* over the D7 chord and adding a bluesy bend just as you would with the A Minor Pentatonic scale over the A7 chord.

Example 1h:

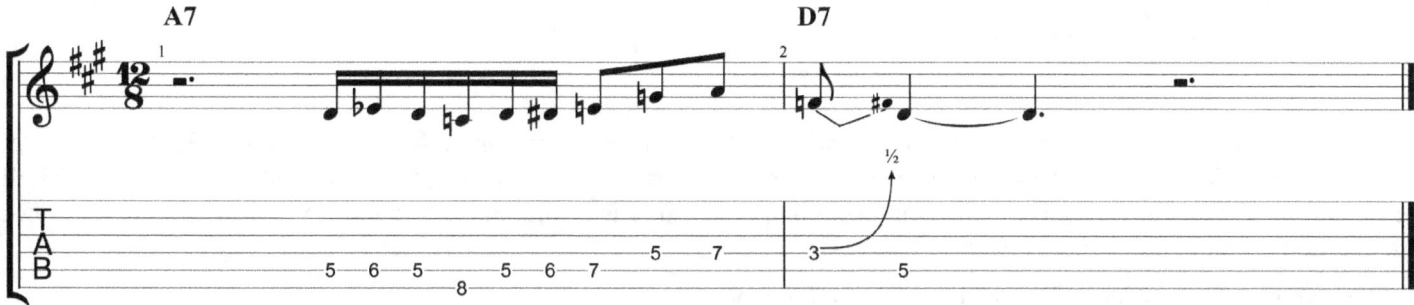

Targeting the major 3rd as the chord changes to D7 is a strong melodic idea because it keeps the melody of our solo aligned closely to the harmonic backing (chord). It can be overused so use it sparingly.

The major 3rd is not the only chord tone that moves by a semitone between A7 and D7.

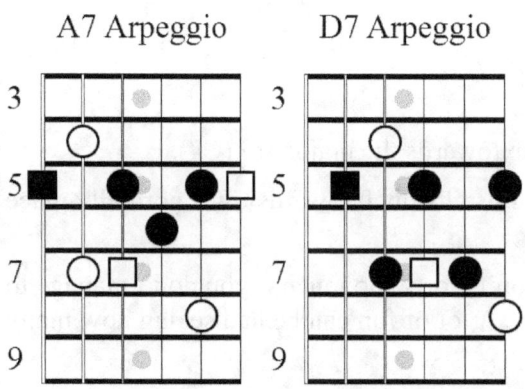

Look at the 3rd string, 6th fret (C#) on the A7 chord.

Can you see how the dark dot falls by a semitone to the 3rd string 5th fret (C) on the D7 chord?

The C# is the major 3rd of the A7 chord and it falls by a semitone to a C natural in the D7 chord.

Even though the C# note does not occur in the A Minor Pentatonic scale you will probably already hint at it over A7 chord, possibly without knowing it.

Here is a short section from **Complete Guide to Blues Guitar Book Two: Melodic Phrasing** where I talk extensively about bending the minor 3rd (C) of the Minor Pentatonic scale slightly towards the major 3rd (C#) of the A7 chord:

"The chords in a blues are normally played as Dominant 7. These are a special kind of major-type chord and contain a major 3rd. The Minor Pentatonic scale, however, contains a minor 3rd (b3) interval. This can be seen clearly on the guitar when you view a dominant 7 chord next to the Minor Pentatonic scale.

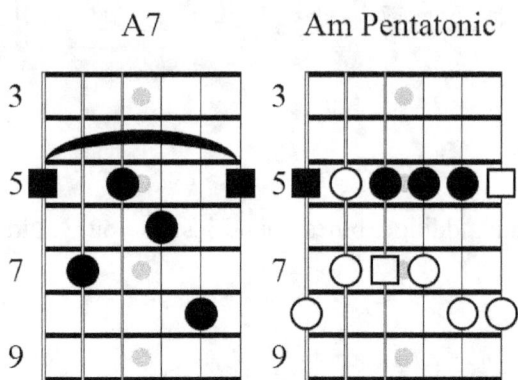

Notice that the C# on the 3rd (6th fret on the 3rd string) of the A7 chord isn't included in the A Minor Pentatonic scale. Instead, it has a C on the 3rd string 5th fret. These two notes, a semitone apart (C# in the chord and C in the melody) will clash and most musicians would say this is undesirable. It certainly isn't the greatest sound if you just 'sit' on the minor 3rd and don't manipulate it in any way.

As you can hear that this isn't the greatest sound in the world!

Example 1i:

Guitarists get around this problem by giving the minor 3rd (C) a little bend up towards the major 3rd (C#).

To do this, use your 1st finger to bend the string towards the floor to slightly raise its pitch towards C#. I normally place my thumb on the top of the fretboard to provide leverage and support.

Adding bends to the b3 helps us catch a glimpse of the blues guitar sound. Don't worry too much if you don't manage to bend all the way to C#. Often we won't push the C all the way to C# anyway. A lot of fun can be had seeing how many different microtones we can find between the b3 and major 3.

Listen carefully to **exercise 1j** which demonstrates the minor 3rd being bent all the way up to the major 3rd.

Example 1j:

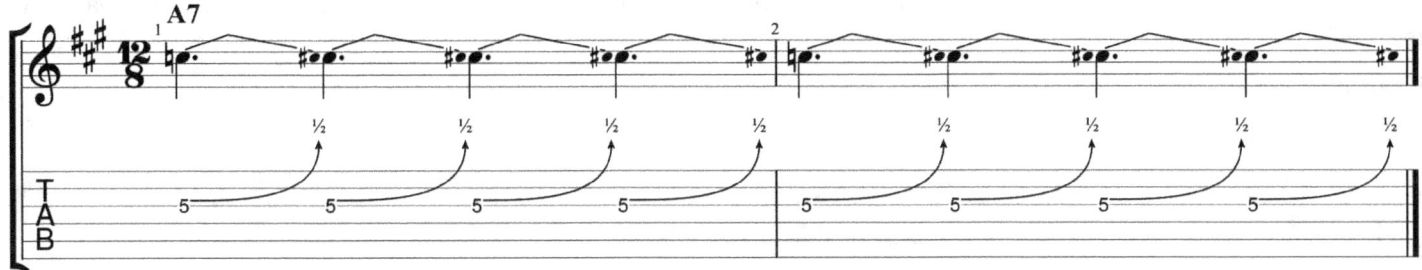

Now compare example 1i with example 1k where we don't necessarily make it all the way to C#.

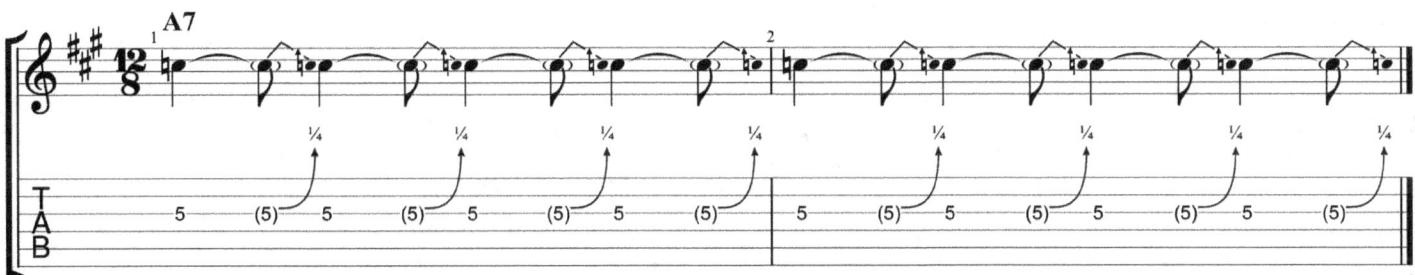

It is good to be aware that we can just give the minor 3rd a little nudge towards major 3rd territory. When we bend a note slightly in this way it is called a curl."

This kind of bend quickly becomes natural and you will often find yourself unconsciously giving the C a little curl towards the C#.

In the following examples we will not be using curls, we will be playing the actual C# note over the A7 and moving it down by step to the C Natural on the D7. This is so you can easily hear the strength of the melodic movement. Later you may wish to explore this same idea but using bends and curls instead.

Here is a simple lick that demonstrates the major 3rd of A7 falling to the b7 of D7.

Example 1l:

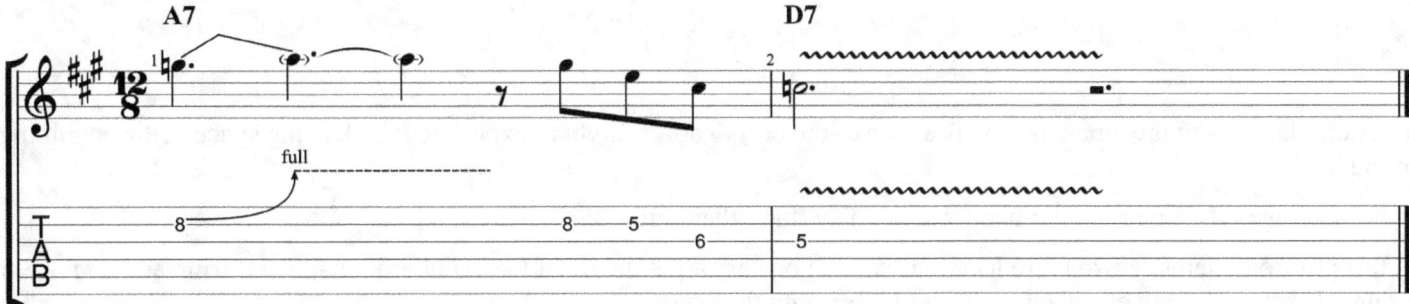

You may feel that the strength of the melodic movement when targeting the b7 is a subtler than when we targeted the 3rd. This is because you will have already heard the b7 note (C) in the solo before, as it is contained in the A Minor Pentatonic scale.

When we targeted the 3rd of D7 (F#) we introduced a completely new note to the melody so it had a little more shock value.

These target notes sound even more subtle if they're contained within a complete line or lick. Here are a few that move from A7 to D7 to get you started.

Example 1m:

Example 1n:

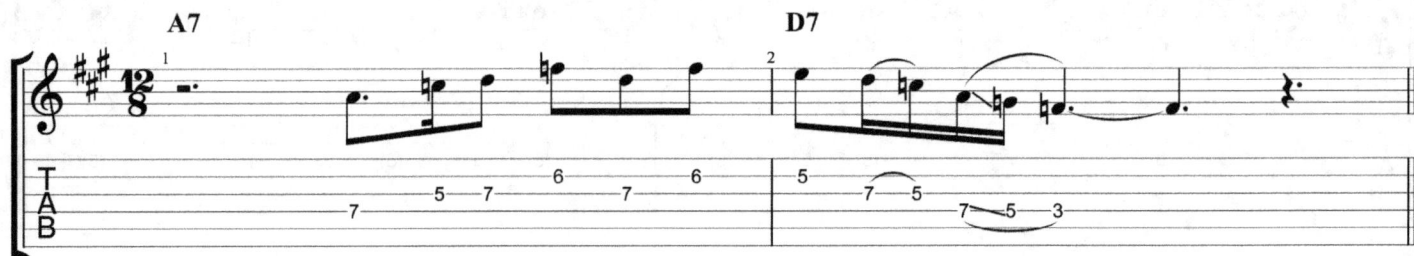

In the next example I do not approach the C natural from C# to show that as long as the C natural is one of the first notes you play in the new bar, you will always get the effect of articulating the chord change.

Example 1o:

You don't have to hit the guide tone on beat one of the bar, so don't forget to experiment by leaving space at the beginning of the bar.

Now you have this sound in your head learn to play it in other octaves.

In this position, there are two more locations where you can target the b7 of the D7 chord: on the 1st string and on the 5th string. Here are some lines to help you get to grips with these positions.

Example 1p:

Targeting the b7 of D7 in the higher octave.

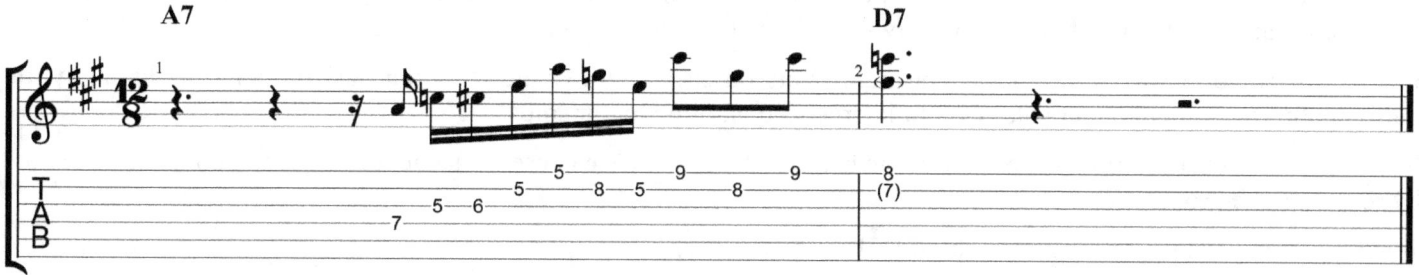

Example 1q:

Targeting the b7 of D7 in the lower octave.

Come up with your own lines with each of the target notes.

Chapter Two: Outlining the Chord IV to Chord I Movement

We have learned that as we move from chord I to chord IV, *the 3rd of chord I (A7) can always fall by a semitone to the b7 of chord IV*, and that the b7 of chord I will always fall by a semitone to the 3rd of chord IV.

In very simple terms, we can target the changing note on each chord change to align our solo with the harmony. By outlining this movement in our solo, we add interest and emotion to our solos.

When the chord changes from D7 back to A7 in bar 7 of the blues, we can use the same technique to outline the A7 chord by reversing the process.

When changing from D7 back to A7 (chord IV back to chord I)

1. The 3rd of Chord IV (D7) rises by a semitone to become the b7 of A7
2. The b7 of D7 rises by a semitone to become the 3rd of A7.

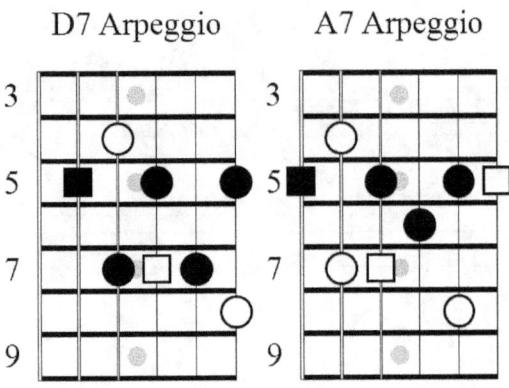

The 3rd of D7 (F#) is located on the 4th string, 4th fret (and on the 2nd string 7th fret).

The b7 of D7 (C) is located on 3rd string, 5th fret (and on the 1st string 8th fret).

The following example demonstrates the movement from the b7 of D7 to the 3rd of A7:

Example 2a:

The next lick highlights a typical line that uses the A Minor Pentatonic scale on the D7 chord then targets the 3rd of the A7 chord. All the lines in the chapter can be practised along with Backing Track 2.

Example 2b:

Example 2b is a similar idea, but this time bounces off the 3rd of A7 to create a bit of forward movement in the solo.

Example 2c:

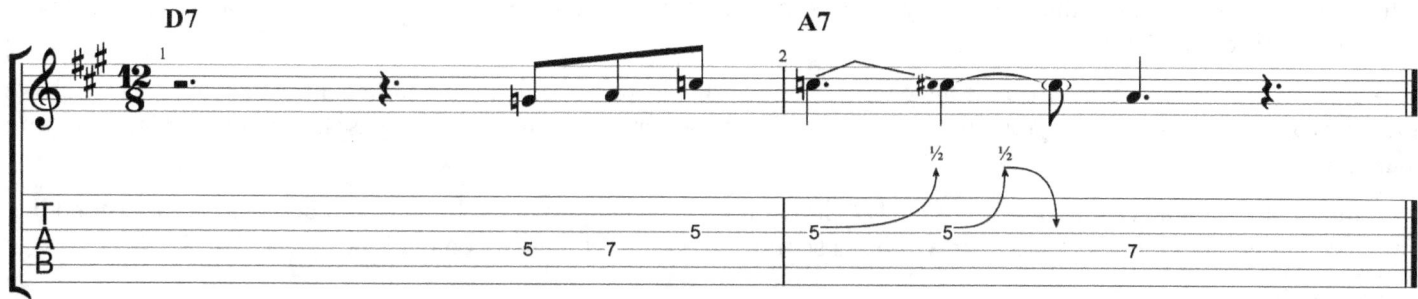

Instead of overtly landing on the major 3rd of the A7 chord, we can target the chord change with a bend for a subtler approach.

Example 2d:

The next line adds a forward motion to the solo by using a combination of the targeted 3rd (C#) and the A Minor Pentatonic scale. Notice how I slide into the lower octave of the 3rd on the final note (5th string, 4th fret).

Example 2e:

When you have the sound of these lines in your ears, try targeting C#s on the A7 chord in the lower and higher octaves. You can do this on the 5th and 1st strings.

Now let's target the b7 of the A7 (G) as the chords change. This is a great effect but a little gentler because you will have already heard the b7 note in the previous bar. Also, the b7 guide tone isn't quite as strong as the 3rd in defining the chord sound.

In example 2f I approach the major 3rd of the D7 chord on beat 4 and then hit the b7 of A7 on beat one of the second bar. The line continues and targets the 3rd of A7 with a semitone bend before resting on the root.

Example 2f:

Example 2g targets the b7 of the A7 chord in the higher octave on the 2nd string. The final note of bar one is the 3rd of D7 which resolves up by step into the b7 of A7.

Example 2g:

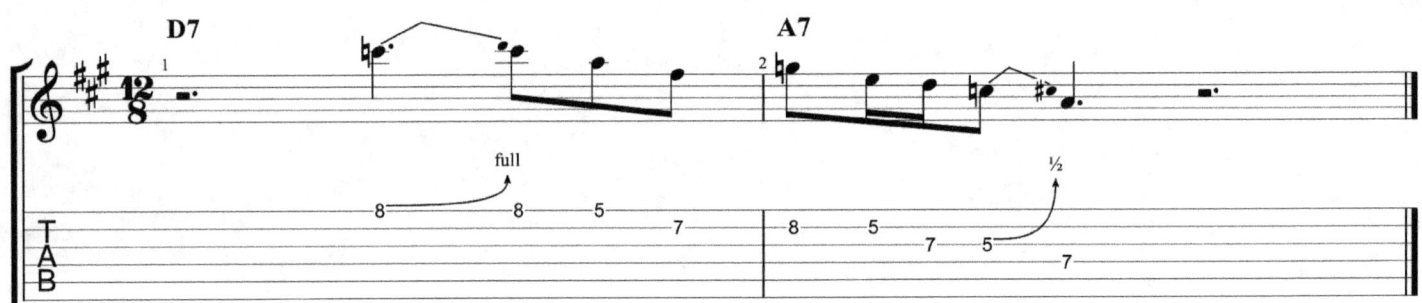

Example 2h is a repeating figure that targets the 3rd of D7 with bends in bar one before hitting the higher octave of the b7 note in bar two.

Example 2h:

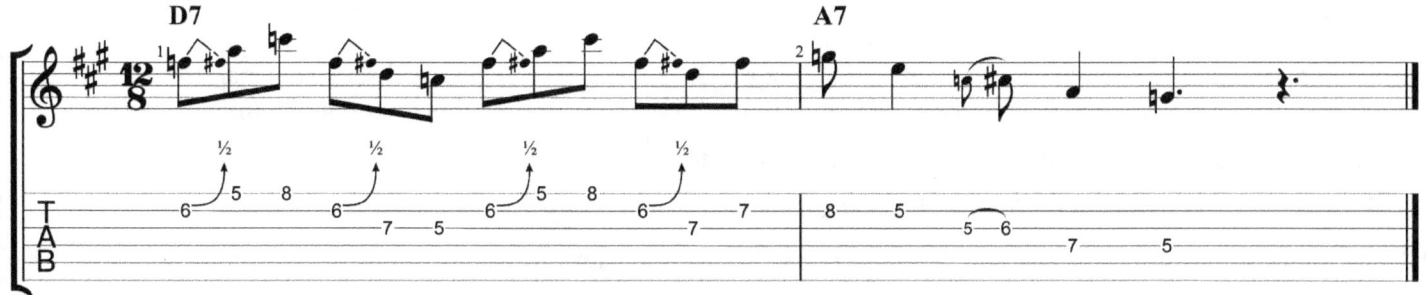

Example 2i is a little jazzier and includes a leap from the b7 to the 3rd on A7.

Example 2i:

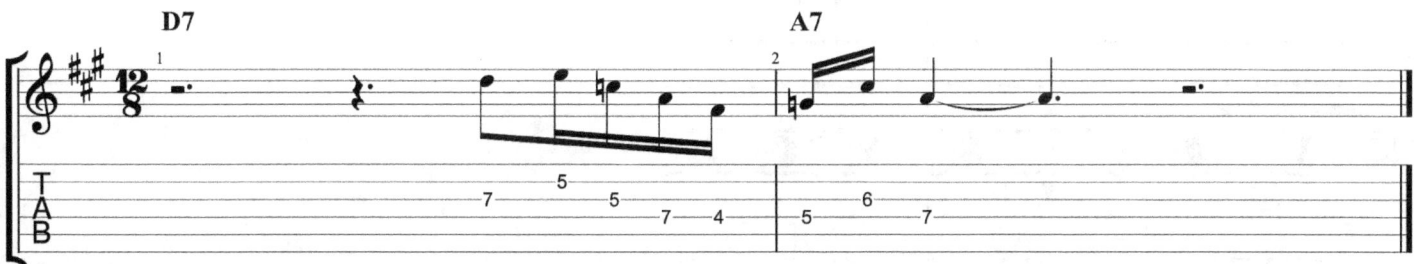

Example 2j begins with a bend using the D *Mixolydian* mode and targets the b7 of A7 with another bend from the 3rd of D7 in the higher octave. We will discuss the Mixolydian mode in a later chapter.

Example 2j:

As always, these ideas are just here to give you an idea of what is possible with target notes. You will get the most immediate musical benefit by memorising a few of these ideas and then incorporating them into your own spontaneous improvisations.

Bring these ideas into your playing while jamming with Backing Track 1. When you have learned the movement on the fretboard, forget the theory and think about these lines as shapes and sounds.

Play these ideas in other keys. Try moving these licks to the keys of E, C and G.

Chapter Three: Outlining the Chord I to Chord V Movement

Chord V (E7 in the key of A) is the strongest chord in the 12-bar blues progression. This is where all the tension in the sequence occurs so targeting the chord change here is one of the most effective ways to add power and interest to your blues solo.

There are many ways to articulate the all-important V chord. Different scale choices are discussed in part two of this book, but for now we will focus on targeting the chord tones of the E7 chord to outline this important harmonic change.

1. There are two methods we can use to target the chord change.
2. Stay in the same fretboard position and introduce a new arpeggio shape

Change fretboard position and translate the arpeggio pattern from D7 up a tone.

While option two is certainly easier, option one more clearly demonstrates how the target notes change between A7 and E7.

Here are the chord shapes of A7 and E7 written out next to the A Minor Pentatonic scale:

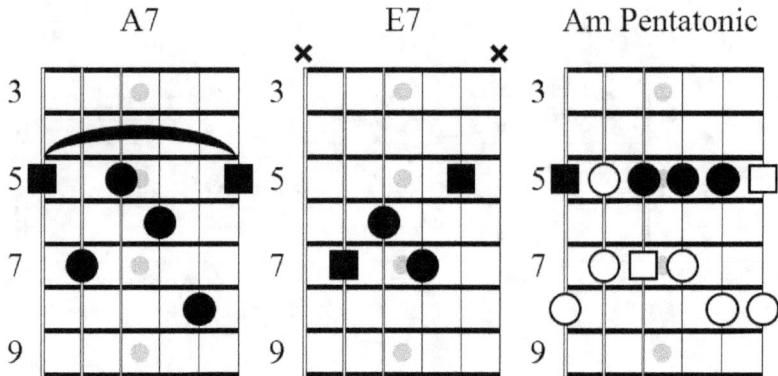

It is easy to see that a new note has been introduced. This note is the 3rd of the E7 chord (G#) and it is located on the 4th string, 6th fret. The higher octave of this note is played on the 1st string, 4th fret.

There is another new note introduced on chord change, but it isn't shown in this voicing of the E7 chord. It can be seen more easily when we compare the full *arpeggios* of each chord:

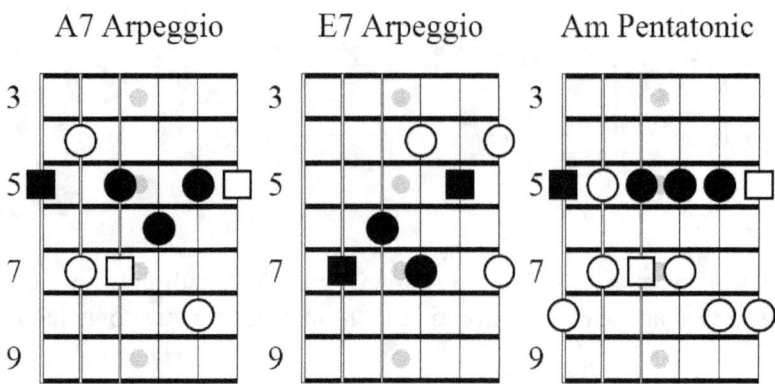

You can see that the new note introduced is the note 'B' played on the 3rd string, 4th fret, and the 1st string, 7th fret. When you compare the E7 arpeggio to the notes in the A7 arpeggio and the A Minor Pentatonic scale, you will see that this note has not been played before.

The note B is the 5th of the E7 chord, and while it is not strictly a guide tone, the fact that this note has not been targeted before in our solo makes it a strong note to play over the E7 chord.

We could target the b7 of the E7 chord (D). However, as D is the root of the *D7* chord it can sometimes sound a bit weak in this context.

The following lines for the A7 to E7 chord movement both target the 3rd of the E7 chord.

Example 3a:

The next lick targets the 3rd of E7 (G#) in the higher octave and then carries a bit more momentum through the chord change.

Example 3b:

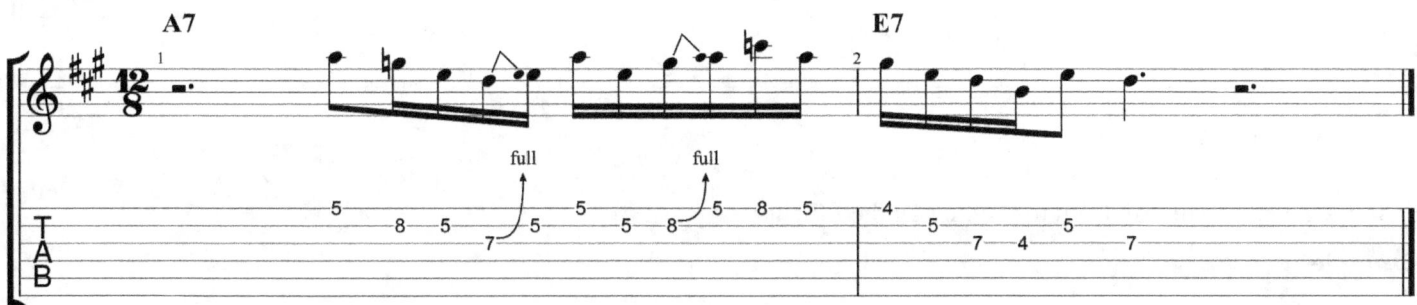

You can practise all the ideas in this chapter over Backing Track 3, a cycle of A7 to E7.

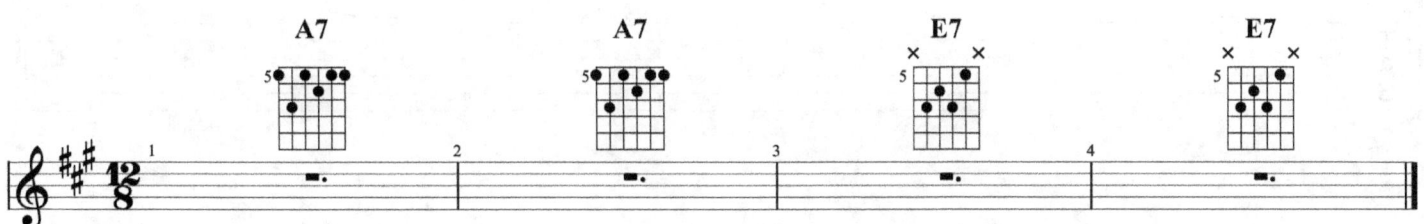

183

Using more interesting rhythms helps add a bit of subtlety to the line:

Example 3c:

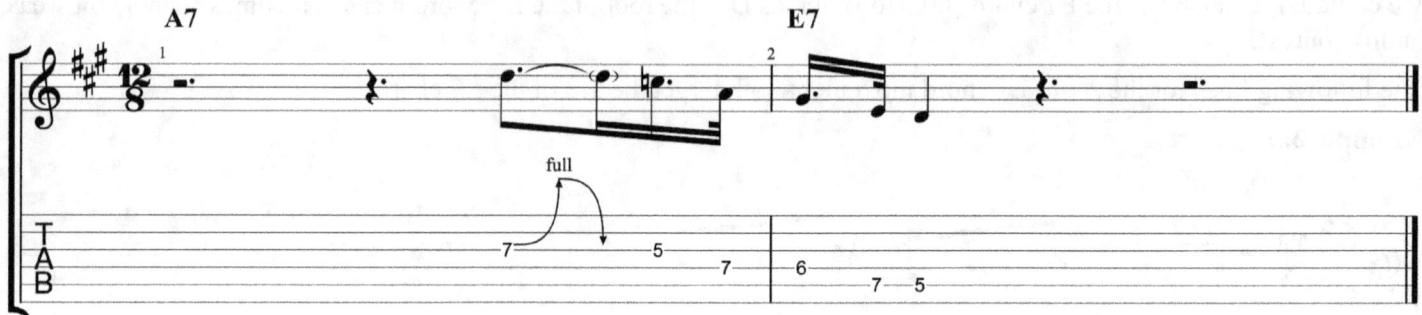

Example 3d:

Example 3e adds a bluesy bend to the line on the E7 chord.

Example 3e:

The following examples target the 5th (B) of the E7 chord.

Example 3f:

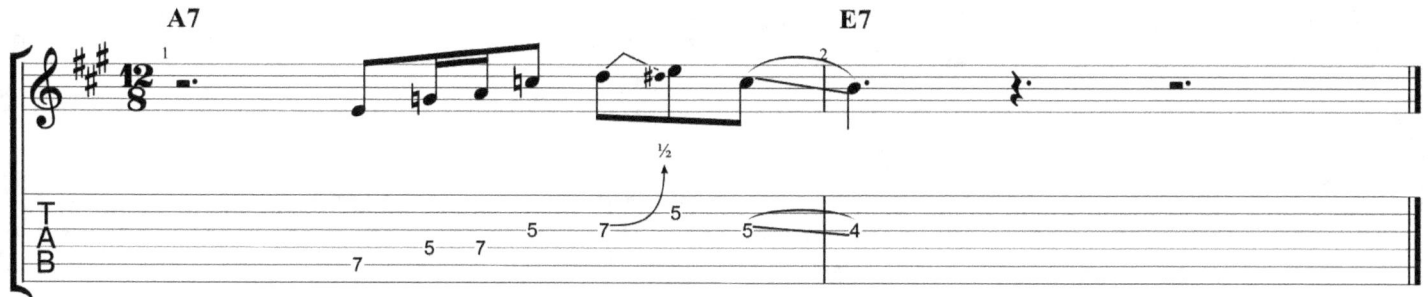

Example 3g combines the E7 arpeggio with the E Mixolydian scale and A Minor Pentatonic scale in bar two.

Example 3g:

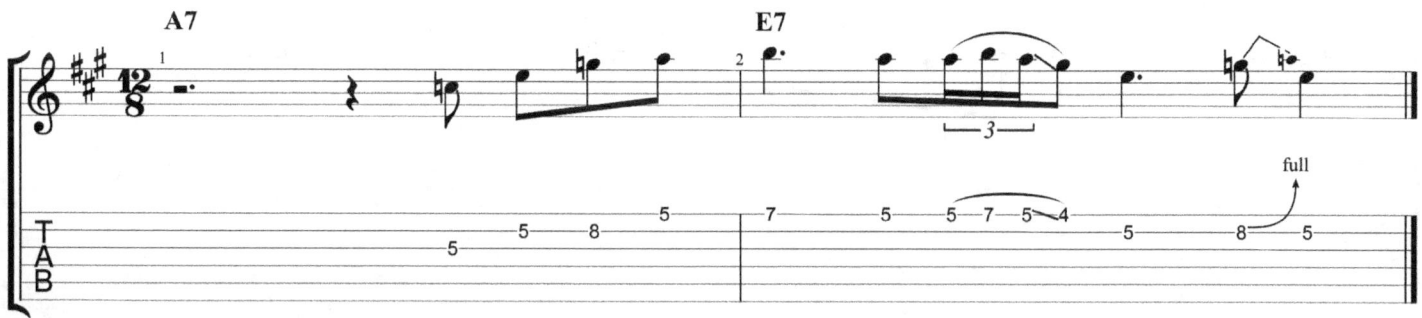

Next, after targeting the B of the E7 chord, the E7 sound is reinforced by descending through the full E7 arpeggio.

Example 3h:

By thinking about chords individually you play notes you may not have considered with a purely Minor Pentatonic approach.

At every other point in the 12-bar blues progression, the bent note in bar two of example 3i will sound awful. By playing it at exactly the right time (targeting the 3rd of the E7 chord) we can add exciting melodic interest and surprise to our solo.

Example 3i:

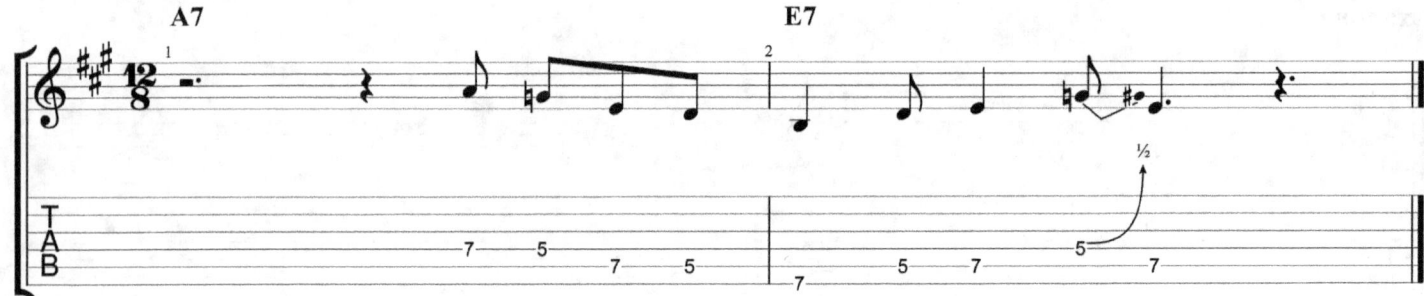

Again in example 3j there is a bent note that might sound bad at other points in the progression. This time I'm bending from the b5 to the 5 on the E7.

Example 3j:

The following examples target the b7 (D) of the E7 chord.

Targeting the D on the E7 chord can sometimes be a little weak because it is the root note of the following chord in the 12-bar blues sequence (D7). To emphasise the change, I often play a C# note on the A chord (the 3rd) which the listener will hear moving to the D. This works better in higher octaves.

Example 3k:

Example 3l:

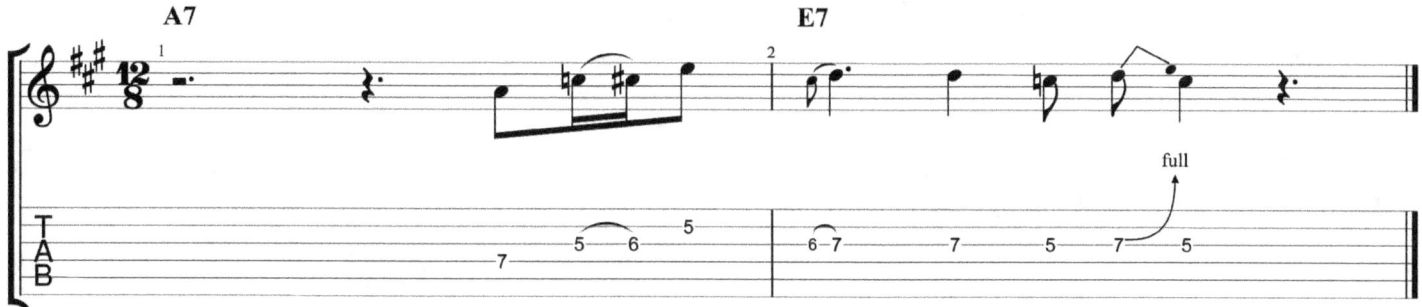

Example 3m:

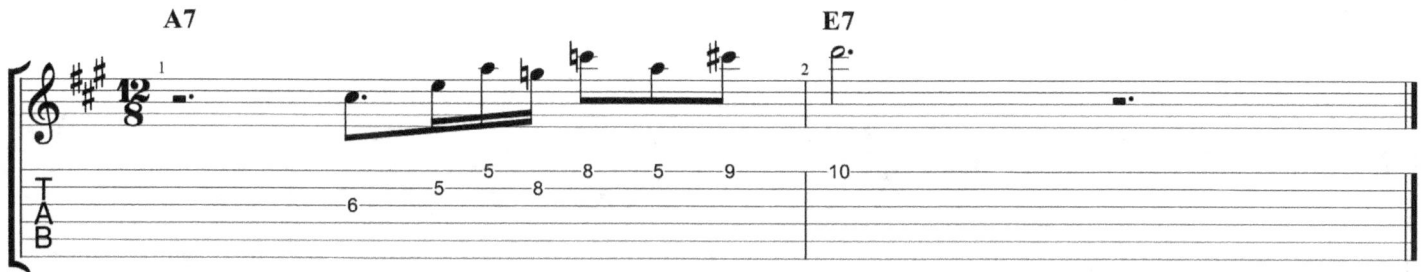

The preceding ideas are useful for targeting the strongest notes on the E7 chord change, but there is another great way to recycle melodic material you already know. You can use the ideas we had for the IV chord (D7) and simply shift them up one tone to E7.

This can be seen clearly when we compare the chord diagrams for E7 and D7:

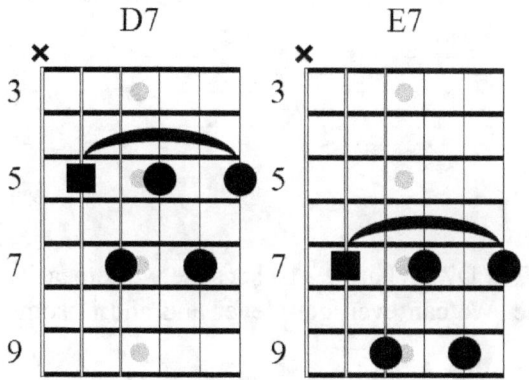

187

The following lines show how to change position on the guitar neck while easily outlining the E7 chord in a similar way to how we outlined the IV chord (D7) earlier.

Example 3n:

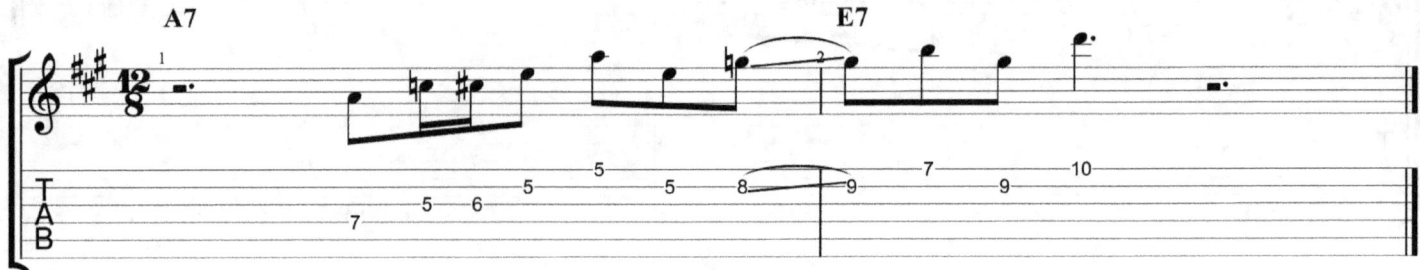

Example 3o:

Example 3p:

This technique comes into its own when we play the change from V to IV (E7 to D7) in bars 9 - 10 because we can easily take an E7 lick and move it down two frets (one tone) to become a D7 line. We can even get clever and add in some chromatic movement between the chords.

Chapter Four: Outlining the Chord V to Chord IV Movement

The movement between chord V (E7) and chord IV (D7) is the strongest harmonic point in the blues progression. The V chord descends by one tone to become the IV and this movement can be outlined easily in a solo with using guide tones and sequences.

We will begin by looking at some solo lines that approach playing the V to IV chord change using the same arpeggio shape and move it down the fretboard as the chord changes from E7 to D7.

When we change positions like this, it is easy to build strong melodic sequences with repeating phrases and patterns.

The following ideas move between the V and IV chords by sliding down the guitar neck and can be practised with Backing Track 4.

Example 4a:

Example 4b:

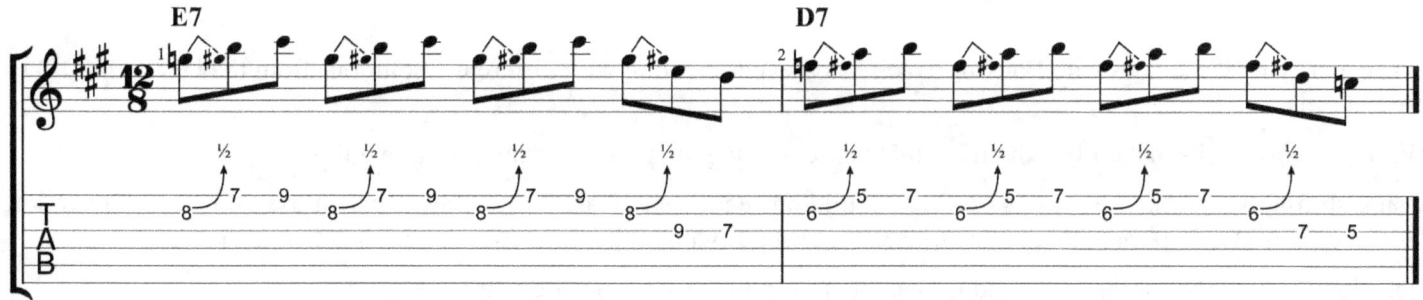

Example 4c:

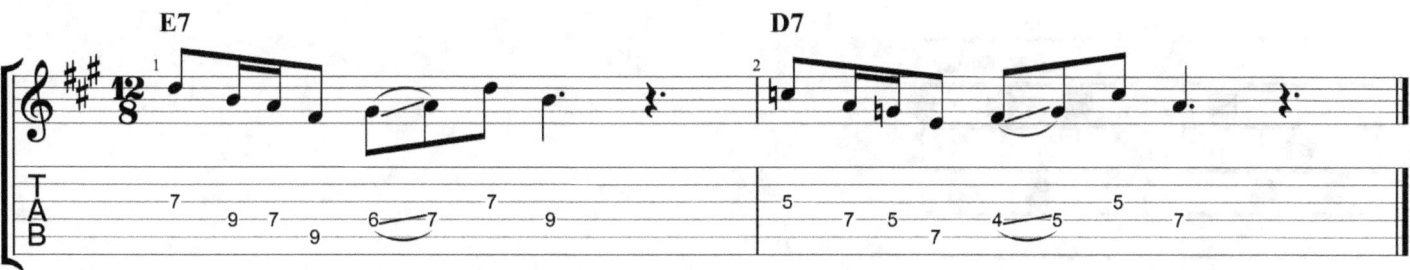

Example 4d:

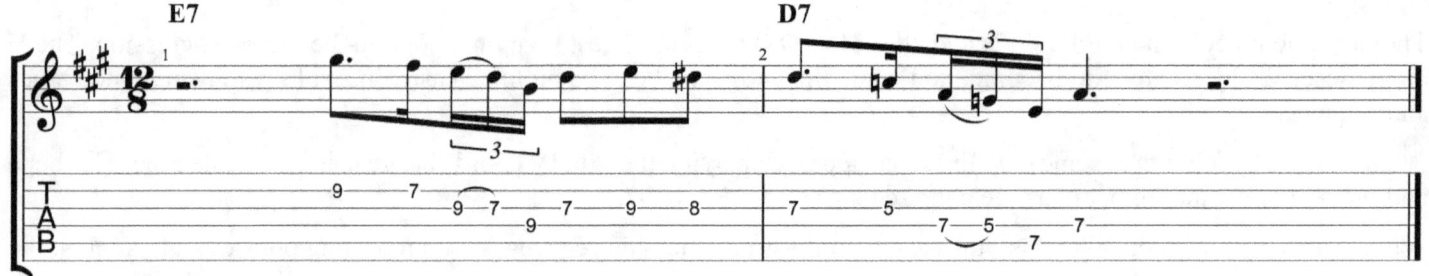

The chord change from V to IV normally only occurs once in a blues chord progression so these ideas can be tricky to practise. To help you practise, Backing Track 8 is a repeating chord sequence of this section which will help you to work specifically on this part of the blues form. The chords are as follows:

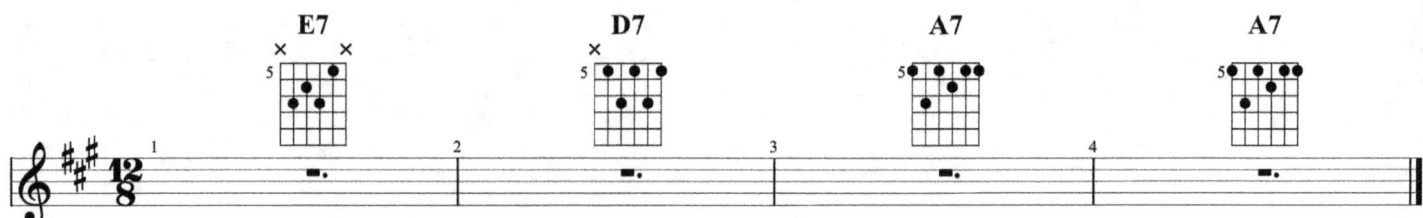

Practise playing these lines with Backing Track 8 and experimenting with different resolutions from the IV chord (D7) to the I chord (A7).

Write your own licks that outline the E7 and D7 chords using the previous examples as a guide.

Using shifting shapes in this way is useful for building sequential ideas. Stevie Ray Vaughan used this technique a lot. However, it is also important to master these chord changes without moving your hand around on the neck.

Let's look at how the chords of E7 and D7 can be played in the same position on the neck.

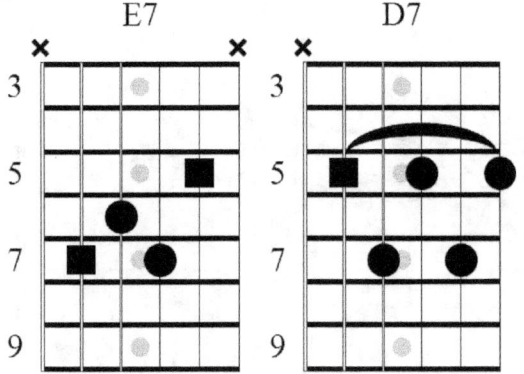

One of the important note-changes between these two chords can be seen clearly from just the chord diagrams. The 3rd of E7 (G#) rises by a semitone to become the 5th (A) of the D7 chord.

This shows that even though the chords may descend harmonically, intervals may still ascend between chords. It is an effective tool to use when you want your melodic line to go in the opposite direction to the bass movement of the chord change.

To see how the other important target notes change we need to take a deeper look at the full arpeggios of each chord:

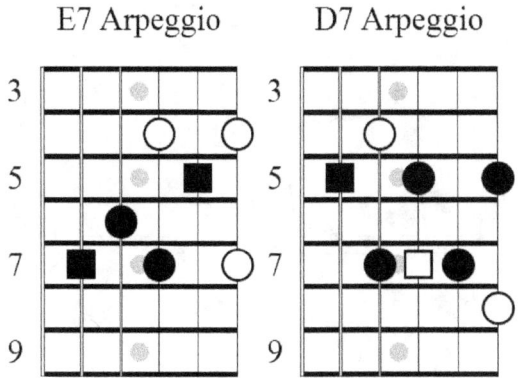

On the 3rd string, 4th fret you can see that the 5th of the E7 (B) chord rises by one semitone to become the b7 of the D7 chord (C).

The root of the E chord (E) on the 2nd string, 5th fret can move in one of two ways.

It can be seen as descending one tone to become the root of the D7 chord.

It can be seen as *ascending* one tone to become the 3rd of the D7 chord (F#). The latter much more interesting because it is in contrary motion to the bass movement.

The following examples highlight each target note in turn, and teach you lines that emphasise the strengths of each particular choice.

Targeting the 3rd of D7 (F#)

Example 4e emphasises the D7 sound with a line based around the arpeggio in bar two.

Example 4e:

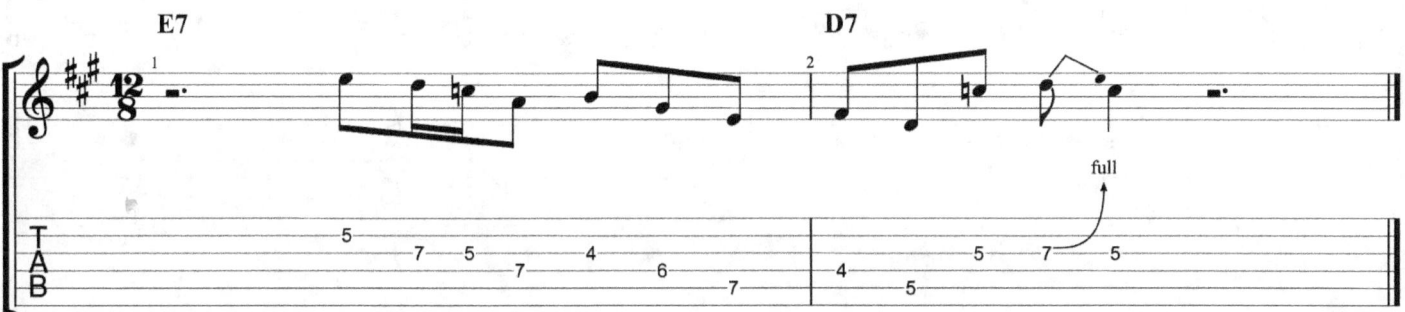

Example 4f once targets the F# and uses the A Minor Pentatonic scale in bar two.

Example 4f:

Example 4g uses a chromatic approach (passing) note to target the F# on the D7 chord.

Example 4g:

In example 4h these is a descending passing note into the lower octave F# on the D7 chord.

Example 4h:

Targeting the 5th of D7 (A)

In example 4i, I target the 5th of the D7 chord with another chromatic approach note.

Example 4i:

Next, the A Minor Pentatonic scale is used over the E7 chord. However, the note G is bent up a semitone to target the 3rd of E7 (G#). The 5th is once again targeted on the D7 chord, however, the b3rd (F) is bent up by a semitone to hit the major 3rd (F#) for a slightly country sound.

Example 4j:

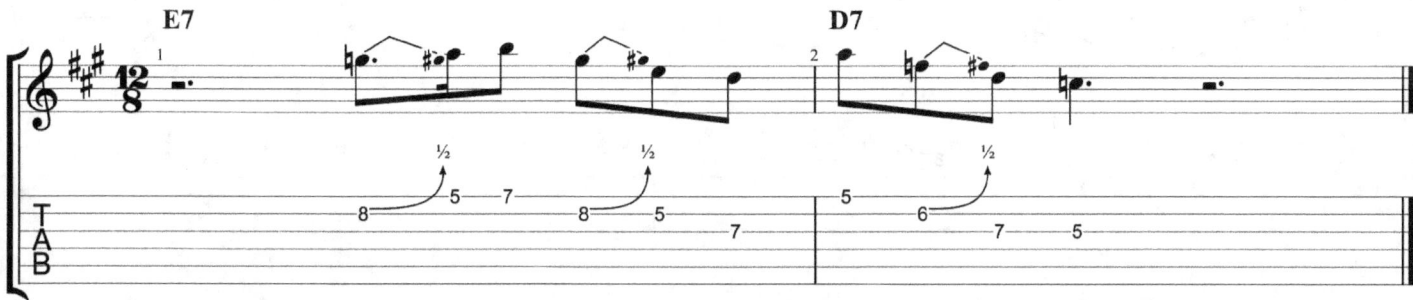

Here's a simple arpeggio idea over the E7 chord.

Example 4k:

Targeting the b7 of D7 (C)

This is a rhythmically simple line that targets the b7 of D7 (C).

Example 4l:

The following idea targets the b7 of the D7 chord in the higher octave.

Example 4m:

Example 4n first targets the b7 of D7 and then the 3rd on beat two.

Example 4n:

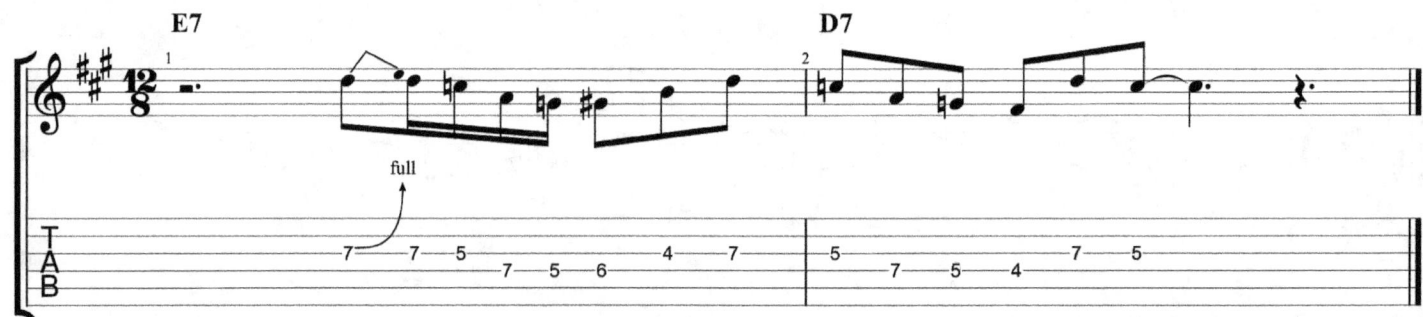

Finally, example 4o is a busier line with powerful forward motion.

Example 4o:

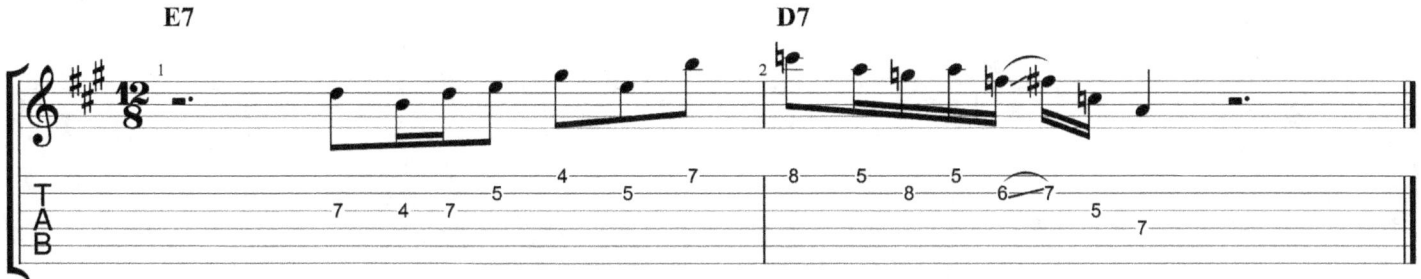

The approaches in the previous four chapters teach you to highligh a chord change by aiming for the strong guide tones of the new chord, or by hitting an arpeggio note on the change.

The method I encourage you to pursue is as follows.

1. Compare the two chord diagrams to see if any obvious notes are changing
2. Write out the arpeggios for each chord and look to see how the guide tones (3rds and 7ths) move.
3. Finally, check to see if other arpeggio notes (the root or 5th) provide a strong movement or can introduce new notes into the solo.

With this process, you will always be able to find interesting, emotive and unexpected notes to play in your solo. These will grab your audience's attention and keep them musically connected to your solo.

Finally, a 'pro tip'! A wonderful musical effect to exploit is to *bend* into the new target note. For example, instead of playing a line from A7 to D7 like this:

Example 4p:

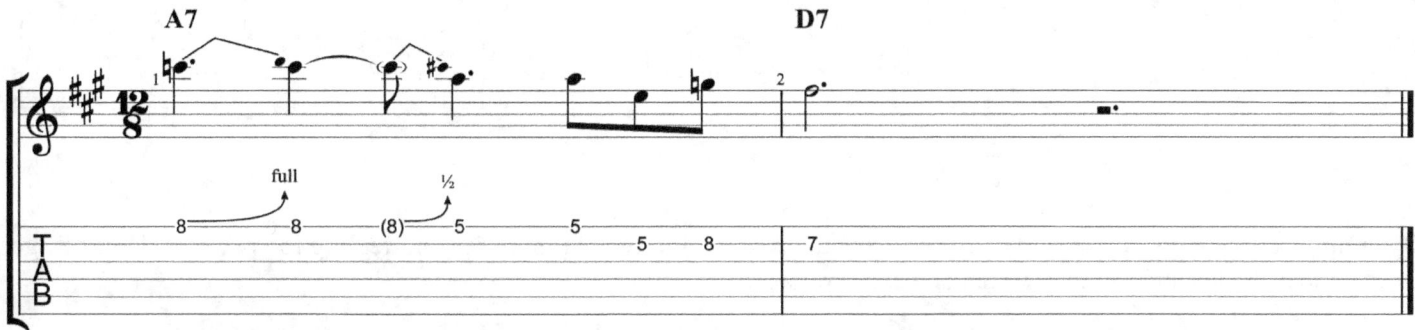

Why not try it like this?

Example 4q:

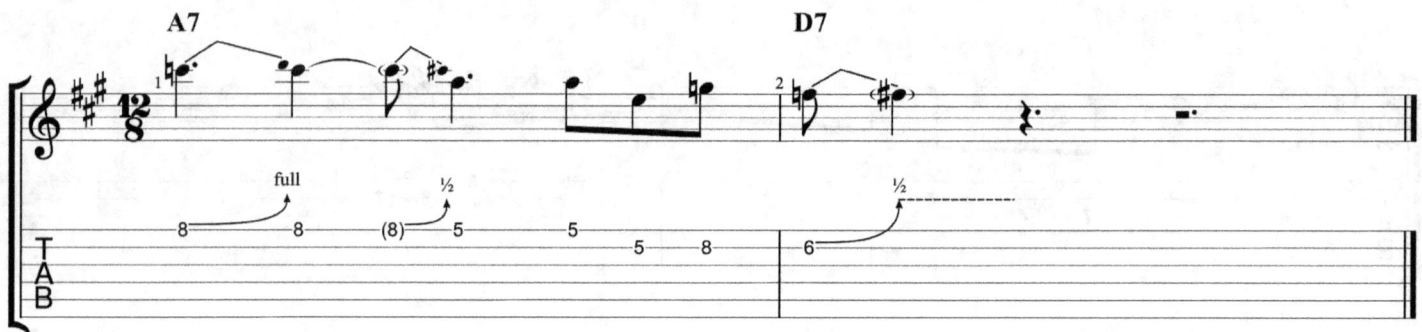

Using a bend to target notes can really add something magical.

Also, by *delaying* the point at which you hit the target note, you can have a huge effect upon the listener.

Experiment with all the displacement ideas and techniques from **The Complete Guide to Blues Guitar Book Two: Melodic Phrasing**.

Here is one idea based around the previous lick to start you off.

Example 4r:

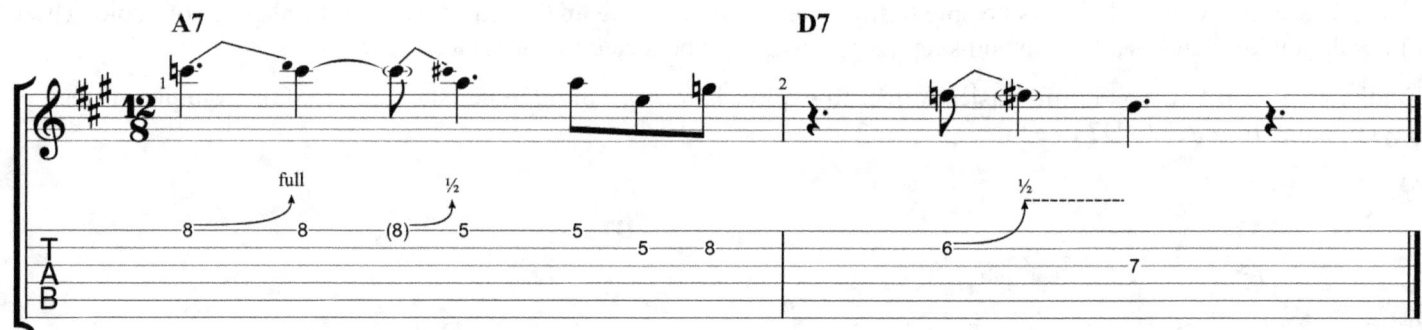

By simply adding a rest at the start of bar two, the delayed resolution adds surprise and feeling to your solo. Don't forget to add slides, bends and vibrato to each and every phrase.

Chapter Five: Chord Changes and Arpeggios in Every Position

All the ideas in the book so far have all been based around the 5th fret area of the guitar. This has been to stay focused on the concept of targeting arpeggio notes in your solos. However, only being able to play these changes in one position of the guitar neck is limiting in terms of range and expression.

The following pages provide chord diagrams and arpeggios for the chord changes of a 12-bar blues in A in each of the five positions on the neck. The 3rds and 7ths are marked to show you how the main target notes are moving.

Read the following diagrams from left to right to see how each important arpeggio note changes between chords I, IV and V in the Key of A. This will teach you how to target the closest note changes between each chord.

You will find many guide tone movements between chords and by incorporating these movements into your solos when the chords change, you will quickly develop an articulate and melodic approach to the blues.

Position One:

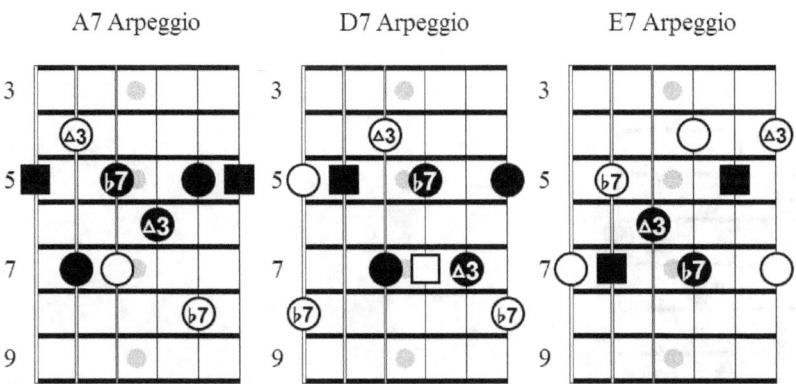

Position Two:

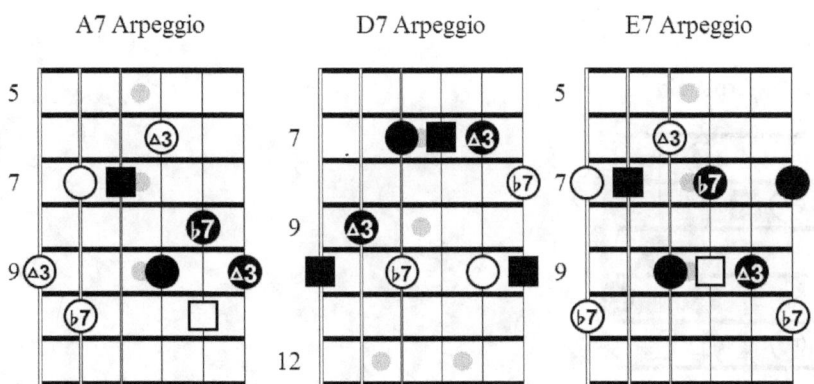

Position Three:

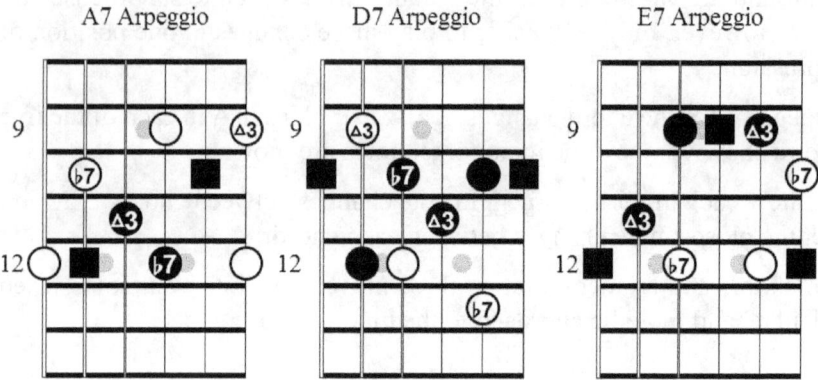

Position Four:

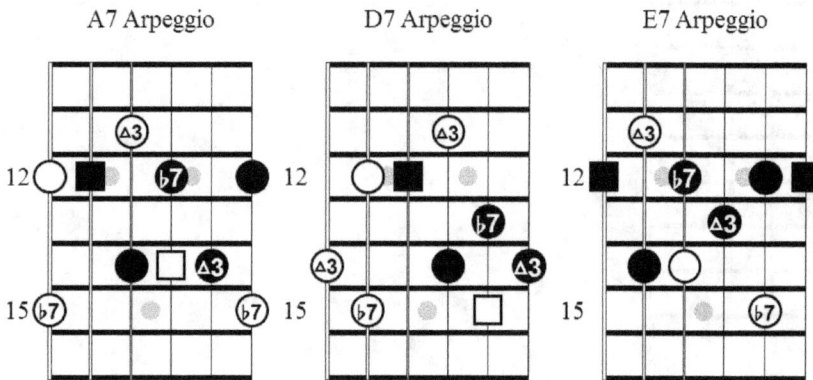

Position Five:

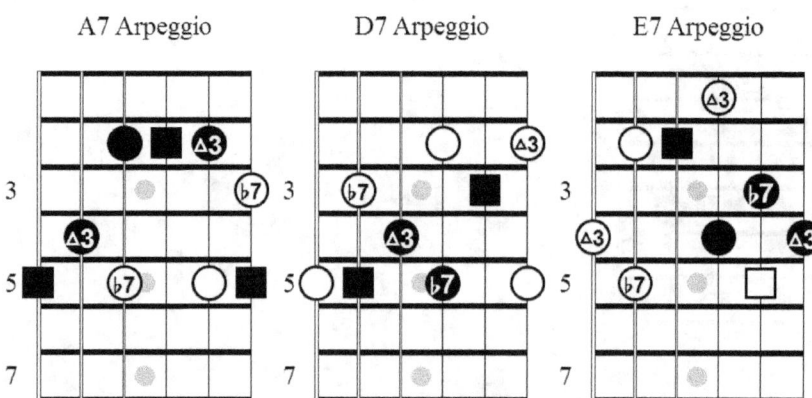

There are also some useful arpeggio exercises you can practise to reinforce the sounds and locations of the moving notes. Practise the following exercises with Backing Track 9, a repeating chord sequence of:

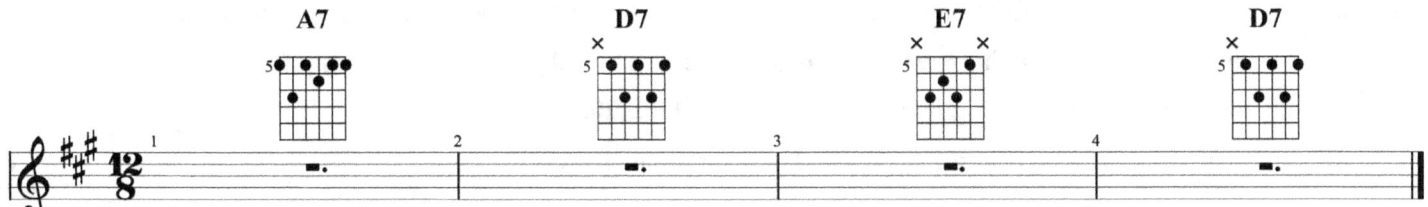

Pick one area of the guitar neck from the diagrams above. In the following examples I use position three.

1. Play each arpeggio ascending from the root with four notes per bar:

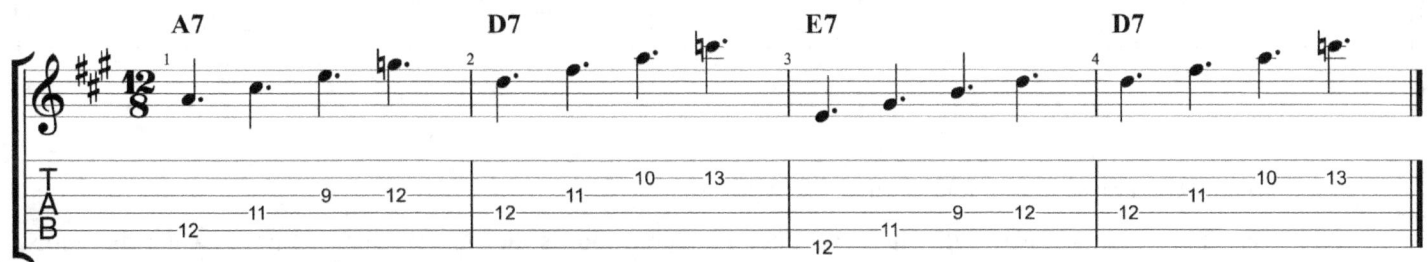

Repeat the exercise descending from the higher root.

1. Play each arpeggio ascending from the 3rd:

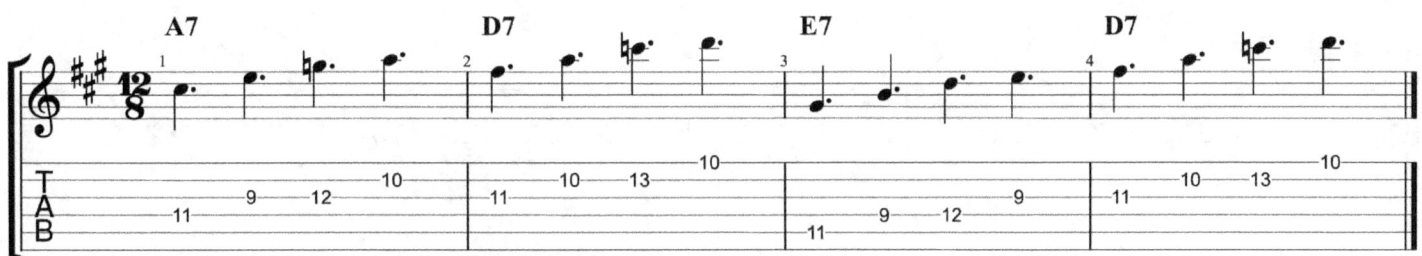

Repeat the exercise descending from the higher octave 3rd.

1. Repeat the previous exercise beginning from the 5th and the b7th of each chord.
2. Now ascend the first arpeggio from the root but *target the closest note in the next chord* when the chords change:

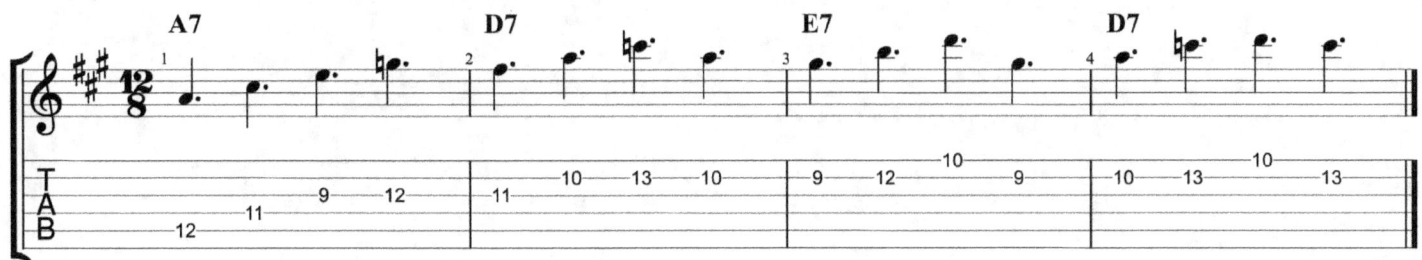

You can travel in any direction or form patterns just so long as you hit a new arpeggio note on every change.

See how long you can keep playing this exercise without a mistake and fully explore each position.

1. Repeat the previous exercise but begin from the 3rd, 5th or b7 of the A7 chord.
2. Limit your playing to just two or three strings and play the same exercises:

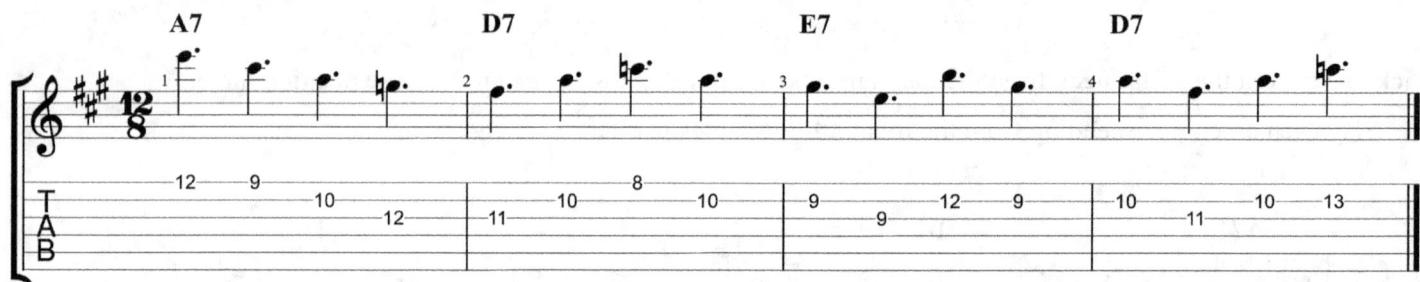

1. Play all the above exercises in 1/8th notes instead of 1/4 notes.
2. Finally, combine these exercises with short A Minor Pentatonic ideas and target arpeggio notes when the chords change for a much more bluesy, musical approach:

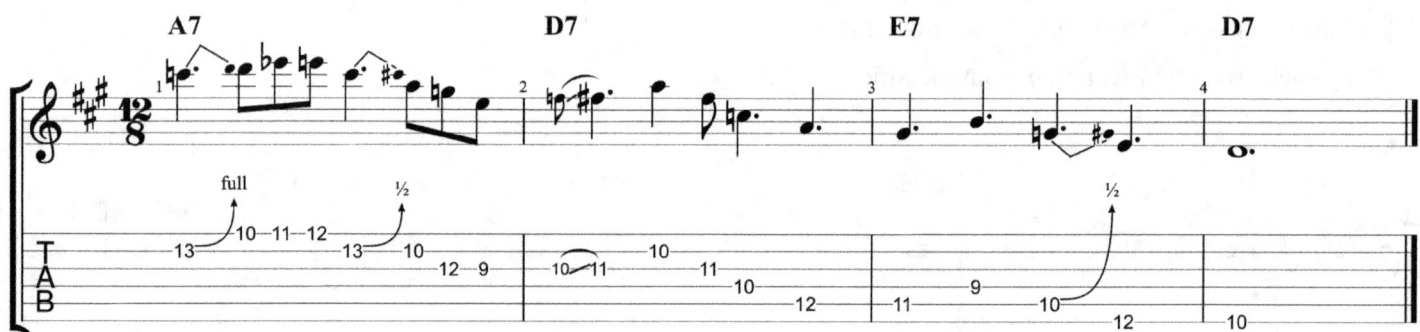

Repeat these exercises in every position and soon you will be able to see, feel and hear the arpeggio changes without having to think about them.

As you can see in the final example, these arpeggio exercises really come alive when the target notes are mixed with Minor Pentatonic licks. Working regularly on the previous eight exercises will improve your playing very quickly.

Part Two - Scales and Soloing Schemes
Chapter Six: Scale Choices for the I Chord

i. The Major Pentatonic Scale

Part one of this book dealt with the concept of articulating a chord change with the notes in our solo. We found that by targeting particular notes from a chord or arpeggio we were able to introduce new, appropriate sounds into our melodies and add interest and feeling to our playing.

However, once we have used a target note to 'play our way' into the new chord, there are often many scale options that can be used to continue the solo. Different scales have different feelings or *colours* and by mastering their different sounds we can manipulate our audiences' emotions to take them on a journey throughout the solo.

Eventually, these sounds will become second nature to you, and you won't think about scales at all when you solo; just moods and expression. However, to begin with, it is important to learn, understand and hear how each scale functions and feels.

After the Minor Pentatonic, the next most common scale choice to use on the I chord (A7) is the *Major Pentatonic* scale.

You may already be aware of this scale and know the easy 'trick' to play it on the guitar. To play an A Major Pentatonic scale simply move an A Minor Pentatonic scale down three frets. For example, here is one way to play the A Major Pentatonic scale:

A Major Pentatonic

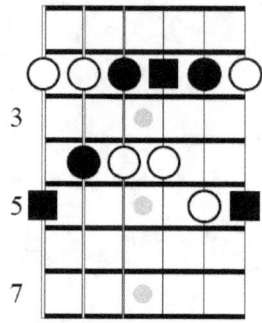

You can see that on paper, this looks very much like the scale of F# Minor Pentatonic, but because we hear it over an A major chord we hear the intervals of the scale in relation to the root note A.

Another way to see that this is an A Major Pentatonic scale is by looking at the location of the root notes (the square dots) of the scale. The root note is on the 5th fret of the 6th string (A) and not on the F# (2nd fret).

Try improvising a solo with the A Major Pentatonic scale over the blues progression in Backing Track 5. It sounds great over the A7 chords but doesn't fit so well over the D7 chords.

If you struggle to get started it can help to take an A Minor Pentatonic lick that you know and simple move it down three frets like this:

Example 6a:

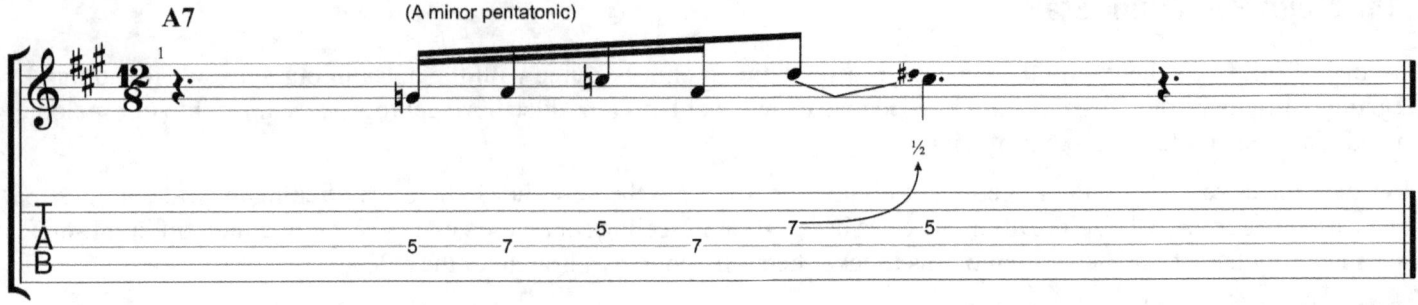

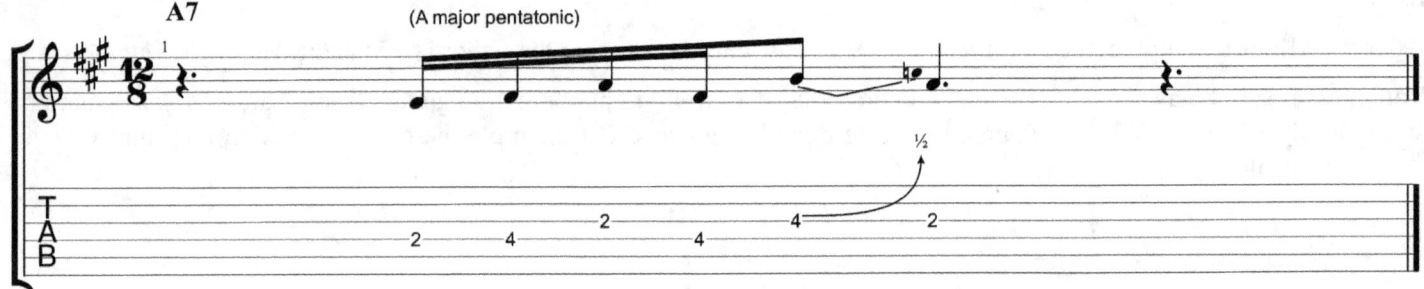

Here are some useful A Major Pentatonic licks that use this scale shape.

Example 6b:

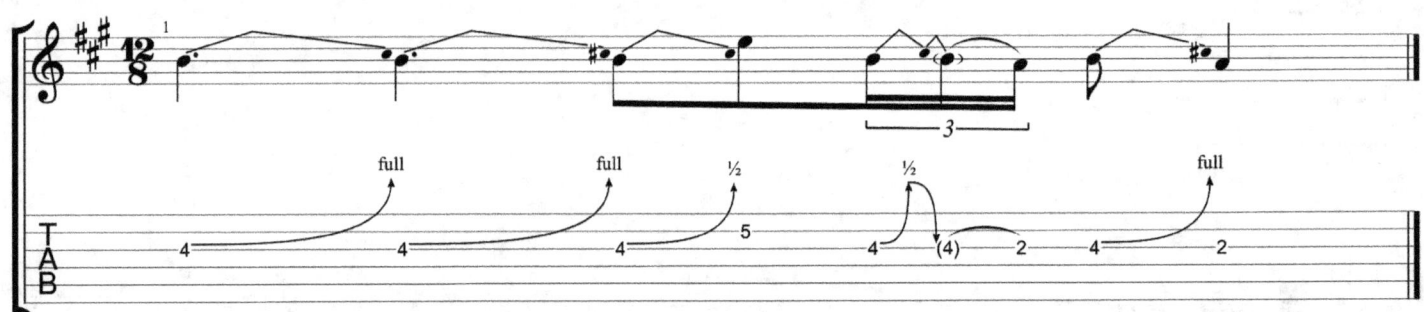

Example 6c:

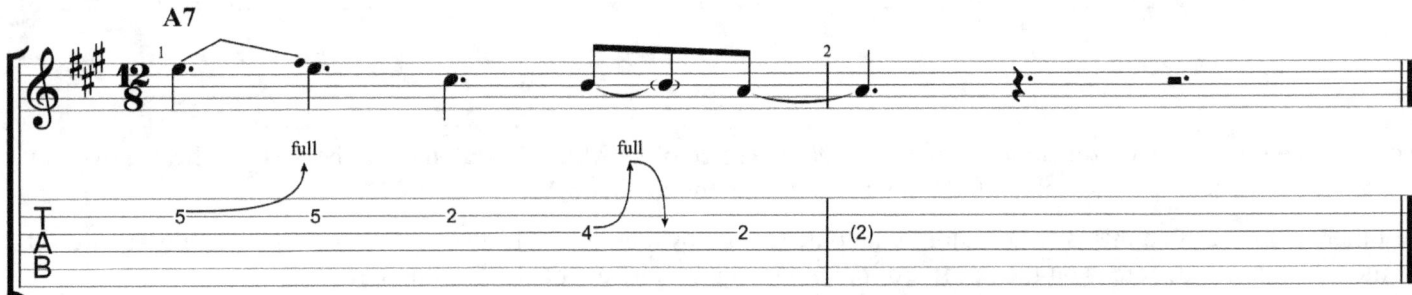

Example 6d:

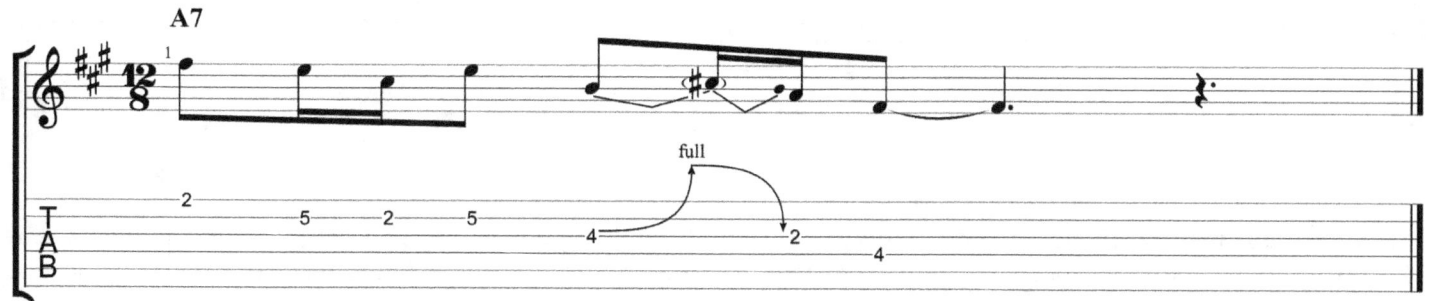

Even with just these few examples and improvising your own Major Pentatonic lines you will quickly realise two things:

1. The A Major Pentatonic scale sounds much happier than the A Minor Pentatonic scale.
2. The A Major Pentatonic scale really doesn't sound that good when the chord changes to D7.

The Major Pentatonic scale sounds happier because it contains different notes to the A Minor Pentatonic scale.

The notes in A Minor Pentatonic are

A C D E and G (formula 1 b3 4 5 b7)

In A Major Pentatonic the notes are

A B C# E and F# (formula 1 2 3 5 6)

By staying away from the b3 and adding the 6th our brain perceives the Major Pentatonic as a happier sound.

The reason that the A Major Pentatonic scale doesn't work well over the D7 chord is because A Major Pentatonic contains the note C#. This C# clashes heavily with the important b7 chord tone C in the D7 chord.

As C (b7) is one of the most important notes in the D7 chord, a C# will introduce a strong, undesired dissonance to the melody.

The solution is to = use a different scale when the chord changes to D7, but we will look at that later.

Moving the A Minor Pentatonic scale down three frets to create an A Major Pentatonic scale is a useful trick, but we don't always want to be *forced* into a specific position on the neck. For this reason, it is beneficial to learn the A Major Pentatonic scale at the fifth fret so it's easy to move between the A Minor and A Major Pentatonic scales in one position.

Here is how to play the A Major Pentatonic scale at the fifth fret:

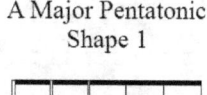

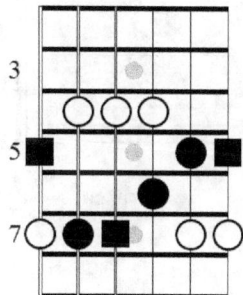

This scale shape may be slightly unfamiliar to you, so learn it ascending and descending until you have it memorised. Don't worry too much about specific fingerings, although I normally like to begin with my second finger on the lowest note.

Here are some useful licks based around this pattern of the A Major Pentatonic scale:

Example 6e:

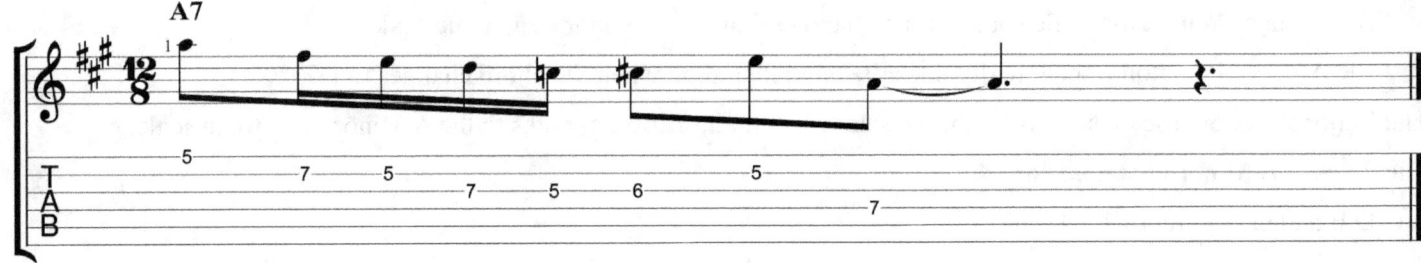

Example 6f:

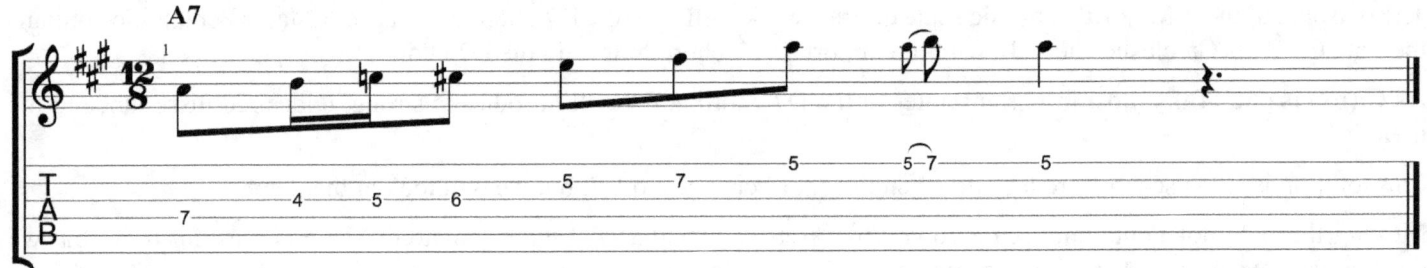

Example 6g:

Example 6h:

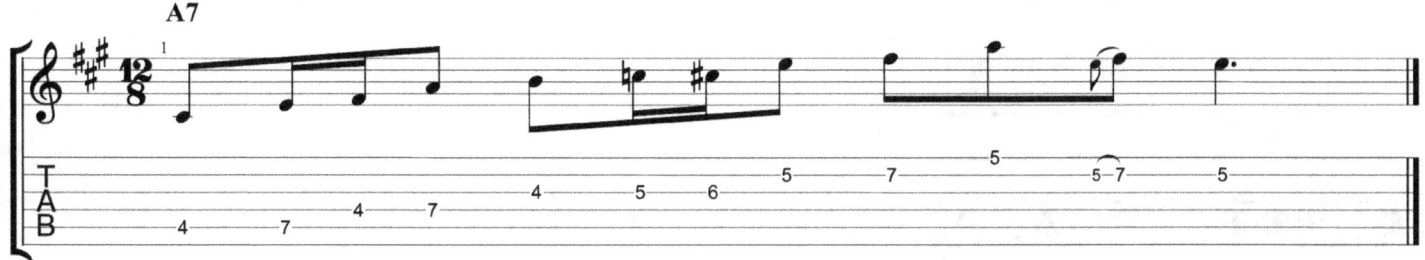

Now learn the Major Pentatonic scale all over the neck in the key of A and try to improvise some solos with it.

Here are the five shapes you need to know:

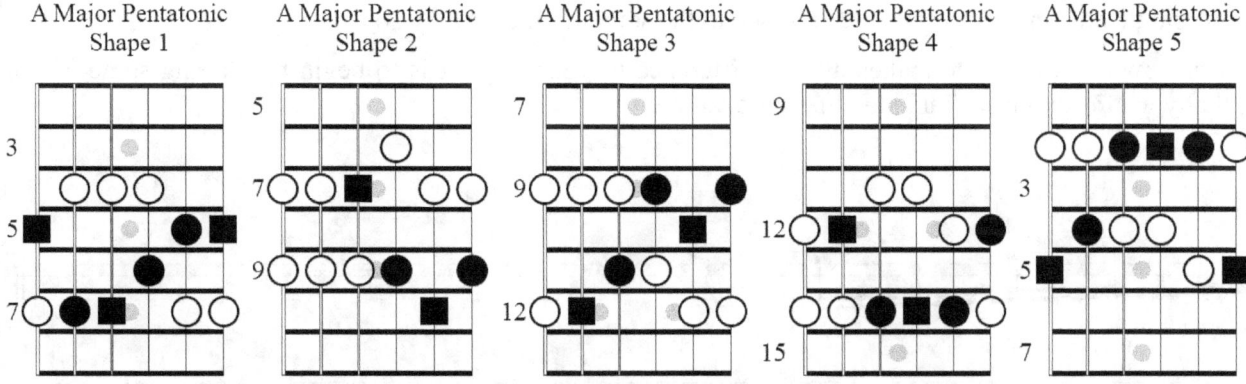

For more Major Pentatonic ideas and a complete guide to the CAGED System, check out my bestselling book **The CAGED System and 100 Licks for Blues Guitar.**

ii. The Blues scale

The Blues scale is interchangeable with the Minor Pentatonic scale. They are identical except for the addition of one note, the 'b5' in the Blues scale.

The Minor Pentatonic scale has the formula

1 b3 4 5 b7

The Blues scale has the formula

1 b3 4 b5 5 b7

Here are the fretboard diagrams of both scales:

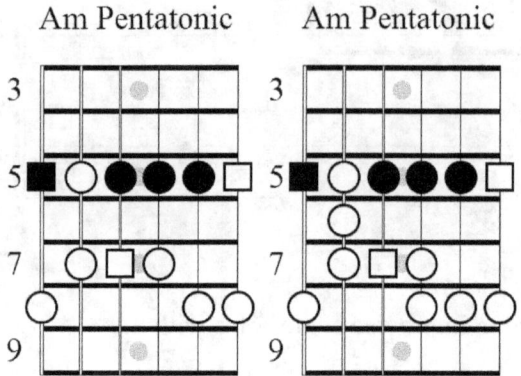

The addition of this single note makes a marked difference to the sound of the melody solos.

A great way to hear how this extra note makes a huge difference to your playing is to begin by altering some Minor Pentatonic licks that you already know. Take this line for example:

Example 6i:

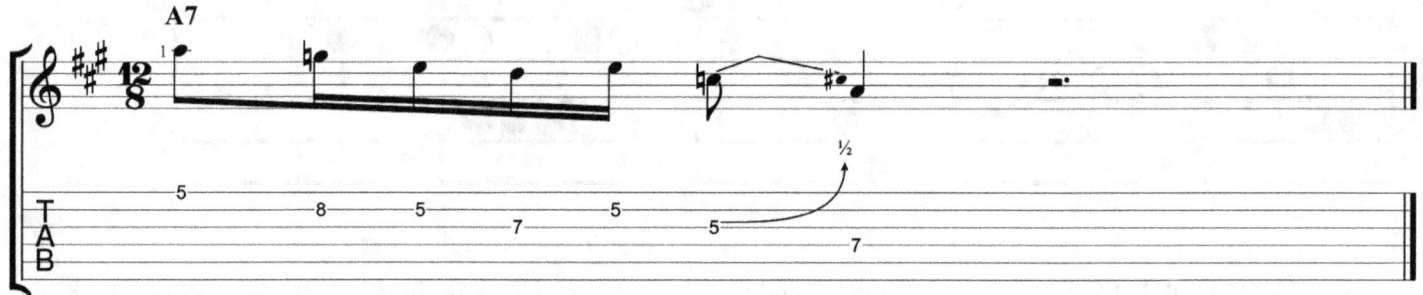

By adding in the *blue note* we create a different sound:

Example 6j:

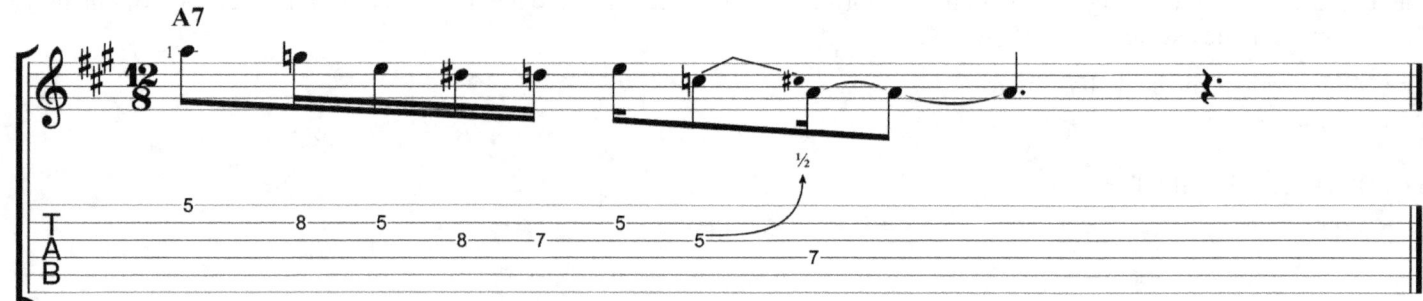

It is also common to bend from the 4th (D) to the b5th (Eb) like this:

Example 6k:

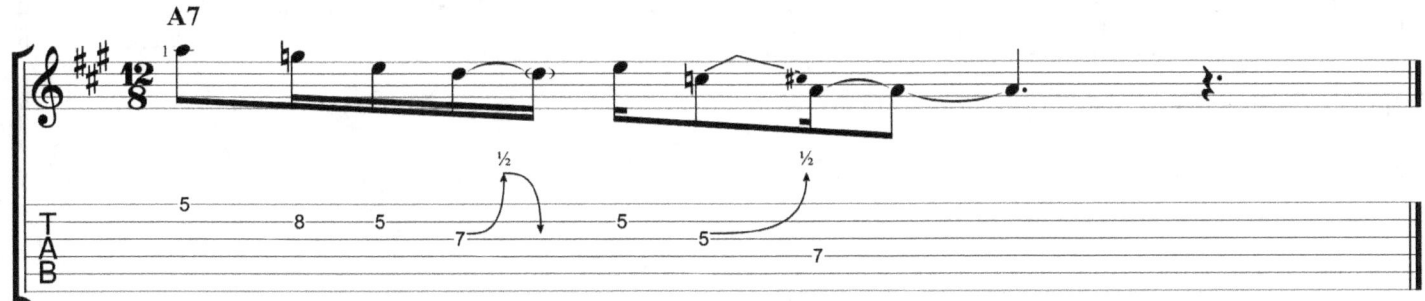

The b5 is also useful when played in the lower octave:

Example 6l:

Example 6m:

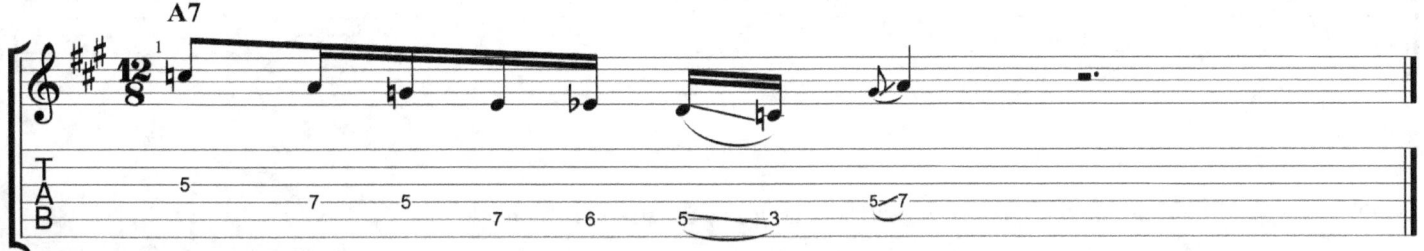

Here are some more useful licks formed from the Blues scale:

Example 6n:

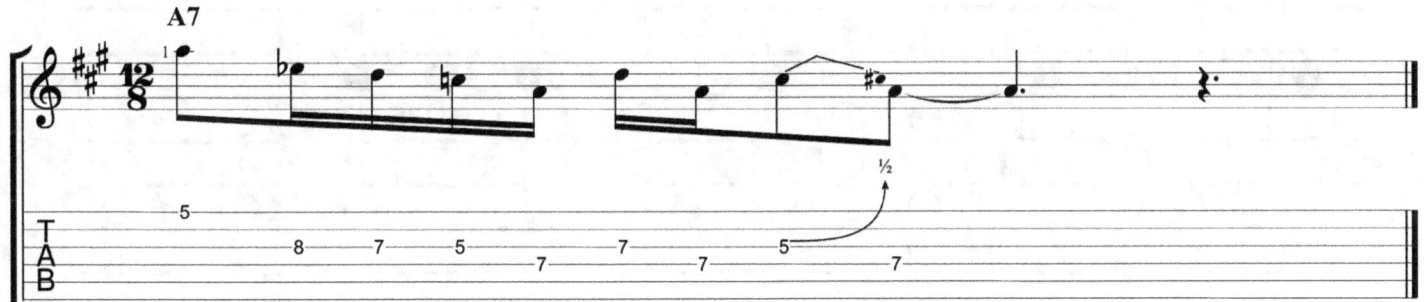

Example 6o:

Example 6p:

Example 6q:

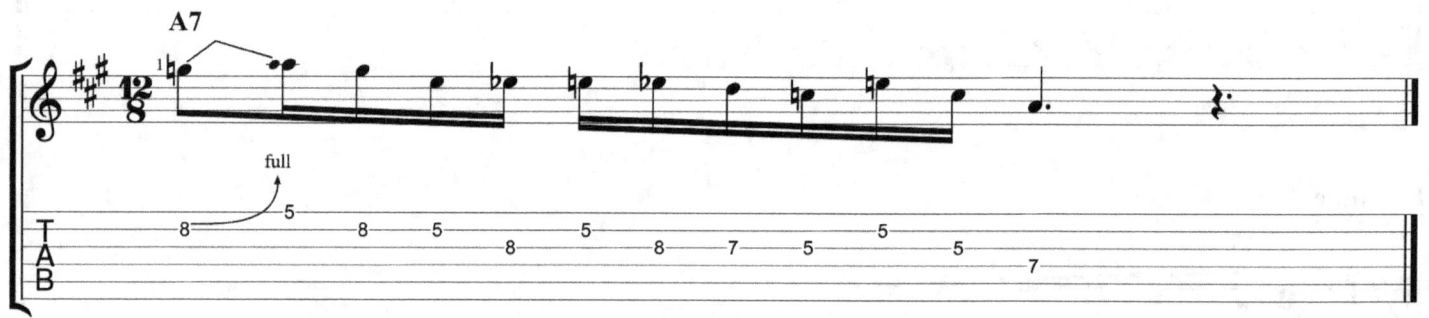

As always, you should practise improvising with the Blues scale all over the neck.

Here are the five scale patterns you need to know.

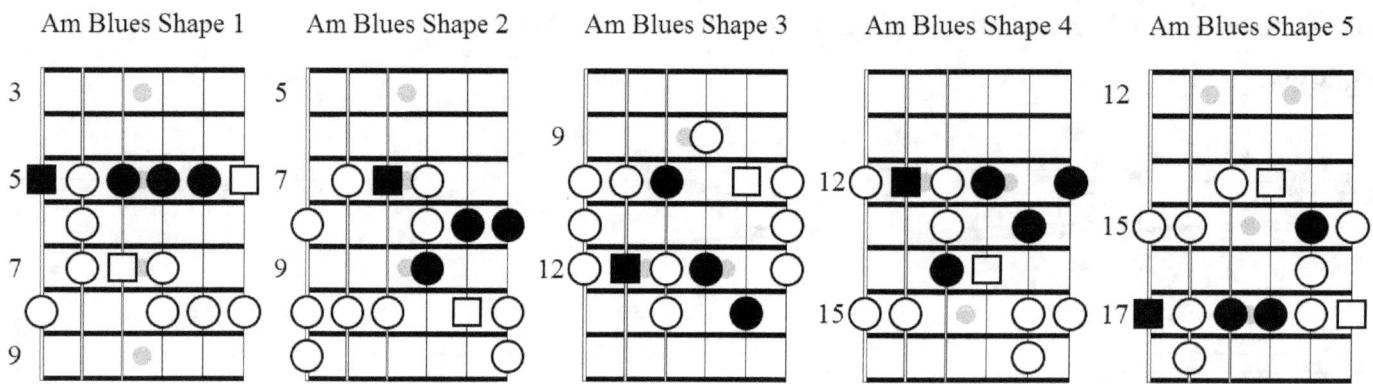

iii. The Mixolydian Mode

A common and important scale choice on the I chord is the scale of A Mixolydian.

Mixolydian is the fifth *mode* of the Major scale and contains all the notes from the A7 arpeggio plus the notes from the A Major Pentatonic scale.

As a formula it is written: 1 2 3 4 5 6 b7

In the key of A the notes are A B C# D E F# G

As you can see, it contains the intervals from A dominant 7 arpeggio:

1 3 5 b7

A C# E G

and the notes from the Major Pentatonic scale

1 2 3 5 6

A B C# E F#

It also includes the 4th from the Minor Pentatonic scale (D)

As the Mixolydian sound is close to the chord arpeggio, the Mixolydian scale is almost always combined with the Minor Pentatonic and Blues scales to give it a little bit of bite, character and aggression.

The scale of A Mixolydian is played in the following way. I have included a diagram of the A Blues scale next to the diagram of the Mixolydian mode to help you see how these scales can be combined. It is useful to see the similarities and differences between the two because Mixolydian is almost always combined with the Minor Pentatonic scale.

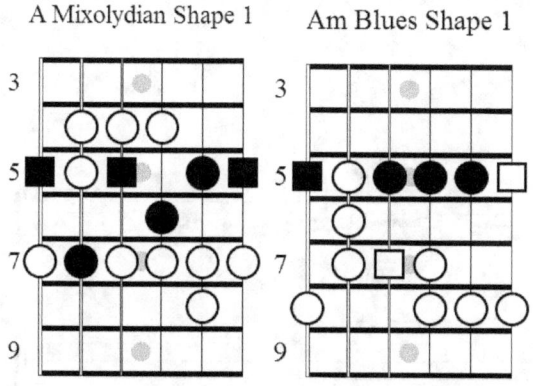

Try playing the Mixolydian scale ascending and descending over the A7 chords in Backing Track 1. It almost sounds a bit too 'correct'.

It is easy to hear that the notes are correct but it doesn't sound very bluesy. When I use the Mixolydian mode in a blues solo I tend to think of the Minor Pentatonic/Blues scale as a framework and stir in some notes of the Mixolydian mode for a brighter colour. It's almost like playing a combination of Minor and Major Pentatonic scales played at the same time.

The following licks are created by combining the A Mixolydian and A Minor Pentatonic/Blues scales.

Example 6r:

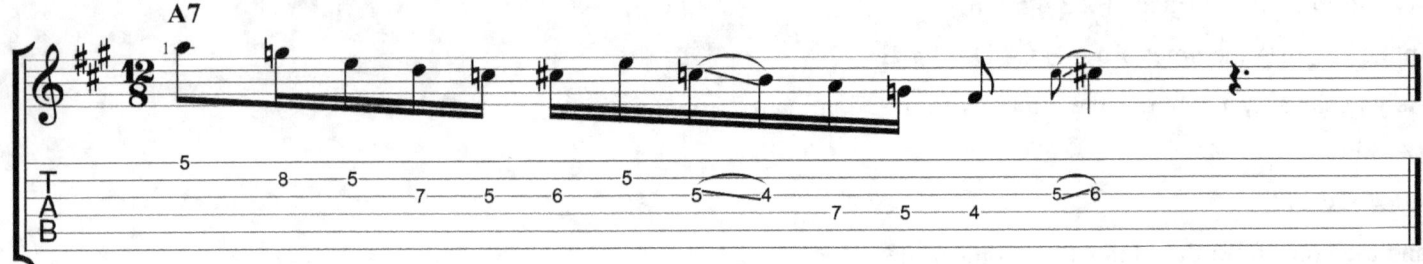

Example 6s:

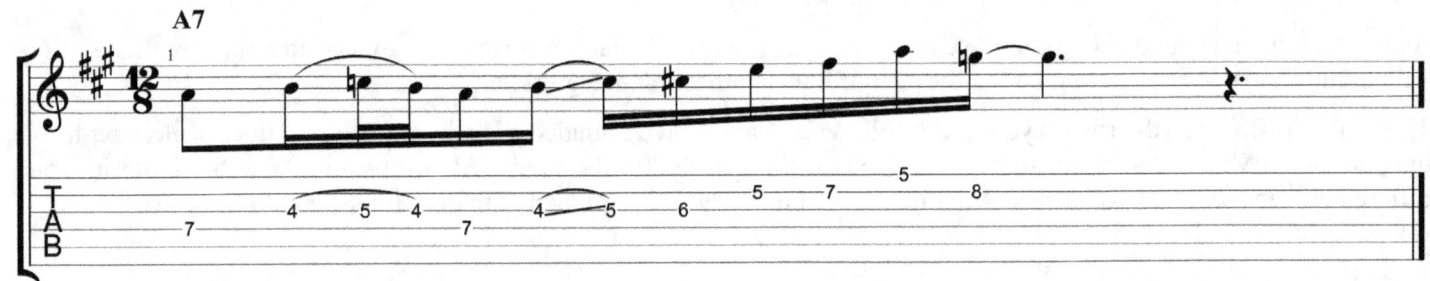

Example 6t:

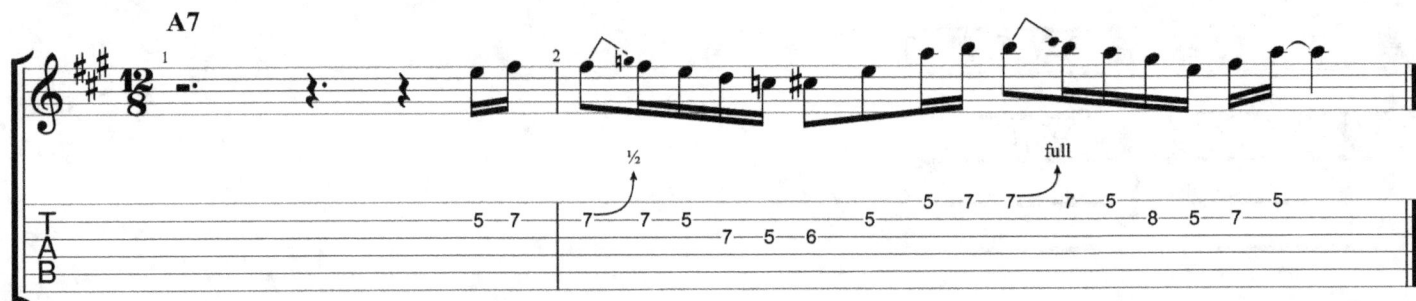

Example 6u:

Example 6v:

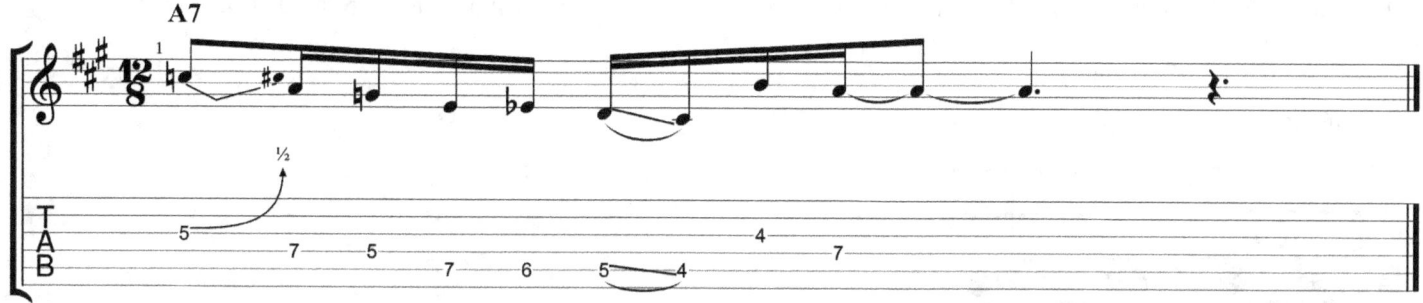

Study the previous examples carefully. Can you see how elements of both the Minor Pentatonic scale and the Mixolydian mode are combined freely to create an authentic blues sound?

These examples are just the tip of the iceberg. One musical way to practise this concept is to look for notes that are contained in the Mixolydian mode but not in the Minor Pentatonic scale. Try bending or sliding from Mixolydian notes into Minor Pentatonic notes and vice versa.

For example, instead of this standard Minor Pentatonic line:

Example 6w:

Convert it into a brighter sounding Mixolydian lick:

Example 6x:

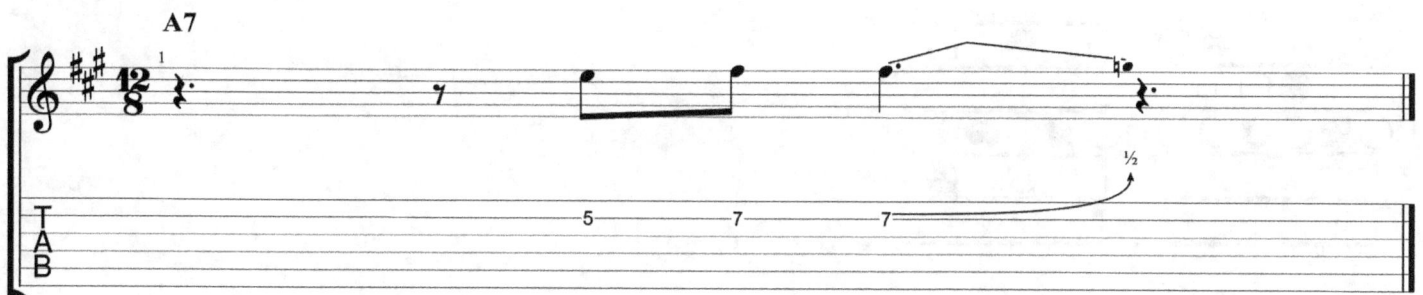

The previous two ideas work on the 1st string too.

There are plenty of opportunities for this kind of conversion and you should practise this concept all over the neck. Here is the scale of A Mixolydian in the five main fretboard positions. Each is shown next to its related Blues scale.

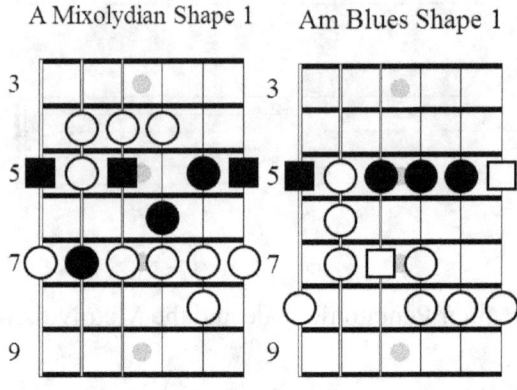

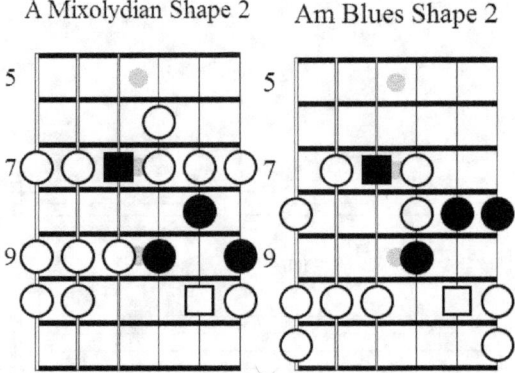

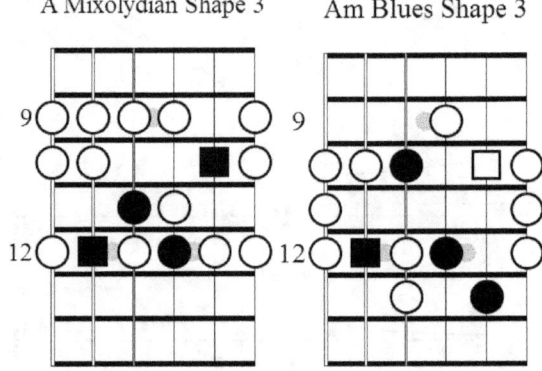

212

A Mixolydian Shape 4   Am Blues Shape 4

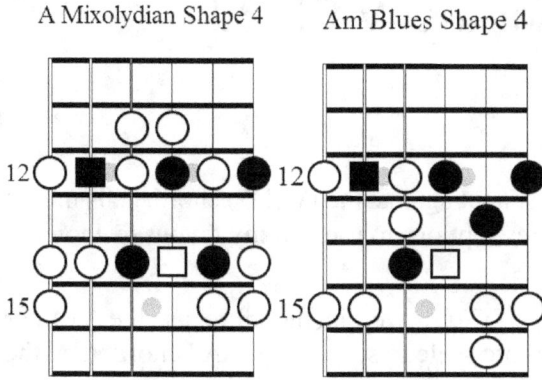

A Mixolydian Shape 5   Am Blues Shape 5

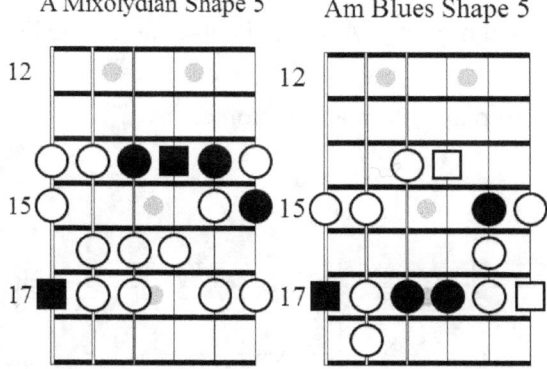

You may have already guessed that you can use the D Mixolydian mode on the D7 (IV) chord and E Mixolydian on the E7 (V) chord. We will look at this in more detail later.

Chapter Seven: Scale Choices for the IV Chord

i. The Tonic Minor Pentatonic on Chord IV

As we learned in Chapter Six, the tonic A Major Pentatonic scale sounds dissonant against the IV (D7) chord. This means that we need to change scale when the harmony changes to D7. There are a few options to use, but my favourite choice is to play the A Minor Pentatonic scale over the D7 chord.

One reason for this is that the A Minor Pentatonic scale contains the b7 note of D7 (C). We can, therefore, use the A Minor Pentatonic to target this note. If we have previously used the A Major Pentatonic scale to solo over the A7 chord, then the note C will not have been played until this point, and its introduction is a nice surprise on the chord change.

It is important to notice that the A Minor Pentatonic scale (A C D E G) does *not* include the important 3rd of the D chord (F#) so it is acceptable to add it in whenever we like.

Here is a simple line that uses the A Major Pentatonic scale on the A7 chord and moves to A Minor Pentatonic on the D7 chord. The line targets the b7 of D7 (C) on the chord change.

I play A Major Pentatonic at the second fret and slide the scale up three frets to play A Minor Pentatonic.

Example 7a:

Here are a couple of ideas that change between the A Major Pentatonic and A Minor Pentatonic scales while staying at the fifth fret:

Example 7b:

Example 7c:

Let's not forget all the work we did in Chapter One. We can still target the major 3rd of the D7 chord (F#) when the chord changes (even though it is not in the A Minor Pentatonic scale), and then continue the line with the A Minor Pentatonic scale.

Example 7d:

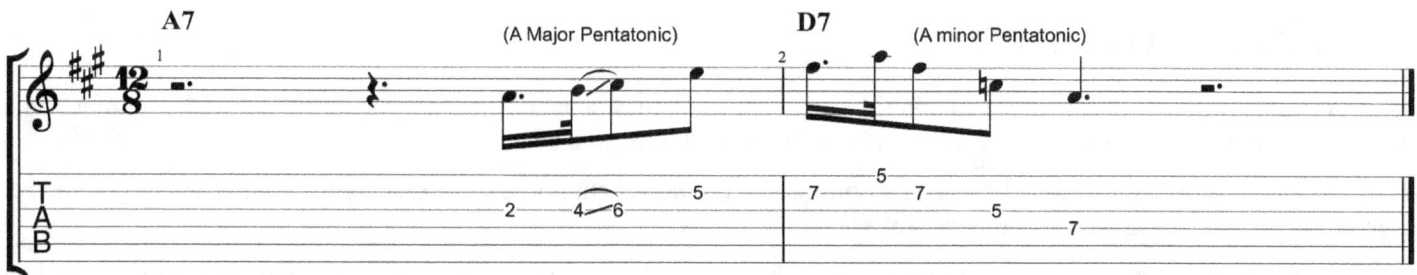

Example 7e:

The key is lots of experimentation and jamming. Remember, just because a scale option is available, you don't have to play it. This is a mistake I often used to make; I'd try to cram in every possible piece of theory into one bar, when in fact a great way to play is to suggest a scale as subtly as possible.

Another important consideration is deciding *when* you're going to play, not *what* you're going to play. By thinking of rhythm and note placement, you take instant command over your solo.

Aim to start your D7 line at a specific point in the bar, for example in the middle of beat three:

Example 7f:

By using this much space between my lines, I effectively highlight the difference in scale choice between bars one and two. I still use A Major Pentatonic in bar one and A Minor Pentatonic in bar two, but by picking the specific point where I will place my notes I give myself room to build my solo and the audience time to appreciate each phrase.

ii. Minor Pentatonic on the IV Chord

As we used the A Major Pentatonic scale over the chord of A7 it may seem obvious to play the D Major Pentatonic scale over the D7 chord. However, This is actually a bit of a musical grey area.

In theory, the scale should work well but in my opinion the D Major Pentatonic scale isn't a great choice for the D7 chord, although you should definitely test this out for yourself.

The D Major Pentatonic does not contain the b7 of the D chord (C) which feels like a powerful note at this point in the progression. Its omission really detracts from the classic blues sound. You'll remember from Chapter One that the movement from the 3rd of A7 (C#) to the b7 of the D7 (C) is one of the defining characteristics and important sounds in the blues.

By playing a D Major Pentatonic scale at this point we lose the opportunity to exploit this movement.

Of course, you could play a D Major Pentatonic scale and add in the b7 (C) note, but this sound is so close to the Mixolydian scale that most people simply play Mixolydian instead.

A good choice for the D7 chord is the D Minor Pentatonic scale, though it tends to work best if we bend the b3 note (F) towards major territory (F#). We looked briefly at this idea earlier when we discussed bending into guide tones from a semitone below.

This is the fretboard diagram for D Minor Pentatonic at the 5th fret. The black note on the 2nd string is the minor 3rd that you'll want to bend towards the major 3rd.

Dm Pentatonic

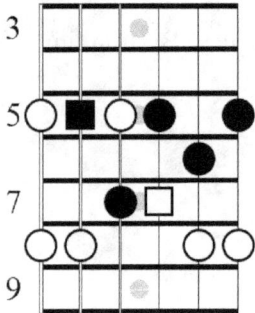

216

Here are some lines for the IV chord based around D Minor Pentatonic scale. Notice how I usually bend the F towards F#.

Example 7g:

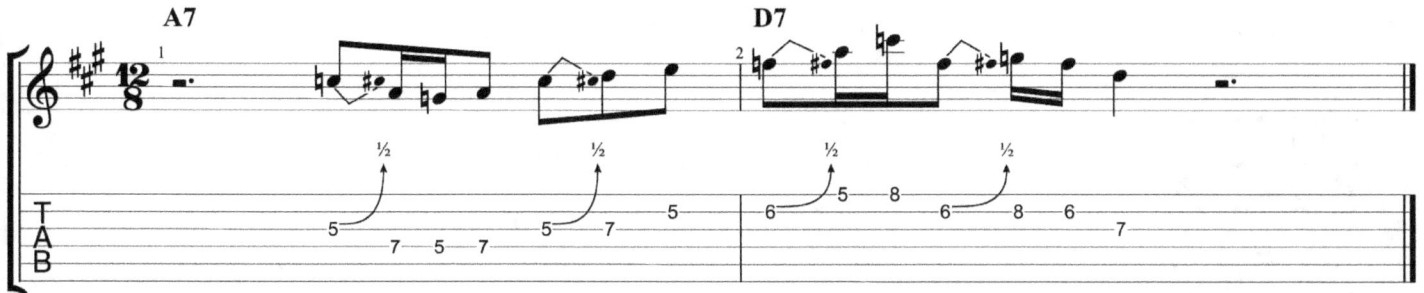

Example 7h:

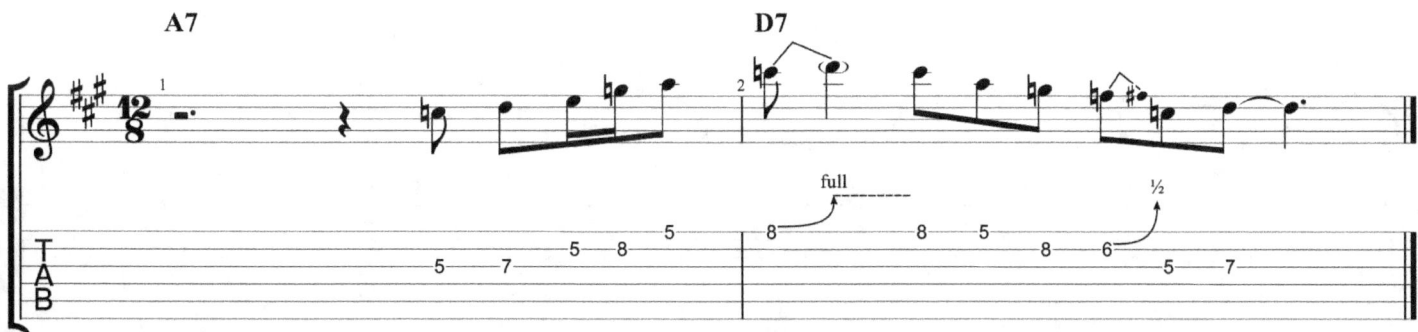

Example 7i:

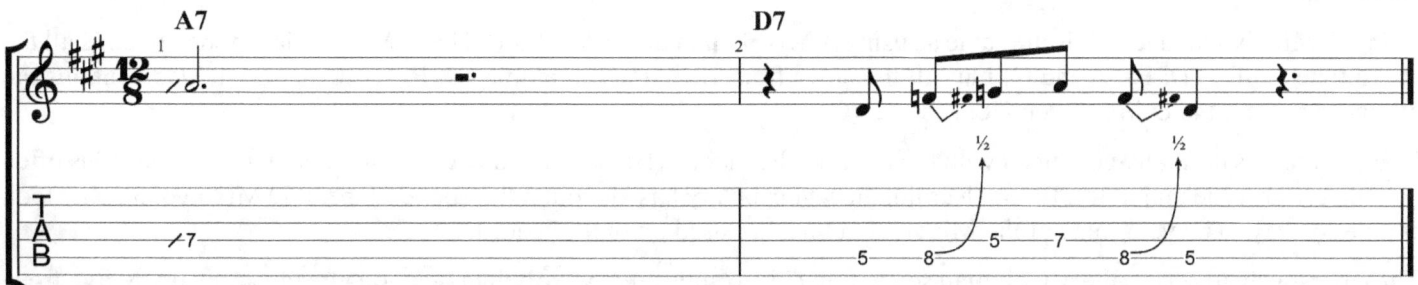

Using a D Minor Pentatonic scale over the D7 chord is a common melodic technique but the b3 (F) does need to be handled with care. The most common way to deal with this note is to bend it up towards the major 3rd (F#) as I have shown.

iii. Mixolydian on the IV chord

Playing the Mixolydian mode on chord IV works much in the same way as playing the Mixolydian mode on chord I. It is a common approach because the Mixolydian scale contains all the notes from the dominant 7 chord plus some great-sounding colours.

Over the chord of D7 we can use the D Mixolydian mode. At the 5th fret, D Mixolydian can be played like this:

D Mixolydian Shape 4

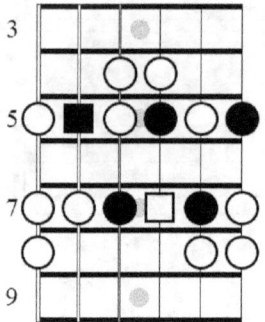

The D Mixolydian mode is not related to the tonic key of A so it is used *only* over the D7 chord. When we play a different scale over each chord, we view each chord change as a temporary modulation (key change) to the tonality of D Mixolydian.

Using D Mixolydian over D7 is the same as using A Mixolydian on an A7 chord. The D Mixolydian mode contains all the chord tones of D7 (D, F#, A and C) plus all the notes from D Major Pentatonic (D, E, F#, A and B). It also contains the 4th interval from the D Minor Pentatonic scale, (G).

Once again, it is normally combined with the D Minor Pentatonic/Blues scale, however, once again, the minor 3rd is often bent up towards the major 3rd. Before learning new vocabulary based around the above shape of D Mixolydian, let's look at an easy way to recycle some of the Mixolydian lines we used on the A7 chord.

The easiest way to access the Mixolydian sound on D7 is to slide an A Mixolydian lick you already know up by five frets. Just as if we were moving a barre chord up the neck from A7 to D7.

For example, Here's the lick from example 6r:

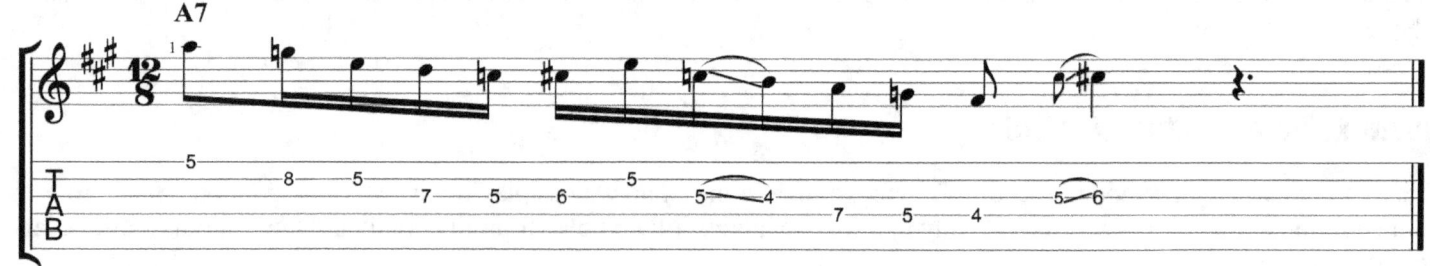

To play it as a D Mixolydian lick, slide it up five frets. Stevie Ray Vaughan was a huge fan of this technique.

Example 7j:

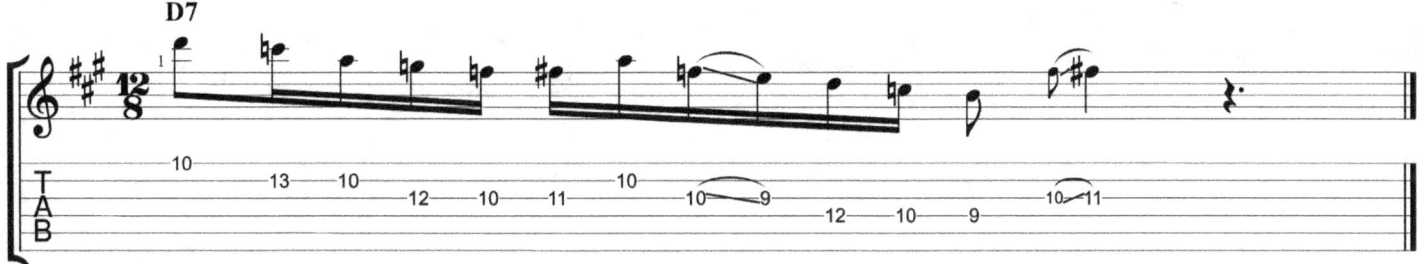

Here is the A Mixolydian from example 6s:

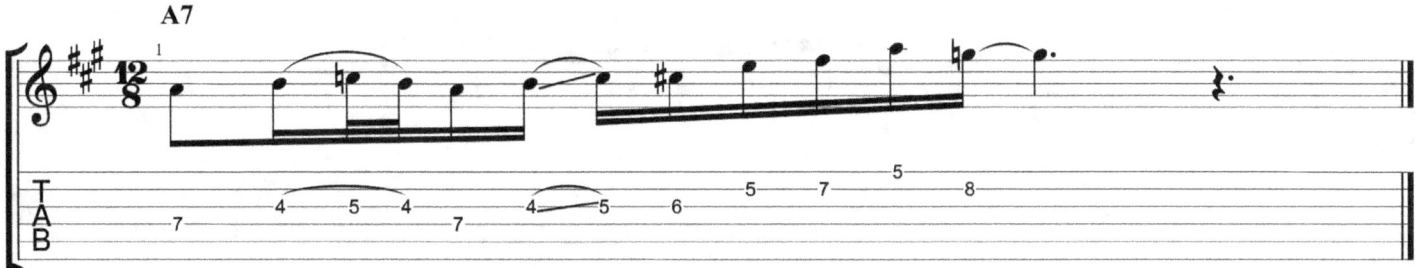

And here it is moved up five frets the neck to become a D Mixolydian line:

Example 7k:

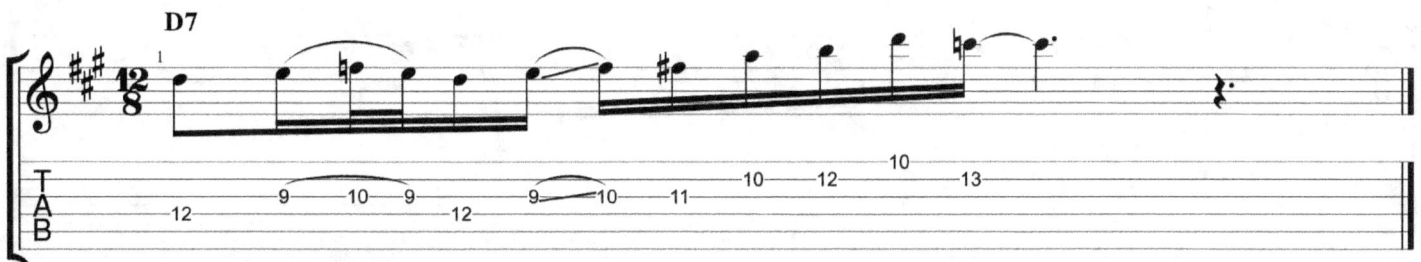

Learning to move lines around the neck into new keys is an essential part of learning the guitar, so try playing all your licks in different keys.

Moving the scale shape up and down the neck is useful, but it is also important to be able to change keys while staying in the same position.

The following lines are based around the D Mixolydian scale shape shown at the beginning of this section. The root note, D is on the 5th string, 5th fret.

These examples all begin on an arpeggio tone of D7, They then continue by using a combination of the D Mixolydian and D Minor Pentatonic scales. I often bend into the arpeggio tone from a semitone below for a more bluesy effect.

Example 7l:

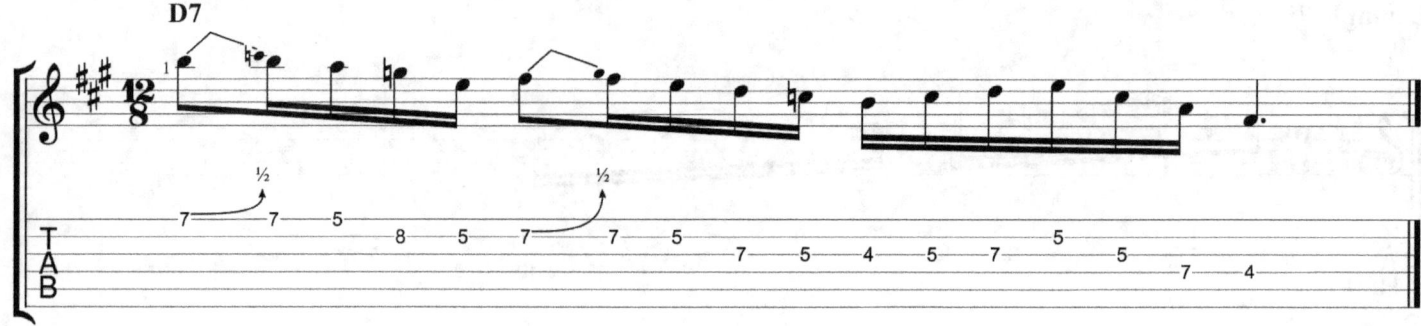

Example 7m:

Example 7n

Example 7o

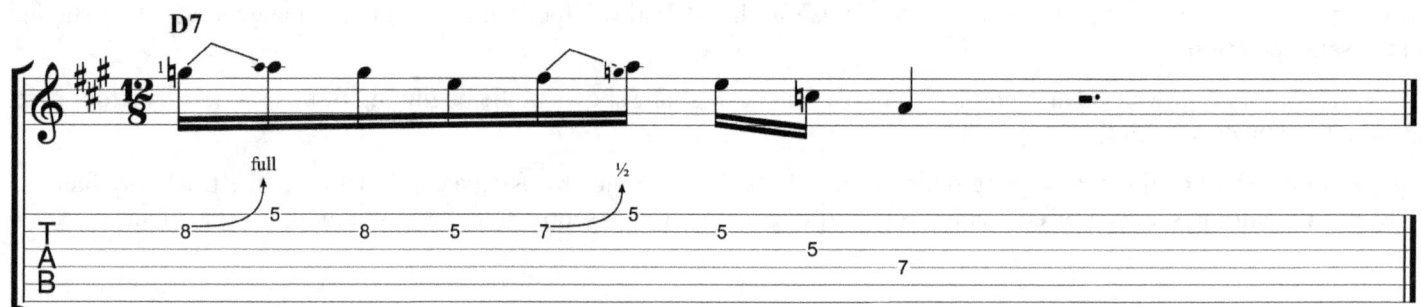

Example 7p:

Example 7q:

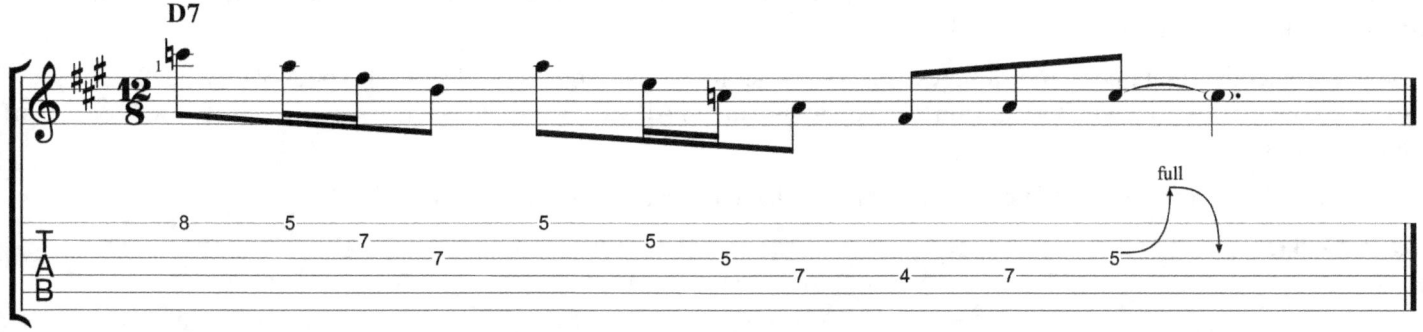

Chapter Eight: Scale Choices for the V Chord

i. The Tonic Minor Pentatonic on Chord V

There are many possible scale choices for the V (E7) chord, and one of the most common sounds is to use the Minor Pentatonic scale played from the key of the song. In our case this is A Minor Pentatonic. We have covered this scale in great depth already.

There is however, a danger in blanketing the blues progression with the tonic Minor Pentatonic scale. By doing so, it is easy to lose sight and sound of the harmonic subtleties that occur when the chords change and that we aim to bring out with intelligent scale choice.

This book has been all about enhancing and articulating these harmonic movements by careful choice of arpeggio notes and guide tones, so in this section we will study a small change we can make to one note of the A Minor Pentatonic scale to make it perfectly outline the E7 chord.

You may remember that one of the strongest notes to target in the E7 chord is the 3rd (G#). The A Minor Pentatonic scale does *not* contain this note but there is a simple way to include it. All we need to do is alter one of the most commonly bent notes in the scale.

When you solo with the A Minor Pentatonic scale you have probably played lines like this:

Example 8a:

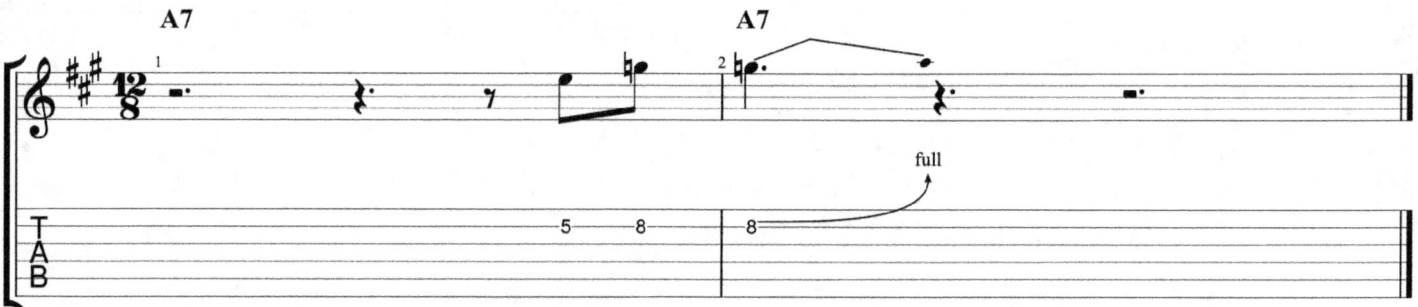

The final note in the previous phrase is a whole tone bend from the note G to the note A. To target the G# note on an E7 chord we simply change this whole-tone bend into a half-tone bend. Instead of bending to G, we bend to G# instead.

This bend is particularly strong if played it right on the chord change:

Example 8b:

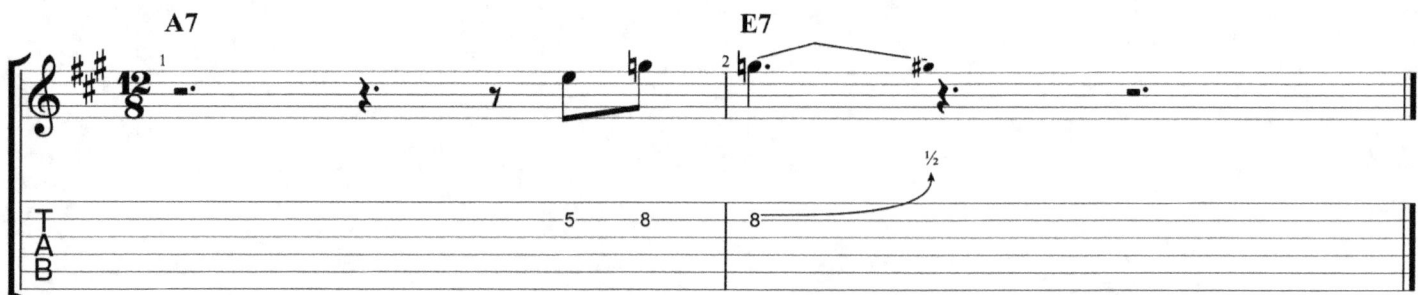

By altering just this one note, it is easy to use A Minor Pentatonic scale to outline the E7 sound. Remember though, the G# will sound terrible at any almost other point in the progression. It only works on the E7 chord.

Here are a couple of lines to get your started. Notice in example 8c how I repeat the G - G# bend in the lower octave.

Example 8c:

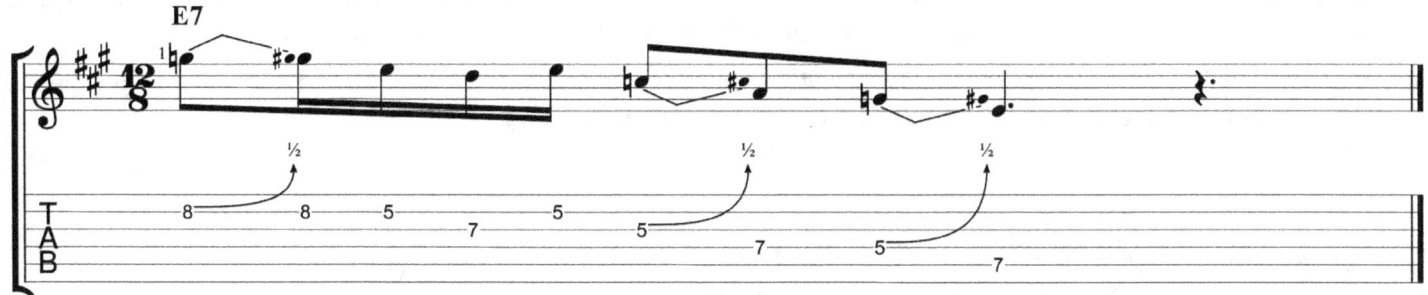

The C natural of the A Minor Pentatonic scale will normally need to be given a little curl towards C# territory as this it a slightly sweeter note against the E7 chord.

Example 8d:

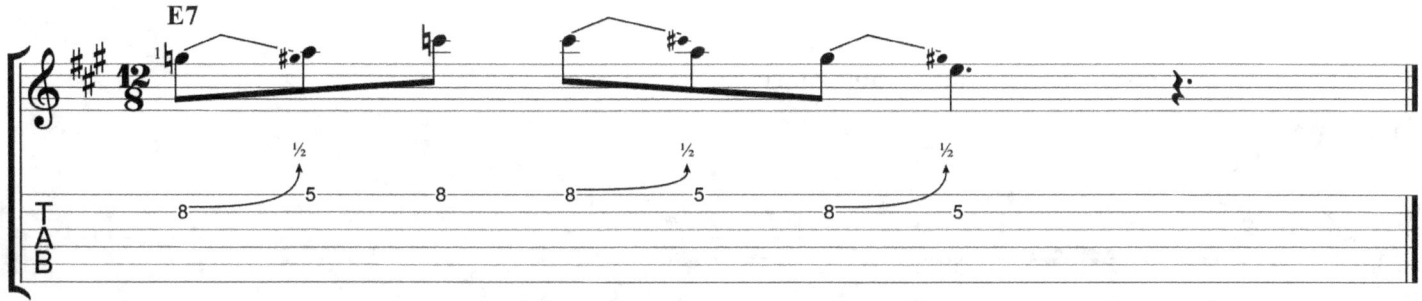

Example 8e:

Example 8f:

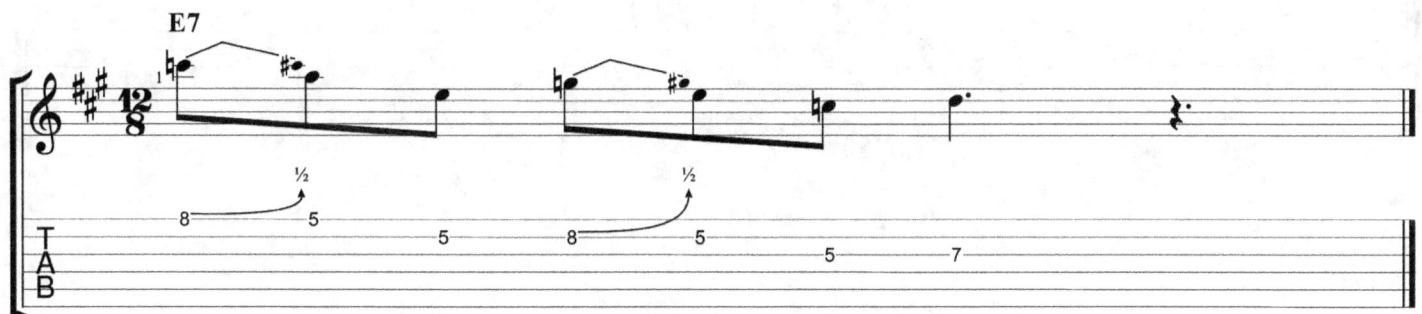

223

ii. Minor Pentatonic on Chord V

Just as we used the D Minor Pentatonic scale over D7, we can also use the E Minor Pentatonic scale over E7. However, it is important to remember that we will nearly always bend the b3 (G) towards the major 3rd territory (G#).

A simple way to access this sound is to take any D Minor Pentatonic lick you know and move it up by a tone to work on the E7 chord. For example, here is a D Minor Pentatonic lick from example 7g.

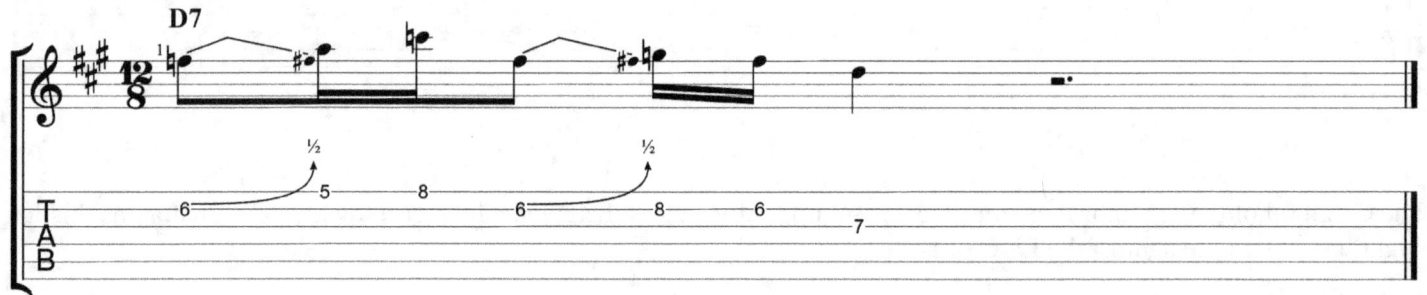

Here it is shifted up a tone to become an E Minor Pentatonic lick:

Example 8g:

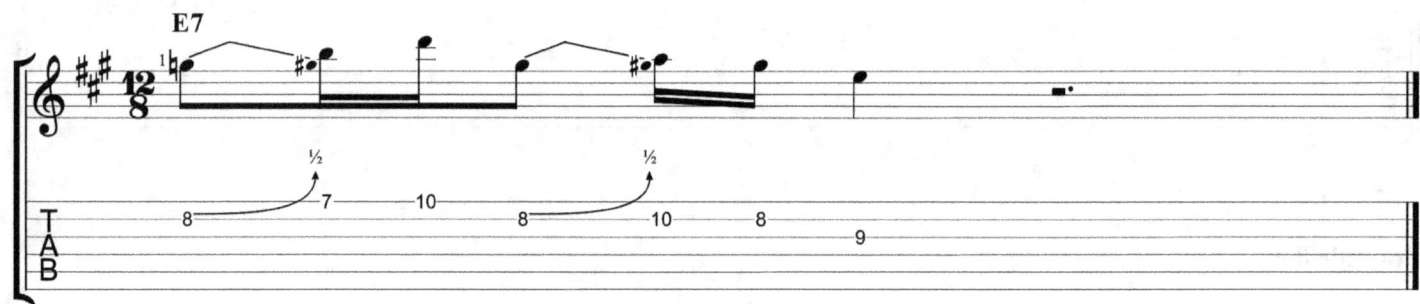

Remember, you can also move an A Minor Pentatonic / Blues scale lick up to the 12th fret area to create an E Minor Pentatonic lick. Let's try it with this example 6j.

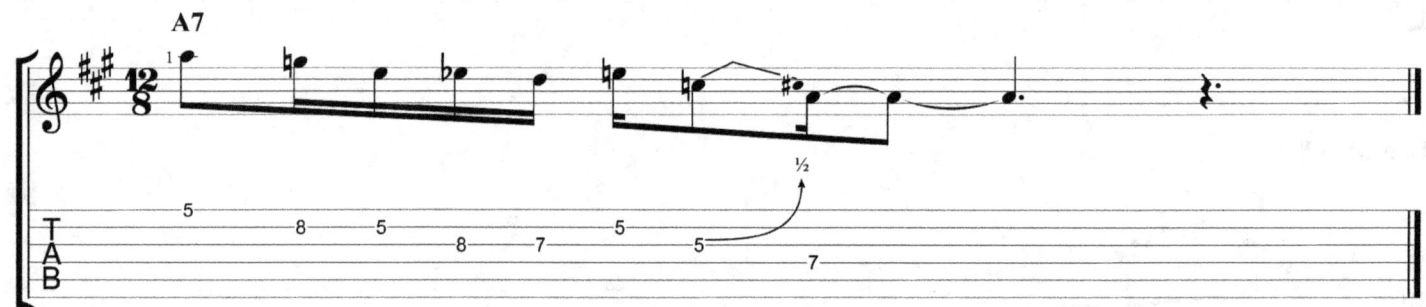

Here is the same line shifted (transposed) up the neck to create an E7 line:

Example 8h:

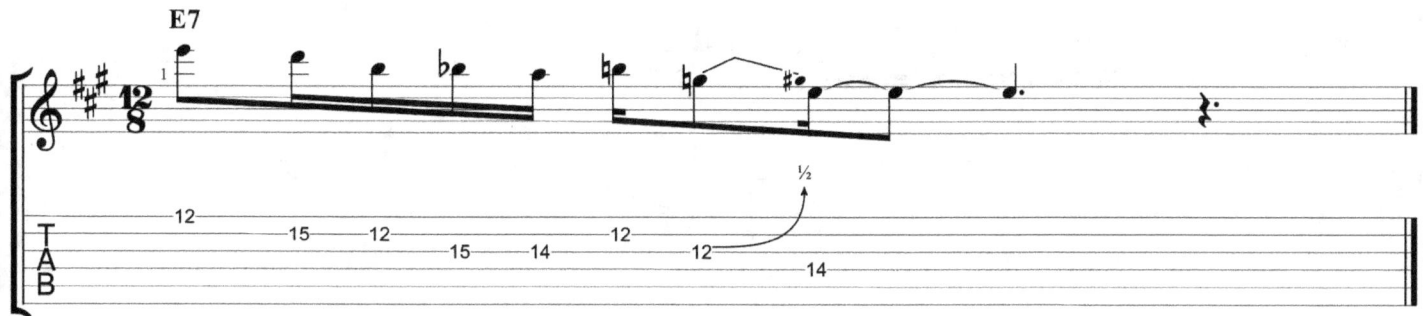

These two techniques are very useful, but we should also learn some E Minor Pentatonic vocabulary at the 5th fret so we don't have to 'chase' licks around the fretboard.

Here's how to play the E Minor Pentatonic / Blues scale at the 5th - 7th fret:

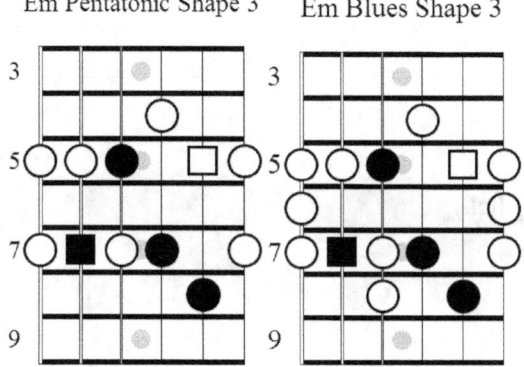

An advantage of using E Minor Pentatonic as opposed to A Minor Pentatonic over the E7 chord is that it contains the 5th of the E7 chord. As we learned earlier, this is an extremely powerful target note as it only occurs in the E7 chord.

The following lines demonstrate how to use the E Minor Pentatonic scale over the E7 chord. Notice that the b3 (G) is normally bent towards the major 3rd (G#) if it occurs at a rhythmically strong point in the bar.

Example 8i:

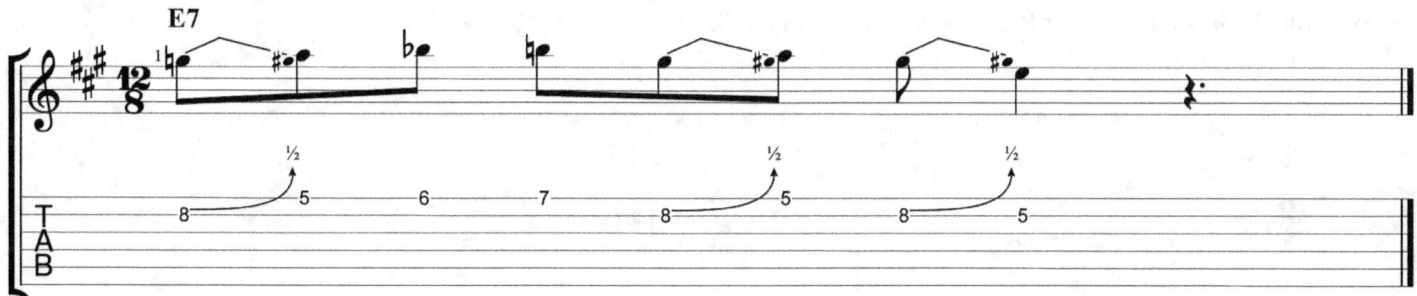

225

Example 8j:

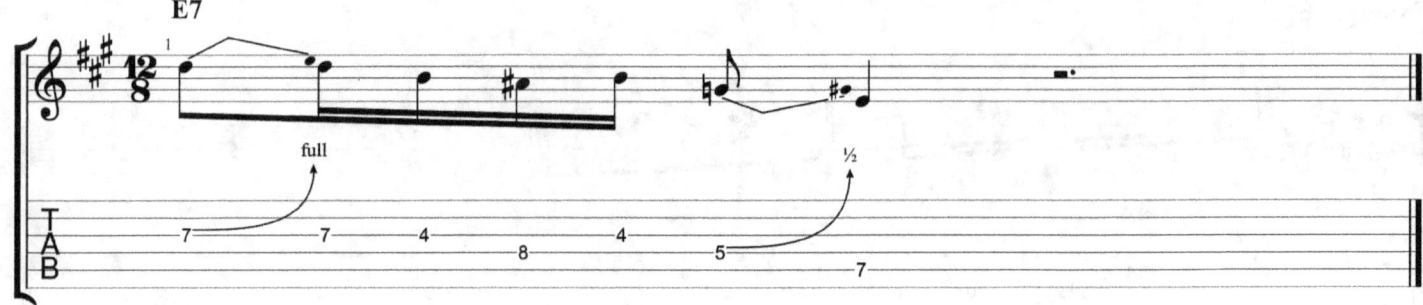

Example 8k:

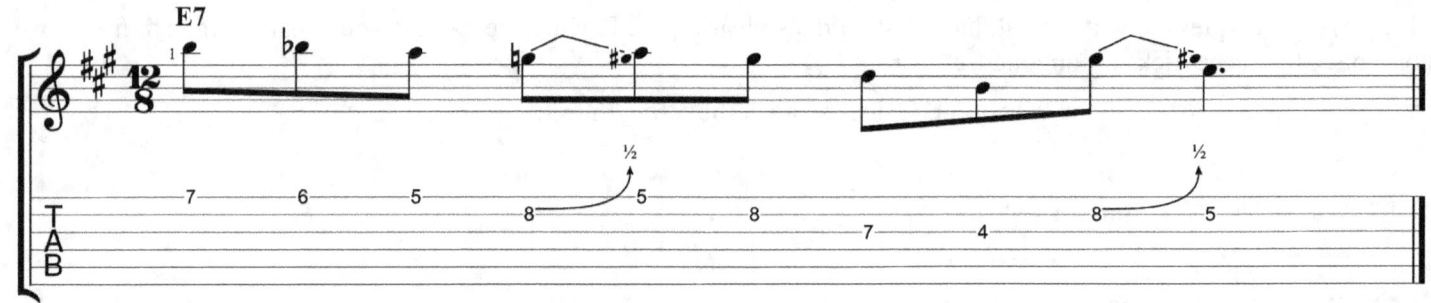

Don't forget, any of these lines can be played a tone (two frets) lower as a D7 lick.

iii. Minor Pentatonic on the 5th of the V Chord

Just as we used the A Minor Pentatonic to play over the D7 chord in Chapter Seven, it possible to use the *B Minor Pentatonic* to solo over the E7 chord.

Playing a Minor Pentatonic scale build from the fifth of the chord is a common technique that's used a lot in rock and explained in more detail in my book, **The Practical Guide to Modern Music Theory**.

The 5th of the E7 chord is the note B, so we can play B Minor Pentatonic over the E7 chord.

The quickest way to hear this relationship is to simply move an A Minor Pentatonic line that we played on the D7 chord up by one tone to become a B Minor Pentatonic line over the E7 chord.

For example, here is an A Minor Pentatonic line (example 7b).

This line uses the A Major Pentatonic scale on the A7 chord and switches to A Minor Pentatonic scale on the D7 chord.

Let's keep the first half of the line the same on the A7 chord, but shift the second half of the line up by a tone to suit an E7 chord:

Example 8l:

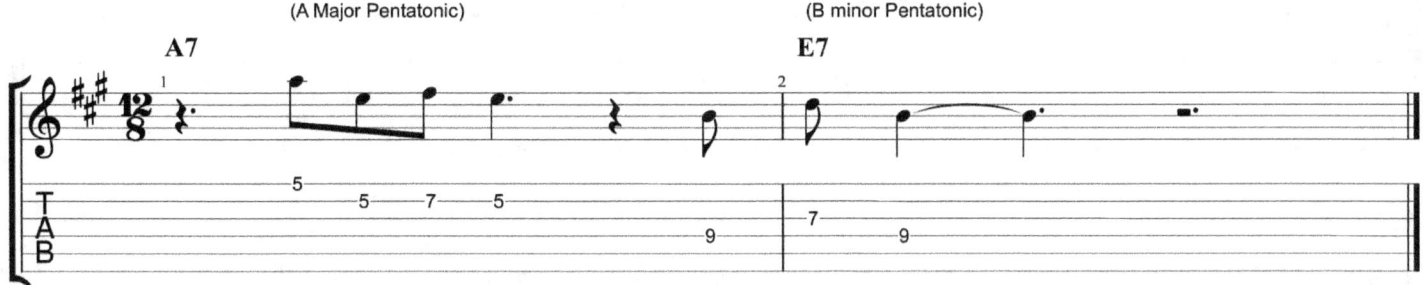

This is a common approach for the dominant chord in a blues. You do have to be a little careful, because the B Minor Pentatonic scale contains the note F# which is an important chord tone of the D7 chord. As we are soloing over an E7 chord I'll avoid hitting the F# note on the chord change as it can sound a bit ambiguous. Essentially, you're playing a strong major 3rd of the IV chord over the V chord.

Use Backing Track 10 to practise this concept, the chord progression on the backing track is:

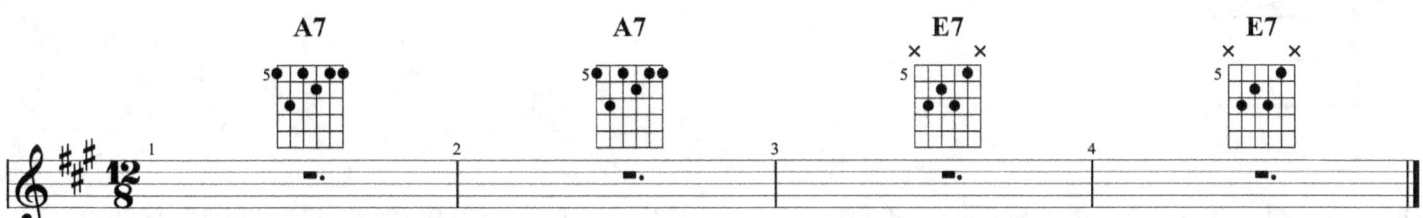

Choose a single idea to play on the A7 chord and move it up a tone so it becomes a B Minor Pentatonic line over the E7 chord.

Use your ears to decide if the notes you are targeting work musically. Here are a few more B Minor Pentatonic lines for you to play on the E7 chord:

Example 8m:

Here I let the E7 chord settle before playing the line to enhance its strength.

Example 8n:

To play the B Minor Pentatonic scale in the same position as the other chords in the blues, it can be played like this:

Bm Pentatonic Shape 5

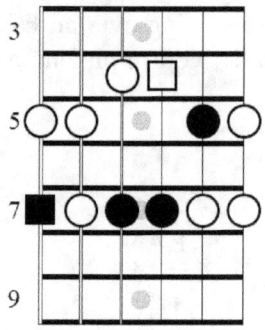

The following lines are based around this scale shape. I also freely add in the 3rd of the E7 chord (G#) to enhance the strength of the line.

Example 8o:

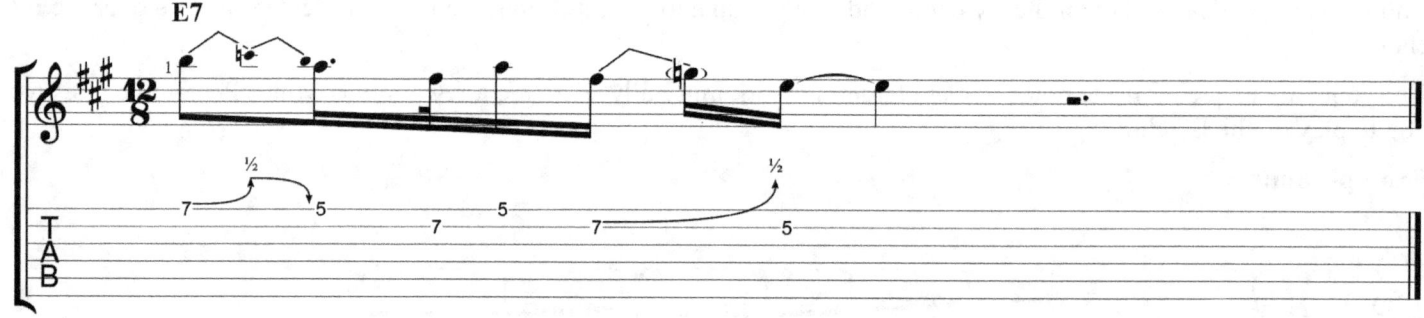

Example 8p:

Example 8q:

You may have noticed that playing the B Minor Pentatonic scale over the E7 is almost like playing the A Major Pentatonic scale over the E7 chord. In fact, there is only one note different between the two scales.

These subtle differences between scale choice become common when we look in so much detail at the soloing possibilities because only a certain amount of notes are be strongly related to the E7 sound.

Try this A Major Pentatonic line over the E7 chord:

Example 8r:

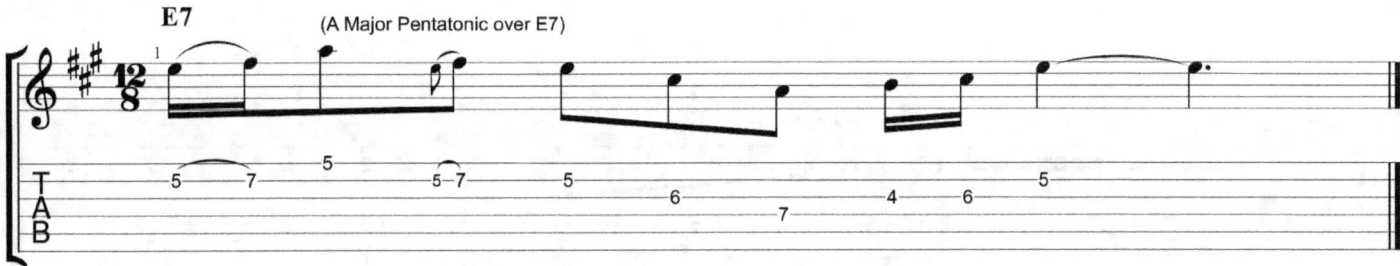

Whether you 'think' A Major Pentatonic or B Minor Pentatonic over the E7 chord will create subtle differences in the feel of your solo over the dominant chord. My advice is to experiment, pick your favourite and stick with it.

iv. Major Pentatonic on the V Chord

Using the Major Pentatonic scale on the V chord is another common choice. It can be a little bright for some people, maybe even a little country-sounding, but when combined with the Minor Pentatonic scale or other previously discussed ideas, it contains all the ingredients of an articulate solo over the Dominant V chord.

The big advantage to using E Major Pentatonic on E7 is that contains the major 3rd. The notes in the scale are:

E F# G# B and C#

These intervals are the root, 9th, 3rd 5th and 13th of the scale.

If you recap Chapter Four, you will see that the 3rd (G#) and the 5th (B) are both strong notes to target on the V (E7) chord. Here is the scale diagram for E Major Pentatonic at the 12th fret:

E Major Pentatonic

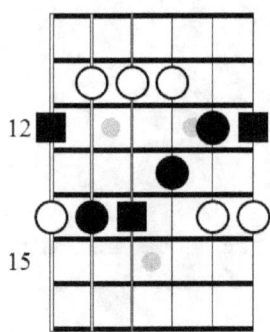

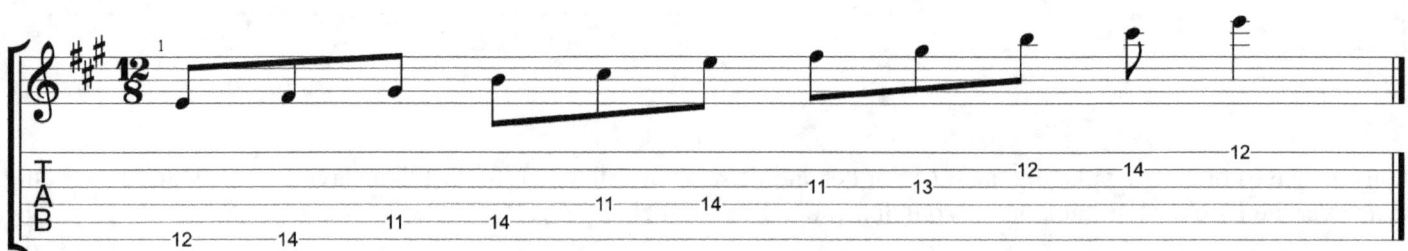

As always, the quickest way to access a new sound is to modify something you already know. Let's move an A Major Pentatonic lick up the neck and play it as an E Major Pentatonic lick. Here is example 6g.

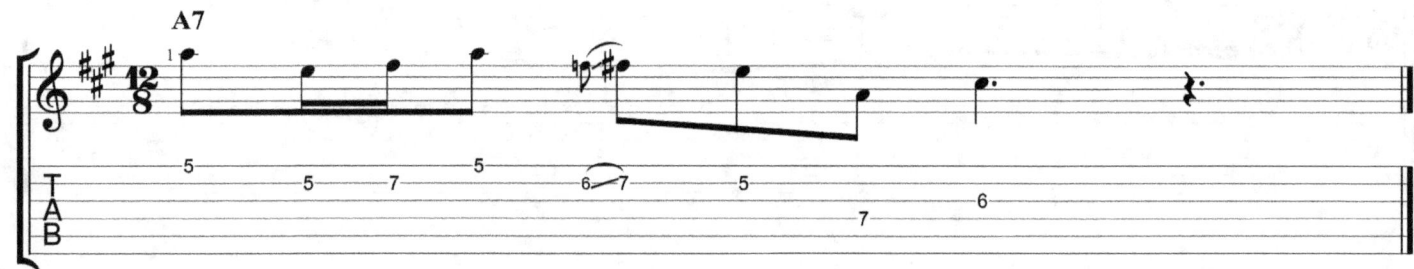

To transpose this line into an E Major Pentatonic lick, move the shape up to the 12 fret like this:

Example 8s:

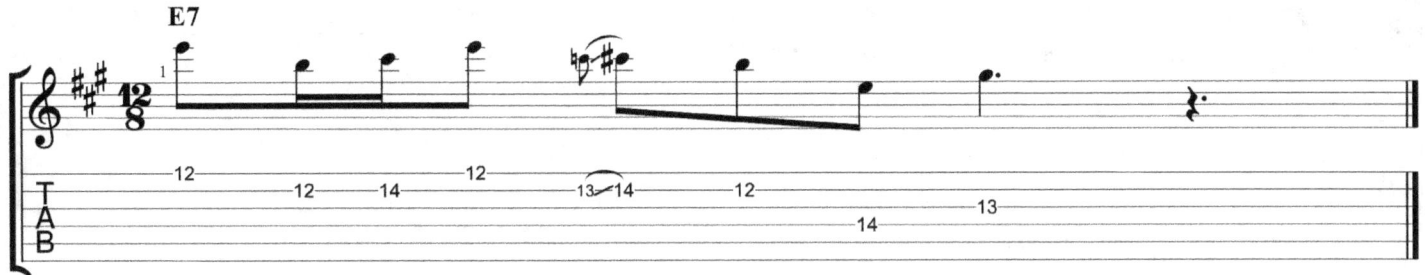

Try transposition with any A Major Pentatonic or D Major Pentatonic licks you learnt in previous chapters. By now you should be finding it easy to move Pentatonic licks into different keys.

To play the E Major Pentatonic scale close to the fifth fret you can use this scale shape:

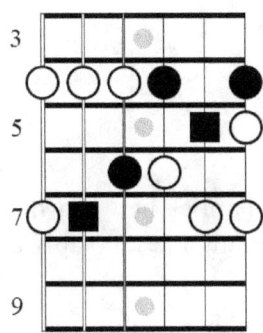

E Major Pentatonic

Here are some lines based around this position. Again, I regularly combine notes from both the Major Pentatonic and Minor Pentatonic scales.

Example 8t:

Example 8u:

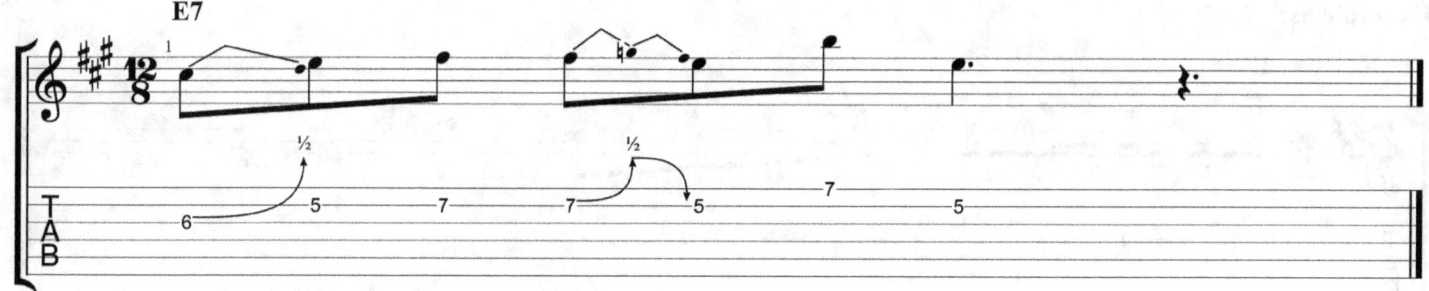

Example 8v:

v. Mixolydian on the V Chord

The final scale choice to explore is E Mixolydian Mode on the E7 chord. There are many similarities between the Mixolydian mode and the Major Pentatonic scale. However, the Mixolydian mode contains a few extra notes, notably a b7 guide tone that helps it fit perfectly around the V7 chord.

To quickly access the Mixolydian sound on the E7 chord, transpose some first position A Mixolydian lines up the neck to the 12th fret area. Try shifting this lick from example 6t:

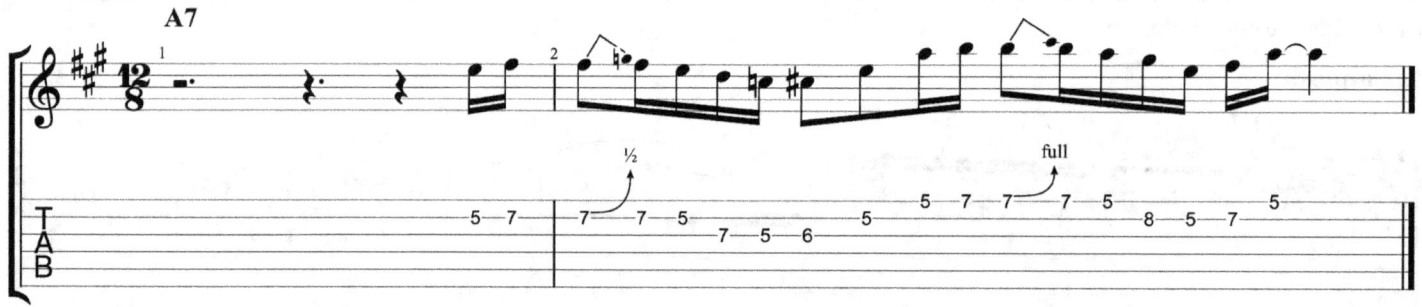

Here is how to play that line with an E root.

Example 8w:

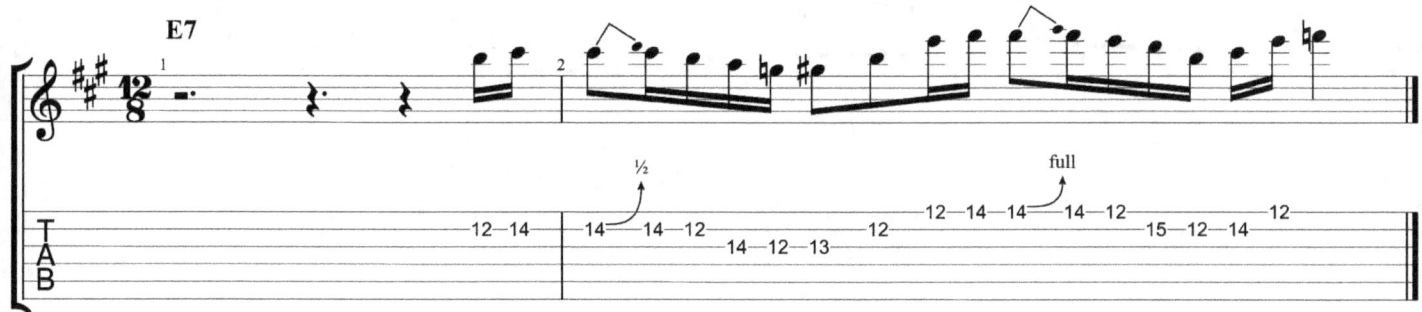

Try moving other A Mixolydian and D Mixolydian licks up the neck to the key of E to access instant vocabulary and get your ears used to this new sound.

The E Mixolydian mode can be played in the 5th-7th fret position in the following way:

E Mixolydian

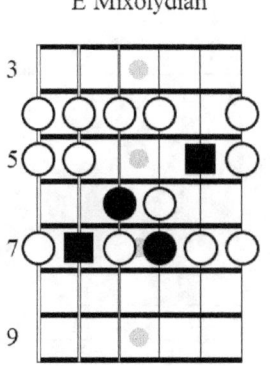

Here are some E Mixolydian licks based around the above scale shape. As always, I freely combine Minor Pentatonic and Blues scale notes into the lines.

Example 8x:

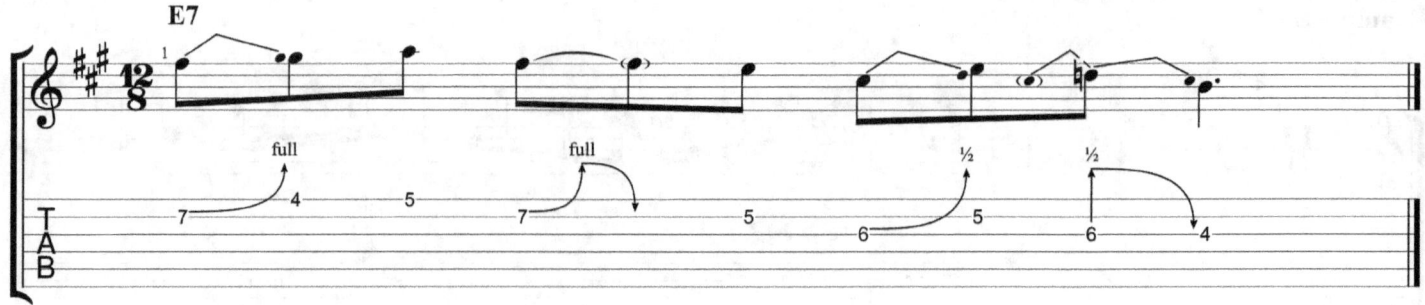

Example 8y:

Example 8z:

Mixolydian on the dominant chord is a favourite sound of many blues guitar players, but the best playing is normally a combination of many different approaches.

In the final chapter, we'll discuss how to practise these concepts efficiently and incorporate them into our playing. If we have a structured approach to practice, then these ideas will quickly combine and become natural to us in our solos.

One important truth that many musicians miss is that all this study just boils down to ear training. Do you really want to be thinking scales when you're playing? Or do you want to simply hear and feel where the right notes are on the guitar?

The type of deep study in this book is an essential stage in your development as a musician. Without studying scale permutations and guide tones you will always be in a situation where 'you don't know what you don't know'. By studying the most important scale choices individually and simply working with the ones you like, you will always be in control of what you play. You will have taught your ears the possible sounds and you will develop a personal language by combining them. Not every scale choice in this book will be to your taste. If you don't like something, do give it a chance and work with it for a while. However, if you still don't like it, simply disregard it and move on to something better.

Chapter 9: How to Practise

There is a vast amount of information in this book. It covers everything from targeting the defining notes of each chord, to multiple different scale choices for every chord in the blues. If you don't develop a structured approach to learning and assimilating all these sounds, then the task of learning all the permutations will feel overwhelming.

My first piece of advice is a warning: Try to avoid the thought, "But what if…?"

I will admit that I'm still guilty of this one, but I'm getting better. Sometimes I'll be soloing, creating melodies and trying to express myself on the guitar. I'll be playing over a blues or a jazz progression and letting my ears guide my playing. Then suddenly I get the thought, "But what if I was using a different scale? Would that sound better? Shouldn't I play *a clever* bit of theory just to show people how knowledgeable I am?"

Maybe you can relate to this. The more we study, the more soloing options we have, and the more we get affected by the thought, "But what if…?"

Unfortunately, at this point I've already lost the game because I've started to think about music theory, and not about playing music and melody.

The way to combat this is to realise that *everything* we practise is just ear training. The time for practising scales and theory is in the practice room. As soon as you sit down to play something meaningful you must switch off that internal dialogue that worries about what you're *not* playing.

You must focus on, and listen to the melody in your head and the notes coming from your guitar. Focus on the music and melody, and hear the next note that you'll play before you play it. If you've done the work in the practice room, the new concepts will eventually get into your ears and under your fingers. If you find it's not coming, practise more slowly. Sing every note before you play it and develop the connection between the brain and fingers.

If you're in any doubt leave silence until you hear the next melody in your head, and then play it. It's difficult at first but practise playing only what you hear inside you.

The quickest way to do this is to sing what you play. This might be embarrassing or awkward at first, but no one has to hear you. It's the one sure-fire way to connect the music inside you to your fingers and your guitar.

If you get stuck when you're on stage, pick one theoretical concept and make music from it. Remember, the most powerful tools you have at your disposal are rhythm, feel and placement. The simplest musical concept will sound incredible when played with impeccable feel.

Above all, switch off from "But what if…?" and focus on the music you're making in the moment.

You may feel that none of this is relevant to you, but in my experience, it has affected every musician I have spoken to. Almost without exception they have all said, "Leave space, keep it simple, and think rhythm."

Let's look at how to incorporate the scales in this book tangibly into our playing.

We have studied many possible scale choices for each chord of the blues progression.

Here they all are written out in the key of A:

Chord I: A7

- A Minor Pentatonic scale
- A Blues scale
- A Major Pentatonic scale
- A Mixolydian scale

Chord IV: D7

- D Minor Pentatonic scale
- A Minor Pentatonic scale
- D Mixolydian scale
- (D Major Pentatonic also possible)

Chord V: E7

- A Minor Pentatonic
- E Minor Pentatonic
- B Minor Pentatonic
- E Major Pentatonic
- E Mixolydian scale

Pick just one soloing approach for each chord. Always begin with your favourite (If you don't have a favourite yet pick one randomly).

Write out the 12-bar blues progression and write in the approach you'll use on each chord. Always use the same approach for the same chord type. For example, if you've decided to use Major Pentatonic on the A7 chord, A Minor Pentatonic on D7 and E Mixolydian on the E7 chords, *stick to it*!

Your soloing scheme will look something like this:

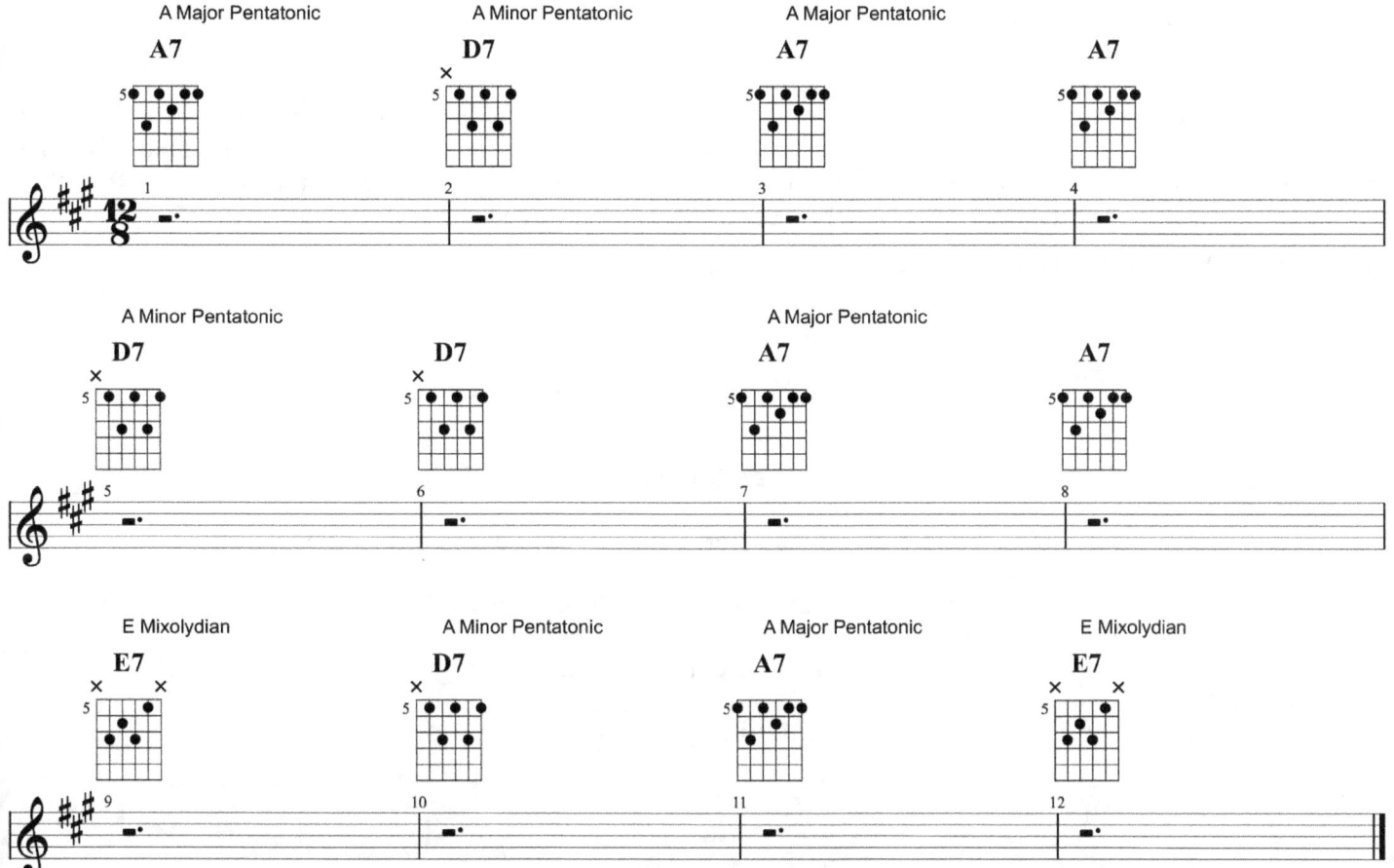

Keep this soloing scheme in front of you and do not deviate from your plan. If other ideas creep in then that's good in one sense, because your musical ear is taking over, but for right now the goal is to make sure that your practice is focused and disciplined.

You may wish to begin by writing out defined licks to play over each chord. This can help at first when it is challenging to improvise smoothly while changing scales over each chord. If you struggle, don't be afraid to use a very slow backing track or simply isolate each chord before putting everything back together.

It may take days, weeks, or months to become fully comfortable with a soloing choice, but if something really isn't working for you don't be afraid to disregard it and try something new. There's no point wasting your time trying to make something you don't like work when the perfect scale choice could be just around the corner!

When you you're starting to get to grips with your initial choices, replace your least favourite scale choice with a new one. If you like all the choices just randomly replace one with something else. For example, in the previous example, you could replace all the A Major Pentatonic scales with A Minor Pentatonic scales.

Next, spend time trying new licks and freely improvising with the scales. Experiment with the rhythmic concepts from **The Complete Guide to Blues Guitar Book Two: Melodic Phrasing** while staying within the chosen set scale choices. This is how you find your own voice and get inside the scale.

Every few weeks switch out one scale and try a new one. Before you know it, your ears and improvisational ability will improve dramatically.

Make a note of your favourite scales and develop your soloing with those. It could be that your favourites sounds are co-dependent. For example, you may only like the sound A Minor Pentatonic on the D7 chord if you played A Mixolydian on the A7. Make a note of these relationships and work on them in different positions on the guitar neck and in different keys. Begin by focusing on the keys of A, E, C and Bb.

Finally, listen!

Listen to the blues players you like. We are all products of who we listen to and how we practise. Treat listening as part of your practice routine. Put your guitar down and see if you can recognise the approaches your favourite musicians use. When you have listened to a tune a few times, pick up your guitar and try to copy short solo phrases you like. B.B. King is great for this because he often leaves big gaps between short, uncomplicated phrases.

Keep it simple, have fun and enjoy the process of developing your musical ears.

Good luck,

Joseph

Be Social

Join over 10,000 people getting six free guitar lessons every day on Facebook:

www.facebook.com/FundamentalChangesInGuitar

Keep up to date on Twitter

@Guitar_Joseph

Other Books from Fundamental Changes

The Complete Guide to Playing Blues Guitar Book One: Rhythm Guitar

The Complete Guide to Playing Blues Guitar Book Two: Melodic Phrasing

The Complete Guide to Playing Blues Guitar Book Three: Beyond Pentatonics

The Complete Guide to Playing Blues Guitar Compilation

The CAGED System and 100 Licks for Blues Guitar

Minor ii V Mastery for Jazz Guitar

Jazz Blues Soloing for Guitar

Guitar Scales in Context

Guitar Chords in Context

The First 100 Chords for Guitar

Jazz Guitar Chord Mastery

Complete Technique for Modern Guitar

Funk Guitar Mastery

The Complete Technique, Theory & Scales Compilation for Guitar

Sight Reading Mastery for Guitar

Rock Guitar Un-CAGED

The Practical Guide to Modern Music Theory for Guitarists

Beginner's Guitar Lessons: The Essential Guide

Chord Tone Soloing for Jazz Guitar

Chord Tone Soloing for Bass Guitar

Voice Leading Jazz Guitar

Guitar Fretboard Fluency

The Circle of Fifths for Guitarists

First Chord Progressions for Guitar

The First 100 Jazz Chords for Guitar

100 Country Licks for Guitar

Pop & Rock Ukulele Strumming

Walking Bass for Jazz and Blues

Guitar Finger Gym

The Melodic Minor Cookbook

The Chicago Blues Guitar Method

Heavy Metal Rhythm Guitar

Heavy Metal Lead Guitar

Progressive Metal Guitar

Heavy Metal Guitar Bible

Exotic Pentatonic Soloing for Guitar

The Complete Jazz Guitar Soloing Compilation

The Jazz Guitar Chords Compilation

Fingerstyle Blues Guitar

The Complete DADGAD Guitar Method

Country Guitar for Beginners

Beginner Lead Guitar Method

The Country Fingerstyle Guitar Method

Beyond Rhythm Guitar

Rock Rhythm Guitar Playing

Fundamental Changes in Jazz Guitar

Neo-Classical Speed Strategies for Guitar

100 Classic Rock Licks for Guitar

The Beginner's Guitar Method Compilation

100 Classic Blues Licks for Guitar

The Country Guitar Method Compilation

Country Guitar Soloing Techniques

www.ingramcontent.com/pod-product-compliance
Lightning Source LLC
Chambersburg PA
CBHW051148290426

44108CB00019B/2653